An Anthology of African and Caribbean
Writing in English

This reader is one part of an Open University integrated teaching system and the selection is therefore related to other material available to students. It is designed to evoke the critical understanding of students. Opinions expressed in it are not necessarily those of the course team or of the University.

An Anthology of African and Caribbean Writing in English

An Anthology edited by
JOHN J. FIGUEROA
for the Third World Studies *course*
at The Open University

HEINEMANN EDUCATIONAL BOOKS
in association with
THE OPEN UNIVERSITY

Heinemann Educational Books Ltd
22 Bedford Square, London WC1B 3HH
PMB 5205, Ibadan · PO Box 45314, Nairobi
PO Box 1028 Kingston · 27 Belmont Circular Road, Port of Spain

EDINBURGH MELBOURNE AUCKLAND
HONG KONG SINGAPORE KUALA LUMPUR NEW DELHI

Heinemann Educational Books Inc.
4 Front Street, Exeter, New Hampshire 03833, USA

British Library Cataloguing in Publication Data
An Anthology of African and Caribbean writing in
  English.—(Open University third world readers; 2)
  1. African literature (English)
  2. Caribbean literature (English)
  I. Figueroa, John II. Series
  820.8'096 PR9340

ISBN 0-435-91297-6

Selection and editorial material copyright © The Open University 1982

First published 1982

Filmset in 9 pt Baskerville by Northumberland Press Ltd, Gateshead
Printed in Great Britain by Richard Clay (The Chaucer Press) Ltd,
Bungay, Suffolk

Poetry, music, and other forms of art are by far
the best-suited media for describing human experience
because they are precise and avoid the abstraction
and vagueness of worn-out coins which are taken
for adequate representations of human experience.

Erich Fromm, *The Revolution of Hope*
(New York: Harper Row, 1968)

Contents

Caribbean Poetry   231

Acknowledgements

While taking full responsibility for this selection and the notes and introduction, I would like to thank many people for their help. John Ramsaran, just retired as Senior Lecturer in English, University of Wales, Swansea; Christopher Heywood, Senior Lecturer in English, Sheffield University; Mbulelo Mzamane, Graduate Student, Sheffield University. These helped particularly with the provision of material from Africa. My colleagues, academic, administrative and secretarial in U204, Third World Studies, The Open University, suggested, read and criticized, copied and typed creatively. Raúl H. Ampuero was particularly helpful on details of editing, and Magnus John, Librarian, in tracing difficult details of publishing. Dorothy Alexander Figueroa not only gave that general support without which one could not work, but also discussed many of the finer points of selection with me.

John J. Figueroa

The editor and publishers would like to thank the following for permission to reproduce copyright material:

African Universities Press for Nos. 8 and 9 from *Reflections* edited by Frances Ademola

Allison & Busby Ltd and George Braziller Inc for No. 10 from *The Slave Girl* by Buchi Emecheta

The editors of BIM journal for Nos. 18, 20 and 21

Bollingen Foundation Inc and Princeton University Press for No. 13 from *African Folktales and Sculptures* edited by Paul Radin

Bolt & Watson Ltd and Doubleday & Co Inc for Nos. 5 and 11 from *Girls at War* by Chinua Achebe

George Campbell for No. 78

Jonathan Cape Ltd for No. 76 from *In a Green Night—Poems 1948–1960* by Derek Walcott

Jonathan Cape Ltd and Farrar, Straus & Giroux Inc for No. 77 from *Sea Grapes* by Derek Walcott © 1971, 1973, 1974, 1975, 1976 by Derek Walcott

H. D. Carberry for No. 95

Estate of Frank Collymore for No. 87

Fontana and Charles Larson for No. 6 from *Modern African Stories* edited by Charles Larson

Rex Collings with Eyre Methuen, and Hill & Wang Inc for No. 62 from *A Shuttle in the Crypt* by Wole Soyinka © Wole Soyinka 1972

Crown Publishers Inc for Nos. 4 and 7 from *Quartet* edited by Richard Rive and No. 25 from *A Treasury of Afro-American Folklore* edited by Harold Courlander © 1976 by Harold Courlander

Curtis Brown Ltd, New York for No. 15 © 1954 by George Lamming

Anderson Desir for No. 99 © Anderson Desir

André Deutsch Ltd for No. 16, and for No. 22 from *Miguel Street* by V. S. Naipaul © V. S. Naipaul

André Deutsch Ltd and Africana Publishing Inc for No. 58 from *Zulu Poems* by
    Mazisi Kunene © Mazisi Kunene
East African Literature Bureau for No. 32 from *Dhana* by Theo Luzuka
East African Publishing House for No. 34 from *Two Songs* by Okot p'Bitek
Gloria Escoffery for No. 88 © Gloria Escoffery
Farrar, Straus & Giroux Inc for No. 103, and for Nos. 104 and 114 from *The
    Star-Apple Kingdom* by Derek Walcott © 1977, 1978, 1979 by Derek Walcott
John J. Figueroa for Nos. 20, 86, 93 and 112
Honor Ford-Smith for No. 81 © Honor Ford Smith
Harper & Row for the epigraph from *The Revolution of Hope*
John Hearne for No. 24
Heinemann Educational Books for No. 1 from *Burning Grass* by Cyprian
    Ekwensi; No. 12 from *Equiano's Travels* edited by Paul Edwards; Nos. 61 and
    63 from *Satellites* by Lenrie Peters; No. 40 from *Poems from East Africa* edited
    by David Cook and David Rubadiri; No. 56 from *Katchikali* by Lenrie
    Peters; Nos. 27, 36, 37, 39, 48, 49, 50, 51, 54 and 74 from *Seven South African
    Poets* collected and selected by Cosmo Pieterse; Nos. 41 and 43 from *A Simple
    Lust* by Dennis Brutus; No. 31 from *Dead Roots* by Arthur Nortje; Nos. 26,
    44, 45 and 65 from *Beneath the Jazz and Brass* by J. C. De Graft; Nos. 42, 67
    and 70 from *Black and White in Love* by Mbella Sonne Dipoko; Nos. 29 and
    46 from *Poets to the People* edited by Barry Feinberg and Nos. 30, 34, 53 and
    63 from *Of Chameleons and Gods* by Jack Mapanje
Heinemann Educational Books and Ethiope Publishing Corporation for Nos.
    38, 60, 64, 66, 69 and 71 from *The Fisherman's Invocation* by Gabriel Okara
Heinemann Educational Books and Mbari Publications for No. 47 from
    Labyrinths by Christopher Okigbo
Heinemann Educational Books and Ngugi wa Thiong'o for No. 2 from *Secret
    Lives* by Ngugi wa Thiong'o
Heinemann Educational Books and Nwamife Publishers for Nos. 28, 55 and 73
    from *Beware Soul Brother* by Chinua Achebe
Heinemann Educational Books (Caribbean) Ltd for Nos. 79, 84, 90 and 91
    from *Jamaica Woman* edited by Pamela Mordecai and Mervyn Morris
Hogarth Press Ltd and Rosica Colin Ltd for No. 14 from *A Morning at the Office*
    by Edgar Mittelholzer © Edgar Mittelholzer
Institute of Jamaica for No. 17 from *Interim* by Neville Dawes
Evan Jones for No. 98 © Evan Jones
Estate of Claude McKay for Nos. 23 from *My Green Hills of Jamaica* by Claude
    McKay 1979, and No. 100
John Robert Lee for No. 97 © John Robert Lee
Estate of Roger Mais for Nos. 92 and 113
Mbari Publications for No. 59
Methuen and Co Ltd and Hill & Wang for No. 72 from *Idanre and other poems*
    by Wole Soyinka © Wole Soyinka
New Beacon Books for No. 89 from *The Pond: A Book of Poems* by Mervyn
    Morris; Nos. 75 and 105 from *Poems of Succession* by Martin Carter and Nos.
    82, 85 and 102 from *Shadow Boxing: Poems* by Mervyn Morris
Oxford University Press for No. 52 from *Sounds of a Cowhide Drum* by Oswald
    Mtshali and Nos. 106, 107, 108, 109 and 110 from *Other Exiles* by Edward
    Brathwaite © Oxford University Press 1975

Oxford University Press (East Africa) for No. 57 from *Zuka* by Jonathan
    Kariara
University of Pittsburgh Press for Nos. 80, 83 and 115 from *Uncle Time* by
    Dennis Scott
Renoster Books for No. 33 from *Yakhal 'inkomo* by Wally Serote
E. M. Roach for No. 116
Sangsters for Nos. 96, 101 and 111 from *Jamaica Labrish* by Louise Bennett
Three Continents Press, Washington DC, 20036 for Nos. 86, 93 and 112 from
    Ignoring Hurts © John Figueroa
Daniel Williams for No. 94
It has not proved possible for us to contact some of the authors or their
dependents, or their publishers by the time of going to press. We have
therefore taken upon ourselves the responsibility of publishing these works,
hoping that by so doing we shall be serving the reputation of the authors. We
shall be very glad to hear from any copyright holders who have been
inadvertently overlooked or incorrectly cited and to make the appropriate
arrangements at the first opportunity.

Introduction

This Third World Anthology aims, in keeping with long-standing rhetorical and educational practice, to afford the reader both pleasure and insight. It arose out of discussions about the Third World: What is it? How did it come about? What are its present-day realities? Such discussions, especially when based on socio-economic theories, tend to sound rather unreal to some persons rooted in the 'Third World'. To me particularly, such discussions, whether they take place at the Open University in England, or in 'Progressive' circles in the 'ex-colonies', always seem heavily Eurocentric. Also they are often, perhaps of necessity, at such a high level of abstraction that they do not capture the flavour of human experiences as they take place in the Third World. These experiences, it should be remembered, do not appear to those having them as either *exotic* or exemplary of any set of theories—least of all those developed and razor-sharpened (at some distance away) by persons having the time and leisure for such things. Not that theories are unimportant. It seems to me that something is too often missing from the theoretical discussions in question. Something which has to do with seeing non-European peoples through their own eyes, and with accepting them as having full existence in their own right, and not simply as illustrating or proving one or other socio-economic theory developed mostly in Europe. It is only too easy, in thinking of underdevelopment, to underplay the real achievements of many Third World countries, and to ignore those particularly human aspects of their existence to which V. S. Reid of Jamaica refers in the introduction to his remarkable novel, *New Day*. 'What I have attempted,' (he says) 'is to transfer to paper some of the beauty, kindliness, and humour of my people, weaving characters into the wider framework ... and creating a tale that will offer as true an impression as fiction can of the way by which Jamaica and its people came to today.' (*New Day* [New York: Alfred A. Knopf, 1949] author's note.)

This Anthology, then, presents what representative and skilful artists from Africa and the Caribbean have to communicate to us, what they have moulded from their own experience whether developed mostly in their own countries or abroad. Their images do not necessarily contradict what the theoreticians have developed as 'explanations' about the existence and state of the Third World. But artists, even the most politically committed of them, *qua* artists, and in contrast to theoreticians, tend to see the world in a rather particular, imagistic way; that is, in the way of *fiction*. And fiction has its truths, which theory dreams not of.

The word fiction, it is important to note, is here used to apply to both prose and verse. It suggests something made; something 'made-up', in a non-pejorative sense. In fiction the active imagination plays an important part—the individual imagination makes meanings and gives significance. But the individual imagination has to resonate with a community of images and a reservoir of shared feelings if it is to move and communicate. Further, fiction in language, while it is being worked, has to respond to the limits and resources of language in general, and also of the particular language in which it is written. Fiction also conforms to, even when it expands, the tradition within which it is produced. It is of necessity conservative and innovative, traditional and subversive. It is perhaps because of the multi-dimensional nature of fiction that it appeals deeply, offers subtle and sometimes intense pleasure, and also affords insights that grow and are enhanced with further reading and further experience. The imagination plays a major role in the making and enjoyment of fiction. Also there is always something rational at work, planning the arrangements, structuring the insights from deep levels of experience, individual and shared; often making judgements about whether to let the image or the story run along in its own way, or to dam its flow for a while; judgements often have to be made about timing, about level of realism, about the reaction and sensibilities of the 'audience'. It is perhaps the ready availability of the last which differentiates the oral making of literature from the written. But central to any kind of literature is the imagination; yet it is not the whole of literature, whether from the point of view of the making of it, the savouring of it, or the critical reaction to it.

In any case it is not often enough remembered that theories, at least in their beginnings, may be as much works of the imagination and as 'made up', as fiction. The great difference between them lies in the abstract nature of the one, as against the particularity of the other, and also in a difference of use, in the domain of each, of such concepts as probability, verisimilitude, verification and, indeed, truth.

But if imagination is not the whole of fiction neither can literature be the whole or major part of Third World studies.

The enjoyment of fiction, and the discussion of it, cannot take the place of sound theorizing or of full discussion about such questions as: Are all the countries of the Third World uncivilized besides being poor, all simple and 'peasant' besides being exploited? Are they all without any real history? Do they have any existence except in relation to European expansionism? Have they not simply copied European and North American mores, having come to, or been persuaded to underrate their own? But even more important than these separate (and partly bogus) questions are the larger questions of how one makes generalizations about the Third World. Where does one find the data from which to theorize, and what kind of data will one admit as evidence?

One source of insight into these questions, often ignored, is the fiction, the art and literature of those countries which make up the Third World. Discussions about the Third World which leave out literature and art, both experientially and critically, tend to be highly abstract, highly contentious and highly Eurocentric.

Such discussions often ignore the variety of individual voices from the Third World and also the achievements of the Third World in the field of art. These achievements tend to be lost in the making of tough abstract models, and in the developing of theories which seem, perhaps understandably, to owe a great deal to the personal and political interests of the Europeans expounding such theories. There is not often enough place in rigorous model-making for the divergent voices which can be found in folk-tales, taped conversations, literature and art of all kinds. Such 'fables' and fiction, significantly, have always worried theoreticians, especially when, like Plato, they are interested in both unearthing the 'realities' (the noumena) beneath phenomena, and in a radically changing society so that it might conform to an ideal pattern. Model-making about the Third World and theorizing about development/underdevelopment often present a paradox that would not have surprised ancient or medieval philosophers: that of the tone and general structures of certain explanations seeming to be at one and the same time as 'idealist' as Plato and as 'materialist' as Marx.

Fiction from the Third World offers to all observers a remarkable variety of individual voices, as well as a very real variety of societies and cultures. This variety should be at once a test of theories and an additional datum for those discussing the Third World. It should also, at the very least, raise the question of squaring the achievements which the fiction represents with the popular image of the Third World as being 'barbarian', 'uncivilized' and 'catastrophe prone'. In the same way one may ask of those who seem to assert that the root, origins and continuation of the Third World are none other than exploitation and alienation, what their explanation might be for the existence and quality of the kind of work presented in this Anthology.

Unfortunately this collection could, as we will see later, contain work from Africa and the Caribbean only, and is but a *selection* of some of the work produced in those areas *in English*. It also contains only two pieces from the extensive oral literature connected with those areas, and does not draw on other rich sources of fiction such as folk tales, taped interviews, songs, praise songs, calypsoes, etc. For informal material the reader is recommended to consult *Third World Lives of Struggle* (eds. Hazel Johnson and Henry Bernstein), as well as *Treasury of American Folklore*, and *African Folktales and Sculpture* which supply Readings 25 and 13 respectively of this Anthology. For more formal, 'literary' fiction a variety of suitable collections and single works is cited in the bibliography. It is enough to mention here *Caribbean Rhythms* (ed. Livingston), *Caribbean Voices Vols. I* and *II* (ed. Figueroa), *Poems of Black Africa* (ed. Soyinka) and *Seven South African Poets* (ed. Pieterse). But in citing these works and in urging the reader to compare what is here presented with other work from the Third World we must not lose sight of three important matters. One, fiction is intended to please as much as to instruct. Two, the insight to be gained from fiction is such insight as is proper to fiction and literature, neither of which is science whether natural or social. Three, one of the main problems of any discussion about the Third World, or of the making of books about it, is simply its vastness. This has no doubt already occurred to the reader. But this vastness is not only territorial; it is also but one aspect of a variety and vastness which shows itself in countless languages and cultures, and in widely differing religious, political and literary traditions.

As far as literary traditions go, one need only think of the classical writings of places like India, and of the recent remarkable harvest of fiction from Latin America: Carpentier, Borges, Neruda, Paz, Vargas Llosa . . . to mention a few. So it is important to call to mind the size of the Third World, and its heterogeneous nature; these cannot be discussed here but are relevant to this Anthology and the choices made in putting it together. There was no way in which one book could have covered the whole of the Third World. For this and other reasons the decision was taken to select only from fiction written in English. A survey was made of such fiction from Africa, the Caribbean and the sub-continent of India. But the size and variety of the material soon made it clear that, regrettably, the Indian material could not be included. One had to concentrate on Africa and the Caribbean. In that way many individual voices could be encouraged to come through to the 'First World', without giving an impression which was too anarchic or too disconnected. It must be stressed once again, however, that in making the selection enjoyment and delight were considered to be as important as, and not at all incompatible with, a deepening of insight and a concern with values.

What of the pieces selected? How are they related to each other and to typical questions which arise when many people think of the Third World? Are they particularly of the Third World and, if so, in what ways?

A few preliminary remarks are needed before trying, even tentatively, to answer these questions—questions which are rather more complicated than they seem at first. Think of selecting any fifteen short stories from England alone and then asking whether, or in what senses, they are really typically *English*!

Notice that mention has already been made of the variety of fiction coming out of the Third World, and of the fact that this Anthology presents a selection of poetry and prose only from the Caribbean and Africa. Although it does not claim to be a comprehensive selection the net has been cast wide. A glance at the table of contents, for instance, will show in the African prose section authors who come from northern Nigeria, Kenya, southern Nigeria, South Africa, eastern Nigeria and Sierra Leone; there are also two pieces connected with a large area of West Africa. The prose pieces in the Caribbean section are from, or connected with, Trinidad, Barbados, Jamaica and Guyana, and also touch upon Caribbean people living in the UK and upon one of the main folk images of the Caribbean, which comes from West Africa, the spider trickster, Anancy. The poetry sections cover an even larger area, adding to those already mentioned: Malawi, Uganda, St Lucia and Tobago. Of course authors do not write about their home countries only; in this collection they react to places as far apart as Moscow, Lagos, Munich and Pretoria.

An attempt has also been made, within the limitations of a single book, to present some newer writers along with the 'older hands'; so that Buchi Emecheta appears as well as Achebe, Anderson Peter Désir as well as Derek Walcott. In the Caribbean section the attempt to show the new takes the form of presenting the work of women poets who are contemporary, and most of whom will be unknown and hitherto unpublished in Great Britain or the USA. So along with the work of established writers such as Louise Bennett and Gloria Escoffery we find that of Honor Ford-Smith and Heather Royes. In the African poetry section we have the comparatively new Jack Mapanje along with such stalwarts as Dennis Brutus and Wole Soyinka. Similarly Kumalo ('Red Our Colour', Reading 29) and Serote ('City Johannesburg', Reading 33) contrast with the quiet authority of Okara ('Once Upon a Time', Reading 66).

The question remains: Even allowing for the scope of the selection and for the fact that the old hands and the new are represented, in what sense can these pieces be called Third World? There is little doubt that they can in some sense be called respectively African and Caribbean!

First of all they are all written by persons from the Third World. To say that none the less some of them are not *Third World* art objects is perhaps to prejudge who or what might be suitably called Third World. But whoever their authors might be, the pieces themselves have concerns which arise quite often in discussions and arguments about the Third World—discussions which take place, for instance, in the Open University's course on Third World Studies. The prose pieces especially give insight into how a variety of groups of persons live in places which are by any definition within the Third World. We have fiction concerned with a group of nomads, their working life and their dreams and aspirations (Reading 1), with city slickers who at first seem naïve and 'bush' (Reading 3 and to some extent Reading 5). The latter two pieces are connected with West African Anancy tales (Readings 13 and 25) in which the power to outwit, while seeming weak and innocent, is humorously and cleverly displayed. This power is much needed by those who live under conditions of hardship and domination, either because of difficult natural surroundings, or because of openness to exploitation.

Likewise the reader will find images of the role of women, of slavery, of the effect of variations of culture, all touched upon in the prose as well as in the poetry. Similarly the effect of 'modern' developed countries, of European customs, known through missionaries or otherwise, on non-Europeans, so-called under-developed countries, can be clearly seen in 'Wedding at the Cross' (Reading 2) and 'The Truly Married Woman' (Reading 6) and 'I Meet an English Gentleman' (Reading 23), as well as in such poems as 'The Motoka' (Reading 32), 'Colonization in Reverse' (Reading 96), 'Mother of Judas, Mother of God' (Reading 82)— to mention but a few examples.

Two other matters of importance to Third World Studies are also to be seen in this collection. One, the effect of the *change* towards European mores and models and two, just as important, the high quality of prose and poetry which has been achieved in the Third World—in this case, in the English language. In fact there can be little doubt of the contribution of such writers as Walcott, Achebe, Brathwaite, Scott, Lamming and Ngugi to English letters and to the English language and its development.

The reader is invited to trace other themes which seem to be particularly connected with the Third World in the material here presented. For instance: What picture is given of ethnicity and its relation to special jobs or crafts? How does this relate to contact and conflict between tribes and other groups? What picture is given of so-called middle class life in, for instance, Readings 8, 14 and 18? How has colonial education and the tendency to look towards the metropolis affected attitudes expressed in these pieces of fiction? How does the image of poverty given in Reading 21, 'The Old Man and the City', and in Reading 98, 'The Song of the Banana Man' compare with what we usually think of in connection with Third World poverty, and with the fiction of Patterson and Mais? In order to help the reader make these connections many of the readings in the Anthology will have placed at the end of them in square brackets the numbers of other readings with which an interesting connection might well be made. For instance Reading 14, Mittelholzer's 'A Morning at the Office', has, amongst others, the number 16 after it, suggesting a connection with Naipaul's 'The Baker's Story'. In both these stories there is a concern with ethnicity and with the way in which in certain countries ethnicity is the basis not only for unfair discrimination but also for a 'division of labour' within the society. The narrator in Naipaul's story explains that he would not be accepted as a baker and seller of bread over the counter because he is black. . . . Naipaul has put it as follows.

And as we walking I see the names of bakers: Coelho, Pantin, Stauble. Potogee or Swiss, or something, and then all those other Chinee places. [. . .] You remember that the Chinee people didn't let me serve bread across the counter? I uses to think it was because they didn't trust me with the rush. But it wasn't that. It was that, if they did let me serve, they would have had no rush at all. You ever see anybody buying their bread off a black man?

Many themes or topics, besides the ones mentioned above, connected with the Third World, suggest themselves. The 'little man or woman' reacting to poverty, or civil war, or other hardships; the regular citizen's behaviour towards the new symbols of wealth, status and power. . . . The (Mercedes) Benz, or the 'road ship'. Then there are those characters who are perhaps more conscious of the predicament into which European expansionism, and/or changes towards the 'modern' way of life, have placed them in what are not only unindustrialized, but perhaps never to be industrialized, communities. Further, there is the movement of people, cultures and languages consequent upon those world trends which, while not being the only factors, are certainly among the main ones responsible for what we now call rather loosely, the Third World. So that there can be no doubt that some of the identifying characteristics which are applied to most of the Third World, whether justly or not, are to be found as concerns in the fiction here presented. Poverty, and local reactions to it, banishment, whether by foreign imperialist forces or by the new home-grown ones, the replacement of older symbols of authority and power by new ones from the industrialized world, either First or Second, the particular relationships between men and women, and between various groups such as tribes. All these and a number of others appear here as the context or expressed concerns of characters or *personae* who are created and presented by Third World authors. These characters sometimes react in their own territories, sometimes they live abroad, sometimes they are visiting (as in Readings 15, 20, 38, 74 and 112). Sometimes the main character is trying desperately to escape from a situation from which there is no escape, as in Reading 114, which bears the realistic and symbolic title, 'The Schooner *Flight*'. This wonderful piece of fiction by Derek Walcott is worthy of the most careful reading. It is written in verse, and in a very special English suitable to its narrator, who is a Trinidadian Shabine, that is, a man of mixed racial and ethnic origins. Its images as well as its rhythms make it poetry. At the same time it can be read as a short story of disclosure, in which the main character slowly reveals to the reader his true, and final, predicament—one shared, incidentally, by all humans whether of the First, Second or Third World.

Not every story or poem will be linked to other items by having a number placed after it in square brackets, although many are so treated. The reader is invited to work out connections for as many items as seem particularly interesting. The connections should not only be with respect to the concerns evinced by the fiction presented. We are dealing with fiction, and with artistic creations in fiction. It would be interesting, for instance, and no doubt instructive, to compare the use of the narrator in Hearne (Reading 24) with Walcott (Reading 114) and Achebe (Reading 11) with Naipaul (Reading 16). The structural development of poems, say, between Brutus's 'By the Waters of Babylon' (Reading 74), Walcott's 'A Letter from Brooklyn' (Reading 103) and Serote's 'City Johannesburg' (Reading 33), would also reward careful attention and analysis. The embodiment of attitudes in images, as well as the evocation of places through them, are likewise among the many satisfying and refreshing aspects of these works of fiction which we must not lose in our anxiety to understand concerns and see messages. Just as a person wearing a mask in the half light might disclose more than when uncovered at noon, so the author of fiction will disclose more to us when allowed to play his role within his mask of author, maker of stories or poems. Fiction speaks not only as it is read, but often afterwards as it is recalled.

So we end as we started. This Anthology aims both to refresh and to enlighten the reader. We are here dealing with fiction and fiction has its truths which are sometimes not dreamt of by theory but are truths of a different kind, which are no more important than the conclusions of theory. It is just that the great theoretical constructions, as models, as abstractions, seem to get all the running in discussions about the Third World. Whatever the theories and models might be—Capitalism,

Socialism, Marxism, Modernization Theory, Industrialization/Resources theories —they are abstract, and rightly so. This Anthology is an attempt to offer something more concrete, and more surely produced in the Third World by people of the Third World. But it does not represent the whole of this field by any means whatsoever; for one thing it has but two pieces of folk material, and nothing of the songs and taped conversations which are now becoming more and more available.

But whatever its shortcomings in terms of representation, one hopes that it will tempt the reader to think again about the Third World, not least about its achievements.

John J. Figueroa

Note

Where an author's work appears more than once, the biography will occur only after the first extract.

African Prose Fiction

Rikku and the Cattle Thieves

CYPRIAN EKWENSI

Night had fallen over Jalla's camp and with it came a feeling of gloom, for Jalla was proposing to strike camp and travel south to Malendo. With heavy hands Shaitu and Leibe were churning the sour milk near the huts, their ears tuned to the conversation of Jalla and Rikku.

'We shall split the herd in two,' Jalla suggested. This was an old ruse, to foil the tax-gatherers who might waylay them. 'Rikku, you will go with some cattle to Ligu's camp. I shall give you a man, a good man too.'

Jalla looked at his mother, and said: 'Shaitu, you and Leibe and the little one will come with me. We shall go to Malendo near the gold mines. It is twenty days' trek from here. There we shall stop till the grass is sour. If all is well, Rikku will join us there.'

Shaitu said, 'By Allah's help, all will be well. But, Jalla, shall we see Mai Sunsaye?'

'Wal-lahi, my mother. You talk as but a child. If Allah wills, we shall find him. If not, then we must be content till he himself returns to us. He is not lost to us!'

'Then you do not believe that he has the sokugo?'

'I do not know what to believe. But when next we find him, let us take him to one who will break this spell and reunite the family.'

Rikku said, 'It wearies me to think that all this strife began because of me!'

They did not speak again, and Jalla rose and walked into the darkness, gazing at the cattle. Rikku followed him, and they stood and talked about the cattle which he was to trek to Ligu's camp. Ligu's camp was in Kontago near the border country, some five days' trek from Malendo, where Jalla would be.

'This trek will prove you a man, my brother.'

'By Allah's help.'

Jalla said, 'Belmuna is a good man, and so funny! He is a hunter with a stout heart, brave as the devil. You will enjoy him on the journey.'

'When do we start?'

'At dawn.'

Rikku went back and sat in front of the fire, listening to the sounds of the night. Gradually a stillness descended, and he dozed away among the ashes.

* * *

They had been on the road now three nights and Rikku's feet were blistered. Belmuna was fresh as on the first day and even now he was crouching behind a rock, taking a steady aim at something Rikku could not see. He had his bow drawn taut and his muscles were tense and glistening.

Silently Rikku tiptoed close behind him, kneeling down at exactly the same time as the arrow hummed away. Still he could see nothing with his untrained eyes.

'Kai!' exclaimed the hunter.

In one bound he leapt out of his hiding position and over the crest of the hill. Rikku stood up and peered after him. A thicket hid him from view, and when he reappeared a duiker was slung across his broad shoulders, a smile furrowed his face.

'Eating for this night,' he smiled.

Rikku stroked the duiker. 'You are a great hunter indeed. But, Belmuna, you brought news of the tax-gatherers. How now do you find time to kill for the pot when we should be fleeing?'

'My little master, you know it is too late to leave this night.' He put down his kill on a rock, and hastily wiping his hunting knife cut off the portions he required leaving the entrails on the rock. 'Good! We go now!'

Although they had been on the road for three nights they did not build their first resting camp till dusk. A light shower had begun to make its soaking felt. The shower developed into a steady downpour, accompanied by claps of thunder and a storm that threatened to root down the very walls of their shelter. Rikku and Belmuna, wrapped in straw rain-capes, went round the fences of the cattle making sure they were safely ensconced for the night.

The rain pelted steadily down. The two of them crouched, one at either end of the enclosure, watching the cattle through the night.

Belmuna said, 'In Allah's name, it will be a happy day when I hand over the cattle to their owner. Kai! A man to risk his life like this! Sleepless in the night harassed in the daytime?'

To pass the time Rikku told Belmuna about Fatimeh and how Hodio had run away with her. He spoke also of his father's quest for the girl. 'My father thinks want Fatimeh. But I do not want her, really.'

Belmuna laughed.

'My father! Allah spare his life!' Rikku said. 'I shall be happy if we can set eye on my father's face again.'

'You think we shall ever cross his way? I tell you your father has vanished Followed the winged creatures. Ha!' There was a pause and then Belmuna asked 'Tell me, Rikku, why did you ever choose to come with me?'

'Because my spirit agrees with your own. And again, you are strong and brave and full of adventure. You understand the hyena and the leopard. You are like an animal yourself.'

Belmuna flung back his head and laughed, holding his sides. He ended his laughter with a little hiccup. 'I am an animal, he, he, he! Hear that one! I am an animal. Oh, by Allah! You are a funny one!' His face suddenly mellowed. 'Allah be praised.'

They talked on into the night and it was Rikku who first shut his eyes and slept

*   *   *

'The sudden rumble of the thunder-storm woke him. He was dazzled by the big sweep of lightning that flashed over the veld, and for a moment, he saw the hump of the Zeebu cattle, their upwardly pointing horns.

'Allah be merciful,' he murmured.

Dawn was a long way off, and this rain made him uneasy. He called out to the old hunter:

'Belmuna! Belmuna! Where are you?'

No one answered him. Instead he saw in the glow of a sudden flash two shapes crouching.

They were men. Momentarily the light fell on their dark faces, silhouetting them. Rikku's heart froze within him. He felt the evil in these thieves, the way they slithered forward under the rain, hissing, signalling fast to each other.

Lightning flashed again and Rikku saw them more clearly. They were severing the cords which held the cattle.

'Raiders!' shouted Rikku. 'Cattle thieves!'

'Belmuna. Belmuna, where are you?'

He heard the patter of feet as the men fled. A sudden sinking feeling in the stomach darkened his spirit. Belmuna might have been surprised and killed. These raiders might have been at work long before he woke. He blamed himself for falling asleep: had he forgotten what the raiders did to his father's cattle?

'Rikku!' cried a voice from the gloom. 'Come here. Hurry!' It was Belmuna. Rikku seized his bow and arrows.

'Belmuna!'

And Belmuna answered: '*Na-am!* . . . I'm here!'

Rikku found that Belmuna had fallen into a thorn scrub. He tried to extricate him without hurting him.

'I—I think I got one of them; I'm not sure,' the hunter confided. 'I chased him and shot him. We shall see in the morning. Ah, thank you. I'm free. Come. Come and see.' He led the way. 'This is where I cut them off. You were sleeping then. Here, by this stream. We should be able to recover the other cattle when the light comes.'

'*Kai*, Belmuna. You are a man!'

'It is Allah that makes men,' the hunter replied. 'Some day when you're grown up like me, you'll be braver than I am. You'll fight for your rights and you'll defend your property. Come with me.'

Rikku felt good. He followed Belmuna. In the darkness they could do little but wait. The rain poured down steadily.

*　　　*　　　*

They rested for two days. On the third day, in the grey of early dawn, Belmuna began to get the cattle on the move. He made clucking noises, his stick slung across both shoulders. There was a mighty rumbling of bodies thudding against bodies, of horns clashing. The cattle lumbered in a thousand opposing directions.

Rikku ran in front and around them, trying to mobilize them, cursing, using all the skill his father had given him. It was a nerve-racking affair. Rikku wanted to sit down and weep.

'*Tau!*' Belmuna exclaimed. 'That is the way, boy! Soon we shall be away. That's the sun, it has risen and is up. Allah has awakened us all. Soon we shall be away.'

He talked on in this encouraging manner until the herd settled down to a good steady pace, except now and again when one of them strayed aside to pluck a juicy bit of grass or young leaves.

Rikku trailed behind, stopping now and again to lean on his stick. His eyes throbbed in his head. He yawned, and his entire body ached for lack of sleep. But the old hunter beside him was cool as ever, his wrinkled face shining, his eyes yellow and quizzical.

He was the first to see the men who were coming towards them from a great distance.

'Rikku, those are the tax-gatherers. They have caught us.'

Rikku shaded his eyes against the morning sun. There were three men, and they looked like officials.

'Belmuna, what shall we do?'

Belmuna's eyes widened. 'We shall play them a trick. *Wai!* They have caught us, but we shall play them a trick.'

His whole body was tense. 'You know, Rikku. I shall stampede the cattle. Ha! How can a man count stampeding cattle, eh? Ah! They have caught us, but they shall see!'

Rikku glanced nervously at the approaching men. Something about the two of them awakened a vague memory in him. 'Belmuna!' He placed a hand over his mouth. 'Belmuna, you recognize those two men?'

'By Allah, I do not know them.'

'The thieves of the other night! They tried to rob us, and when they failed, they went to the tax-gatherers.'

'The rats! Gently now, here they come. Smile at them. Be pleasant.' He leaned a hand on Rikku. 'I shall stampede the cattle. Listen. You know that ravine, the one near the rocks, the one we passed yesterday? We meet there.'

Rikku's eyes fixed on the face of the official.

'Welcome!' He smiled. 'Sannu!'

The official nodded. He looked tired. Rikku and the two traitors exchanged glances of hate.

'What's your name?' asked the tax official.

One of the thieves came forward eagerly. 'He said your name!'

'My name?' Rikku turned that over.

'Your name!'

'R-i-k-k-u- S-sunsaye!' The official wrote that down. Without lifting his head, he said: 'All these your cattle?'

'All this lot? Yes.' He winked at Belmuna to stand by.

'Aren't you too young to own all this?'

'They are mine.' Rikku glared at the thieves. 'I did not steal them. When a man marries in our tribe, his father gives him cattle—'

'You are married?'

Rikku smiled. He must play for time. Out of the corner of his eye he saw Belmuna girding his loins tighter with the wet cloth.

'My wife is at the camp.'

The thieves exchanged glances, while the official lifted his red fez cap and scratched his head. Rikku saw his lips moving. He was counting the cattle.

'How many?' he asked.

'You will have to count them. I cannot say exactly. Last night the thieves came. I do not know how many they stole.' He talked directly at the two men who immediately busied themselves with the counting. 'A man starts with twenty cattle, they have young and increase; or they have the rinderpest sickness, and they are wiped out. One gets confused.'

'True,' the official said. He folded his notebook and yelled at the men. 'Get busy.'

Rikku signalled to Belmuna. At the same time, he and Belmuna began to speak in guttural tones. There was a strange wave of movement throughout the herd. The cattle began to get jittery.

'The time has come, Rikku.'

The official strode forward. 'Control them! Keep them together—'

'My Lord,' said Rikku, smiling. 'Don't panic so. Cattle are sensitive. They don't like strangers.'

'Look out!' shouted one of the thieves as a big-horned bull charged him and knocked him down.

Rikku gave five taps on his stick, light taps seen only by Belmuna. It was the agreed signal. The cattle surged. They were now raging around.

The official sprang back as they stampeded past him into the veld. Swearing, with the wicked smile of vengeance, Rikku watched his herd, watched the gasp of dismay on the tax-collector's face as his precious calculation vanished with the wind.

'Till next time!' Rikku waved his stick, and away he darted, tearing down the hill in a direction opposite to that which the herd had taken.

Far out and away from them all, Rikku doubled back on his paces, ran fast along the dry bed of the stream, now and again pausing to make sure he was not being followed. He could see nothing of his pursuers. If they decided to follow the cattle, they would get nowhere. He had trained them to disperse in different ·directions, but to reassemble in one spot.

Close on midday he arrived at the agreed ravine. It was very hot with the sun directly overhead. Tsetse flies were buzzing about his ears. He crouched under a tree, watching the cattle return one by one, and counting them as they came.

In the early hours of the evening, Rikku milked one of the cows, and having drunk his fill, set out for the north country. He would have to march very hard, if he hoped to get safely to Ligu.

Belmuna would never show up. Unknown to Rikku, the old friendly hunter was dead. A few yards from the scene where the tax-gatherer had accosted Rikku two men lay dead. One of them was the thief. The other was Belmuna. Both had been gored to death.

From *Burning Grass*, pp. 65–75.

CYPRIAN EKWENSI *Born in 1921 in Minna, Nigeria, of Ibo parents living in the Moslem north. Universities: Ibadan (BA), Ghana, and Chelsea School of Pharmacy. The above extract shows his understanding of the nomad Fulani, but he is also very much a man of the new African cities as his first novel,* People of the City *(1954), shows.*

[5, 11]

NGUGI WA THIONG'O

Everyone said of them: what a nice family; he, the successful timber merchant; and she, the obedient wife who did her duty to God, husband and family. Wariuki and his wife Miriamu were a shining example of what co-operation between man and wife united in love and devotion could achieve: he tall, correct, even a little stiff, but wealthy; she, small, quiet, unobtrusive, a diminishing shadow beside her giant of a husband.

He had married her when he was without a cent buried anywhere, not even for the rainiest day, for he was then only a milk clerk in a settler farm earning thirty shillings a month—a fortune in those days, true, but drinking most of it by the first of the next month. He was young; he did not care; dreams of material possessions and power little troubled him. Of course he joined the other workers in collective protests and demands, he would even compose letters for them; from one or two farms he had been dismissed as a dangerous and subversive character. But his heart was really elsewhere, in his favourite sports and acts. He would proudly ride his Raleigh bicycle around, whistling certain lines from old records remembered, yodelling in imitation of Jim Rogers, and occasionally demonstrating his skill on the machine to an enthusiastic audience in Molo township. He would stand on the bicycle balancing with the left leg, arms stretched about to fly, or he would simply pedal backwards to the delight of many children. It was an old machine, but decorated in loud colours of red, green and blue with several Wariuki home-manufactured headlamps and reflectors and with a warning scrawled on a sign-board mounted at the back seat: Overtake Me, Graveyard Ahead. From a conjurer on a bicycle, he would move to other roles. See the actor now mimicking his white bosses, satirizing their way of talking and walking and also their mannerisms and attitudes to black workers. Even those Africans who sought favours from the whites were not spared. He would vary his acts with dancing, good dancer too, and his mwomboko steps, with the left trouser leg deliberately split along the seam to an inch above the knee, always attracted approving eyes and sighs from maids in the crowd.

That's how he first captured Miriamu's heart.

On every Sunday afternoon she would seize any opportunity to go to the shopping square where she would eagerly join the host of worshippers. Her heart would then rise and fall with his triumphs and narrow escapes, or simply pound in rhythm with his dancing hips. Miriamu's family was miles better off than most squatters in the Rift Valley. Her father, Douglas Jones, owned several groceries and tea-rooms around the town. A God-fearing couple he and his wife were: they went to church on Sundays, they said their prayers first thing in the morning, last thing in the evening and of course before every meal. They were looked on with favour by the white farmers around; the District Officer would often stop by for a casual greeting. Theirs then was a good Christian home and hence they objected to their daughter marrying into sin, misery and poverty: what could she possibly see in that Murebi, Murebi bii-u? They told her not to attend those heathen Sunday scenes of idleness and idol worship. But Miriamu had an independent spirit,

though it had since childhood been schooled into inactivity by Sunday sermons—
thou shalt obey thy father and mother and those that rule over us—and a proper
upbringing with rules straight out of the Rt Reverend Clive Schomberg's classic:
British Manners for Africans. Now Wariuki with his Raleigh bicycle, his milkman's
tunes, his baggy trousers and dance which gave freedom to the body, was the light
that beckoned her from the sterile world of Douglas Jones to a neon-lit city in a far
horizon. Part of her was suspicious of the heavy glow, she was even slightly
revolted by his dirt and patched-up trousers, but she followed him, and was
surprised at her firmness. Douglas Jones relented a little: he loved his daughter
and only desired the best for her. He did not want her to marry one of those useless
half-educated upstarts, who disturbed the ordered life, peace and prosperity on
European farms. Such men, as the Bwana District Office often told him, would
only end in jails: they were motivated by greed and wanted to cheat the simple-
hearted and illiterate workers about the evils of white settlers and missionaries.
Wariuki looked the dangerous type in every way.

He summoned Wariuki, 'Our would-be-son-in-law', to his presence. He wanted
to find the young man's true weight in silver and gold. And Wariuki, with knees
weakened a little, for he, like most workers, was a little awed by men of that
Christian and propertied class, carefully mended his left trouser leg, combed and
brushed his hair and went there. They made him stand at the door, without
offering him a chair, and surveyed him up and down. Wariuki, bewildered, looked
alternately to Miriamu and to the wall for possible deliverance. And then when he
finally got a chair, he would not look at the parents and the dignitaries invited to sit
in judgement but fixed his eyes to the wall. But he was aware of their naked gaze
and condemnation. Douglas Jones, though, was a model of Christian graciousness:
tea for our—well—our son—well—this young man here. What work? Milk clerk?
Ahh, well, well—no man was born with wealth—wealth was in the limbs, you know,
and you, you are so young—salary? Thirty shillings a month? Well, well, others
had climbed up from worse and deeper pits: true wealth came from the Lord on
high, you know. And Wariuki was truly grateful for these words and even dared a
glance and a smile at old Douglas Jones. What he saw in those eyes made him
quickly turn to the wall and wait for the execution. The manner of the execution
was not rough: but the cold steel cut deep and clean. Why did Wariuki want to
marry when he was so young? Well, well, as you like—the youth today—so
different from our time. And who 'are we' to tell what youth ought to do? We do
not object to the wedding: but we as Christians have a responsibility. I say it again:
we do not object to this union. But it must take place at the cross. A church
wedding, Wariuki, costs money. Maintaining a wife also costs money. Is that not
so? You nod your head? Good. It is nice to see a young man with sense these days.
All that I now want, and that is why I have called in my counsellor friends, is to see
your savings account. Young man, can you show these elders your post office book?

Wariuki was crushed. He now looked at the bemused eyes of the elders present.
He then fixed them on Miriamu's mother, as if in appeal. Only he was not seeing
her. Away from the teats and rich udders of the cows, away from his bicycle and the
crowd of rich admirers, away from the anonymous security of bars and tea-shops,
he did not know how to act. He was a hunted animal, now cornered: and the
hunters, panting with anticipation, were enjoying every moment of that kill. A
buzz in his head, a blurring vision, and he heard the still gracious voice of Douglas
Jones trailing into something about not signing his daughter to a life of misery and
drudgery. Desperately Wariuki looked to the door and to the open space.

Escape at last: and he breathed with relief. Although he was trembling a little, he was glad to be in a familiar world, his own world. But he looked at it slightly differently, almost as if he had been wounded and could not any more enjoy what he saw. Miriamu followed him there: for a moment he felt a temporary victory over Douglas Jones. They ran away and he got a job with Ciana Timber Merchants in Ilmorog forest. The two lived in a shack of a room to which he escaped from the daily curses of his Indian employers. Wariuki learnt how to endure the insults. He sang with the movement of the saw: kneeling down under the log, the other man standing on it, he would make up words and stories about the log and the forest, sometimes ending on a tragic note when he came to the fatal marriage between the saw and the forest. This somehow would lighten his heart so that he did not mind the falling saw-dust. Came his turn to stand on top of the log and he would experience a malicious power as he sawed through it, gingerly walking backwards step by step and now singing of Demi na Mathathi who, long ago, cleared woods and forests more dense than Ilmorog.

And Miriamu the erstwhile daughter of Douglas Jones would hear his voice rising above the whispering or uproarious wind and her heart rose and fell with it. This, this, dear Lord, was so different from the mournful church hymns of her father's compound, so, so, different and she felt good inside. On Saturdays and Sundays he took her to dances in the wood. On their way home from the dances and the songs, they would look for a suitable spot on the grass and make love. For Miriamu these were nights of happiness and wonder as the thorny pine leaves painfully but pleasantly pricked her buttocks even as she moaned under him, calling out to her mother and imaginary sisters for help when he plunged into her.

And Wariuki too was happy. It always seemed to him a miracle that he, a boy from the streets and without a father (he had died while carrying guns and food for the British in their expeditions against the Germans in Tanganyika in the first European World War), had secured the affections of a girl from that class. But he was never the old Wariuki. Often he would go over his life beginning with his work picking pyrethrum flowers for others under a scorching sun or icy cold winds in Limuru, to his recent job as a milk clerk in Molo: his reminiscences would abruptly end with that interview with Douglas Jones and his counsellors. He would never forget that interview: he was never to forget the cackling throaty laughter as Douglas Jones and his friends tried to diminish his manhood and self-worth in front of Miriamu and her mother.

Never. He would show them. He would yet laugh in their faces.

But soon a restless note crept into his singing: bitterness of an unfulfilled hope and promise. His voice became rugged like the voice-teeth of the saw and he tore through the air with the same greedy malice. He gave up his job with the Ciana Merchants and took Miriamu all the way to Limuru. He dumped Miriamu with his aged mother and he disappeared from their lives. They heard of him in Nairobi, Mombasa, Nakuru, Kisumu and even Kampala. Rumours reached them: that he was in prison, that he had even married a Muganda girl. Miriamu waited: she remembered her moments of pained pleasure under Ilmorog woods, ferns and grass and endured the empty bed and the bite of Limuru cold in June and July. Her parents had disowned her and anyway she would not want to go back. The seedling he had planted in her warmed her. Eventually the child arrived and this together with the simple friendship of her mother-in-law consoled her. Came more rumours: whitemen were gathering arms for a war amongst themselves, and black men, sons of the soil, were being drafted to aid in the slaughter. Could this be true? Then Wariuki returned from his travels and she noticed the change in her man. He was now of few words: where was the singing and the whistling of old tunes remembered? He stayed a week. Then he said: I am going to war. Miriamu could not understand: why this change? Why this wanderlust? But she waited and worked on the land.

Wariuki had the one obsession: to erase the memory of that interview, to lay for ever the ghost of those contemptuous eyes. He fought in Egypt, Palestine, Burma and in Madagascar. He did not think much about the war, he did not question what it meant for black people, he just wanted it to end quickly so that he might resume his quest. Why, he might even go home with a little loot from the war. This would give him the start in life he had looked for, without success, in towns all over colonial Kenya. A lucrative job even: the British had promised them jobs and money-rewards once the wicked Germans were routed. After the war he was back in Limuru, a little emaciated in body but hardened in resolve.

For a few weeks after his return, Miriamu detected a little flicker of the old fires and held him close to herself. He made a few jokes about the war, and sang a few soldiers' songs to his son. He made love to her and another seed was planted. He again tried to get a job. He heard of a workers' strike in a Limuru shoe factory. All the workers were summarily dismissed. Wariuki and others flooded the gates to offer their sweat for silver. The striking workers tried to picket the new hands, whom they branded traitors to the cause, but helmeted police were called to the scene, baton charged the old workers away from the fenced compound and escorted the new ones into the factory. But Wariuki was not among them. Was he born into back luck? He was back in the streets of Nairobi joining the crowd of the unemployed recently returned from the War. No jobs no money-rewards: the 'good' British and the 'wicked' Germans were shaking hands with smiles. But questions as to why black people were not employed did not trouble him: when young men gathered in Pumwani, Kariokor, Shauri Moyo and other places to ask questions he did not join them: they reminded him of his old association and flirtation with farm workers before the war: those efforts had come to nought: even these ones would come to nought: he was in any case ashamed of that past: he thought that if he had been less of a loafer and more enterprising he would never have been so humiliated in front of Miriamu and her mother. The young men's talk of processions, petitions and pistols, their talk of gunning the whites out of the country, seemed too remote from his ambition and quest. He had to strike out on his own for moneyland. On arrival, he would turn round and confront old Douglas Jones and contemptuously flaunt success before his face. With the years the memory of that humiliation in the hands of the rich became so sharp and fresh that it often hurt him into sleepless nights. He did not think of the whites and the Indians as the real owners of property, commerce and land. He only saw the picture of Douglas Jones in his grey woollen suit, his waistcoat, his hat and his walking stick of a folded umbrella. What was the secret of that man's success? What? What? He attempted odd jobs here and there: he even tried his hand at trading in the hawk market at Bahati. He would buy pencils and handkerchiefs from the Indian Bazaar and sell them at a retail price that ensured him a bit of profit. Was this his true vocation?

But before he could find an answer to his question, the Mau Mau war of national liberation broke out. A lot of workers, employed and unemployed, were swept off the streets of Nairobi into concentration camps. Somehow he escaped the net and was once again back in Limuru. He was angry. Not with the whites, not with the

Indians, all of whom he saw as permanent features of the land like the mountains and the valleys, but with his own people. Why should they upset the peace? Why should they upset the stability just when he had started gathering a few cents from his trade? He now believed, albeit without much conviction, the lies told by the British about imminent prosperity and widening opportunities for blacks. For about a year he remained aloof from the turmoil around: he was only committed to his one consuming passion. Then he drifted into the hands of the colonial regime and cooperated. This way he avoided concentration camps and the forest. Soon his choice of sides started bearing fruit: he was excited about the prospects for its ripening. While other people's strips of land were being taken by the colonialists, his piece, although small, was left intact. In fact, during land consolidation forced on women and old men while their husbands and sons were decaying in detention or resisting in the forest, he, along with other active collaborators, secured additional land. Wariuki was not a cruel man: he just wanted this nightmare over so that he might resume his trade. For even in the midst of battle the image of D. Jones never really left him: the humiliation ached: he nursed it like one nurses a toothache with one's tongue, and felt that a day would come when he would stand up to that image.

Jomo Kenyatta returned home from Maralal. Wariuki was a little frightened, his spirits were dampened: what would happen to his kind at the gathering of the braves to celebrate victory? Alas, where were the Whites he had thought of as permanent features of the landscape? But with independence approaching, Wariuki had his first real reward: the retreating colonialists gave him a loan: he bought a motor-propelled saw and set up as a timber merchant.

For a time after Independence, Wariuki feared for his life and business as the sons of the soil streamed back from detention camps and from the forests: he expected a retribution, but people were tired. They had no room in their hearts for vengeance at the victorious end of a just struggle. So Wariuki prospered undisturbed: he had, after all, a fair start over those who had really fought for Uhuru.

He joined the Church in gratitude. The Lord had spared him: he dragged Miriamu into it, and together they became exemplary Church-goers.

But Miriamu prayed a different prayer, she wanted her man back. Her two sons were struggling their way through Siriana Secondary School. For this she thanked the Lord. But she still wanted her real Wariuki back. During the Emergency she had often cautioned him against excessive cruelty. It pained her that his singing, his dancing and his easy laughter had ended. His eyes were hard and set and this frightened her.

Now in Church he started singing again. Not the tunes that had once captured her soul, but the mournful hymns she knew so well; how sweet the name of Jesus sounds in a believer's ear. He became a pillar of the Church Choir. He often beat the drum which, after Independence, had been introduced into the church as a concession to African culture. He attended classes in baptism and great was the day he cast away Wariuki and became Dodge W. Livingstone, Jr. Thereafter he sat in the front bench. As his business improved, he gradually worked his way to the holy aisle. A new Church elder.

Other things brightened. His parents-in-law still lived in Molo, though their fortunes had declined. They had not yet forgiven him. But with his eminence, they sent out feelers: would their daughter pay them a visit? Miriamu would not hear of it. But Dodge W. Livingstone was furious: where was her Christian forgiveness?

He was insistent. She gave in. He was glad. But that gesture, by itself, could not erase the memory of his humiliation. His vengeance would still come.

Though his base was at Limuru, he travelled to various parts of the country. So he got to know news concerning his line of business. It was the year of the Asian exodus. Ciana Merchants were not Kenya Citizens. Their licence would be withdrawn. They quickly offered Livingstone partnership on a fifty-fifty share basis. Praise the Lord and raise high his name. Truly God never ate Ugali. Within a year he had accumulated enough to qualify for a loan to buy one of the huge farms in Limuru previously owned by whites. He was now a big timber merchant: they made him a senior elder of the church.

Miriamu still waited for her Wariuki in vain. But she was a model wife. People praised her Christian and wifely meekness. She was devout in her own way and prayed to the Lord to rescue her from the dreams of the past. She never put on airs. She even refused to wear shoes. Every morning, she would wake early, take her Kiondo, and go to the farm where she would work in the tea estate alongside the workers. And she never forgot her old strip of land in the Old Reserve. Sometimes she made lunch and tea for the workers. This infuriated her husband: why, oh why did she choose to humiliate him before these people? Why would she not conduct herself like a Christian lady? After all, had she not come from a Christian home? Need she dirty her hands now, he asked her, and with labourers too? On clothes, she gave in: she put on shoes and a white hat especially when going to Church. But work was in her bones and this she would not surrender. She enjoyed the touch of the soil: she enjoyed the free and open conversation with the workers.

They liked her. But they resented her husband. Livingstone thought them a lazy lot: why would they not work as hard as he himself had done? Which employer's wife had ever brought him food in a shamba? Miriamu was spoiling them and he told her so. Occasionally he would look at their sullen faces: he would then remember the days of the Emergency or earlier when he received insults from Ciana employers. But gradually he learnt to silence these unsettling moments in prayer and devotion. He was aware of their silent hatred but thought this a natural envy of the idle and the poor for the rich.

Their faces brightened only in Miriamu's presence. They would abandon their guarded selves and joke and laugh and sing. They gradually let her into their inner lives. They were members of a secret sect that believed that Christ suffered and died for the poor. They called theirs the *Religion of Sorrows*. When her husband was on his business tours, she would attend some of their services. A strange band of men and women: they sang songs they themselves had created and used drums, guitars, jingles and tambourines, producing a throbbing powerful rhythm that made her want to dance with happiness. Indeed they themselves danced around, waving hands in the air, their faces radiating warmth and assurance, until they reached a state of possession and heightened awareness. Then they would speak in tongues strange and beautiful. They seemed united in a common labour and faith: this was what most impressed Miriamu. Something would stir in her, some dormant wings would beat with power inside her, and she would go home trembling in expectation. She would wait for her husband and she felt sure that together they could rescue something from a shattered past. But when he came back from his tours, he was still Dodge W. Livingstone, Jr., senior church elder, and a prosperous farmer and timber merchant. She once more became the model wife listening to her husband as he talked business and arithmetic for the day:

what contracts he had won, what money he had won and lost, and tomorrow's prospects. On Sunday man and wife would go to church as usual: same joyless hymns, same prayers from set books; same regular visits to brothers and sisters in Christ; the inevitable tea-parties and charity auctions to which Livingstone was a conspicuous contributor. What a nice family everyone said in admiration and respect: he, the successful farmer and timber merchant; and she, the obedient wife who did her duty to God and husband.

One day he came home early. His face was bright—not wrinkled with the usual cares and worries. His eyes beamed with pleasure. Miriamu's heart gave a gentle leap, could this be true? Was the warrior back? She could see him trying to suppress his excitement. But the next moment her heart fell again. He had said it. His father-in-law, Douglas Jones, had invited him, had begged him to visit them at Molo. He whipped out the letter and started reading it aloud. Then he knelt down and praised the Lord, for his mercy and tender understanding. Miriamu could hardly join in the Amen. Lord, Lord, what has hardened my heart so, she prayed and sincerely desired to see the light.

The day of reunion drew near. His knees were becoming weak. He could not hide his triumph. He reviewed his life and saw in it the guiding finger of God. He the boy from the gutter, a mere milk clerk . . . but he did not want to recall the ridiculous young man who wore patched-up trousers and clowned on a bicycle. Could that have been he, making himself the laughing stock of the whole town? He went to Benbros and secured a new Mercedes Benz 220S. This would make people look at him differently. On the day in question, he himself wore a worsted woollen suit, a waistcoat, and carried a folded umbrella. He talked Miriamu into going in an appropriate dress bought from Nairobi Drapers in Government Road. His own mother had been surprised into a frock and shoe-wearing lady. His two sons in their school uniform spoke nothing but English. (They affected to find it difficult speaking Kikuyu, they made so many mistakes.) A nice family, and they drove to Molo. The old man met them. He had aged, with silver hair covering his head, but he was still strong in body. Jones fell on his knees; Livingstone fell on his knees. They prayed and then embraced in tears. Our son, our son. And my grandchildren too. The past was drowned in tears and prayers. But for Miriamu, the past was vivid in the mind.

Livingstone, after the initial jubilations, found that the memories of that interview still rankled a little. Not that he was angry with Jones: the old man had been right, of course. He could not imagine himself giving his own daughter to such a ragamuffin of an upstart clerk. Still he wanted that interview erased from memory forever. And suddenly, and again he saw in that revelation the hand of God, he knew the answer. He trembled a little. Why had he not thought of it earlier? He had a long intimate conversation with his father-in-law and then made the proposal. Wedding at the cross. A renewal of the old. Douglas Jones immediately consented. His son had become a true believer. But Miriamu could not see any sense in the scheme. She was ageing. And the Lord had blessed her with two sons. Where was the sin in that? Again they all fell on her. A proper wedding at the cross of Jesus would make their lives complete. Her resistance was broken. They all praised the Lord. God worked in mysterious ways, his wonders to perform.

The few weeks before the eventful day were the happiest in the life of Livingstone. He savoured every second. Even anxieties and difficulties gave him pleasure. That this day would come: a wedding at the cross. A wedding at the cross, at the cross where he had found the Lord. He was young again. He bounced in health and a sense of well-being. The day he would exchange rings at the cross would erase unsettling memories of yesterday. Cards were printed and immediately dispatched. Cars and buses were lined up. He dragged Miriamu to Nairobi. They went from shop to shop all over the city: Kenyatta Avenue, Muindi Bingu Streets, Bazaar, Government Road, Kimathi Street, and back again to Kenyatta Avenue. Eventually he bought her a snow-white long-sleeved satin dress, a veil, white gloves, white shoes and stockings and of course plastic roses. He consulted Rev. Clive Schomberg's still modern classic on good manners for Africans and he hardly departed from the rules and instructions in the matrimonial section. Dodge W. Livingstone, Jr. did not want to make a mistake.

Miriamu did not send or give invitation cards to anybody. She daily prayed that God would give her the strength to go through the whole affair. She wished that the day would come and vanish as in a dream. A week before the day, she was driven all the way back to her parents. She was a mother of two; she was no longer the young girl who once eloped; she simply felt ridiculous pretending that she was a virgin maid at her father's house. But she submitted almost as if she were driven by a power stronger than man. Maybe she was wrong, she thought. Maybe everybody else was right. Why then should she ruin the happiness of many? For even the church was very happy. He, a successful timber merchant, would set a good example to others. And many women had come to congratulate her on her present luck in such a husband. They wanted to share in her happiness. Some wept.

The day itself was bright. She could see some of the rolling fields in Molo: the view brought painful memories of her childhood. She tried to be cheerful. But attempts at smiling only brought out tears: What of the years of waiting? What of the years of hope? Her face-wrinkled father was a sight to see: a dark suit with tails, a waist jacket, top hat and all. She inclined her head to one side, in shame. She prayed for yet more strength: she hardly recognized anybody as she was led towards the holy aisle. Not even her fellow workers, members of the *Religion of Sorrows*, who waited in a group among the crowd outside.

But for Livingstone this was the supreme moment. Sweeter than vengeance. All his life he had slaved for this hour. Now it had come. He had specially dressed for the occasion: a dark suit, tails, top hat and a beaming smile at any dignitary he happened to recognize, mostly MPs, priests and businessmen. The church, Livingstone had time to note, was packed with very important people. Workers and not so important people sat outside. Members of the *Religion of Sorrows* wore red wine-coloured dresses and had with them their guitars, drums and tambourines. The bridegroom as he passed gave them a rather sharp glance. But only for a second. He was really happy.

Miriamu now stood before the cross: her head was hidden in the white veil. Her heart pounded. She saw in her mind's eye a grandmother pretending to be a bride with a retinue of aged bridesmaids. The Charade. The Charade. And she thought: there were ten virgins when the bridegroom came. And five of them were wise— and five of them were foolish—Lord, Lord that this cup would soon be over—over me, and before I be a slave . . . and the priest was saying: 'Dodge W. Livingstone, Jr., do you accept this woman for a wife in sickness and health until death do you part?' Livingstone's answer was a clear and loud yes. It was now her turn. . . . Lord that this cup . . . this cup . . . over meeeee. . . . 'Do you Miriamu accept this man for a husband. . . . She tried to answer. Saliva blocked her throat . . . five virgins . . . five virgins . . . came bridegroom . . . groom . . . and the Church was now silent in fearful expectation.

Suddenly, from outside the Church, the silence was broken. People turned their eyes to the door. But the adherents of the *Religion of Sorrows* seemed unaware of the consternation on people's faces. Maybe they thought the ceremony was over. Maybe they were seized by the spirit. They beat their drums, they beat their tambourines, they plucked their guitars all in a jazzy bouncing unison. Church stewards rushed out to stop them, ssh, ssh, the wedding ceremony was not yet over—but they were way beyond hearing. Their voices and faces were raised to the sky, their feet were rocking the earth.

For the first time Miriamu raised her head. She remembered vaguely that she had not even invited her friends. How had they come to Molo? A spasm of guilt. But only for a time. It did not matter. Not now. The vision had come back . . . At the cross, at the cross where I found the Lord . . . she saw Wariuki standing before her even as he used to be in Molo. He rode a bicycle: he was playing his tricks before a huge crowd of respectful worshippers . . . At the cross, at the cross where I found the Lord . . . he was doing it for her . . . he had singled only her out of the thrilling throng . . . of this she was certain . . . came the dancing and she was even more certain of his love . . . He was doing it for her. Lord, I have been loved once . . . once . . . I have been loved, Lord . . . And those moments in Ilmorog forest and woods were part of her: what a moaning, oh, Lord what a moaning . . . and the drums and tambourines were now moaning in her dancing heart. She was truly Miriamu. She felt so powerful and strong and raised her head even more proudly; . . . and the priest was almost shouting: 'Do you Miriamu . . .' The crowd waited. She looked at Livingstone, she looked at her father, and she could not see any difference between them. Her voice came in a loud whisper: 'No.'

A current went right through the church. Had they heard the correct answer? And the priest was almost hysterical: 'Do you Miriamu . . .' Again the silence made even more silent by the singing outside. She lifted the veil and held the audience with her eyes. 'No, I cannot . . . I cannot marry Livingstone . . . because . . . because . . . I have been married before. I am married to . . . to . . . Wariuki . . . and he is dead.'

Livingstone became truly a stone. Her father wept. Her mother wept. They all thought her a little crazed. And they blamed the whole thing on these breakaway churches that really worshipped the devil. No properly trained priest, etc. . . . etc. . . . And the men and women outside went on singing and dancing to the beat of drums and tambourines, their faces and voices raised to the sky.

From *Secret Lives*, pp. 97–112.

NGUGI WA THIONG'O   *This major East African writer was born in 1938 in Limuru, Kenya. Universities: Makerere and Leeds. Politically committed, especially to the Kikuyu cause, he has shown some of the corruption emerging since Independence and was recently imprisoned in Kenya. He has recently decided to concentrate his efforts on writing in Gikuyu rather than English so as to communicate more widely in his homeland. This decision, like that of Soyinka's to promote Swahili as the Pan-African language, could have very interesting effects on English.*

[6, 8, 10, 11, 18, 19]

3 *The Crooks*

GABRIEL OKARA

Their hair was all brown with dust. The clothes they had on were dirty and torn. Their bare feet were as dirty and as brown as their hair. The only luggage they had was a bulging haversack. It was neatly buckled down, and one of them carried it on his shoulder as they walked along the bridge towards Idumota. They were two men who had apparently just arrived from the provinces by lorry.

Traders arriving dirty and dusty from head to foot, and carrying haversacks, are a familiar sight in Lagos. But these two had an air about them of being in a strange place. They walked one behind the other as if they were picking their way in a forest. They avoided bodily contact with the people walking briskly to and fro past them, and were startled over and over again by the strident horns of the cars. They gazed at the lagoon and at the stream of cars, motorcycles and bicycles rushing in both directions across the gigantic bridge.

On the other side, a man was cycling leisurely along on a brand-new bicycle from the Idumota end of the bridge. His shirt and trousers were a dazzling white, and his two-tone black and white shoes were spotless. Tilted over his forehead was a white cork helmet. He put on his brakes as his practised eyes caught the two men on the other side, stopping now and again to allow people to pass, or looking for an opening through the milling throng on the pavement. The man on the bicycle studied them for a few minutes from his side of the bridge and waited for a break in the traffic. His eyes never left them. An old car wheezed past. He looked quickly left and right. Another car was approaching, but he dashed across narrowly missing death. Safe on the other side he cycled up to the two men.

'Hallo,' he said, with a broad smile.

The two men were startled and moved on faster. But the cyclist stuck to them.

'I know you from somewhere,' he said, smiling. 'I tink na Enugu. I get friend dere and you resemble 'am.'

The man carrying the haversack moved to the railings and his partner, turning to the cyclist, said, 'Yes, na from Enugu we come. You go for Enugu before?'

'Yes,' the cyclist said, 'I stay for Enugu long time. Okonkwo be my big friend an' you resembl'am for face. You be him broder?'

'Yes,' said the stranger, 'one Okonkwo be one farder one moder with me. He be big contractor for Enugu an' we stay for Asata. Na him be your frien'?'

'Ah, na him!' said the cyclist, 'we be big frien's. All the lorry wey he get na me arrange for 'am. I be agent for lorry. Dis na firs' time you come for Lagos?'

'Yes, dis na firs' time an'na lorry I wan buy sef.'

'Ah, you be lucky man!' said the cyclist. 'Waiten be your name?'

'Okonkwo.'

'An' your friend?'

'Okeke.'

'You be lucky, man. Na lorry I go give person for Ebute Metta jus' now. Na God say make you meet me. Wayo plenty for here. They wayo you an' take your money for nothin'. How many lorry you wan' buy?'

'Na only one,' said Okonkwo.

'Na only one you want. I go fit arrange ma quick for you if na today or tomorrow. Only today late small. But tomorow I go fit getam for you easy . . . You get place for stay?'

'The person wey I know, I no know the place he stay. But we go look for am,' said Okonkwo.

'Make you no worry,' said the cyclist, 'you stay for my place. Your broder be my big frien' and he go vex when he hear say I see you an' no keep you for my house. Come we go.'

At this invitation Okonkwo shook his head and said, 'I fer for dis town. They tell me say wayo plenty. I no know you. You say you be my broder frien' but I dey fear.'

'You right,' said the cyclist, 'you right for fear. But your broder an' me be big frien's an even 'e write me letter say him broder dey come. I forget for tell you de firs' time I see you. So make you no fear. Na God make wey I see you.'

'I dey fear O,' said Okonkwo, 'I dey fear but make I tell Okeke firs'.'

With this he went over to Okeke and told him. But Okeke replied with a vigorous shake of his head and said loudly that it was all a trick to get their money. But after much persuasion he reluctantly agreed and they went with the cyclist.

It was evening. Okonkwo and Okeke had eaten a well-pounded *foofoo* and *egusi* soup specially prepared for them and were sitting close together with the haversack between them in their host's parlour. The latter, who had been out for some little time, had just come in with a party of other people. The newcomers were dressed in heavily embroidered *agbadas* and slippers.

'Dis na my frien's,' their host said introducing the people to Okonkwo and Okeke. 'I tell dem say I get big 'tranger so they come salute you. All be big people. Na we dey sell motor for dis town.'

As the men went forward to shake hands with them, Okonkwo and Okeke looked awed and fidgeted. The hand shaking over their host beckoned one of his friends into his bedroom.

'You see how them be?' he said, after shutting the door. 'They be moo-moo and they get plenty money for bag. Now listen, as I say before we go play big. We go make them win hundred "redboys". When you wan' kill big fish you use big hook and big bait. So you know waiten you go do. Tomorrow we go rich.' Then he opened a small wooden box and bringing out three cards, said, 'Dis na the cards,' as he handed them over to his partner who took them and put them in his pocket. Then the other two men went back into the parlour to join the others. Soon drinks were produced from their bag-like pockets and as they drank and boasted of their riches the cards were brought out. They invited Okonkwo and Okeke to play, but they refused as they didn't know how.

'Very easy,' said the man with the cards. 'When I cutam putam for ground, you pick dis one,' showing them an ace of spades as he continued, 'you pick dis one you win, you pick another I win, easy you see.'

Still Okonkwo and Okeke were reluctant, but they soon seemed to be impressed by the easy way some of the people won money and joined the game.

'Na one one poun',' said the man with the cards. 'Put your money for ground. You take dis you win, you take dis you lose.' Okonkwo and Okeke watched carefully as the man cut the cards and put them face downwards on the floor. After studying them for a minute or two Okonkwo picked one card. It was the ace of spades and so he won. So it went on until Okonkwo and Okeke won one hundred pounds between them.

'E do now,' said the host as the hundredth pound was being handed over to Okonkwo and Okeke. 'E do now. You be lucky people. Tomorrow you go get lorry.' So they stopped playing and the people left. The host also went to bed after showing Okonkwo and Okeke a place to sleep in the parlour.

When he thought that Okonkwo and Okeke would be asleep, their host opened the door quietly and peered in. The haversack was chained to a chair. He shut the door. But soon he was back again unable to resist the anticipation of the money he would trick them out of the next day. Okonkwo and Okeke snored. They were the greenest things he'd ever come across, he thought. He already felt the seven hundred and fifty pounds in the haversack in his palms. Tomorrow, tomorrow, he thought, and shutting the door gently, went to bed a rich man. . . .

But when he went to greet his guests in the morning, the room was empty!

In the lavatory of the 'Up Limited' train, Okonkwo and Okeke were grooming themselves.

'Free food, free lodging, and a gift of a hundred pounds!' Okonkwo was saying, as he washed his face.

'When he was peeping in again and again, I thought he was going to be tough,' said Okeke, as he rubbed his chin before the mirror.

'They'll never learn,' said Okonkwo, as he wiped his face. 'They are green as peas, the whole batch of them. See how they left the door only bolted.'

So they bantered as the train jogged along. Swaying on the handle of the door was their haversack now emptied of the stones and old rags that had won them the hundred pounds.

From *More Voices of Africa*, pp. 66–70.

GABRIEL OKARA   *Born in 1921 in Ijaw District, western Nigeria, Gabriel Okara is one of Nigeria's outstanding poets in English. Educated Nigeria and USA, he travelled abroad on behalf of Biafra during the Civil War. He is now Writer in Residence in Rivers, Nigeria, at the Council on Arts and Culture.*

[13, 21, 25, 38, 60, 64, 69, 71]

4   *Debut*

ALF WANNENBURGH

It was only after he had searched the back streets of Cape Town for half an hour that Paul found Governor's Lane. He counted the houses from the corner and parked his car.

Somewhere inside the semi-detached cottage a recorded saxophone wailed its plaintive appeal. He climbed the three steps from the pavement and knocked cautiously on the front door. Then he moved slightly to one side, so that the first light from the opened door would not fall directly on him, and stood, whistling softly to himself, allowing his eyes to wander over the jungle of potted ferns on the stoep. Deep in his stomach he could feel the fortifying warmth of the brandy he had drunk in preparation for the party. There was no answer to his knock. Inside, the saxophone continued to plead.

He knocked again, this time more boldly, and glanced at his watch. It was eight o'clock. Right on time, he thought. A brief, late visit could so easily be interpreted as that of a self-opinionated junior clerk who condescends to accept a messenger's invitation to his sister's engagement party. Well, arriving early like this should prove to Lionel that he came because he really wanted to spend the evening with them, and that he was not merely dropping in out of curiosity, or as a matter of form. Slumming.

What Paul feared most was that his moves would be misunderstood. Originally, he had pressed Lionel for an invitation because he wanted to penetrate the official status-barrier between them, and he had been confident that his request would be regarded as sincere. But as the time between the invitation and the party had shortened, his confidence had diminished. 'Are you quite sure it's all right?' he had asked on a number of occasions. And each time Lionel would stare blankly at him for a moment and then hasten, in his servile fashion, to assure him that it really was so. He wasn't sure whether Lionel's expression *was* blank, or dead pan. What did he think? What did he feel? Now he was thankful for the brandy's added reassurance.

As he raised his hand to knock a third time, the door opened about three inches and a small, brown face looked up at him. Looked up at him, and said nothing.

'Is Lionel Petersen home?' he asked, after a moment of mutually uncertain silence.

The child continued to stare up at him. She did not reply.

'Does Lionel Petersen live here?'

He stepped into the light. Without moving her body, the child swept him with her eyes, as if she was trying to divine his reason for being there from his appearance.

'Please, I'm looking for Lionel Petersen!'

The child turned her face from the opening and shouted: 'Lionel, there's a white man here by the door to see you.'

The door opened a few inches further to reveal an apple-green, linoleum-covered entrance hall. There were no signs of a party. Not the slightest indication. But surely Lionel had confirmed it only the previous afternoon. Paul couldn't possibly have made the mistake of coming on the wrong night?

'Lionel! A white man!'

Paul winced. There was no answer from inside and the small, brown face disappeared. The door closed, leaving the stoep in darkness. He altered the position of his feet indecisively and fumbled for his cigarettes. The saxophone wept tremulously into a blues passage.

Then suddenly the door swung wide open. 'I'm terribly sorry for keeping you waiting like this, sir, but I wasn't expecting you to come so early.'

'That's quite all right, Lionel. I was just beginning to wonder whether I had come to the right house.'

'Oh yes, sir.'

Paul was ushered into a small pink sitting room. The carpet had been rolled up along one wall in anticipation of dancing, and the room was empty of furniture, save for a highly-polished gram-radio and a pair of easy chairs in which sprawled two youths, wearing blue jeans and pictured shirts, who were reading vividly coloured American comics. They turned their eyes towards him and nodded. Lionel did not introduce them. Self-consciously, they gathered their scattered comics from the floor and left the room.

Lionel turned down the volume of the record player. 'My younger brothers,' he said, jerking his head in the direction of the doorway.

'I see—but there was really no need for them to go out.'

'They have to go and change, anyway, sir.'

Lionel began smoothing the upholstery of one of the easy chairs. 'If you will just make yourself comfortable, sir.' He patted the cushion back into shape. 'You see, sir, no one else has arrived yet. My sister and her friends have gone to an early show at the Gem. They should be back in about half an hour. I've just been helping with things in the kitchen.'

'Please don't let me get in your way.'

'Not at all, sir.'

'Another thing, Lionel—' Paul felt decidedly ill at ease. He had known before he came that he would have to say this, and had carefully rehearsed his words; but now he felt that he was only erecting another barrier by repeating them. 'My name tonight is Paul. Please don't call me anything else in front of your friends. I want to be treated exactly like your other guests. Please.'

'Yes, sir.'

'Yes . . .?'

'It's not easy for me to change my whole way of thinking just like that, sir.'

Paul shrugged. He could feel the colour rising in his cheeks. This was not as he had wanted it to be. It was all so damn formal. He had expected to arrive in the middle of the party, when all the stiffness of their work-day relationship would be dissolved in an exciting swirl of enjoyment. Instead, they were alone together. Alone, with the wedge of rank thrusting itself between them. 'Please try,' he said.

'Can I get you a drink, sir?'

'Thank you, yes.'

'Something in particular?'

'I'll have some—what is it you coloured people usually drink?' He vaguely recalled some smug office joke, and remembered bottle store window displays he had seen. 'Oh, yes, I'll have some of that wine. Oom Tas, isn't it?'

'I can give you anything you like, sir. Brandy, gin, vodka?'

'No. No. I want to be like everybody else. Just give me a glass of Oom Tas, please.'

Lionel stiffened. 'I'm sorry, but we never keep any Oom Tas, sir. If you want wine, I can get you some sherry.'

Paul noticed the curl of distaste that came to his lips and the note of restrained contempt in the way he said 'Oom Tas', and he felt that Lionel was being, deliberately, very patient with him, as if he were teaching him a lesson. Paul hoped that he had not said anything which had offended him.

'Make it brandy then.'

While Lionel went to fetch him a drink from another room, Paul sat and looked at the framed Tretchikoff print and illuminated text, *God is Head of This House,* which faced each other from opposing walls. Damn it, why couldn't he relax? Faint female laughter rippled nervously in the entrance hall and Lionel returned with a bottle and glass. He was followed, hesitantly, by a plump woman whose white apron accentuated the bulbous prominence of the maternal breasts that pressed against the restraining floral fabric of her dress.

'Mr Anderson, this is my mother.'

'Very pleased to meet you, Mrs Petersen.'

She bobbed her head and gave him a toothless smile. For a moment no one said anything and she began shyly backing toward the door. 'I'm very glad you were able to come,' she managed. 'Lionel often speaks about you.'

'Thank you.' And then, turning to Lionel as Mrs Petersen slipped from view, Paul said: 'I'm sorry if I said anything that offended you.'

'That's quite all right, sir.'

'I also find it difficult to change my whole way of thinking, you know.'

'I understand, sir.'

Lionel poured some brandy into the glass and handed it to him. Paul felt the warm flush of his embarrassment meet and mingle with the already present glow of the brandy in his stomach. Just a few more should loosen him up nicely. He took the glass and drank deeply, feeling the raw flame of the spirits blazing through his throat and chest. That was much better. Already he could feel the difference.

'Thanks. Just what I needed.'

Lionel refilled his glass.

'I think we're beginning to understand each other, don't you?'

'Yes, sir,' Lionel repeated dutifully.

There was a knock at the front door. A youth of about twenty, wearing a carefully pressed, diamond-black suit and silver tie, was admitted to the room. He glanced apologetically from one to the other, nodded timidly, slunk across to the vacant chair opposite Paul and sat down. He did not raise his eyes, and apparently he expected to be ignored.

'Would you introduce us?' Paul said to Lionel.

Immediately the youth looked up and gave him an ingratiating smile.

'I'm sorry, sir. Tony Williams, this is Mr Anderson—from the office where I work.'

Paul clasped the extended hand firmly, and felt it crumple. It was damp and boneless, and he dropped it as soon as he felt its texture. Tony Williams continued to smile.

'Lionel!' a voice called from somewhere at the back of the house. Lionel excused himself. Tony Williams and Paul glanced uncertainly at each other.

'You're not at the cinema with the others?' said Paul.

'No, Mr Anderson,' Tony Williams responded eagerly. 'You see, they only told me they were going after they had booked their seats already.' He seemed relieved and grateful to Paul for having spoken to him.

'You a close friend of Lionel and his sister?'

'No, our mothers are friends.'

'I see.' Paul lapsed into silence, searching for a new topic with which to continue the conversation. He felt unpleasantly drowsy, and he knew if he closed his eyes he would experience a languid, floating sensation. Brandy always affected him that way.

'Cigarette, Mr Anderson?' Tony Williams flashed an ornate cigarette case in front of Paul. 'Solid silver,' he said, proudly tapping the lid. 'Belonged to my grandfather.'

'Very nice.'

'He was a European, like you.'

'I beg your pardon?'

'I said my grandfather was white. He was Irish. I'm mostly white myself, though you wouldn't say so to look at me. Would you?'

Paul looked at the dark-skinned youth and was quite certain that he would not. 'I don't know,' he said.

'Well, I am. Well, almost—my grandfather came from Ireland.'

Paul found the conversation embarrassing. He disliked the way Tony Williams claimed his white ancestry. 'It doesn't matter to me, really.'

'You see, a lot of coloured people have native blood,' Tony Williams continued. 'You can tell by their hair. Now there's nothing like that in my family.'

Paul wished that the conversation would end. 'I don't see that it's important.'

'But it is, Mr Anderson, because those who haven't got straight hair are mostly the skollies. Those with native hair. That's why I'm glad when a European gentleman like you comes to one of our parties, because then you can see that some of us are respectable, and that all coloured people aren't like that. You know, sometimes I feel ashamed that I'm coloured. But as I told you about my grandfather. . . .'

Paul was swept by a sudden feeling of revulsion. Why? Why did they have to keep reminding him that he was different? 'A European gentleman.' Did they think he had come to censor their enjoyment? To confirm or discard a previously held prejudice? All he wanted was to belong, to be accepted simply as another guest at the party. Just another guest.

'Is something wrong, Mr Anderson?' Tony Williams was leaning forward with exaggerated concern. 'Another drink?'

Paul held out his glass. Outside there were sounds of laughter, and a moment later a crowd of young people swarmed into the room. They hesitated briefly when they saw Paul and Tony Williams, and their exuberance dissolved. A few of them nodded indefinitely at Paul, the remainder ignored him—not deliberately, as a slight, but rather as if they had been caught in an unfamiliar situation, and not knowing what they should do, did nothing. Tony Williams was pointedly ignored. He lowered his eyes and seemed to shrink into his chair. He made no attempt to greet them.

After the first shock of finding a stranger in the room, their chatter revived quickly. The men made their exit in a group and went toward the room that served as a bar, while the girls pressed around the record player, excitedly disagreeing about the title of the first tune they wanted to play.

Paul jumped to his feet and, with an extravagant display of chivalry, offered his chair to any of the ladies who might wish to sit. A few giggled. None accepted.

He was disconcerted by their reticence and wanted to escape. Women had a way of humiliating one with just the faintest suggestion of laughter. They were so adept at it.

'Come, shall we join the men in the bar?' he said to Tony Williams, who appeared indifferent as to whether he was ignored by the men or the women. He unwound from his chair, slowly and without enthusiasm, and followed Paul at a short distance.

The bar was crowded. A table had been placed across one corner of the room, and its top was covered by a brightly coloured beach towel, on which were arranged rows of sparkling tumblers, a basin of water for rinsing them, and assorted bottles of liquor. When Paul paused in the doorway, the clamour for drinks terminated suddenly and the crowd parted to allow him immediate access to the table.

'Yes, sir. What can I do for you, sir?' asked the plump, red-faced man with rolled-up shirt sleeves who stood behind the table, his trousers suspended, beneath a protruding stomach, by a pair of broad black braces.

Paul flushed. 'First come, first served,' he said with strained casualness. 'I'll wait my turn.'

Lionel appeared beside him suddenly and touched him lightly on the arm. 'Go ahead, sir, let him fill your glass. It's the first time we've had a European at one of our parties.'

Paul wanted to protest but found himself being led by Lionel through the parted crowd, which closed behind them as they passed, leaving Tony Williams alone at the door. He accepted the drink Lionel handed to him and then turned. 'Please,' he said to all who were in the room, his voice choking self-consciously, 'don't treat me like a European. I have that all day at work. This is the first time I'm coming to one of your parties, and I want you to think of me as one of yourselves.' He added a second 'please'. Then they parted again, and he returned through the crowd to the door.

'That was very good, Mr Anderson,' Tony Williams said, feeling for Paul's hand. 'Most of these people don't deserve you treating them like they were equals. But it was very nice what you just said.'

The crowd had closed again behind Paul. Backs were turned toward him. Drinks were being served and consumed.

'The only good white man is a dead one,' said someone in the thick of the crowd, and everybody laughed, a trifle nervously, because perhaps that was going a little too far. Paul also laughed. He laughed louder than anyone else because he wanted them to know that he understood the quip in the spirit of a joke. He was still laughing when they had stopped. But when he stopped, they all started again. He handed his empty glass to Tony Williams and began searching for the bathroom, followed by the sounds of their amusement.

There he sat for a while, feeling the damp chill of the cement floor seeping through the seat of his trousers, his forehead resting on the white enamel coolness of the rim of the bath. Once there was an urgent knocking at the bathroom door. Then he heard someone being directed to go outside, and after that he was not disturbed again.

When he had resolved the threatening conflict in his stomach, he stood up and placed his ear against the door. All sounds seemed to be coming from the front of the house. He inched the door open gingerly, and seeing that nobody was in the vicinity, with hands outstretched for support from the walls on both sides of the passage, he began feeling his way toward the room in which they were dancing.

Bright-eyed young people spun and writhed before him in a confusion of movement and colour, while the older, more sedate couples glided effortlessly between the gyrating figures, lost in the somnambulent smoothness of their rhythm. Then, suddenly, it was not only the dancers who were moving; grey streaks like heavy rain shot across his vision, and the music receded into the background and was replaced by a monotonous, low humming in his ears. Then the whole room began to turn. Around, and around, and around and around; his head seemed to be revolving with rapidly increasing momentum through a narrowing tunnel of sound in ever tightening spirals—faster, faster, faster. Where to? He fought down the mounting pangs of nausea and pushed his head back hard against the wall, fixing his eyes on the illuminated text opposite him, *God is Head of This House*. It was as if he was standing in a constantly shaken kaleidoscope. And then, slowly, he gained control over his own internal movement, and he was able to separate the stationary objects from the dancers who continued to move, swaying and twisting.

As Paul watched, he noticed that some of the dancers glanced occasionally in his direction and then turned and whispered to their partners, who looked at him with furtive, suppressed smiles. But although these smiles were directed at him, they did not invite his participation. He inspected his clothing, but could find no possible cause for mirth. But then, they were not quite smiles of mirth. They were rather of the sort that set him apart—that isolated him. And as he watched, he longed to participate, to be accepted as one of them. Maybe they thought that he was holding himself aloof? Yes. That was it. He must show them that he was not aloof.

Slowly, he allowed his eyes to wander around the edge of the room, and he noticed that the only other person who seemed to be left outside the general excitement was a girl who was darker than the rest, and who had what Tony Williams had called 'native' hair. Was that the reason why no one paid her any attention? Then he would dance with her. That would show them that he wasn't aloof.

He stumbled across the room and seized her hand. 'Come. Let's dance,' he shouted above the din.

'No,' she said. 'Please, I'm not feeling well.'

But already he had pulled her out on to the floor, and they were caught in the vortex of swirling bodies.

'Please,' she said again, more urgently.

He smiled abandonedly. 'We'll show them,' he said, flinging her out at arm's length and then suddenly jerking her back toward him. The brandy throbbed behind his temples. 'Let's go!' His heels flashed up alternately behind him in a preposterous distortion of the Charleston. The other dancers edged away from them. His right heel caught the net apron of a satin dress. It hooked for a fraction of a second, and then he felt the materials part. There was a short, sharp scream of protest. 'Sorry!' he shouted over his shoulder, and then his feet continued to work like flails, a piece of pink net flying from the heel of his shoe like a flag.

Then Paul and his dark partner were alone on the floor. The other dancers stood around the fringes of the room and waited for them to stop.

'Please!' his partner repeated, struggling.

'We'll show them! Don't be shy,' he shouted, raising her arm to form an arch and ducking beneath it.

'Please!' she said again. And then her feet stopped moving. But he clung to her limp arm and pranced about her, calling encouragement. Then, as the music reached its climax, he grabbed her in his arms and spun her round and round in a final flourish that ended with a kiss on her cheek.

She turned her face away from him and tried to free her hands.

When the music stopped, the room continued to revolve against the direction in which he felt himself to be turning. He dropped the girl's arms, and leaving her standing alone in the centre of the floor, he reeled toward the door. He had to get to the bathroom, quickly. Christ, he had to get to the bathroom. But the doorway and the passage were choked with laughing people, all of whom seemed to be clutching at his arms and coat sleeves. God, how they were laughing! Cluster upon cluster of laughing brown faces. Row upon row of laughing brown faces. God how they were laughing! But he didn't mind their being brown. Anyone could have any damn colour face he liked. Please, God, he had to get to the bathroom Blue, pink, white, green, and even brown, what did he care, as long as he got to the bathroom. And then he was going to be nice to those brown faces. He liked them, and he was going to show them that he liked them. They would see. And still the faces were laughing—rows of white teeth like endless piano keyboards.

He staggered between them, pulling the tails of his unbuttoned jacket behind him, shrugging off the hands that grabbed at his shoulders, until he came at last to the bathroom door.

It was locked.

He rattled the handle and beat on the panels with the palms of his hands. I remained locked. Then he twisted around so that his shoulders were flat against the wall, slid slowly down to a sitting position on the apple-green linoleum beside the door, and placed his head between his knees.

The laughter came to him from the passage in terrifying waves of unreality.

God, he would show them!

He felt the saliva running thin in his mouth and his stomach heaved.

Then suddenly the laughing stopped.

Now Lionel and Tony Williams were beside him. 'Just a moment and we'l make you comfortable, sir.'

He was being lifted. 'No. No. Jus' a faintin' spell. Wan' t' be like ever'body else . . .' He saw Mrs Petersen shaking stiff white sheets out over the bed. And then he was alone in the dark room.

'Why these whites always got to show off!' shrilled a high-pitched female voice on the other side of the door.

He closed his eyes and the bed spun. Again his stomach heaved. O Christ, no The sheets were clean, and they were white . . .

In the other room the recorded saxophone recommenced its plaintive appeal.

From *Quartet*, pp. 117–28

ALF WANNENBURGH   *Born in 1936 in Cape Town, South Africa. Attended University of Cape Town.*

[14, 24]

5 *Civil Peace*

CHINUA ACHEBE

Jonathan Iwegbu counted himself extra-ordinarily lucky. 'Happy survival!' meant so much more to him than just a current fashion of greeting old friends in the first hazy days of peace. It went deep to his heart. He had come out of the war with five inestimable blessings—his head, his wife Maria's head and the heads of three out of their four children. As a bonus he also had his old bicycle—a miracle too but naturally not to be compared to the safety of five human heads.

The bicycle had a little history of its own. One day at the height of the war it was commandeered 'for urgent military action'. Hard as its loss would have been to him he would still have let it go without a thought had he not had some doubts about the genuineness of the officer. It wasn't his disreputable rags, nor the toes peeping out of the one blue and one brown canvas shoes, nor yet the two stars of his rank done obviously in a hurry in biro, that troubled Jonathan; many good and heroic soldiers looked the same or worse. It was rather a certain lack of grip and firmness in his manner. So Jonathan, suspecting he might be amenable to influence, rummaged in his raffia bag and produced the two pounds with which he had been going to buy firewood which his wife, Maria, retailed to camp officials for extra stock-fish and corn meal, and got his bicycle back. That night he buried it in the little clearing in the bush where the dead of the camp, including his own youngest son, were buried. When he dug it up again a year later after the surrender all it needed was a little palm-oil greasing. 'Nothing puzzles God,' he said in wonder.

He put it to immediate use as a taxi and accumulated a small pile of Biafran money ferrying camp officials and their families across the four-mile stretch to the nearest tarred road. His standard charge per trip was six pounds and those who had the money were only glad to be rid of some of it in this way. At the end of a fortnight he had made a small fortune of one hundred and fifteen pounds.

Then he made the journey to Enugu and found another miracle waiting for him. It was unbelievable. He rubbed his eyes and looked again and it was still standing there before him. But, needless to say, even that monumental blessing must be accounted also totally inferior to the five heads in the family. This newest miracle was his little house in Ogui Overside. Indeed nothing puzzles God! Only two houses away a huge concrete edifice some wealthy contractor had put up just before the war was a mountain of rubble. And here was Jonathan's little zinc house of no regrets built with mud blocks quite intact! Of course the doors and windows were missing and five sheets off the roof. But what was that? And anyhow he had returned to Enugu early enough to pick up bits of old zinc and wood and soggy sheets of cardboard lying around the neighbourhood before thousands more came out of their forest holes looking for the same things. He got a destitute carpenter with one old hammer, a blunt plane and a few bent and rusty nails in his tool bag to turn this assortment of wood, paper and metal into door and window shutters for five Nigerian shillings or fifty Biafran pounds. He paid the pounds, and moved in with his overjoyed family carrying five heads on their shoulders.

His children picked mangoes near the military cemetery and sold them to soldiers' wives for a few pennies—real pennies this time—and his wife started making breakfast akara balls for neighbours in a hurry to start life again. With his family earnings he took his bicycle to the villages around and bought fresh palm-wine which he mixed generously in his rooms with the water which had recently started running again in the public tap down the road, and opened up a bar for soldiers and other lucky people with good money.

At first he went daily, then every other day and finally once a week, to the offices of the Coal Corporation where he used to be a miner, to find out what was what. The only thing he did find out in the end was that that little house of his was even a greater blessing than he had thought. Some of his fellow ex-miners who had nowhere to return at the end of the day's waiting just slept outside the doors of the offices and cooked what meal they could scrounge together in Bournvita tins. As the weeks lengthened and still nobody could say what was what Jonathan discontinued his weekly visits altogether and faced his palm-wine bar.

But nothing puzzles God. Came the day of the windfall when after five days of endless scuffles in queues and counter-queues in the sun outside the Treasury he had twenty pounds counted into his palms as *ex gratia* award for the rebel money he had turned in. It was like Christmas for him and for many others like him when the payments began. They called it (since few could manage its proper official name) *egg-rasher*.

As soon as the pound notes were placed in his palm Jonathan simply closed it tight over them and buried fist and money inside his trouser pocket. He had to be extra careful because he had seen a man a couple of days earlier collapse into near-madness in an instant before that oceanic crowd because no sooner had he got his twenty pounds than some heartless ruffian picked it off him. Though it was not right that a man in such an extremity of agony should be blamed yet many in the queues that day were able to remark quietly on the victim's carelessness, especially after he pulled out the innards of his pocket and revealed a hole in it big enough to pass a thief's head. But of course he had insisted that the money had been in the other pocket, pulling it out too to show its comparative wholeness. So one had to be careful.

Jonathan soon transferred the money to his left hand and pocket so as to leave his right free for shaking hands should the need arise, though by fixing his gaze at such an elevation as to miss all approaching human faces he made sure that the need did not arise, until he got home.

He was normally a heavy sleeper but that night he heard all the neighbourhood noises die down one after another. Even the night watchman who knocked the hour on some metal somewhere in the distance had fallen silent after knocking one o'clock. That must have been the last thought in Jonathan's mind before he finally carried away himself. He couldn't have been gone for long, though, when he was violently awakened again.

'Who is knocking?' whispered his wife lying beside him on the floor.

'I don't know,' he whispered back breathlessly.

The second time the knocking came it was so loud and imperious that the rickety old door could have fallen down.

'Who is knocking?' he asked then, his voice parched and trembling.

'Na tief-man and him people,' came the cool reply. 'Make you hopen de door.' This was followed by the heaviest knocking of all.

Maria was the first to raise the alarm, then he followed and all their children.

'Police-o! Thieves-o! Neighbours-o! Police-o! We are lost! We are dead! Neighbours, are you asleep? Wake up! Police-o!'

This went on for a long time and then stopped suddenly. Perhaps they had scared the thief away. There was total silence. But only for a short while. 'You done finish?' asked the voice outside. 'Make we help you small. Oya, everybody!'

'Police-o! Tief-man-o! Neighbours-o! we done loss-o! Police-o! ...'

There were at least five other voices besides the leader's.

Jonathan and his family were now completely paralysed by terror. Maria and the children sobbed inaudibly like lost souls. Jonathan groaned continuously.

The silence that followed the thieves' alarm vibrated horribly. Jonathan all but begged their leader to speak again and be done with it.

'My frien,' said he at long last, 'we don try our best for call dem but I tink say dem all done sleep-o . . . So wetin we go do now? Sometaim you wan call soja? Or you wan make we call dem for you? Soja better pass police. No be so?'

'Na so!' replied his men. Jonathan thought he heard even more voices now than before and groaned heavily. His legs were sagging under him and his throat felt like sand-paper.

'My frien, why you no de talk again. I de ask you say you wan make we call soja?'

'No.'

'Awrighto. Now make we talk business. We no be bad tief. We no like for make trouble. Trouble done finish. War done finish and all the katakata wey de for inside. No Civil War again. This time na Civil Peace. No be so!'

'Na so!' answered the horrible chorus.

'What do you want from me? I am a poor man. Everything I had went with this war. Why do you come to me? You know people who have money. We . . .'

'Awright! We know say you no get plenty money. But we sef no get even anini. So derefore make you open dis window and give us one hundred pound and we go commot. Orderwise we de come for inside now to show you guitar-boy like dis . . .'

A volley of automatic fire rang through the sky. Maria and the children began to weep aloud again.

'Ah, missisi de cry again. No need for dat. We done talk say we na good tief. We just take our small money and go nwayorly. No molest. Abi we de molest?'

'At all!' sang the chorus.

'My friends,' began Jonathan hoarsely. 'I hear what you say and I thank you. If I had one hundred pounds . . .'

'Lookia my frien, no be play we come play for your house. If we make mistake and step for inside you no go like am-o. So derefore . . .'

'To God who made me; if you come inside and find one hundred pounds, take it and shoot me and shoot my wife and children. I swear to God. The only money I have in this life is this twenty-pounds egg-rasher they gave me today . . .'

'OK. Time de go. Make you open dis window and bring the twenty pound. We go manage am like dat.'

There were now loud murmurs of dissent among the chorus: 'Na lie de man de lie; e get plenty money . . . Make we go inside and search properly well . . . Wetin be twenty pound? . . .'

'Shurrup!' rang the leader's voice like a lone shot in the sky and silenced the murmuring at once. 'Are you dere? Bring the money quick!'

'I am coming,' said Jonathan fumbling in the darkness with the key of the small wooden box he kept by his side on the mat.

*

At the first sign of light as neighbours and others assembled to commiserate with him he was already strapping his five-gallon demijohn to his bicycle carrier and his wife, sweating in the open fire, was turning over akara balls in a wide clay bowl of boiling oil. In the corner his eldest son was rinsing out dregs of yesterday's palm wine from old beer bottles.

'I count it as nothing,' he told his sympathizers, his eyes on the rope he was tying. 'What is *egg-rasher*? Did I depend on it last week? Or is it greater than other things that went with the war? I say, let *egg-rasher* perish in the flames! Let it go where everything else has gone. Nothing puzzles God.'

From *Girls at War*, pp. 82–9.

CHINUA ACHEBE   *Born in 1930 in Agidi, in the Ibo section of eastern Nigeria. His father was an Ibo Mission teacher. He therefore had early experience of both the pagan and Christian in Nigerian life. Learnt English very early in life, and holds the view that the English language is one of the main things keeping Nigeria together as a country. Was very much involved in the Civil War on the side of Biafra in whose service he acted as a diplomat.*

[1, 8, 9]

6   *The Truly Married Woman*

ABIOSEH NICOL

Ajayi stirred for a while and then sat up. He looked at the cheap alarm clock on the chair by his bedside. It was six fifteen, and light outside already; the African town was slowly waking to life. The night watchmen roused from sleep by the angry crowing of cockerels were officiously banging the locks of stores and houses to assure themselves and their employers, if near, of their efficiency. Village women were tramping through the streets to the market place with their wares, arguing and gossiping.

Ajayi sipped his cup of morning tea. It was as he liked it, weak and sugary, without milk. With an effort of will, he got up and walked to the window, and standing there he took six deep breaths. This done daily, he firmly believed, would prevent tuberculosis. He walked through his ramshackle compound to an out-house and took a quick bath, pouring the water over his head from a tin cup with which he scooped water from a bucket.

By then Ayo had laid out his breakfast. Ayo was his wife. Not really one, he would explain to close friends, but a mistress. A good one. She had borne him three children and was now three months gone with another. They had been

THE TRULY MARRIED WOMAN

together for twelve years. She was a patient, handsome woman. Very dark with very white teeth and open sincere eyes. Her hair was always carefully plaited. When she first came to him—to the exasperation of her parents—he had fully intended marrying her as soon as she had shown satisfactory evidence of fertility, but he had never quite got round to it. In the first year or so she would report to him in great detail the splendour of the marriage celebrations of her friends, looking at him with hopeful eyes. He would close the matter with a tirade on the sinfulness of ostentation. She gave up after some time. Her father never spoke to her again after she had left home. Her mother visited her secretly and attended the baptismal ceremonies of all her children. The Church charged extra for illegitimate children as a deterrent; two dollars instead of fifty cents. Apart from this, there was no other great objection. Occasionally, two or three times a year, the pastor would preach violently against adultery, polygamy, and unmarried couples living together. Ajayi and Ayo were good churchpeople and attended regularly, but sat in different pews. After such occasions, their friends would sympathize with them and other couples in similar positions. There would be a little grumbling and the male members of the congregation would say that the trouble with the Church was that it did not stick to its business of preaching the Gospel, but meddled in people's private lives. Ajayi would indignantly absent himself from Church for a few weeks but would go back eventually because he liked singing hymns and because he knew secretly that the pastor was right.

Ayo was a good mistress. Her father was convinced she could have married a high-school teacher at least, or a pharmacist, but instead she had attached herself to a junior Government clerk. But Ayo loved Ajayi, and was happy in her own slow, private way. She cooked his meals and bore him children. In what spare time she had she either did a little petty trading, visited friends, or gossiped with Omo, the woman next door.

With his towel round his waist, Ajayi strode back to the bedroom, dried himself and dressed quickly but carefully in his pink tussore suit. He got down the new bottle of patent medicine which one of his friends who worked in a drug store had recommended to him. Ajayi believed that to keep healthy, a man must regularly take a dose of some medicine. He read the label of this one. It listed about twenty diseased conditions of widely differing pathology which the contents of the bottle were reputed to cure if the patient persevered in its daily intake. Ajayi underlined in his own mind at least six from which he believed he either suffered or was on the threshold of suffering: dizziness, muscle pain, impotence, fever, jaundice, and paralytic tremors. Intelligence and courage caused him to skip the obviously female maladies and others such as nervous debility or bladder pains. It said on the label too that a teaspoonful should be taken three times a day. But since he only remembered to take it in the morning and in any case believed in stock treatment, he took a swig and two large gulps. The medicine was bitter and astringent. He grimaced but was satisfied. It was obviously a good and strong medicine or else it would not have been so bitter.

He went in to breakfast. He soon finished his maize porridge, fried beans, and cocoa. He then severely flogged his eldest son, a ten-year-old boy, for wetting his sleeping-mat last night. Ayo came in after the boy had fled screaming to the back yard.

'Ajayi, you flog that boy too much,' she said. 'He should stop wetting the floor, he is a big boy,' he replied. 'In any case, no one is going to instruct me on how to bring up my son.' 'He is mine too,' Ayo said. She seldom opposed him unless she felt strongly about something. 'He has not stopped wetting although you beat him every time he does. In fact, he is doing it more and more now. Perhaps if you stopped whipping him he might get better.' 'Did I whip him to begin doing it?' Ajayi asked. 'No.' 'Well, how will stopping whipping him stop him doing it?' Ajayi asked triumphantly. 'Nevertheless,' Ayo said, 'our own countrywoman Bimbola, who has just come back from England and America studying nursing, told us in a women's group meeting that it was wrong to punish children for such things.' 'All right, I'll see,' he said, reaching for his sun helmet.

All that day at the office he thought about this and other matters. So Ayo had been attending women's meetings. Well, what do you know. She would be running for the Town Council next. The sly woman. Always looking so quiet and meek and then quoting modern theories from overseas doctors at him. He smiled with pride. Indeed Ayo was an asset. Perhaps it was wrong to beat the boy. He decided he would not do so again.

Towards closing time the chief clerk sent for him. Wondering what mistake he had made that day, or on what mission he was to be sent, he hurried along to the forward office. There were three white men sitting on chairs by the chief clerk, who was an ageing African dressed with severe respectability. On seeing them, Ajayi's heart started thudding. The police, he thought; heavens, what have I done?

'Mr Ajayi, these gentlemen have enquired for you,' the chief clerk said formally. 'Pleased to meet you, Mr Ajayi,' the tallest said, with a smile. 'We represent the World Gospel Crusading Alliance from Minnesota. My name is Jonathan Olsen.' Ajayi shook hands and the other two were introduced.

'You expressed an interest in our work a year ago and we have not forgotten. We are on our way to India and we thought we would look you up personally.'

It transpired that the three Crusaders were *en route* and that their ship had stopped for refuelling off the African port for a few hours. The chief clerk looked at Ajayi with new respect. Ajayi tried desperately to remember any connection with WGCA (as Olsen by then had proceeded to call it) whilst he made conversation with them a little haltingly. Then suddenly he remembered. Some time ago he had got hold of a magazine from his subtenant who worked at the United States Information Service. He had cut a coupon from it and posted it to WGCA asking for information, but really hoping that they would send illustrated bibles free which he might give away or sell. He hoped for at least large reproductions of religious paintings which, suitably framed, would decorate his parlour or which he might paste up on his bedroom wall. But nothing had come of it and he had forgotten. Now here was WGCA as large as life. Three lives. Instantly and recklessly he invited all three and the chief clerk to come to his house for a cold drink. They all agreed.

'Mine is a humble abode,' he warned them. 'No abode is humble that is illumined by Christian love,' Olsen replied. 'His is illumined all right, I can assure you,' the chief clerk remarked drily.

Olsen suggested a taxi, but Ajayi neatly blocked that by saying the roads were bad. He had hurriedly whispered to a fellow clerk to rush home on a bicycle and tell Ayo he was coming in half an hour with white men and that she should clean up and get fruit drinks. Ayo was puzzled by the message as she firmly imagined all white men drank only whisky and iced beer. But the messenger had said that there was a mixture of friendliness and piety in the visitors' mien, which made him suspect that they might be missionaries. Another confirmatory point was that they were walking instead of being in a car. That cleared up the anomaly in Ayo's mind and she set to work at once. Oju, now recovered from his morning disgrace, was dispatched with a basket on his head to buy soft drinks. Ayo whisked off the wall all their commercial calendars with suggestive pictures. She propped up family photographs which had fallen face downwards on the table. She removed the Wild West novels and romance magazines from the parlour and put instead an old copy of Bunyan's *Pilgrim's Progress* and a prayer book which she believed would add culture and religious force to the decorations. She remembered the wine glasses and the beer-advertising table-mats in time and put those under the sofa. She just had time to change to her Sunday frock and borrow a wedding ring from her neighbour when Ajayi and the guests arrived. The chief clerk was rather surprised at the change in the room—which he had visited before—and in Ayo's dress and ring. But he concealed his feelings. Ayo was introduced and made a little conversation in English. This pleased Ajayi a great deal. The children had been changed too into Sunday suits, faces washed and hair brushed. Olsen was delighted and insisted on taking photographs for the Crusade journal. Ayo served drinks and then modestly retired, leaving the men to discuss serious matters. Olsen by then was talking earnestly on the imminence of Christ's Second Coming and offering Ajayi ordination into deaconship.

The visit passed off well and soon the missionaries left to catch their boat. Ajayi had been saved from holy orders by the chief clerk's timely explanation that it was strictly against Government regulations for civil servants to indulge in non-official organizations. To help Ajayi out of his quandary, he had even gone further and said that contravention might result in a fine or imprisonment. 'Talk about colonial oppression,' the youngest of the missionaries had said, gloomily.

The next day Ajayi called at the chief clerk's office with a carefully wrapped bottle of beer as a present for his help generally on the occasion. They discussed happily the friendliness and interest the white men had shown.

This incident and Ayo's protest against flagellation as a specific against enuresis made Ajayi very thoughtful for a week. He decided to marry Ayo. Another consideration which added weight to the thought was the snapshot Olsen took for his magazine. In some peculiar way Ajayi felt he and Ayo should marry, as millions of Americans would see their picture—Olsen had assured him of this—as 'one saved and happy African family'. He announced his intention of marrying her to Ayo one evening, after a particularly good meal and a satisfactory bout of belching. Ayo at once became extremely solicitous and got up looking at him with some anxiety. Was he ill? she asked. Was there anything wrong at the office? Had anyone insulted him? No, he answered, there was nothing wrong with his wanting to get married, was there? Or had she anyone else in mind? Ayo laughed, 'As you will,' she said; 'let us get married, but do not say I forced you into it.'

They discussed the wedding that night. Ajayi wanted to have a white wedding with veil and orange blossom. But Ayo with regret decided it would not be quite right. They agreed on grey. Ayo particularly wanted a corset to strap down her obvious bulge; Ajayi gave way gallantly to this feminine whim, chucking her under the chin and saying, 'You women with your vanity!' But he was firm about no honeymoon. He said he could not afford the expense and that one bed was as good as another. Ayo gave way on that. They agreed, however, on a church wedding and that their children could act as bridal pages to keep the cost of clothes within the family.

That evening Ajayi, inflamed by the idea and arrangements for the wedding, pulled Ayo excitedly to him as they lay in bed. 'No,' said Ayo, shyly, pushing him back gently, 'you mustn't. Wait until after the marriage.' 'Why?' said Ajayi, rather surprised, but obedient. 'Because it will not somehow be right,' Ayo replied seriously and determinedly.

Ayo's father unbent somewhat when he heard of the proposed marriage. He insisted, however, that Ayo move herself and all her possessions back home to his house. The children were sent to Ayo's married sister. Most of Ajayi's family were in favour of the union, except his sister, who, moved by the threat implicit in Ayo's improved social position, advised Ajayi to see a soothsayer first. As Ayo had got wind of this through friends at market on Saturday, she saw the soothsayer first and fixed things. When Ajayi and his sister called at night to see him, he consulted the oracles and pronounced future happiness, avoiding the sister's eye. The latter restrained herself from scratching the old man's face and accepted defeat.

The only other flaw in a felicitous situation had been Ayo's neighbour Omo, who had always on urgent occasions at short notice loaned Ayo her wedding ring. She had suddenly turned cold. Especially after Ayo had shown her the wedding presents Ajayi intended to give her. The neighbour had handled the flimsy nylon articles with a mixture of envy and rage.

'Do you mean you are going to wear these?' she had asked. 'Yes,' Ayo had replied simply. 'But, my sister,' she had protested, 'you will catch cold with these. Suppose you had an accident and all those doctors lifted your clothes in hospital. They will see everything through these.' 'I never have accidents,' Ayo answered, and added, 'Ajayi says all the 'Ollywood cinema women wear these. It says so there. Look—"Trademark Hollywood".' 'These are disgraceful; they hide nothing, it is extremely fast of you to wear them,' the jealous girl said, pushing them back furiously over the fence to Ayo.

'Why should I want to hide anything from my husband when we are married?' Ayo said triumphantly, moving back to her own kitchen and feeling safe in future from the patronizing way the wedding ring had always been lent her.

The arrangements had to be made swiftly, since time and the corset ribs were both against them; Ajayi's domestic routine was also sorely tried, especially his morning cup of tea which he badly missed. He borrowed heavily from a money-lender to pay the dowry and for the music, dancing, and feasting, and for dresses of the same pattern which Ayo and her female relations would wear after the ceremony on the wedding day.

The engagement took place quietly, Ajayi's uncle and other relations taking a Bible and a ring to Ayo's father and asking for her hand in marriage, the day before the wedding. They took with them two small girls carrying on their heads large hollow gourds. These contained articles like pins, farthings, fruit, kola nuts, and cloth. The articles were symbolic gifts to the bride from the bridegroom, so that she might be precluded in future marital disputes from saying, 'Not a pin or a farthing has the blackguard given me since we got married.'

On arrival at Ayo's father's house, the small procession passed it first as if uncertain, then returned to it. This gave warning to the occupants. Ajayi's uncle then knocked several times. Voices from within shouted back and ordered him to name himself, his ancestry, and his mission. He did this. Argument and some abuse followed on either side. After his family credentials had been seriously examined, questioned, doubted, and disparaged, Ajayi's uncle started wheedling and cajoling. This went on for about half an hour to the enjoyment and mock trepidation of Ajayi's relations. He himself had remained at home, waiting. Finally, Ayo's father opened the door. Honour was satisfied and it was now supposed to be clearly evident

to Ajayi's relations, in case it had not been before, thet they were entering a family
and household which was distinguished, difficult, and jealous of their distinction.
'What is your mission here?' Ayo's father then asked sternly.
Ajayi's uncle answered humbly:

'We have come to pluck a red, red rose
That in your beautiful garden grows.
Which never has been plucked before,
So lovelier than any other.'

'Will you be able to nurture our lovely rose well?' another of Ayo's male
relations asked.
Ajayi's family party replied:

'So well shall we nurture your rose
'Twill bring forth many others.'

They were finally admitted; drinks were served and prayers offered. The gifts
were accepted and others given in exchange. Conversation went on for about thirty
minutes on every conceivable subject but the one at hand. All through this, Ayo and
her sisters and some young female relations were kept hidden in an adjoining bedroom. Finally with some delicacy, Ajayi's uncle broached the subject after Ayo's
father had given him an opening by asking what, apart from the honour of being
entertained by himself and his family, did Ajayi's relations seek. They had heard,
the latter replied, that in this very household there was a maiden chaste, beautiful,
and obedient, known to all by the name of Ayo. This maiden they sought as wife for
their kinsman Ajayi. Ayo's father opened the bedroom and brought forth Ayo's
sister. Was this the one? he asked, testing them. They examined her. No it was not
this one they replied, this one was too short to be Ayo. Then a cousin was brought
out. Was this she? No, this one is too fat, the applicants said. About ten women in
all were brought out. But none was the correct one. Each was too short or too fat or
too fair, as the case was, to suit the description of the maiden they sought. At this
point, Ajayi's uncle slapped his thigh, as if to show that his doubts were confirmed;
turning to his party, he stated that it was a good thing they had insisted on seeing for
themselves the bride demanded, or else the wrong woman would have been foisted
on them. They agreed, nodding. All right, all right, Ayo's father had replied, there
was no cause for impatience. He wanted to be sure they knew whom they wanted.
Standing on guard at the bedroom door, he turned his back to the assembly, and
with tears in his eyes beckoned to Ayo sitting on the bed inside. He kissed her lightly
on the forehead to forgive the past years. Then he led her forth and turned fiercely to
the audience. Was this then the girl they wanted, he asked them sternly?
'This *is* the very one,' Ajayi's uncle replied with joy. 'Hip, hip, hip, hooray,'
everybody shouted, encircling Ayo and waving white handkerchiefs over her head.
The musicians smote their guitars instantly; someone beat an empty wine bottle
rhythmically with a corkscrew; after a few preliminary trills the flutes rose high in
melody; all danced round Ayo. And as she stood in the centre, a woman in her
mid-thirties, her hair slightly streaked grey, undergoing a ceremony of honour she
had often witnessed and long put outside her fate, remembering the classic
description of chastity, obedience, and beauty, she wept with joy and the unborn
child stirred within her for the first time.

The next morning she was bathed by an old and respected female member of her family and her mother helped her to dress. Her father gave her away at the marriage service at church. It was a quiet wedding with only sixty guests or so. Ajayi looked stiff in dinner jacket with buttonhole, an ensemble which he wore only on special occasions. Afterwards they went to Ayo's family home for the wedding luncheon. At the door they were met by another of Ayo's numerous elderly aunts, who held a glass of water to their lips for them to sip in turn, Ajayi being first. The guests were all gathered outside behind the couple. The aunt made a conveniently long speech until all the guests had foregathered. She warned Ayo not to be too friendly with other women as they would inevitably steal her husband; that they should live peaceably and not let the sun go down on a quarrel between them. Turning to Ajayi, she told him with a twinkle in her eye that a wife could be quite as exciting as a mistress, and also not to use physical violence against their daughter, his wife.

After this they entered and the Western part of the ceremony took place. The wedding cake (which Ayo had made) was cut and speeches made. Then Ajayi departed to his own family home where other celebrations went on. Later he changed into a lounge suit and called for Ayo. There was weeping in Ayo's household as if she were setting off on a long journey. Her mother in saying goodbye, remarked between tears, that although she would not have the honour next morning of showing the world evidence of Ayo's virginity, yet in the true feminine powers of procreation none except the blind and deaf could say Ayo had lacked zeal.

They called on various relations on both sides of the family and at last they were home. Ayo seemed different in Ajayi's eyes. He had never really looked at her carefully before. Now he observed her head held erectly and gracefully through years of balancing loads on it in childhood; her statuesque neck with its three natural horizontal ridges—to him, signs of beauty; her handsome shoulders. He clasped her with a new tenderness.

The next morning, as his alarm clock went off, he stirred and reached for his morning cup of tea. It was not there. He sprang up and looked. Nothing. He listened for Ayo's footsteps outside in the kitchen. Nothing. He turned to look beside him. Ayo was there and her bare ebony back was heaving gently. She must be ill, he thought; all that excitement yesterday.

'Ayo, Ayo,' he cried, 'are you ill?' She turned round slowly still lying down and faced him. She tweaked her toes luxuriously under the cotton coverlet and patted her breast slowly. There was a terrible calm about her. 'No, Ajayi,' she replied, 'are you?' she asked him. 'Are your legs paralyzed?' she continued. 'No,' he said. He was puzzled and alarmed, thinking that her mind had become unhinged under the strain.

'Ajayi, my husband,' she said, 'for twelve years I have got up every morning at five to make tea for you and breakfast. Now I am a truly married woman you must treat me with a little more respect. You are now a husband and not a lover. Get up and make yourself a cup of tea.'

From *Modern African Stories*, pp. 28–39

ABIOSEH NICOL   *Abioseh Nicol is the pseudonym for Davidson Nicol. Born in 1924 in Freetown, Sierra Leone. Writer, physician, scientist (research into insulin). Universities: London and Cambridge. He has served Africa as administrator, medic, writer and intellectual.*

[2, 10, 11, 18, 81]

RICHARD RIVE

Rain poured down, blotting out all sound with its sharp and vibrant tattoo.
Dripping neon signs reflecting lurid reds and yellows in mirror-wet streets.
Swollen gutters. Water overflowing and squelching on to pavements. Gurgling
and sucking at storm-water drains. Table Mountain cut off by a grey film of mist
and rain. A lost City Hall clock trying manfully to chime nine over an indifferent
Cape Town. Baleful reverberations through a spluttering all-consuming drizzle.
Yellow light filters through from Solly's 'Grand Fish and Chips Palace'. Door
tight-shut against the weather. Inside stuffy with heat, hot bodies, steaming
clothes, and the nauseating smell of stale fish oil. Misty patterns on the plate-glass
windows and a messy pool where rain has filtered beneath the door and mixed with
the sawdust.
Solly himself in shirt sleeves, sweating, vulgar, and moody. Bellowing at a
dripping woman who has just come in.
'Shut 'e damn door. Think you live in a tent?'
'Ag, Solly.'
'Don' ag me. You coloured people can never shut blarry doors.'
'Don't bloomingwell swear at me.'
'I bloomingwell swear at you, yes.'
'Come. Gimme two pieces 'e fish. Tail cut.'
'Two pieces 'e fish.'
'Raining like hell outside,' the woman said to no one.
'Mmmmmm. Raining like hell,' a thin befezzed Malay cut in.
'One an' six. Thank you. An' close 'e door behin' you.'
'Thanks. Think you got 'e on'y door in Hanover Street?'
'Go to hell!' Solly cut the conversation short and turned to another customer.
The northwester sobbed heavy rain squalls against the windowpanes. The
Hanover Street bus screeched to a slithery stop and passengers darted for shelter in
a cinema entrance. The street lamps shone blurredly.
Solly sweated as he wrapped parcels of fish and chips in a newspaper. Fish and
chips. Vinegar? Wrap? One an' six please. Thank you! Next. Fish and chips. No?
Two fish. No chips? Salt? Vinegar? One an' six please. Thank you! Next. Fish an'
chips.
'Close 'e blarry door!' Solly glared daggers at a woman who had just come in.
She half smiled apologetically at him.
'You coloured people are worse than Kaffirs.'
She struggled with the door and then stood dripping in a pool of wet sawdust.
Solly left the counter to add two presto logs to the furnace. She moved out of the
way. Another customer showed indignation at Solly's remark.
'You blooming Jews are always making coloured people out.'
'Go to hell!' Solly dismissed the attack on his race. Fish an' chips. Vinegar?
Salt? One an' six. Thank you.
'Yes, madam?'
'Could you tell me when the bioscope comes out?'

'Am I the blooming manager?'

'Please.'

'Half pas' ten,' the Malay offered helpfully.

'Thank you. Can I stay here till then? It's raining outside.'

'I know it's blarrywell raining, but this is not a Salvation Army.'

'Please, baas!'

This caught Solly unawares. He had had his shop in that corner of District Six since most could remember and had been called a great many unsavoury things in the years. Solly didn't mind. But this caught him unawares. *Please, baas.* This felt good. His imagination adjusted a black bow tie to an evening suit. *Please, baas.*

'Okay, stay for a short while. But when 'e rain stops you go!' She nodded dumbly and tried to make out the blurred name of the cinema opposite, through the misted windows.

'Waitin' for somebody?' Solly asked. No response.

'I ask if yer waitin' fer somebody!' The figure continued to stare.

'Oh go to hell,' said Solly, turning to another customer.

Through the rain blur Siena stared at nothing in particular. Dim visions of slippery wet cars. Honking and wheezing in the rain. Spluttering buses. Heavy, drowsy voices in the Grand Fish and Chips Palace. Her eyes travelled beyond the street and the water cascades of Table Mountain, beyond the winter of Cape Town to the summer of the Boland. Past the green grapelands of Stellenbosch and Paarl and the stuffy wheat district of Malmesbury to the lazy sun and laughter of Teslaarsdal. A tired sun here. An uninterested sun. Now it seemed that the sun was weary of the physical effort of having to rise, to shine, to comfort, and to set.

Inside the nineteenth-century, gabled mission church she had first met Joseph. The church is still there, and beautiful, and the ivy climbs over it and makes it more beautiful. Huge silver oil lamps suspended from the roof, polished and shining. It was in the flicker of the lamps that she had first become aware of him. He was visiting from Cape Town. She sang that night like she had never sung before. Her favourite psalm.

'All ging ik ook in een dal der schaduw des doods . . . Though I walk through the valley of the shadow of death . . . *der schaduw des doods.'* And then he had looked at her. Everyone had looked at her, for she was good in solos.

'Ik zoude geen kwaad vreezen . . . I will fear no evil.' And she had not feared, but loved. Had loved him. Had sung for him. For the wide eyes, the yellow skin, the high cheekbones. She had sung for a creator who could create a man like Joseph. *'Want gij zijt met mij; Uw stok en Uw staf, die vertroosten mij.'*

Those were black and white polka-dot nights when the moon did a golliwog cakewalk across a banjo-strung sky. Nights of sweet remembrances when he had whispered love to her and told her of Cape Town. She had giggled coyly at his obscenities. It was fashionable, she hoped, to giggle coyly at obscenities. He lived in one of those streets off District Six and was, he boasted, quite a one among the girls. She heard of Molly and Miena and Sophia and a sophisticated Charmaine, who was almost a schoolteacher and always spoke English. But he told her that he had only found love in Teslaarsdal. She wasn't sure whether to believe him. And then he had felt her richness and the moon darted behind a cloud.

The loud screeching of the train to Cape Town. Screeching loud enough to drown the protest of her family. The wrath of her father. The icy stares of Teslaarsdal matrons. Loud and confused screechings to drown her hysteria, her ecstasy. Drowned and confused in the roar of a thousand cars and a hundred thousand lights and a summer of carnival evenings that is Cape Town. Passion in a tiny room off District Six. Desire surrounded by four bare walls and a rickety chair and a mounted cardboard tract that murmured *Bless this House.*

And the agony of the nights when he came home later and later and sometimes not at all. The waning of his passion and whispered names of others. Molly and Miena and Sophia. Charmaine. The helpless knowledge that he was slipping from her. Faster and faster. Gathering momentum.

'Not that I'm saying so but I only heard . . .'

'Why don't you go to bioscope one night and see for yourself . . .'

'Marian's man is searching for Joseph . . .' Searching for Joseph. Looking for Joseph. Knifing for Joseph. Joseph. Joseph! JOSEPH! Molly! Miena! Sophia! Names! Names! Names! Gossip. One-sided desire. Go to bioscope and see. See what? See why? When! Where!

And after he had been away a week she decided to see. Decided to go through the rain and stand in a sweating fish and chips shop owned by a blaspheming Jew. And wait for the cinema to come out.

The rain had stopped sobbing against the plate-glass window. A skin-soaking drizzle now set in. Continuous. Unending. Filming everything with dark depression. A shivering, weeping neon sign flickered convulsively on and off. A tired Solly shot a quick glance at a cheap alarm clock.

'Half pas' ten, bioscope out soon.'

Siena looked more intently through the misty screen. No movement whatsoever in the deserted cinema foyer.

'Time it was bloomingwell out.' Solly braced himself for the wave of after-show customers who would invade his Palace.

'Comin' out late tonight, missus.'

'Thank you, baas.'

Solly rubbed sweat out of his eyes and took in her neat and plain figure. Tired face but good legs. A few late stragglers catching colds in the streets. Wet and squally outside.

'Your man in bioscope?'

She was intent on a khaki-uniformed usher struggling to open the door.

'Man in bioscope, missus?'

The cinema had to come out some time or other. An usher opening the door, adjusting the outside gate. Preparing for the crowds to pour out. Vomited and spilled out.

'Man in bioscope?'

No response.

'Oh, go to hell!'

They would be out now. Joseph would be out. She rushed for the door, throwing words of thanks to Solly.

'Close the blarry door!'

She never heard him. The drizzle had stopped. An unnatural calm hung over the empty foyer, over the deserted street. Over her empty heart. She took up her stand on the bottom step. Expectantly. Her heart pounding.

Then they came. Pouring, laughing, pushing, jostling. She stared with fierce intensity, but faces passed too fast. Laughing, roaring, gay. Wide-eyed, yellow-skinned, high-cheekboned. Black, brown, ivory, yellow. Black-eyed, laughing-eyed, gay, bouncing. No Joseph. Palpitating heart that felt like bursting into a thousand pieces. If she should miss him. She found herself searching for the wrong face. Solly's face. Ridiculously searching for hard blue eyes and a sharp white chin in a sea of ebony and brown. Solly's face. Missing half a hundred faces and then again searching for the familiar high cheekbones. Solly. Joseph. Molly. Miena. Charmaine.

The drizzle restarted. Studying overcoats instead of faces. Longing for the pale blue shirt she had seen in the shop at Solitaire. A bargain at £1. 5s. She had scraped and scrounged to buy it for him. A week's wages. Collecting her thoughts and continuing the search for Joseph. And then the thinning out of the crowd and the last few stragglers. The ushers shutting the iron gates. They might be shutting Joseph in. Herself out. Only the ushers left. And the uncompromising iron gates.

'Please, is Joseph inside?'

'Who's Joseph?'

'Is Joseph still inside?'

'Joseph who?'

They were teasing her. Laughing behind her back. Preventing her from finding him.

'Joseph is inside!' she shouted frenziedly.

'Look, merrim, it's raining cats an' dogs. Go home.'

Go home. To whom? To what? An empty room? An empty bed? A tract that shrieked its lie, *Bless this House?*

And then she was aware of the crowd on the corner. Maybe he was there. Running and peering into every face. Joseph. The crowd in the drizzle. Two battling figures. Joseph. Figures locked in struggle slithering in the wet gutter. Muck streaking down clothes through which wet bodies were silhouetted. Joseph. A blue shirt. And then she wiped the rain out of her eyes and saw him. Fighting for his life. Desperately kicking in the gutter. Joseph. The blast of a police whistle. A pickup van screeching to a stop.

'Please, sir, it wasn't him. They all ran away. Please, sir, he's Joseph. He done nothing. He done nothing, my baas. Please, sir, he's my Joseph. Please, baas!'

'*Maak dat jy weg kom.* Get away. *Voetsak!*'

'Please, sir, it wasn't him. They ran away!'

Alone. An empty bed. An empty room.

Solly's Grand Fish and Chips Palace crowded out. People milling inside. Rain once more squalling and sobbing against the door and windows. Swollen gutters unable to cope with the giddy rush of water. Solly sweating to deal with the after-cinema rush.

Fish an' chips. Vinegar? Salt? One an' six. Thank you. Sorry, no fish. Wait five minutes. Chips on'y. Vinegar? Ninepence. Tickey change. Thank you. Sorry, no fish. Five minutes' time. Chips? Ninepence. Thank you. Solly paused for breath and stirred the fish.

'What's 'e trouble outside?'

'Bioscope, Solly.'

'No, man, outside!'

'I say, bioscope.'

'What were 'e police doin'? Sorry, no fish yet, sir. Five minutes' time. What were 'e police doin'?'

'A fight in 'e blooming rain.'

'Jeeesus, in 'e rain?'

'Ja.'

'Who was fightin'?'

'Joseph an' somebody.'
'Joseph?'
'Ja, fellow in Arundel Street.'
'Yes, I know Joseph. Always in trouble. Chucked him outta here a'reddy.'
'Well, that chap.'
'An' who?'
'Dinno.'
'Police got them?'
'Got Joseph.'
'Why were 'ey fightin'? Fish in a minute, sir.'
'Over a dame.'
'Who?'
'You know Miena who works by Patel? Now she. Her boyfriend caught 'em.'
'In bioscope?'
'Ja.'
Solly chuckled deeply, suggestively.
'See that woman an' 'e police?'
'What woman?'
'Dame cryin' to 'e police.'
'They say it's Joseph's dame.'
'Joseph always got plenty 'e dames. F–I–S–H—R–E–A–D–Y!!! Two pieces
for you, sir? One an' six. Shilling change. Fish an' chips? One an' six. Thank you.
Fish on'y? Vinegar? Salt? Ninepence. Tickey change. Thank you!'
'What you say about 'e woman?'
'They say Joseph's girl was crying to 'e police.'
'Oh, he got plenty 'e girls.'
'This one was living with him.'
'Oh, what she look like? Fish, sir?'
'Okay. Nice legs.'
'Hmmmmm,' said Solly, 'Hey, close e' damn door. Oh, you again.' Siena
came in. A momentary silence. Then a buzzing and whispering.
'Oh,' said Solly, nodding as someone whispered over the counter to him. 'I see.
She was waiting here. Musta been waitin' for him.' A young girl in jeans giggled.
'Fish an' chips costs one an' six, madam.'
'Wasn't it one an' three before?'
'Before the Boer war, madam. Price of fish go up. Potatoes go up an' you expect
me to charge one an' three?'
'Why not?'
'Oh, go to hell! Next, please!'
'Yes, that's 'e one, Solly.'
'Mmmm. Excuse me, madam'—turning to Siena—'like some fish an' chips?
Free of charge, never min' 'e money.'
'Thank you, my baas.'
The rain now sobbed wildly as the shop emptied, and Solly counted the cash in
his till. Thousands of watery horses charging down the street. Rain drilling into
cobbles and pavings. Miniature waterfalls down the sides of buildings. Blurred
lights through unending streams. Siena listlessly holding the newspaper parcel of
fish and chips.
'You can stay here till it clears up,' said Solly.
She looked up tearfully.

Solly grinned, showing his yellow teeth. 'It's quite okay.'
A smile flickered across her face for a second.
'It's quite okay by me.'
She looked down and hesitated for a moment. Then she struggled against the
door. It yielded with a crash and the northwester howled into Solly's Palace.
'Close 'e blarry door!' he said, grinning.
'Thank you, my baas,' she said as she shivered out into the rain.

From *Quartet*, pp. 142–50.

RICHARD RIVE   *Born in 1931 in Cape Town, South Africa. Son of a black American
father and coloured South African mother. Did his BA at University of Cape Town. His novel,*
Emergency, *is built around the Sharpeville massacre.*

[16]

8   *Lagos Interlude*

RALPH OPARA

My cousin Nwankechukukere spent forty-eight hours in Paris. She is now an
expert on the slim-look, the full-length look and all the possible combinations of
'looks' usually associated with Parisian *haute couture*. She also made an overnight
stop in Rome and heard Maria Callas warbling her mellisonant way through
Verdi's 'Aida' at La Scala. La Scala, unfortunately happens to be in Milan, and
Milan is quite some way from Rome. But then you never know the number of
activities that could be fitted into an overnight stop. She is also an accomplished
dancer, she probably tripped the light fantastic to the accompaniment of bedouin
strings, in a tent somewhere north of Timbuctoo. But the Kano-bound plane
makes no provision for refuelling in the middle of the Sahara.

Cousin Nwankechukukere came back with a wardrobe the size of the Eiffel
Tower and such impressive ideas indicative of her profound study of de Gaulle,
the Common Market and slimming. She had become a woman. She even changed
her name. There was no fanfare about this. I had expected the usual insertion in
the papers: 'I, formerly known, called, addressed as . . . shall from today hence-
forward be known, called, addressed, etc' and the bit about 'former documents
remaining valid'. But no. Cousin Nwankechukukere just changed her name to
'Nwa'. To me there was a delightful crunchiness in 'Nwan-ke-chu-ku-ke-re', a
crunchiness redolent of fried corn and groundnuts eaten with coconut. It was a
pity to lose all that. Furthermore Nwankechukukere as a name should give the

bearer a superiority complex. It is a name which literally means 'She-who-is-made-by-God'.

Her new unpoetic and uncrunchy name she pronounced firmly with a French accent—which was rather like saying *s'il vous plaît* with an Ibo accent. Indeed she taught me the gentle art of punctuating my sentences in English with *s'il vous plaît*. This was a *sine qua non* in polite conversation. I have even heard her on occasions, at her abusive best, call an offending houseboy 'a pig-headed son-of-a-bitch, *s'il vous plaît*'!

She did me the honour one day, of asking me to take her in my car into the shopping centre on Lagos Island. My first reaction was naturally an appropriate one—surprise. It seemed to me most strange that after her pilgrimage to the Champs Elysées and Arc de Triomphe (from where a Frenchman took off on an orbital flight), that she should ask for a form of transport much slower than a moon rocket. In fact I had misgivings over the ability of my decrepit four-cylinder wagon to live up to its reputation of good behaviour. It might develop stage fright or throw a tantrum. My reward for trouble-free motoring with my cousin as passenger to the Island and back to Lagos Mainland was a free lesson in the cha-cha-cha. They say that driving, like love, is a many splendoured thing. If a Dr Jekyll wanted a catalyst for his transformation into a Mr Hyde, he only needs to get behind a wheel and on to a road in Lagos. I have no reason to disbelieve this. I do know that driving in Lagos can be more than a many splendoured thing. It brings out the best in a man and the beast too—and the beast is the fellow in the driver's seat of the car behind. On this occasion, a veritable King Kong in the car behind, sat with all his King Kongly might on the horn of his car, playing, no doubt, a salutation to the African sun. My driving mirror told me that the fellow was not a taxi driver—only taxi drivers have the distinction of transforming car horns into battle sirens. My mirror also told me that the fellow was shaking his fist—the well-known gesture of impatient motorists. All this began when I drove into Herbert Macaulay Road on Lagos Mainland—and cousin Nwa thought it was all *ça ne va pas*!

As we crawled to a busy road junction, a woman who had a basket on her head, a baby on her back and wings on her feet, decided to fly across the road. But with one hand clutching her basket and the other holding the baby, her feet seemed to lose all sense of direction. She zigzagged into head-on collision with a school boy in green uniform, turned right round, her arms flapping and ran for the kerb screaming, '*Olorun, Olorun-o*' (God, God).

I stepped sharply on my brakes. This sent cousin Nwa flying into the windscreen and the driver behind into another fit of horn blowing. Now was my chance to do something about the nuisance behind me. I flung open my door nearly knocking over a cyclist; he rode away invoking the goddess of Lagos waters to flood me out of my house. But I had no time for him. I strode purposefully towards the horntooter. I raised my right hand to point a big finger at him when—we recognized each other. 'Oh, hallo,' he said, 'I have been trying to attract your attention. I think the back tyre of your car is going flat.'

Now, that was hardly fair; I mean, the fellow might at least have let me unburden myself of some of the morning's accumulated irritations. I felt unjustly repressed, and apprehensive of the effect of this on my heart. I had read a few psychologists and their injunctions never to bottle-up one's feelings. In the circumstances, all I could do was to say, 'Well, thank you very much Olu'. I turned to do something about parking the car properly and getting out the spare wheel.

'Hey there.' This was from a policeman who suddenly appeared from nowhere. He was armed to the teeth with notebooks and ball pens. 'Park there,' he said, pointing at a section of the road. 'Yes, certainly—of course—em, if you say so.' I smiled. 'I say so!' He barked. I stopped smiling. He carefully selected a pen to match the notebook in his hand. 'Obstruction; that's what it is. Obstruction. Do you know you are causing obstruction—in traffic—eh?' 'Wait a minute constable—eh, officer, I merely stopped to—em—park to change a flat tyre.' 'Obstruction—causing obstruction—don't you know traffic must go on?' At this he flicked open a blank page of his notebook, and turned the bonnet of my car into a writing desk. 'Give me your *particular*.' He fixed a gaze at Cousin Nwa. 'I beg your pardon,' I said. I think Cousin Nwa almost giggled but thought better of it.

'You don't hear me? Give your particular,' repeated the policeman and he flicked open another page of his notebook and changed his blue pen for a red one. Cousin Nwa now switched on what she thought was a most disarming smile, turned to our man and said:

'Please officer, my cousin is driving me into Lagos Island to shop, *s'il vous plaît*.' He fixed her with a look which implied: 'Young lady, you better look out,' but he said, 'That question is not relevant to this matter sir—madam.' And cousin Nwa did a most surprising thing. She shut up—and sought refuge in the centre pages of a daily paper. 'Well, well, well, where is your particular?' He flicked open a third page but did not change pens. 'Give me your licence, driving licence, motor licence, insurance licence—everything.'

At this point a police van in which our policeman had driven up and which was parked not very far from the scene, passed by. The man at the wheel smiled and nodded to our man. The smile meant everything in the sentence 'Carry on, old chap, you have landed your fish.'

'You see officer,' I began—'You are wasting time. Give me the particular. Your name? Age, address?' He paused as he wrote these down. The next thing naturally would be to inquire into my marital status, financial status, age next birthday, father's tribe, mother's tribe, religious denomination . . . but he did not seem to want these. 'OK,' he said, 'where the licence?' I reached for my brief case on the back seat of the car, but the licence was not in it. That confirmed his suspicion; I did not possess any. 'I'm sorry officer, but the licence is on my writing desk at home. It should have been in my brief case.' 'Ho,' he cried, 'you think you fool me.' A third notebook appeared; the red pen disappeared. 'Well, your licence is not here. Therefore you are a learner. Therefore you are driving without a licence,' he paused, 'then you are a learner!'

A few passers-by were taking some interest in all this. A man in a yellow shirt got off his bicycle, rolled up to Cousin Nwa's side and took a solid front-line position. It was not clear whether he wanted to hear every word that passed between the officer and myself. Detectives have been known to wear yellow shirts. The next cyclist who had obviously seen this sort of motorist-policeman situation on several occasions, did not try to stop, he merely shouted 'I-go drive myself' which was his way of telling everybody within ear-shot that I could not afford a driver. This was the truth of course. But his tone of voice suggested that this was an unpardonable sin. Perhaps he was a dedicated Trade Unionist who had made a pilgrimage to a certain place behind the Iron Curtain and now spoke out loud and clear on behalf of down-trodden commercial drivers, deprived of jobs by the likes of me. Anyway the policeman's voice was louder and clearer as he declared: 'Yes, that is how you people drive in Lagos. No licence! You are a learner. Yes I think so.' He looked at cousin Nwa to confirm this, but she instead opened her handbag, took out a dainty little handkerchief and dabbed at a small bead of perspiration on her forehead. Mr Yellow-shirt thought this was most elegant and said in admiration, 'Ah, sissy!' The word 'Sissy', a corrupt form of sister, was a general term for 'young lady'. But Cousin Nwa did not take kindly to this form of address and did the most inelegant thing that day. She told Yellow-shirt, 'Go home and mind your own business.' Whether she expected Yellow-shirt to execute a D'Artagnan bow, I don't know. But what Yellow-shirt did do was not to be found in any Encyclopaedia of Good Manners. He made a rude sign at cousin Nwa and made her taste a few choice expressions from his larder of Yoruba invectives. He rounded the whole business off with; 'Get away, you think I no know you. I see you before at Yaba roundabout'; which was his way of saying that Cousin Nwa walked the streets at night, s'il vous plaît!

The audience cheered—especially a hawker with an assortment of articles ranging from clothes pegs to leather watch straps. Now he did not exactly show the kind of tact expected of an experienced salesman. He sidled up to cousin Nwa, thrust a pair of sunglasses in her hand, and said: 'Madam will buy? Four shillings and sixpence only.' My cousin, who had passed through a thousand and one emotional stages in the few seconds following Yellow-shirt's insult, did what came naturally. She threw the sunglasses out of the car, and covered her face with her hands. The hawker did a marvellous dive, a smart wicketkeeper he was, and caught the sunglasses. But then he dropped quite a few of the clothes pegs, woollen socks, watch straps and other sunglasses. Yellow-shirt quickly picked these up for him and with a grin the hawker promptly asked Madam to buy a ladies' watch since she did not like sunglasses.

Cousin Nwa was a thoroughly confused woman, not knowing what to do about Yellow-shirt or the hawker. But swiftly and surely, inspiration came and with a voice which would have done credit to any drill-major, she shouted: 'Officer, arrest this man.'

This request did not exactly specify whether she meant Yellow-shirt or the hawker. The hawker looked at Yellow-shirt; Yellow-shirt looked at the hawker. And I thought they were going to toss a coin to determine to whom the honour was due. Now the policeman, still standing on my side of the car was just then assuring me for the fourth time that he was convinced I was a learner driver. He was in fact prepared to have a bet on it. This was a financial proposition that interested me very much. But cousin Nwa cut into this frank and fair discussion with: 'Officer, arrest this man.'

Yellow-shirt and the hawker did not like this insistent appeal to the policeman. Apparently they were, in their private lives, God-fearing, water-drinking, law-abiding, tax-paying citizens and nothing must tarnish their record. Perhaps this accounted for the strange turn of events. The hawker appealed to everyone around to bear witness that he meant no offence and that if a man asked a young lady to purchase a pair of sunglasses to protect her eyes from the wicked sun, did the man do wrong? Yellow-shirt thought the hawker was trying to pass the buck. 'Me and you,' he declared, holding the front of the hawker's singlet, 'me and you, na who make the sissy vex. Eh?'

The audience refused to take sides. Said the hawker, 'Leave me.' Replied Yellow-shirt, 'Leave me.' And they left each other; this they did either to emphasize the peace-loving aspects of their characters or because the policeman had brought out another notebook and a blue pen. The audience was naturally disappointed—and one or two muttered under their breath, 'Ojo', 'Ojo', the Yoruba for 'coward'.

Cousin Nwa could not quite see why the Black Maria had not rolled up to whisk away the miscreants. So she urged, for the umpteenth time, 'Officer, arrest this man.'

The policeman opened the fifth page of his notebook, wrote something and said to me 'Bring your licence and show me at the station by 5 p.m. today.' At that he shut his notebook, returned the pen to his pocket and marched away to deal with more obstructions farther up the road.

And that you may say was the end of my privilege of taking Cousin Nwa shopping, *s'il vous plaît.*

From *Reflections*, pp. 100–5.

RALPH C. OPARA   *Born in 1933 in eastern Nigeria. BA, University College, Ibadan.*

[2, 5, 10, 11, 15, 21, 22, 81]

9   *Rain*

NKEM NWANKWO

The land-boat caused a stir throughout Aniocha as it wound its way through snaky pathways, brushed past scorched bushes, swerved from tall palms and then came to rest in the shade of an ogbu tree in front of a big iron house. The owner climbed out, and as he did so, he gave a sharp order to the driver. Then he turned and waved cheerfully to the many people who had gathered to admire his boat. He was of medium height, stocky, with scarred face and sharp eyes which were not sure whether to twinkle or to be suspicious. His agbada, of brown print, seemed to belong to a smaller man so that it hadn't many of the usual superfluous folds. The man walked briskly with an impetuous gait and soon entered the iron house. The many people who had followed the progress of the land-boat with awe now came from several directions and surrounded it. They had seen many of its like before but this was the first to be owned by an Aniocha man. 'Ahai,' said a herdsman, 'it shines like lightning.' 'I wonder how much it costs. Can the money in all Aniocha buy it?' 'Impossible.' 'I look like a spirit,' said an old woman peering dimly at her image distorted on the body of the car. 'Wait, people of my land,' said the herdsman, listening, 'our man!' Bells were heard tinkling in unison in the distance. The attention of the crowd was at once drawn away from the boat. 'Rain!' they said, turning delighted, expectant faces towards the direction from which it blew. A little later, a lithe, tall man turned a corner and lunged towards the group. The tinkles came with him. They were produced by small, bronze bells which were sewn on to a blue cloak lined with white which draped him from shoulder to ankle. 'Rain!' many shouted again, and some, 'Is he drunk?' 'Hoa!' roared the newcomer. His clear-cut features were very expressive, his eyes laughing, 'kliklikli!'

'Yiii!' returned the crowd.

'Kliklikli!'

'Yiii!'

'I give to each man his own. Goodness to all. If there is any man to whom what is good is not good let him put his head into the fire and see how he likes it.' There was much more flourish after this, some wits in the audience chaffing Rain and he riposting aptly. Then he said, pointing to the land-boat:

'Do they say this is our brother's?'

'It belongs to Ndulue Oji.'

'Man of our family?'

'True word.'

'So this world is ours?'

'Ahai!'

Rain stood thinking for a moment. Then coming to a decision he walked to the car, opened its back door and climbed in. 'Ahai,' he sighed trying the cushion, 'world that is good.' 'That is the way it is done,' said the herdsman, grinning. 'If my bottom were strong, I would do the same.' The driver of the car had gone somewhere to drink water, and soon returned. He was dressed in white overalls and peaked cap. 'What next?' he said as he saw Rain. 'You are brave!' Rain peeped out of the window. 'Does he say it is what?' he said. 'Come out,' roared the driver. 'If I were angered too, I would break his head,' said Rain. 'Do you come out or may I chuck you out!' shouted the driver, beside himself. 'People of our land,' said Rain, 'but for my bowing to your eyes I would break this boy's head. He has fired my anger.' The old woman intervened. 'You can't talk to him that way, my son,' she said to the driver. 'He is not your age group.' 'And while we are talking, the land-boat does not belong to you,' said another woman, 'I can't understand these boys.' 'Get going, old bones,' said the driver. The women shrank away.

At this moment two men came by, one of whom wore the anklets of the ozo. The driver appealed to them. 'There is a rascal dirtying my master's car,' he said. 'What does he look like?' They poked their heads into the car. 'Ah, it is Danda.' 'Come out,' the ozo man said, 'can't you see you have not grown fit for this type of thing?' 'Men who go about in land-boats have horns?' said Danda, turning to the crowd and inviting them to applaud the quip. They did. 'Come out,' said the ozo. He disliked Danda's persistence, the more so as he would have liked the chance to get into the land-boat himself. 'If every akalogholi is to ride a land-boat, there will be nothing left for the world but to turn upside down.' 'Men of our land,' said Danda, still keeping the sympathy of the crowd, 'did you not tell me that this land-boat belongs to one of my brothers?' 'Therefore it is yours,' roared the herdsman deliberately. 'What belongs to one belongs to one's kindred. Ho ha.'

The appearance of the owner of the car put an end to further altercation. Ndulue Oji had just said farewell to his host and come waddling out. He saw the people gathered about his car and was pleased. Some ten years ago he gazed like them at one of the wonders of the white man. It hadn't occurred to him that he would one day own it. But the war had enriched him, the eyes of his fathers had been open. 'People of our land, I greet you,' he said with a great laugh, shaking hands with a few. Then he put his hand to the handle of the door of his car but stopped, furious. 'Who is this fellow?' he said glaring at the driver. 'He got in when I went to drink water. And I cannot pull him out.' Ndulue looked more closely and, recognizing the intruder, smiled. 'Ah it is you, brother,' he said. He liked Danda.

'Is it Ndulue's voice I hear?' asked Danda.

'Yes, come out!'

'Take me home in this our land-boat.'

'No, you can ride in it any other day but not today.'

'Now.'

'No, come out,' said Ndulue, raising his voice slightly.

'Well, if I were you I would listen, Danda,' said the herdsman conciliating Ndulue.

Danda thought for a moment and then said, 'You think you can turn me out of this land-boat?'

'Yes.'

'You are not fit to.'

'Danda is right,' murmured the old woman. 'Does the law say now that when a man has a land-boat he should forget his kindred!'

Ndulue was beaten. He had made his mark in the world and like most Aniocha 'arrivers' he was now busy cultivating the goodwill of his neighbours. The last thing he wanted was for it to get about that he had refused a member of his kindred hospitality. So, smiling, he nodded to the driver, got in himself and sat beside Danda. The crowd clapped their hands. 'Thank you,' said Danda. 'And farewell. Stay on the ground and eat sand. Danda is flying to the land of the spirits on the wings of the eagle.'

The car cruised past the new beautiful church of the Anglican mission, past the small haberdashery that had recently been opened by one of Ndulue's friends, and past the huge signpost that directed people to the Roman Catholic mission on the other side of the village. 'It is a fine world,' said Danda. 'True,' agreed Ndulue.

Soon they arrived at the big compound walled round with iron, and drove through the stylish door. The house was two-storeyed and was famous all over Aniocha. The plan was after that of a District Officer whom Ndulue had known when he was abroad. This was the man who used to kick him playfully on the shins. But the agonies had won Ndulue the contracts for building prisoners' quarters.

There was a garage at the right and the car was parked in it. The men came out. 'We have done it, son of our fathers,' said Ndulue, watching Danda. 'It was good. We ate the world,' said Danda, leading the way into the two-storeyed house. 'There are people in the shed,' continued Ndulue. Since he completed the house he had become increasingly annoyed with the villagers coming into it, sometimes still carrying their work dirt, sitting firmly on the new cushioned chairs and saying challengingly: 'This house is as much mine as yours.' To stop them he had built a long shed which faced the main building, and had given orders that anybody who wanted palm wine should go there. But a few of the men, of whom Danda was one, had never recognized the demarcation. 'I have no Oji in my parlour,' said Ndulue. 'Never mind,' said Danda.

Two strangers were already in the parlour. Danda greeted them in his usual way. 'Kliklikli!' 'Yiii!' 'Welcome, strangers,' said Danda. 'Aniocha is safe for you. The man who comes to visit should not bring in evil neither should he carry evil away.'

At the sight of his visitors Ndulue was excited. One was a merchant friend of his, a thin man who wore an oversize agbada and an old pair of spectacles. The other was a young 'Senior Service' man dressed quietly in a black suit. 'Are these your faces?' Ndulue roared. He embraced the trader and shook hands with the young man. 'We came a short while ago,' said the former, 'and they said you had not gone far so we decided to wait.' 'You did well, hai.' He embraced the trader again and laughed loud and long. After that he bustled about with a strained, preoccupied expression. 'There is no Oji in this house. This is too bad,' then he said, 'Very well. Okoli Oka!' A stalwart servant in shorts and singlet burst into the room. 'What!' bawled Ndulue, 'Go and dress well, damn fool!' The steward ran back to the servants' quarters. Some minutes later he came back dressed in white overalls and white trousers but no shoes. 'Go and get me the hot drink.' 'We were invited for the feast by our relative here,' the merchant said after the steward had gone. 'Your relatives?' said Ndulue. 'Have you relatives in Aniocha?' 'Yes, didn't you know? My great grandmother on the father's side was married from here.' 'True word?'

The steward came in carrying a tray with a bottle of brandy and three glasses. 'Martell!' announced Ndulue grabbing the bottle roughly. 'Make friends with Martell!' He uttered this phrase a little self-consciously. It was one of the few English expressions he knew. The brandy was to be drunk neat. He carefully measured out a portion into the three glasses. Then he took one and waved the other two on to his guests.

There was in the parlour a long massive table which ran the whole length of the room. The visitors sat on one side of it, Danda and Ndulue on the other. Now before the steward could reach the guests he had to pass Danda and walk right round the table. Danda had been standing, telling the merchant a story. As soon as the steward came abreast of him he took one of the glasses and continued his story. The steward stared, undecided. 'Why did you bring only three glasses?' shouted Ndulue. 'Have I now become so poor that I have to stint glasses. Isn't he very stupid?' he said to his visitors. The merchant laughed. 'Come, take this and serve my own friends. Get another glass for me. And mind, I am tired of your fumbling. I will sack you.' 'Yes sir.' The steward disappeared again to fetch the fourth glass. Ndulue filled it for himself and then said in English, 'Cheers!' 'Cheers!' responded his guests standing. 'Cheers!' said Danda also standing. 'Long life and prosperity,' said Ndulue again in English. The guests raised their glasses aloft.

At the end of the ritual they were about to sit down but Danda said, 'Wait, people of our land. Let us do this thing as it is done.' They were puzzled but remained standing. Danda turned to Ndulue and said, 'Let's have one more drink. If we have to have wine we may as well have enough to fill our mouths.' 'True word,' said the trader measuring out some more drops of brandy. 'That's how it is,' said Danda raising his glass. 'When a man brings Oji we must pray to his ofo. We thank you Ndulue. We pray that from where you got this Oji there will be more of it for you. A hundred more. Let us pray to Chineke Olisaebuluwa who made all things. Chineke, come down from the sky and eat Oji. Spirits of the dead come and eat Oji.' Danda tipped some liquid on the floor. Ndulue had waited with some impatience for the end of the story. At last he said: 'Son of our fathers.' 'The

world is bad nowadays,' said Danda. 'Let the world be good. Let this Oji cleanse
the world. Let it make us friends. May each man have what is due to him. The
hawk shall perch and the eagle shall perch. Whichever bird says to the other, don't
perch, let its wings break.' And Danda tossed the drink into his mouth and sighed
gustily. The others sat down.

'How is our business?' Ndulue said to the civil servant who till now had said
nothing. 'It goes on.' 'Have they seen the face of our paper yet?' 'Not yet.' He
was an Assistant District Officer. A month before, his superior had advertised for
contractors to build some culverts in a Native Authority road. Ndulue had
prepared his tender and had passed it to the young officer asking him to try his best
to see it through. 'We shall see what can be done,' said the ADO. But apparently
this reply was not sufficiently re-assuring. Ndulue had waited on the young man,
pressed him to his house, given him Martell. 'We shall see what can be done.' The
man stuck to this noncommital position. The trouble was that though he had often
accepted gifts he hadn't learnt how to give them. They said that the safest way was
to deal through the District Officer's steward. But even this method spelled its own
peril. 'We shall do our best,' he repeated warily. 'It is well,' said Ndulue. 'I don't
understand white men. I have never been to England. You have been and I know
you know how to deal with our man. It is good for a man to have legs in many
places.'

There was a lull in the conversation after this. And Danda who could not bear
silence dispelled it. He sang in a husky-sweet voice shaking his head from side to
side and occasionally stopping to bawl: 'ewe ewe ewe! that's the way we do it!'
'Rain,' said Ndulue smiling. And then to the guests as if explaining Danda's
aberration: 'He is my brother.' 'Ewe, ewe ewe!' Danda continued braying. After
some minutes he made an end. Then he carefully untied from a thick knot at the
edge of his wrapper a beautifully carved oja and began to flute with it. The silvery
sounds darted up to the ceiling ruffling the cobwebs at the four corners of the room
and ringing to life the clod-like statues that stood in framed family pictures on the
wall. 'O! O! O!' cried Danda, moved to ecstasy by his own fluting. Then he drew
an impudent finale and waited for the type of applause he was used to. There was
none. Danda burst out. 'Why are we solemn? Why are we dressed up? Have we
forgotten how to stand on our heads?' Danda stood on his head, and waved his
legs in the air. 'Why don't we eat pepper?' he said as he regained his feet. 'No, I
am not drunk. But why are we dumb. Dance, shout, laugh. Eat pepper. Shake
hands!' He shook hands with all of them. At last the visitors took their leave.
Ndulue, fussing insistently saw them out.

Danda stood on the top of the cement steps in front of the house and watched the
golden ridges moulded by the departing sun. 'Rain has been entertained in the
house,' whispered an occupant of the shed to a friend. 'He doesn't go for small
things, Rain.' 'God created the world,' cried Danda. He cleaned the saliva off the
oja and began to flute again, calling the praise names of the men who sat in the
shed.

One of them leapt out and ran towards the farther wall of the compound
shouting, 'Ewe ewe ewe!' His praise name had been mentioned by the oja and this
had made him mad—'ewe ewe ewe!' he roared stopping precariously only a pace
from the corrugated iron cover of the wall. Then he ran back to his place still
bawling. Ndulue had come back now and was free to work himself up to the same
level of excitement as the rest. 'That's how it is, flute man,' he cried as he heard
his praise name fluted, 'I hear you!' He ran into his house, and a minute later

returned, carrying a double-barrelled gun, loaded it, and let off two volleys into the heavens. 'Sing on. You are in my house and no evil can fall on you. It is I, Ndulue, who say you should sing.' He thumped his chest for emphasis and laughed his mighty laugh. The last strains of the song trailed away. Then Danda, crying 'o! o! o!' sprinted out of the compound. Nnoli Nwego, a giant of a man with huge shoulders and a small head, detached himself from the other people in the shed and joined him. 'I have eaten the world,' Danda said to him. 'Did Ndulue give you palm wine?' 'I am not drunk.' 'You said you ate the world!' 'I fled to the land of the spirits on the wings of the eagle,' Danda said.

From *Reflections*, pp. 18–24.

NKEM NWANKWO   *Born in 1936 in Onitsha, Nigeria. Teacher and writer, studied for his degree at University of Ibadan.*

[3, 5, 32, 45]

10   A Short Journey. . .

BUCHI EMECHETA

It was still dark when they started on their winding, red-earthed journey to Onitsha. [. . .]

The silence was profound. The night animals had gone into hiding and the day ones were still reluctant to come out into the open to start their early morning business. Ojebeta and her brother were not unaware of the animals' sleepy movements in the thick walls of the green forest as the subdued noise of their footsteps startled one or two creatures into temporary wakefulness. Except for these minor signs of activity, there was stillness everywhere. As they padded through the bush tracks, they seemed to be entering the very belly of the earth. It was as if they were being gradually but nonetheless determinedly swallowed by a dark, mysterious, all-green world, the walls of which were enveloping them, fencing them in, closing them up. Overhead hung the tangled branches of huge tropical trees, on both sides of them were large leaves, creeping plants and enormous tree-trunks, all entwined together to form this impenetrable dark green grove.

The foot track they were following was like a thin red snake hemmed in by the two sides of this green presence so that they could not even see its head, because that end was blocked by the meeting of the two green walls ahead.

[. . .] The silence of their surroundings had affected Ojebeta somewhat. Gone were her usual bird-like prattles, her bat-like bumping into things, her teasing of adults. She felt that she was in the presence of a Power mysterious. She felt that she was being watched by that hushed, hidden someone. Had she ever been taught how, her reaction might have been to kneel and pray to that lurking Power who had made the plants so lush, the animals so quiet, the stars so retiring. But she was not Christian; neither was her big brother Okolie, though she sensed his need for silence now too, and knew somehow that the feeling was mutual, She tried hard, and effectively, to subdue the jangling sounds made by the little bells and the empty tobacco tins tied round her arms.

They trekked for what seemed ages until they came to the stream. Here at least they were in the presence of something moving. Clear, glistening water tumbled among tiny rocks and washed the small green plants by the bank. The fact that the area was a kind of clearing which allowed a direct view of the sky, a gap in the green canopy, added to the feeling of openness.

'We must wash,' Okolie said, and ran down the slope that led to the stream without looking behind to find out if his sister was following. His voice, even to himself, sounded alien and unused.

[. . .] She was so taken aback by the purity of it all that she hated to disturb it by wading in to have a wash. Encouraged by her brother's voice, she asked the question that all of a sudden formed in her mind.

'Why is the water so pure and clean?' Her voice was rather loud, and a nearby frog protested by starting to croak furiously, so much so that it awakened several others who joined in the chorus until the stream was filled with the croaky wailings of frogs.

Okolie looked at her accusingly as if to say, 'See what you have done?' Nonetheless he replied patiently to her question. 'It is because there is no one about yet. We are the first people to disturb its calm.'

She thought about this answer for a while and was puzzled at its correctness. Why, had not her mother, her friends, even all the professional storytellers of Ibuza told her that when they and all humans were asleep the people of the dead—Ndi-Nmo—took over? They came to the stream at night to wash themselves and their clothes, just like the living humans did in the day. And when the first cock crowed, they disappeared and returned to their natural habitat, the land of the dead. If that was so, thought Ojebeta, surely they would have left the stream a little disturbed?

'What of the people of the dead?' she piped now. 'They must have been using the stream all night, when we were sleeping. I know that my mother and all those people killed off by the felenza cannot go one day without having a bath. Surely Mother must have been to have her daily bath, even though she has died? I saw the burial. They put all her cooking pots and washing calabashes in her burial mat. My big mother Uteh even put a great calabash of soap in it, so that Mother wouldn't lack any.'

Her brother stopped in his tracks, looked at Ojebeta thoughtfully and said reassuringly: 'The people of the dead are not as dirty and noisy as we are. They don't go about disturbing the peace or stirring up mud. They float, almost like birds.' Then he added, with a little authority, and indicating that he would rather not be asked any more questions on the subject, 'Have your bath: I'm going to the men's bathing place. You must hurry.' [. . .]

Ojebeta stood wondering what it would be like to go into the men's bathing place. She would have liked a glimpse of what it was that the men kept there is such a secret place. Why did they have to go so deep into the dark belly of the forest to bathe, when women and children made do with this open place where the sand was clean and the water clear and shallow? She was not particularly keen on having her bath so early in the morning when almost all the rest of the world was still asleep. Where were they going anyway to warrant this secrecy, this early rising from their sleeping mats? Her brother had simply told her that they were going to see a relative of theirs living in Onitsha.

[. . .] Quite often these days he snapped at her and told her that her questions were childish. So she had begun holding conversations with her mother—had she not been told that the dead do see?—especially when she was as puzzled as she felt now.

'Why, Mother, am I going to see this woman—this Ma Palagada, or whatever her name is? She never came to visit us, not even when Father was alive. Why should I go to see her now, and maybe stay with her? I don't want to stay away from home, away from where you and Father were buried. Mother, Father, answer me, both of you, please . . .'

She listened with both ears and with breath abated, but apart from the half-hearted early songs of birds and the now slowly rising croaks of frogs and the buzzing of water insects, there was no answer. Instead her brother's head showed itself from the grove like the head of a tortoise coming out of its shell. He shouted at her, crossly:

'When will you start your wash? We're going to Onitsha, you know, not to the farm.'

Quickly she threw her small cloth on to the bank, cupped some water over her body and began to rub herself with her palm. Okolie's patience was by now exhausted, and he came towards her hurriedly knotting his loin cloth like someone preparing for a fight, bent down to scoop up some sand from the bottom of the stream, and walked up to her.

'Bend down,' he said rather impatiently.

She obeyed at once, noting the irritation in his voice. He poured the fine sand on to her back and rubbed it gently all over, so that it pleasantly scratched the prickly heat rashes on her dark skin. [. . .]

After her wash, Okolie picked up her small *npe* waist cloth which she had left by the bank, and after shaking off the clinging grass tied it round her. When she smiled her thanks, watching him tie his *otuogwu* in his usual toga fashion, he looked at her but did not return her smile. She sensed that all was not well in his mind but did not ask what. Even if he had told her of his financial worries, she would not have understood. Once more they resumed their path in silence.

[. . .] The dazzling sunshine almost blinded Ojebeta, and she lagged behind, so that her brother was forced to slow down his big strides in order for her to catch up with him.

'Come, little sister, I will carry you on my shoulders,' he said with concern.

She shook her head defiantly, implying that she was capable of walking all the way, but Okolie knew that it was a poor show of reluctance to accept his offer. He knew that her feet must indeed be aching by now, even though her pride would not let her admit it. He smiled sadly. The thought of what he was planning to do to her began to nag at his mind and torment him again, however much he tried to suppress it. He was only doing the right thing, he told himself, the only possible thing. He had no alternative. He begged their dead parents to forgive him, but what else was there for a young bachelor like himself to do with a little sister of merely seven years of age? A spoilt child who was still sucking at her mother's breast when all other children of her age had long been weaned? Mixed up with these feelings of self-justification was the conviction that he desperately needed whatever money came his way to prepare himself for his coming-of-age dance, one of the most important events in his age-group. He could not afford to do anything else . . . .

He looked at Ojebeta again and, as if in compensation for his anticipated sins, he relented his critical thoughts of her and began to address her with her praise names.

'Come on, our beautiful visitor. Who has skin like that of the beautiful wives of the king of Idu? Who is the girl with the cleanest teeth in all the seven lands of the world? Who is our mother's pet and our father's heart? Who is my only sister, who originally came as a visitor but has now decided to stay? Come. Come and ride on your big brother's shoulders, like the queen of the gods on her horse that is part human and part animal. Come!' [. . .]

'Come,' he begged again.

She could no longer refuse. She ran into the protection of his wide arms. He gathered her into his *otuogwu* and his thin red lips spread into a sad smile as he hugged her on to his shoulder.

[. . .] Still Okolie hurried. [. . .] He must catch one of the early canoes owned by the Ijaws which were used to ferry market women on their way to the big Onitsha market.

By Cable Point, he was busy speculating about how much he was going to ask this relative, now very distant, to pay for Ogbanje Ojebeta. He had never sold anyone before, and now he persuaded himself that what he was about to do was not selling in its actual sense. He was giving his sister away into the keeping of this rich lady, and getting some money for her so that, when she grew up, she might be given to a suitable husband and could collect the bride price. Okolie was not unaware of the fact that he was not the eldest of his father's two sons, but he reasoned to himself, 'Where is Owezim now? He left when the felenza was at its height, and I alone was the one who had to gather up our father when he died; I alone had to cover our mother's nakedness when she lay there dead on the mud floor. So I deserve to have the money I need so badly for my coming-of-age dance. What does it matter if I have to trade my sister to get it? She will be well looked after there, better than I can afford to do in Ibuza. Let her go. This is the only way she can survive and grow into adulthood.'

Another thought crossed his mind then. Suppose his sister was sold into slavery to the Potokis, and they took her away across the seas and he never saw her again? He deadened his conscience and reminded himself that the new white men who were now penetrating into their small towns and villages were trying hard to abolish that type of trade. People were not going missing as before. Okolie recollected how in his childhood many young women had been kidnapped in the middle of the night when they went out to their toilet. He could still remember his grandfather coming home with strings of captives after raiding neighbouring villages; some of the captives—the lucky ones—were kept as house slaves, but most of them were either taken down to Bonny or sold to people going to Idu. Those were the times when the human market was at its height. Not now. Nobody would dream of treating this little sister of his that way, because she was special. If it occurred to him that so might the little girls his grandfather had captured in other villages have been special to their people, Okolie stifled the idea. He had now worked his guilty conscience up to such an extent that he found himself running, hurrying to get it over with and forget about it. Life, he said under his breath to himself, is a chance. Ogbanje Ojebeta was now being offered a chance to make the best of her life.

'What is all this hurry and talking to yourself for so early in the day? I have been watching your approach and could not believe my eyes that it was you. And where are you carrying your sister to? Is she not well?'

Okolie in his rush and self-analysis had not seen his in-law Eze coming towards him. In fact he had deliberately set out from Ibuza early to avoid meeting market women whom he knew would start asking questions and maybe offering to take Ojebeta from him—though they would not have given him any money for her, which was what he wanted most. And if he dreaded meeting the Ibuza market women, the worst person on earth he could come across was this in-law of his.

Like many of their sex, the sons of Okwuekwu and their father himself when he was alive did not think much of this man who had had the audacity to marry a girl from their family. After all, Uteh was a beauty; and not only was she a beauty, but she was a daughter born along the Eke market. Yet she had condescended to marry this man with brown skin and eyes that watered all the time like those of wet chicks. His body was of the kind that after each bath looked as if he poured ashes over it. He was never healthy, neither in looks nor in reasoning. Uteh on the other hand had the jet-black skin of the family, and a small intelligent head with a very high forehead. When she walked her heels never reached the ground, only the balls of her feet. She was always standing straight and looking over people's heads for she was tall, so narrow and her body so polished that she had the nickname of 'the black snake that glides'. That she had deigned to marry this fool, however, had alienated her from her blood relatives, who said she had married the most idiotic person in the whole of Ibuza.

Of course, no one actually knew what else was expected of Uteh, since her father accepted the bride price before she was able to make any choice. And what obedient daughter of any family, good or bad, would be allowed to marry a man of her choice? She was only obeying her father's instructions. Okwuekwu was then too young to have a say in such adult matters. And when the bride price was paid by her prospective husband's people, Eze too was a youth and no one knew he would grow up to have short legs, ashy skin and eyes that watered. He was kind to Uteh, and that was all she wanted. It still pained her, however, that in important family matters in which the first daughter of the house ought to have been consulted they always ruled her out.

In fact she had been thinking of taking Ojebeta as her own child, the daughter she had never had. She had borne one son, in her younger days, but had never been pregnant again since then; rumour said it was because she was so narrow that she could not carry children. However, her husband Eze was so satisfied with her that he never even thought of getting himself another wife. This was one of the reasons why people thought him stupid, that he worshipped his woman and did not wish to expand his family. What man in his right senses would entrust his whole future to one son only, and at that a son who had been pampered and spoilt by his mother? He must be a stupid man. And since his wife Uteh visited the medicine man more frequently than was considered good for any woman, who was to say she was not mixing concoction into his food so that he would have eyes for no one but her? Did one ever see a person with such eyes that watered all the time? So people speculated.

Eze, knowing the way people regarded him, at times tended to act somewhat comically just to attract a little respect, but it was always done in such an unorthodox way that all he did for himself was to attract more ridicule. After a while, though, he stopped caring, and rested content to be himself, which meant speaking the truth as tactlessly as he liked, not minding if others laughed and called him 'River Niger eye'.

Now here he stood in the middle of the road and demanded to know where Okolie was going with his sleeping sister.

'We are going on a very important errand to Onitsha,' faltered Okolie, 'and we're in a great hurry, otherwise we shall be late for the early canoes.'

Eze might have watery eyes but he did not have a watery brain. He was thinking. He screwed up his ashy face in such a way as to create a mass of lines like those formed by time. Though he was not a young man, he was by no means aged enough to have acquired such wrinkles: it was one of his comical faces. Then he spoke in a voice, again put on purposely, that sounded like a rabbit that was being strangled.

'And your little sister is part of this errand, too? I mean, is she going to say something at this urgent meeting that warranted your leaving Ibuza when everybody was still asleep?' [. . .]

Okolie saw the situation. Making a clean breast of it would condemn him for ever in the eyes of his people. They would stop calling him Okolie the son of Okwuekwu Oda, and best horn-blower in the Uloko age-group. They would instead call him Okolie who sold his sister for money. But he *needed* this money, he argued with himself. The only alternative to getting it this way would have been to go and steal, and that could result in anything, including death, for if you were caught stealing from another person the owner of the property could hit you with anything he could lay his hands on, even a cutlass. He did not want to work hard at farming, as most members of his age-group did to raise money for their outing preparations; not only would that take a long time but the work was too strenuous. Had not his late father always called him a good-for-nothing, with strong legs and hefty arms which he refused to put to proper use, fit only to go about blowing horn pipes for funeral ceremonies and at bride departures? 'What are those strong arms for, Okolie?' he used to ask. Often he would threaten his son, 'You will not eat from the yam I worked for with my own sweat.' But having said that he would hasten to court to do his 'Order' bit, and behind his back Okolie would convince his mother that he intended to improve his ways. His mother would relent, and give him hot pounded yam and spicy fish soup; and then Okolie would go out with his horn pipe under his cloth, in search of any celebrations in Ibuza. Now that both his parents were dead, he was left to manage a big farm that he did not know how to manage. Some small children had already started calling him 'Okolie Ujo Ugbo'—Okolie the farm truant—for when other young men were out on their farms during the day he was seen walking about doing nothing. Sometimes he took consolation in his horn pipe, though who could enjoy blowing horn pipes when there was no audience to listen, no dancers to dance to the melody?

He would go back to the farm; but first he needed the money his sister would fetch, to see him through the beginning of another farming season and to buy a new horn pipe, and some women's head-scarves which he would have to tie round his waist for the dance. He would also need strings of cowries and little bells for his feet. Essential too were large, colourful ostrich feathers to complete his Uloko outfit. He reasoned with himself now, did anyone ever come of age twice? It happened only once in one's lifetime, and it was the duty of each person to make it as memorable as he could possibly afford. He looked again at this bandy-legged man standing in his path and his patience snapped.

'Move out of my way, you old tortoise, and let me pass.'

'No, Okolie, not before you let me take Ogbanje Ojebeta to her big mother, my wife Uteh. The way you are holding her, one would think you were going to sell her or something. But no blood brother would think of doing such a thing.'

Eze's way of talking artificially slowly gave Okolie time to recover from the shock of being found out in advance. Putting on a bluff, he started to laugh, so heartily that Ojebeta woke up.

'No, in-law, you know that your wife is not the only big mother she has. You remember our relative Olopo who married a Kru man? She is very rich now. They say she has built many houses in Otu at Onitsha. She heard of all the mishaps that were befalling us, with everybody dying and sent me a messenger last market day to tell me that I should bring Ojebeta to Onitsha since she wished to see and buy her this and that, to console her for the loss of her mother. That is why we are going to her. I am hurrying now so that I can catch the Ijaw canoes, and we shall be back in Ibuza in time for the evening meal. Ojebeta will stay with your wife, but first I want her to get over the loss of our mother. Remember they were so close that when she died we found Ojebeta lying across her and clinging to her breast? She has missed Mother so, haven't you?' he asked his little sister, chucking her under the chin. [. . .]

Eze was thinking again, and whatever his thoughts were, they were apparently sad thoughts. He looked at Ojebeta and simply said to her: 'Those who are born to survive will always survive. Your big mother will always welcome you, and the door of my hut is open always to you. The little pieces of yam you would eat would not be wanting in my hut. If you need anywhere to stay, come to us.'

With that he dipped his hand into the jute hunter's bag that hung on his shoulder, brought out a piece of dried fish and gave it to her.

'Take this and break your fast with it.'

He walked away quickly, with no word for Okolie.

Okolie's heart sank. Should he or should he not go ahead with his plans? But who wanted to be saddled with a little seven-year-old sister? And he did not want her living with Uteh, because he did not like Eze. No, let her go to Ma Palagada, and he would collect some money from her. Ogbanje Ojebeta's fate was decided. She must be sold. [. . .]

Onitsha Market

The Onitsha market called Otu, one of West Africa's big meeting places, was situated on the bank of the River Niger and served not only the people of Onitsha but those from the surrounding Ibo towns and villages as well. They regarded this place as the centre of their world. A market day was an occasion to dress up and meet with friends, as well as to buy and sell. The market was where people who wanted to display their dances went, be it an age-group or a family showing the end of their mourning for a departed relative. And there were many superstitions attached to the market place. For example, if a person was insane then so long as the madness was not shown in the market there was hope of a cure. The big markets were places where the visible living met and among them moved the dead and the invisible. [. . .]

Okolie and his charge Ojebeta did not regret leaving the flat-bottomed canoe that had ferried them across the river from Asaba. At first Ojebeta had liked the enthusiastic rowing of the canoe men, so much so that she had allowed her finger; to run through the water as they sped. But after a while, when she had begun to feel dizzy, and a market woman carrying a pot of red palm oil to sell had warned her to take care lest she was thrown into the river, Ojebeta had become scared Her fear was not lessened by the strange loud songs of the canoe men in tune with their stylish rowing. [. . .]

The Eke market was the biggest market Ojebeta had previously ever seen before, but this one looked to her like a whole city. It was a complete market landscape that seemed to stretch for miles. People swarmed and buzzed like insects. Most were dressed up fashionably but some, like the canoe men and the people selling fresh fish, wore only very meagre cloths wrapped kite-like round their loins. Apart from the Ibo traders, there were Yoruba stalls where you could buy different kinds of root medicine and the black dyed cloth called *iyaji* (in fact it was more a navy blue but to the Ibos, who loved things colourful, bright and flowery, anything darkish and plain was black). Even the Northerners—the Hausas, and the tall, graceful Fulani shepherds with their leather knapsacks leather slippers, long whitish robes and dark brown turbans—had stalls. Some of their families had settled permanently in the houses along Otu market and sold delicious Hausa dishes, such as corn and bean dumplings laced with roasted meat in honey, and the beef known as *efi Awusa*. Their women had large holes in their ears through which they wedged bright coral beads bought with the money they made buying and selling in Ibo towns.

[. . .] Ojebeta, though frightened and clutching Okolie, found it fascinating So many people and so many different kinds of Ibo dialect! Her hold on her brother became tighter as she began to notice that people were staring at her. She felt humiliated when she saw a group of women with trays of cassava pulp on their heads laughing and pointing in her direction; one of them, trying to be modest was looking away to hide her laughter.

Ojebeta glanced at her brother, then down at herself, and asked, 'Why are they staring at me so, and laughing?'

Okolie was finding it hard to control his nagging guilt, and as he guided her through the noisy crowds—through the stalls of the fish sellers and the yam sellers towards a more open space in the market—he did not at first hear her question. He heard eventually, after she had tugged him and shouted louder; he knew however, that to give her a full explanation would take long minutes, so he patted her shoulder as if to say she should not worry about those silly people who had nothing better to do than stand there laughing like people with broken heads.

He knew why they were laughing. It was not just because of Ojebeta's safety charms, the bells and cowrie shells that jingled and clanged when she made the slightest movement. It was because his sister also had a very interesting face. All over her features were traced intricate tattoos, the pattern of spinach leaves, with delicate branches running down the bridge of her nose, spreading out on her forehead and ending up at the top of her ears. On each cheek was drawn the outline of a large spinach leaf looking ready to be picked. It was not that many Ibo did not have facial tribal marks of different kinds, rather that few would have put so many on the face of one little girl. But Ojebeta's mother Umeadi, when she realized that her daughter was going to live, had had a reason for going to the expense of engaging the services of the most costly face-marker in Ibuza. For, with such a riot of tribal spinach marks on her only daughter's face, no kidnapper would dream of selling her into slavery. [. . .]

The thought of cutting off Ojebeta's charms occurred to her brother Okolie. Among her own people they were not such a strange affair, but they were out of place in the middle of one of the largest markets in West Africa. They were supposed to be for domestic purposes. Usually it was thought safe to remove such charms from a child when that child could talk coherently enough for any living adult to understand, so that if her persecutors from the other world should ask her to come with them, she could shout, 'Go away, I don't want you. I am happy here.' Then the adult could take a broom or whatever and start to beat all the corners of the room saying, '*Asha, Asha,*' until the child stopped calling for help. [. . .]

But Ogbanje Ojebeta was dearer to her mother than that. She had wanted to make assurance doubly sure, and had allowed her daughter to carry the charms for so long as insurance that she would survive. It was almost as if her mother, without meaning to, had wanted to keep Ojebeta a baby as long as possible, since no little brother or sister followed her. Now Okolie was too frightened of the possible consequences to risk removing the bells and cowries himself.

'Suppose anything should happen to her,' he thought. 'They would say that I killed her. No, let her wear them until I get her into the house of a master.'

Moreover, who could tell what trick their dead parents might be contriving now they were both on the other side? They might be longing to have their only daughter with them and might frighten her to death in her sleep. Who could foretell the thoughts of the dead, even if they were our loved ones? He believed that the living should belong to the living. [. . .]

Their last push and jostle through the crowd round those selling fresh meat brought Okolie and Ojebeta to some stalls that looked very clean and elegant and less noisy. It was as if the women of these stalls were of a different breed, well dressed like people having a special outing. At many of the stalls there were very young girls sitting on low stools with heads bowed, doing some kind of sewing. Ojebeta watched avidly as they passed these colourful stalls of the cloth sellers. They halted rather abruptly in front of one of them, and she guessed that they had reached their destination.

It was a strange destination for a child of seven. She could not have imagined in her most wild dream that this was where they were going. They had walked for miles and for hours and through various kinds of forests, waded streams and been ferried in a canoe to come this far. And now they stood before this gaily coloured stall where thousands of cloths of different patterns hung in rows on wooden shelves. They were so many colours and designs that they all seemed to merge into each other. Some had patterns of leaves on them, some had birds, some fish, some had a design like the mortar used to pound yam—whatever object you could think of, there was bound to be an abada material that had that design.

Sitting on a long bench on the floor were four young girls, aged between nine and fourteen. They were all dressed identically in material with a pattern of cowries on it: the background of the cloth was white and the cowries were deep blue shapes with their edges tinged in yellow. Ojebeta noticed these details only on a closer look, for at first the cloth just looked bluish. They had stopped in front of one of these girls.

'Where is your mother?' Okolie asked in a low, dry voice.

Two girls looked up, and one of the younger ones gave a conspiratorial nudge to the largest and apparently the eldest girl. The latter looked up from her sewing and covered her mouth to prevent the laugh that wanted to escape at the sight of this queer-looking pair at their stall. She could tell from their clothes and from their tribal markings, particularly those on the little girl's face, that they were not from the bush interior but from the Aniocha area. But they certainly were an odd pair, with this big healthy man, in his prime of youth, walking up to stalls in Otu and asking people, 'Where is your mother?' without any form of greeting.

'Look,' whispered the smallest girl, loudly enough for Okolie and Ojebeta to hear, 'look she is wearing bells like market dancers.'

The big girl, who had by now composed herself again, told the small girl to keep quiet and keep her eyes on her work or she would take her to Pa Palagada when they got home. At the mention of that name there was such an unnatural hush that one would have thought that whoever this person or apparition called 'Pa Palagada' was his powers must be immense. Peace suddenly descended; even the girl sniggering and pointing at nothing bent her neck and glued her eyes to her sewing.

The fat girl seemed to think Okolie wished to buy some abada material for Ojebeta, for she took out the wooden measure and waited for him to tell her which he wanted of the innumerable cloths supplied to them mainly by the United Africa Company Europeans.

Okolie studied her with interest. She was an attractive grown girl of about fourteen with large breasts. She looked well fed and so fresh and plump that her skin reminded him of smooth, ripe mangoes, ready to burst open oozing out rich, creamy, sugary juice. He wondered why Ibuza girls were not like that; they were usually thin, with long legs and narrow faces. Well, he debated within himself, this girl probably sat here all day and maybe the most work she did was to fetch firewood for the family or pound yam for the evening meal. An Ibuza girl of her age would have to help her mother plant cassava, help her father peel corn from the cobs when they were ripe, and on her way back from the farm she would carry heads of ripe palm kernels ready to be pressed into oil which could be sold here in the Otu market, apart from that oil kept for the family's cooking and oil lamps. But these girls in Otu did not have to lead such itinerant lives. Although some of them were in fact slaves—Ma Palagada would have paid a sum on their heads, just as he was expecting her to pay something for his sister Ojebeta—yet they appeared to be treated just like the children in any family.

This strengthened his belief that he was doing the right thing for Ojebeta. He was sure Ma Palagada would treat her like one of these girls under her care. He imagined his sister in one of the outfits the girls were wearing; in Ibuza she could only dress like that for big important days, whereas here the girls were well turned out for the Otu market. He also liked their way of speaking the Ibo language, with a tinge of foreign sophistication, not the brash, harsh and pointed accents of his own people who because they were people of the interior did not have to live and trade with as many foreigners as these Ibos of Otu Onitsha. Many Ibo traders came from wherever their homes were just to make money at the Otu market, so that they could buy lands, build fine modern Victorian houses and live very modern, clean and foreign lives.

The big girl went on to say, like someone chanting, that they had just had a brand new supply of abada from the coast.

'You see this one—we call it "*Ejekom be loya*" ("I have a date with a lawyer"),' she sang, pointing with the long wooden measure to a cloth with a plain white background and a border of yellow, pale blue and pink. 'You can't get this from any other stall here in Otu market. Our Ma Palagada has bought the sole right to it for the next four markets from those white UAC people. So if you buy it now for yourself and a yard or two for your girl-wife, you will both be in the height of fashion. People will never stop looking at you and admiring you both because they will never have seen a cloth so smooth and beautiful as this. It looks very like the white *otuogwu* your people like to wear. Just feel its smoothness. It is a cloth in a million.' Then she paused, both for breath and to assure herself that she had been saying the right thing.

Okolie had to smile. [. . .]

He stepped right into the shed that formed the stall. The other girls held their breath, ready to let out a scream just in case they were going to be attacked by a market thief in broad daylight. They had all heard stories from other stalls where there were usually crowds about thieves who would move in on the seller, shouting for her attendance while other members of the gang were making away with goods meant for sale; that was mostly at the stalls of the dry fish sellers, not in the section of those selling cloth. You might also be given counterfeit paper money or even coins minted by some clever persons; but few thieves would think of coming this way and dragging a little girl with cowrie charms and spinach face along. The girls were alarmed, and puzzled, though without losing their outward composure.

'Get out of the stall,' said the big girl menacingly, holding on fast to the wooden measure, 'or I will call the market police.'

Okolie ignored her and sat down in a space at the edge of the bench. 'I have a special message for your mother,' he announced. 'I have come all the way from Ibuza to give her the message. I am a relative of hers. That is why I have come, not to steal cloth. Steal my relative's cloth? Tah! I would never do a thing like that. And this is my sister, not my wife.'

This latest statement intensified the laughter which had been bubbling within the girls, who were not very keen on their sewing anyway. First, they found it difficult to see any kind of resemblance between Ma Palagada and this farmer, the fact too that the big girl could have imagined the man's little sister was his wife made them laugh the more.

'Don't blame me,' said the big girl, defending herself. 'The Owerri people marry their wives like that, and then come to the market for her to be equipped.'

Okolie nodded. 'Not just Owerri people. Many of our people do it.' To himself he said, *Is it not almost the same as I am now about to do to my little sister, young as she is—marry her away to this woman relative? So why condemn the Owerri people or anyone else who does that kind of thing.*

As a gesture of affection, and to help assuage his guilt, he pulled Ogbanje Ojebeta on to his lap and they sat there on the bench, watching the bustle and jostle of the market. He wondered why God had created so many people, and for what reason. And why some of the people created could be as rich as this Ma Palagada and her husband and others as poor as those in Ibuza where he came from, so many farmers all struggling for survival. Then the thought occurred to him that after his Uloko dance he could consider becoming a trader himself. After all, he was going to get some money from Ma Palagada today. His imaginings were not disappointed as he watched the number of customers who came to the stall to buy yards and yards of cloth. One or two even bought the handkerchiefs which the girls were making from scraps of material. The big girl mended some torn cloths for a few people; and all the time the customers paid money, all money. Yes, he was going to get so much money for his sister.

He drew the tired little girl Ojebeta closer to him, and she put her head on his broad shoulder, trusting him as any sister would trust her brother, her only visible relative.

A Necessary Evil

It was now past midday, and it was still very hot. [. . .]

Ojebeta noticed that the water here tasted different, as if something had been added to it. She was about to ask her brother about it when they heard a group of laughing female voices approaching. One of the girls called in a voice so low, so urgent and so sibilantly formed that Ojebeta thought something terrible must be about to happen:

'Chiago, Nwayinuzo—shh . . . shh . . . They are coming. They are coming. . . .'

At once heads were once more bent to work. The big girl called Chiago stood with the wooden cloth measure in her hand like a soldier on guard, almost behind Okolie and his sister. The owners of the jocular voices were still hidden by a stall that jutted into the middle of the passageway. Many other people came and went. Ojebeta was silent in expectation. Okolie's stomach started to rumble in apprehension.

They heard the leave-takings and farewells; and then a very big lady appeared from around the corner—a lady who was tall of bearing, a lady who was very proud. She had a large, very sensuous mouth, and the laughter was still on her lips. She was also the most well-dressed person Ojebeta had ever seen. She was wearing a brown abada with fish patterns on it, a yellow blouse, and silk scarf on her head. She walked with easy steps, saying hello to this stall and how-do-you-do to that person. She seemed to know everybody and they responded to her warmth.

'There she is,' said Chiago unnecessarily under her breath, while keeping a straight face and not looking in the direction of the woman who was their owner.

At last Ma Palagada strolled into her stall and greeted them fulsomely.

'Oh, oh—have you been waiting for me long? Why did you not tell the girls to come for me? I was at a meeting with the UAC people. Welcome! Welcome! Have they given you something to eat? Is this the little sister you talked about? Welcome. Oh, my! She is just a baby. For her to have lost everyone. . . . Still, God knows best. Welcome!'

A velveteen cushion on a bench was plumped up for her to sit on. Okolie watched and answered her in monosyllables, indicating that, no, they had not eaten anything: the girls had not known who he was.

At this Ma Palagada laughed; it was not a very loud sound but it had a mellow richness in it. It was the laughter of the well fed, the laughter of someone who had not known for a very long time what it was to be hungry. 'We shall soon take care of that. These thoughtless girls should have given you something.'

She looked down again at Ojebeta, appraising her from head to foot, then called her to come to her.

Ojebeta did not want to go and she clung to her brother. It was not that she did not like her relative but that the whole show was just too sudden for the poor child. What did this woman want with her? She might be a relative, but Ojebeta had never seen her before; moreover, she did not look like any relative she had even seen before. All this cloth on her stall and the amount she had on herself, and her way of speaking the Ibo language—Ojebeta was overwhelmed. No, she did not want to go to her.

It was at this point that she had the first clue of what was in store for her, for here something like suppressed anger escaped from her brother. His voice was direct and businesslike, almost as if he were someone who did not know who she was, a stranger to her. Ojebeta was so startled that she burst into tears and called out:

'My mother, please come to me. I am lost!'

Ma Palagada was moved and told Okolie to be gentle with his sister. 'Come,' she urged Ojebeta, 'I only want to greet you. You haven't even said a single word to me. Come. I am your relative, you know. Come. You mustn't be frightened of us. We are not bad people. Just come here ...'

Okolie pulled and half carried Ojebeta to the lady who, with a smile on her face, felt her arms and peered into her eyes, then smiled again and asked, 'Are you hungry?'

Ojebeta was a child brought up with so much love and so much trust that it never occurred to her to distrust a smiling face. Her tears had been a reaction to this new voice she heard her brother whom she had known all her life use to her; now the voice had stopped. She nodded her head vigorously up and down like a mad lizard. Yes, of course she was hungry.

She heard the other girls giggling again. Now what had she done? Ojebeta wondered in bewilderment, hating the smallest girl who sniggered the most. She felt like fighting that girl, for she was not much bigger than herself, but she ignored her and kept on nodding.

'You shall have some food,' Ma Palagada said. 'Chiago, go to the food stalls and buy Ogbanje—is that your name?—buy her a piece of agidi from those people from Accra. Have you eaten their agidi before? It is very nice.'

Ojebeta nodded once more; she had tasted 'agidi Akala', as her dead mother used to call it. On the days her mother used to go to Onitsha she would buy one large piece, and Ojebeta and all her friends and her father would sit up and wait for her to come home from Otu, just to have their little bits of Accra agidi. In those days it had been a real delicacy for her; and now she was once more going to have some to eat, her mouth watered like a dog's. Ma Palagada gave some money to the big girl Chiago, who ran among the other stalls, turned a corner and disappeared into the market. They all waited. More customers came. Okolie and Ma Palagada talked blatant nothings to gain time. Sitting away from her brother, apart from the other girls, Ojebeta thought of her mother, her father, of the 'agidi Akala' she was going to have.

Chiago soon arrived with the corn dough steaming. It was the first time Ojebeta had seen it hot, for the agidi her mother used to buy was always cold by the time she reached home from the market. She watched Chiago peeling the wrapping leaves off and putting them into another white bowl.

'Do you want pepper on it?' asked Chiago then.

Ma Palagada, who had seemed to be unaware of the goings on, intervened: 'Let her do it the way she wants. Give her the pepper and salt. She can spice it herself.'

So Chiago handed Ojebeta the whitest and the best agidi she had ever seen in her life. At first Ojebeta did not know what to do. Should she eat it all, or share it with the others, her brother in particular?

Okolie saw her dilemma and said, with his mouth watering, 'Eat it, it's all for you.'

Ojebeta could not believe her ears. The other girls did not even look as if they were at all interested. Why, in her home five people would have shared this, for agidi was regarded as something special, not heavy enough to be everyday food. She did the only thing that she felt was right: she scooped one big handful and gave it to her brother. The latter looked this way and that way, felt ashamed and said with little heart:

'No, my sister, you eat it. Your relative bought it for you.'

That was strange, thought Ojebeta. But if Okolie had gone off his food, what of the new relative she had just acquired, who had been kind enough to buy all this hot agidi with fresh pepper and salt? She walked up to her with the innocence of a child who had never been taught to fear adults and said, 'Have some, it's nice.' Ma Palagada smiled, called her a good little girl but said that she had eaten; they had had their midday meal before she went to the meeting. So Ojebeta could eat it all. She hurried back to the bench and, sitting with her head bent to one side, busied herself with her day's good luck—a whole piece of agidi Akala to herself.

Ma Palagada and Okolie talked and talked in voices so low that Ojebeta did not bother to make any attempt to find out what they were saying. It was too much of an effort, and besides what did it matter at the moment. So immersed was she in the agidi that she scarcely heard her brother announce:

'I am going to the food stalls to eat some pounded yam. I shall not be long.'

Ojebeta looked up and nodded.

'I will show you the way,' Ma Palagada said casually to Okolie. 'Chiago, take care of the stall. I shall not be long.'

'Yes, Ma,' said Chiago.

Ojebeta went on scooping the agidi into her mouth, showing it off as she did so to the youngest girl, whom she had heard them refer to as Amanna. But Amanna did not even seem to envy her, and instead laughed each time Ojebeta scooped the food up. The urge to fight this cheeky girl was becoming strong, though once more she managed to ignore her while polishing the bowl with her fingers, at the same time making a great deal of noise with her mouth. It had been a delicious meal and Ojebeta was now full; though the last bit had been cold and not as tasty as when she first started it, she finished it all.

Now she looked about her, pleased with the world. The other girls still giggled, but she had decided to take no notice of their foolish behaviour. She sat perched on the wooden bench by the edge of the stall so that she would be the first to catch a glimpse of her brother and Ma Palagada when they showed up eventually. She watched people come in and out of the stall and was fascinated by the fast method the girl Chiago used to mend torn clothes, for she had never before seen a sewing machine. She wished she too could have a go at the black monster with yellow patterns on it. When Chiago wound it, it made sounds as if it was singing, and after it sang on each piece of cloth they came out stitched together so well and so quickly. This way, she noticed, it was not necessary to use needles like her mother had used for sewing tears in her cloth.

After Ojebeta had watched this for a while, the longing for her brother and for them to be going home from the market began to increase. She could see that some other people were already starting to leave. Yet Ma Palagada's girls sat there, doing their sewing, intermittently singing scraps of song, but looking as if they were willing to wait the whole day if necessary. Ojebeta was fed up of waiting. The sweet sensation the hot agidi had given her was fast evaporating and giving way to a kind of boredom, tinged somewhat with rebellion. Not wanting to ask the permission of these unfriendly strangers, she scrambled up from her seat, determined to go and find her brother. Had he not promised Uteh's husband that they would be back home before the evening meal? Well, it was fast approaching sundown and she knew they had a very long trek ahead of them. She then realized

ow tired her feet were, but the urge to go home was far more pressing than her
need to give in to fatigue.

As she took a few steps from the stall, the girls looked at her and all of a sudden
stopped their endless chatter. Chiago was the first to find her tongue.

'Where are you going, little girl from Ibuza?'

'I am going to look for my brother,' came the unpolished reply.

For once the other girls did not laugh at her. Only Amanna made a slight
tittering sound but was quickly hushed by Chiago's stern glance. The latter was
thinking fast to herself: *Poor parentless child. They probably did not tell her. She probably
does not know she may never see her brother again. Poor girl.*

Aloud she said, not without pity, 'Come back, little Ibuza girl. Your big brother
will soon be here. Come back, or you will get lost in the market, and the child-
catchers from the coast will take you away in their canoes. Come back.'

Ojebeta stood and looked at her for a moment, wondering why the child-
catchers should want to take her away. She had, it was true, heard stories of people
going missing even in Ibuza, but that such a fate could befall her was beyond
belief. After all, she was only going to get her brother, over there round the corner.
She would run faster than any child-catcher in the world, and once she had found
her big brother Okolie who would dare catch her?

'Will my "little father" be here soon?' she asked, seeking further reassurance.

'Of course he will. What have we been telling you?' replied Chiago, her eyes
averted.

Ojebeta did not know what came over her then, except that it was connected
with her having been brought up by simple people who looked you straight in the
eye because they had nothing to hide. The way this big girl spoke to her, the way
the others all at once seemed to be made of mechanical wood, working without
feeling at their work and not daring to look at her, made her uneasy. She did not
want to wait to find out what they were being so cagey about; all she wanted was
her brother and for them both to go back home to Ibuza, where her aunt Uteh
would be waiting for her with pounded yam and palm soup and little crabs from
the Oboshi stream. All the girls were seemingly engrossed in their sewing, and she
told herself that they were not watching her. She knew where her brother Okolie
was—just round the corner, at the stalls of the food sellers. If she ran that way she
would surely find him, still sitting there eating yam and stew. She would find him,
before these girls ever caught up with her. She would find him....

And just like a hunter's arrow that had been quivering impatiently in its bow
while the hunter covered his prey until the opportune moment to let fly, so did
Ogbanje Ojebeta dash out of the Palagada cloth stall. She ran, almost flew like an
arrow, her little legs like wings, her heart beating fast in fear and anticipation,
going as she thought to her brother—her brother, the only person she knew in this
market full of strange people, the only person who would take her home to their
own, the only person who had brought her here. She made music with her metal
charms and cowries as she ran to meet him. She was an unusual sight among the
sophisticated, rich, fat mammy traders who formed the backbone of Onitsha
market.

'If I can't find him, my big brother,' she said to herself as she ran, 'I shall go
back to Ibuza to the hut of my big mother and wait for him.'

But it was to be an abortive attempt at freedom.

At the end of the line of cloth stalls was a very big one belonging to a fat mammy
called Ma Mee, who was one of the richest Onitsha marketwomen at the time.

She, like Ma Palagada, had a double stall, but her twin stalls curved into the pathway, almost blocking the way from the riverside. Hers was a corner site, and the fact that she occupied this privileged position had been the cause of a great deal of backbiting and bickering among the other cloth traders, particularly the smaller fry who had only a single stall. [...] there were occasions when each trader needed the goodwill of the others, for example when robbers—well aware that the cloth stalls contained valuable materials and belonged mainly to a few wealthy and privileged women—would organize themselves for raids. But if one stall could raise the alarm and the thief was seen, God have mercy on his soul. These were women who did not have time for the police; they could not afford to lose a day' trade by going to court or going to see a chief. They invariably dealt with the culprit in the way they themselves thought fit.

The same fate awaited any runaway domestic slave. Many of the market women had slaves in great number to help them with the fetching and carrying that went with being a full-time trader—and also in the vain hope that one day the British people at the coast would go and some of these house slaves could be sold abroad, just as their fathers and grandfathers had done, so profitably that the abundance of capital and property they had built could still be seen in many families round Onitsha and Bonny and Port Harcourt.

On this hot afternoon, a tiresome and very hungry Ibo beggar of a fisherman had caught a sizeable thorn fish which he had brought to the prosperous cloth sellers. He had expected to sell it at a higher price than Ma Mee was offering [...]. The fisherman became more despondent as Ma Mee would not agree to the price he wanted and as he saw that the fish's resistance was growing more feeble, whether because it now realized it was fighting a losing battle or because of the effects of having been out of the water for so long on such a hot afternoon. He stopped dangling the fish on the powerful wire which he had strung through its open mouth and was summoning up the courage to touch its slimy body, at the same time as Ma Mee was beginning to feel compelled to buy it from him, when they all—the fisherman, Ma Mee and the girl slaves who had been passive throughout the preceding argument—heard the cries of alarm of the girls at Ma Palagada's stalls.

Everyone's first involuntary reaction was to look for a club, a knife, even the wooden measuring stick, to arm themselves with ready to fight to protect their own territory, as it were. They all dashed out, led by the poor fisherman who wanted to play the role of a gallant man preserving the women from robbers.

Ma Mee was a big woman, so big that she never stopped perspiring. But there were certain happenings which appeared to make her weightless: happenings such as market thieves and runaways. For if you did not help your neighbour in such a situation, the day the same trouble befell you, people would turn a blind eye rather than offer assistance; it was an unwritten law among the traders on the banks of the Niger. So, tightening her voluminous lappa round her substantial posterior her breasts heaving in unison to her great haste, she rushed forward prepared to do battle with and if necessary maim this market thief causing this outcry, if she could lay hands on whoever it was, for daring to go into her absent colleague's stall.

However, it was not a market thief that they saw; it was a sight so peculiar that people simply stared bemused as it sped past their stalls—Chiago tearing along the pathway chasing a small, helpless and terrified child: a little girl festooned with bells and cowrie shells, just like a slave prepared for sacrifice! They stared, and did not understand.

Chiago's cries soon put them in the picture.

'Hold her! Please hold her for me, she is new—hold her!'

But she did not look at all like any slave girl Ma Mee had ever seen before, this little creature who more or less ran into her arms for protection and cried out:

'Oh, my mother, I am lost.'

For a split second, Ma Mee held her, as she would have embraced her very own child; then she let go of the fugitive but still barred her way with her great bulk.

'You are not lost, little girl with pagan charms,' she replied. 'You are just a domestic slave.'

Almost fainting with that kind of disappointment and sense of unfairness which is sometimes inexplicable, Ojebeta the only living daughter of Umeadi cried out once more in despair, this time to her dead mother:

'Save me, Mother, for now I am lost.'

Unable to go forward past Ma Mee, she had no alternative but to allow herself to be caught by her pursuer.

'Let me go, let me go!' Ojebeta screamed as she wriggled violently in the hands of Chiago, the biggest of the Palagada girls.

Chiago would have held Ojebeta gently except that she knew it was likely to have resulted in real trouble for herself. So she gripped her tightly, masking her pity for this parentless child by explaining unnecessarily to the crowd, and especially to Ma Mee, that Ojebeta had only just arrived that very afternoon.

Ma Mee did not envy her neighbour for having four girl slaves; and this new little one would bring the total number of Palagada slaves to seven, since they also had two male slaves who had been bought or captured—she was not quite sure of the story—from among the people called the Urhobos. It was said that Pa Palagada had bought the men from some Potokis who were leaving the country and returning to their own land. The two, who were young boys at the time, could not remember where they had originally come from, so they were given Ibo names and were put to work on the Palagada farms. Sometimes Ma Palagada would bring to the Otu market the big yams that these two hardworking and now hefty men had produced. So far as Ma Mee was concerned the Palagadas already had as many slaves as they needed; after all, one couldn't sell them abroad as in the old days. However, she kept all these thoughts to herself.

Chiago thanked Ma Mee in the way she had been taught to greet important ladies like her, with a curtsy, and half pulled, half carried Ojebeta back to their own stall, knowing that the eyes of all the other women were following her. As she tried to lessen the shock for the poor girl, Chiago too was near tears, remembering how it had come about that she herself had been sold. [. . .]

Chiago remembered that she had had to cross another river, and they had walked what seemed endless numbers of miles. For days they had walked and they were so tired that for part of the journey Pa Palagada had to be carried by local bearers in a hammock. At a town called Arochukwu they had stayed for days, and it was here that she had a bitter taste of what life held in store for her. She did not see the so-called daughter of Pa Palagada; in fact she seldom saw him at all. She was thrust into a small room at the back of the house with other strange people, who all seemed unhappy and, like her, scantily dressed. They all ate together, and had to go to the stream to fetch water, and she had to help in the large cooking place they called the 'kinsheni', or something like that. She had stayed there with Pa Palagada and his entourage for just five days, and then they had set off again walking and walking and only resting at occasional drinking and eating places. They crossed another fairly small river in a canoe, and by this time Chiago had not

even been able to remember from which direction she had originally come. [. . .]
The picture of her family, however, had dimmed after eleven years with her
mistress and her husband. The long stay had taught her a great many things. The
most important was that a slave who made an unsuccessful attempt to run away
was better off dead. Such a slave would be so tortured that he or she would be
useless as a person, or else might be used for burial.

She had watched one such horrible burial when she had been about twelve and
was travelling with Ma Palagada in the Ibo interior. The chief wife of the master o
the house had died, and it was necessary for her husband to send her to the land o
the dead accompanied by a female slave. The one chosen was a particularly
beautiful slave, with smooth skin and black closely cropped hair, who was said to be
a princess captured in war from another Ibo village; she had made attempts to
return to where she came from, but unfortunately her new owner caught her and
she lost her freedom of movement. On the eve of the burial she was brought and
ordered to lie down in the shallow grave. As might be expected, she resisted, but
there was no pity on the faces of the men who stood by watching, amused by her
cries. She made appeals to the gods of her people to save her, she begged some o
the mourners to spare her life, saying that her father the chief of another village
would repay them, but to no avail. One of the sons of the dead woman lost his
patience and, maybe out of mercy and a wish to have it all done with as quickly as
possible, took a club and struck the defenceless woman hard at the back of her
shaved head. The more Chiago thought about it in later years, the more convinced
she was that the woman slave must have had seven lives. She did not drop down
into the grave she was later to share with her dead mistress as was then expected.
Instead she turned to look at the chief, who was calling on his son to cease his
brutality, and she said to him, 'For showing me this little mercy, chief, I shall come
again, I shall come again. . . .'

She was not allowed to finish her valedictory statement, for the stubborn young
man, disregarding his father's appeal, gave the woman a final blow so that she fell
by the side of the grave. But she was still struggling even when the body of her dead
mistress was placed on her. She still fought and cried out, so alive. Soon her voice
was completely silenced by the damp earth that was piled on both her and the dead
woman.

Chiago never quite recovered from this early shock, not even when sometime
later she heard Ma Palagada talking to another woman trader about it and ending
up by saying that one of the chief's younger wives now had a baby daughter very
like the slave princess who had been buried alive; to clinch the resemblance this
little girl was born with a lump on the back of her head, in the same place as where
the slave princess had been struck. . . .

Chiago had seen, too, many slaves who had become successful, who had worked
so well with their masters that they themselves became wealthy traders at Otu
market, given their freedom when their masters grew old. The majority of them
particularly the male slaves, did not wish to go home, if they could even remember
which part of the country they had come from originally. Some of them stayed
because they could not return to their region as a result of some atrocity they had
committed. One of the Palagada slaves was born a twin and her people, somewhere
among the Efiks, did not accept twins; her mother had nursed her secretly and later
had her sold, simply to give her a chance in life.

If only Chiago could have communicated all that passed through her mind to this
struggling little girl. She wished she could tell her that the only course left for her

was to make the best of everything, by being docile and trouble-free. She had stopped holding her too tightly but had her arms round the girl's naked waist, looking at her with pity as if she were her own sister. In fact they would soon be like sisters—did not the same fate await them?

'I shall tell my father of you,' Ojebeta whimpered in between exhausted hiccoughs. In her confusion after the long, wearying journey and her escape attempt, she imagined her father was still alive and well in Ibuza. She stared at everyone in front of the stalls they passed, hoping that one of them would be her brother.

If the girls felt like reminding Ojebeta that her parents were long dead, they restrained themselves. They had seen scenes like this played out before their very eyes too often, and they knew from experience that to indulge in a little fantasy would do her no harm at all; if anything, it would do her good. So they let her wallow in her own world of wishful thinking. She went on repeating that she would tell her father, her mother and her big mother Uteh, until she was completely exhausted.

Ma Mee soon strolled round to their stall to find out how they were coping and whether Ma Palagada was back. Chiago replied that she was sure she would be back soon, and this statement awakened in Ojebeta a last, futile hope to gain sympathy.

'Please, kind mother, can you bring my brother back to me? He only went there round your stall to eat pounded yam.'

'Yes,' Ma Mee replied in a soft voice, 'I shall bring your brother back. But do you want me to buy you anything to eat? Do you want honeyed meat balls from the Hausa people down the coast?'

Ojebeta shook her head vigorously as though she would snap it off from her body. She did not want anything, not any more, not from these people who had tricked her into letting Okolie out of her sight because of some hot agidi.

'I don't want anything. I only want to go home.' She little realized in what circumstances and how long it would be before that going home took place.

Ma Mee walked back to her stall telling herself that buying and selling people could not be helped. 'Where would we be without slave labour, and where would some of these unwanted children be without us?' It might be evil, but it was a necessary evil.

From *The Slave Girl*, pp. 29–65.

BUCHI EMECHETA   *Born in 1944 near Lagos, Nigeria. Has been living in England since 1962, gaining a BSc in Sociology, being a teacher and librarian, and raising five children.*

[2, 6, 7, 8, 11, 12, 15]

CHINUA ACHEBE

The first time their paths crossed nothing happened. That was in the first heady days of warlike preparation when thousands of young men (and sometimes women too) were daily turned away from enlistment centres because far too many of them were coming forward burning with readiness to bear arms in defence of the exciting new nation.

The second time they met was at a check-point at Awka. Then the war had started and was slowly moving southwards from the distant northern sector. He was driving from Onitsha to Enugu and was in a hurry. Although intellectually he approved of thorough searches at road-blocks, emotionally he was always offended whenever he had to submit to them. He would probably not admit it but the feeling people got was that if you were put through a search then you could not really be one of the big people. Generally he got away without a search by pronouncing in his deep, authoritative voice: 'Reginald Nwankwo, Ministry of Justice.' That almost always did it. But sometimes either through ignorance or sheer cussedness the crowd at the odd check-point would refuse to be impressed. As happened now at Awka. Two constables carrying heavy Mark 4 rifles were watching distantly from the roadside leaving the actual searching to local vigilantes.

'I am in a hurry,' he said to the girl who now came up to his car. 'My name is Reginald Nwankwo, Ministry of Justice.'

'Good afternoon, sir. I want to see your boot.'

'Oh Christ! What do you think is in the boot?'

'I don't know, sir.'

He got out of the car in suppressed rage, stalked to the back, opened the boot and holding the lid up with his left hand he motioned with the right as if to say After you!

'Are you satisfied?' he demanded.

'Yes, sir. Can I see your pigeon-hole?'

'Christ Almighty!'

'Sorry to delay you, sir. But you people gave us this job to do.'

'Never mind. You are damn right. It's just that I happen to be in a hurry. But never mind. That's the glove-box. Nothing there as you can see.'

'All right sir, close it.' Then she opened the rear door and bent down to inspect under the seats. It was then he took the first real look at her, starting from behind. She was a beautiful girl in a breasty blue jersey, khaki jeans and canvas shoes with the new-style hair-plait which gave a girl a defiant look and which they called—for reasons of their own—'air force base'; and she looked vaguely familiar.

'I am all right, sir,' she said at last meaning she was through with her task. 'You don't recognize me?'

'No. Should I?'

'You gave me a lift to Enugu that time I left my school to go and join the militia.'

'Ah, yes, you were the girl. I told you, didn't I, to go back to school because girls were not required in the militia. What happened?'

'They told me to go back to my school or join the Red Cross.'

'You see I was right. So, what are you doing now?'

'Just patching up with Civil Defence.'

'Well, good luck to you. Believe me you are a great girl.'

That was the day he finally believed there might be something in this talk about revolution. He had seen plenty of girls and women marching and demonstrating before now. But somehow he had never been able to give it much thought. He didn't doubt that the girls and the women took themselves seriously, they obviously did. But so did the little kids who marched up and down the streets at the time drilling with sticks and wearing their mothers' soup bowls for steel helmets. The prime joke of the time among his friends was the contingent of girls from a local secondary school marching behind a banner: WE ARE IMPREGNABLE!

But after that encounter at the Awka check-point he could not sneer at the girls again, nor at the talk of revolution, for he had seen it in action in that young woman whose devotion had simply and without self-righteousness convicted him of gross levity. What were her words? We are doing the work you asked us to do. She wasn't going to make an exception even for one who once did her a favour. He was sure she would have searched her own father just as rigorously.

When their paths crossed a third time, at least eighteen months later, things had got very bad. Death and starvation having long chased out the headiness of the early days, now left in some places blank resignation, in others a rock-like, even suicidal, defiance. But surprisingly enough there were many at this time who had no other desire than to corner whatever good things were still going and to enjoy themselves to the limit. For such people a strange normalcy had returned to the world. All those nervous check-points disappeared. Girls became girls once more and boys boys. It was a tight, blockaded and desperate world but none the less a world—with some goodness and some badness and plenty of heroism which, however, happened most times far, far below the eye-level of the people in this story—in out-of-the-way refugee camps, in the damp tatters, in the hungry and bare-handed courage of the first line of fire.

Reginald Nwankwo lived in Owerri then. But that day he had gone to Nkwerri in search of relief. He had got from Caritas in Owerri a few heads of stock-fish, some tinned meat, and the dreadful American stuff called Formula Two which he felt certain was some kind of animal feed. But he always had a vague suspicion that not being a Catholic put one at a disadvantage with Caritas. So he went now to see an old friend who ran the WCC depot at Nkwerri to get other items like rice, beans and that excellent cereal commonly called Gabon gari.

He left Owerri at six in the morning so as to catch his friend at the depot where he was known never to linger beyond 8.30 for fear of air-raids. Nwankwo was very fortunate that day. The depot had received on the previous day large supplies of new stock as a result of an unusual number of plane landings a few nights earlier. As his driver loaded tins and bags and cartons into his car the starved crowds that perpetually hung around relief centres made crude, ungracious remarks like 'War Can Continue!' meaning the WCC! Somebody else shouted 'Irevolu!' and his friends replied 'shum!' 'Irevolu!' 'shum!' 'Isofeli?' 'shum!' 'Isofeli?' 'Mba!'

Nwankwo was deeply embarrassed not by the jeers of this scarecrow crowd of rags and floating ribs but by the independent accusation of their wasted bodies and sunken eyes. Indeed he would probably have felt much worse had they said nothing, simply looked on in silence, as his boot was loaded with milk, and powdered egg and oats and tinned meat and stock-fish. By nature such singular good fortune in the midst of a general desolation was certain to embarrass him. But what could a man do? He had a wife and four children living in the remote village of Ogbu and completely dependent on what relief he could find and send them. He couldn't abandon them to kwashiokor. The best he could do—and did do as a matter of fact—was to make sure that whenever he got sizeable supplies like now he made over some of it to his driver, Johnson, with a wife and six, or was it seven?, children and a salary of ten pounds a month when gari in the market was climbing to one pound per cigarette cup. In such a situation one could do nothing at all for crowds; at best one could try to be of some use to one's immediate neighbours. That was all.

On his way back to Owerri a very attractive girl by the roadside waved for a lift. He ordered the driver to stop. Scores of pedestrians, dusty and exhausted, some military, some civil, swooped down on the car from all directions.

'No, no, no,' said Nwankwo firmly. 'It's the young woman I stopped for. I have a bad tyre and can only take one person. Sorry.'

'My son, please,' cried one old woman in despair, gripping the door-handle.

'Old woman, you want to be killed?' shouted the driver as he pulled away, shaking her off. Nwankwo had already opened a book and sunk his eyes there. For at least a mile after that he did not even look at the girl until she finding, perhaps, the silence too heavy said:

'You've saved me today. Thank you.'

'Not at all. Where are you going?'

'To Owerri. You don't recognize me?'

'Oh yes, of course. What a fool I am ... You are ...'

'Gladys.'

'That's right, the militia girl. You've changed, Gladys. You were always beautiful of course, but now you are a beauty queen. What do you do these days?'

'I am in the Fuel Directorate.'

'That's wonderful.'

It was wonderful, he thought, but even more it was tragic. She wore a high-tinted wig and a very expensive skirt and low-cut blouse. Her shoes, obviously from Gabon, must have cost a fortune. In short, thought Nwankwo, she had to be in the keep of some well-placed gentleman, one of those piling up money out of the war.

'I broke my rule today to give you a lift. I never give lifts these days.'

'Why?'

'How many people can you carry? It is better not to try at all. Look at that old woman.'

'I thought you would carry her.'

He said nothing to that and after another spell of silence Gladys thought maybe he was offended and so added: 'Thank you for breaking your rule for me.' She was scanning his face, turned slightly away. He smiled, turned, and tapped her on the lap.

'What are you going to Owerri to do?'

'I am going to visit my girl friend.'

'Girl friend? You sure?'

'Why not? ... If you drop me at her house you can see her. Only I pray God she hasn't gone on weekend today; it will be serious.'

'Why?'

'Because if she is not at home I will sleep on the road today.'

'I pray to God that she is not at home.'

'Why?'

'Because if she is not at home I will offer you bed and breakfast . . . What is that?' he asked the driver who had brought the car to an abrupt stop. There was no need for an answer. The small crowd ahead was looking upwards. The three scrambled out of the car and stumbled for the bush, necks twisted in a backward search of the sky. But the alarm was false. The sky was silent and clear except for two high-flying vultures. A humorist in the crowd called them Fighter and Bomber and everyone laughed in relief. The three climbed into their car again and continued their journey.

'It is much too early for raids,' he said to Gladys, who had both her palms on her breast as though to still a thumping heart. 'They rarely come before ten o'clock.'

But she remained tongue-tied from her recent fright. Nwankwo saw an opportunity there and took it at once.

'Where does your friend live?'

'250 Douglas Road.'

'Ah! that's the very centre of town—a terrible place. No bunkers, nothing. I won't advise you to go there before 6 p.m.; it's not safe. If you don't mind I will take you to my place where there is a good bunker and then as soon as it is safe, around six, I shall drive you to your friend. How's that?'

'It's all right,' she said lifelessly. 'I am so frightened of this thing. That's why I refused to work in Owerri. I don't even know who asked me to come out today.'

'You'll be all right. We are used to it.'

'But your family is not there with you?'

'No,' he said. 'Nobody has his family there. We like to say it is because of air-raids but I can assure you there is more to it. Owerri is a real swinging town and we live the life of gay bachelors.'

'That is what I have heard.'

'You will not just hear it; you will see it today. I shall take you to a real swinging party. A friend of mine, a Lieutenant-Colonel, is having a birthday party. He's hired the Sound Smashers to play. I'm sure you'll enjoy it.'

He was immediately and thoroughly ashamed of himself. He hated the parties and frivolities to which his friends clung like drowning men. And to talk so approvingly of them because he wanted to take a girl home! And this particular girl too, who had once had such beautiful faith in the struggle and was betrayed (no doubt about it) by some man like him out for a good time. He shook his head sadly.

'What is it?' asked Gladys.

'Nothing. Just my thoughts.'

They made the rest of the journey to Owerri practically in silence.

She made herself at home very quickly as if she was a regular girl friend of his. She changed into a house dress and put away her auburn wig.

'That is a lovely hair-do. Why do you hide it with a wig?'

'Thank you,' she said leaving his question unanswered for a while. Then she said: 'Men are funny.'

'Why do you say that?'

'You are now a beauty queen,' she mimicked.

'Oh, that! I mean every word of it.' He pulled her to him and kissed her. She neither refused nor yielded fully, which he liked for a start. Too many girls were simply too easy those days. War sickness, some called it.

He drove off a little later to look in at the office and she busied herself in the kitchen helping his boy with lunch. It must have been literally a look-in, for he was back within half an hour, rubbing his hands and saying he could not stay away too long from his beauty queen.

As they sat down to lunch she said: 'You have nothing in your fridge.'

'Like what?' he asked, half-offended.

'Like meat,' she replied undaunted.

'Do you still eat meat?' he challenged.

'Who am I? But other big men like you eat.'

'I don't know which big men you have in mind. But they are not like me. I don't make money trading with the enemy or selling relief or . . .'

'Augusta's boy friend doesn't do that. He just gets foreign exchange.'

'How does he get it? He swindles the government—that's how he gets foreign exchange, whoever he is. Who is Augusta, by the way?'

'My girl friend.'

'I see.'

'She gave me three dollars last time which I changed to forty-five pounds. The man gave her fifty dollars.'

'Well, my dear girl, I don't traffic in foreign exchange and I don't have meat in my fridge. We are fighting a war and I happen to know that some young boys at the front drink gari and water once in three days.'

'It is true,' she said simply. 'Monkey de work, baboon de chop.'

'It is not even that; it is worse,' he said, his voice beginning to shake. 'People are dying every day. As we talk now somebody is dying.'

'It is true,' she said again.

'Plane!' screamed his boy from the kitchen.

'My mother!' screamed Gladys. As they scuttled towards the bunker of palm stems and red earth, covering their heads with their hands and stooping slightly in their flight, the entire sky was exploding with the clamour of jets and the huge noise of home-made anti-aircraft rockets.

Inside the bunker she clung to him even after the plane had gone and the guns, late to start and also to end, had all died down again.

'It was only passing,' he told her, his voice a little shaky. 'It didn't drop anything. From its direction I should say it was going to the war front. Perhaps our people are pressing them. That's what they always do. Whenever our boys press them, they send an SOS to the Russians and Egyptians to bring the planes.' He drew a long breath.

She said nothing, just clung to him. They could hear his boy telling the servant from the next house that there were two of them and one dived like this and the other dived like that.

'I see dem well well,' said the other with equal excitement. 'If no to say de ting de kill porson e for sweet for eye. To God.'

'Imagine!' said Gladys, finding her voice at last. She had a way, he thought, of conveying with a few words or even a single word whole layers of meaning. Now it was at once her astonishment as well as reproof, tinged perhaps with grudging admiration for people who could be so light-hearted about these bringers of death.

'Don't be so scared,' he said. She moved closer and he began to kiss her and squeeze her breasts. She yielded more and more and then fully. The bunker was dark and unswept and might harbour crawling things. He thought of bringing a mat from the main house but reluctantly decided against it. Another plane might pass and send a neighbour or simply a chance passer-by crashing into them. That would be only slightly better than a certain gentleman in another air-raid who was seen in broad daylight fleeing his bedroom for his bunker stark-naked pursued by a woman in a similar state!

Just as Gladys had feared, her friend was not in town. It would seem her powerful boy friend had wangled for her a flight to Libreville to shop. So her neighbours thought anyway.

'Great!' said Nwankwo as they drove away. 'She will come back on an arms plane loaded with shoes, wigs, pants, bras, cosmetics and what have you, which she will then sell and make thousands of pounds. You girls are really at war, aren't you?'

She said nothing and he thought he had got through at last to her. Then suddenly she said, 'That is what you men want us to do.'

'Well,' he said, 'here is one man who doesn't want you to do that. Do you remember that girl in khaki jeans who searched me without mercy at the check-point?'

She began to laugh.

'That is the girl I want you to become again. Do you remember her? No wig. I don't even think she had any earrings ...'

'Ah, na lie-o. I had earrings.'

'All right. But you know what I mean.'

'That time done pass. Now everybody want survival. They call it number six. You put your number six; I put my number six. Everything all right.'

The Lieutenant-Colonel's party turned into something quite unexpected. But before it did things had been going well enough. There was goat-meat, some chicken and rice and plenty of home-made spirits. There was one fiery brand nicknamed 'tracer' which indeed sent a flame down your gullet. The funny thing was looking at it in the bottle it had the innocent appearance of an orange drink. But the thing that caused the greatest stir was the bread—one little roll for each person! It was the size of a golf-ball and about the same consistency too! But it was real bread. The band was good too and there were many girls. And to improve matters even further two white Red Cross people soon arrived with a bottle of Courvoisier and a bottle of Scotch! The party gave them a standing ovation and then scrambled to get a drop. It soon turned out from his general behaviour, however, that one of the white men had probably drunk too much already. And the reason it would seem was that a pilot he knew well had been killed in a crash at the airport last night, flying in relief in awful weather.

Few people at the party had heard of the crash by then. So there was an immediate damping of the air. Some dancing couples went back to their seats and the band stopped. Then for some strange reason the drunken Red Cross man just exploded.

'Why should a man, a decent man, throw away his life. For nothing! Charley didn't need to die. Not for this stinking place. Yes, everything stinks here. Even these girls who come here all dolled up and smiling, what are they worth? Don't I know? A head of stock-fish, that's all, or one American dollar and they are ready to tumble into bed.'

In the threatening silence following the explosion one of the young officers walked up to him and gave him three thundering slaps—right! left! right!—pulled him up from his seat and (there were things like tears in his eyes) shoved him outside. His friend, who had tried in vain to shut him up, followed him out and the silenced party heard them drive off. The officer who did the job returned dusting his palms.

'Fucking beast!' said he with an impressive coolness. And all the girls showed with their eyes that they rated him a man and a hero.

'Do you know him?' Gladys asked Nwankwo.

He didn't answer her. Instead he spoke generally to the party:

'The fellow was clearly drunk,' he said.

'I don't care,' said the officer. 'It is when a man is drunk that he speaks what is on his mind.'

'So you beat him for what was on his mind,' said the host, 'that is the spirit, Joe.'

'Thank you, sir,' said Joe, saluting.

'His name is Joe,' Gladys and the girl on her left said in unison, turning to each other.

At the same time Nwankwo and a friend on the other side of him were saying quietly, very quietly, that although the man had been rude and offensive what he had said about the girls was unfortunately the bitter truth, only he was the wrong man to say it.

When the dancing resumed Captain Joe came to Gladys for a dance. She sprang to her feet even before the word was out of his mouth. Then she remembered immediately and turned round to take permission from Nwankwo. At the same time the Captain also turned to him and said, 'Excuse me.'

'Go ahead,' said Nwankwo, looking somewhere between the two.

It was a long dance and he followed them with his eyes without appearing to do so. Occasionally a relief plane passed overhead and somebody immediately switched off the lights saying it might be the Intruder. But it was only an excuse to dance in the dark and make the girls giggle, for the sound of the Intruder was well known.

Gladys came back feeling very self-conscious and asked Nwankwo to dance with her. But he wouldn't. 'Don't bother about me,' he said, 'I am enjoying myself perfectly sitting here and watching those of you who dance.'

'Then let's go,' she said, 'if you won't dance.'

'But I never dance, believe me. So please enjoy yourself.'

She danced next with the Lieutenant-Colonel and again with Captain Joe, and then Nwankwo agreed to take her home.

'I am sorry I didn't dance,' he said as they drove away. 'But I swore never to dance as long as this war lasts.'

She said nothing.

'When I think of somebody like that pilot who got killed last night. And he had no hand whatever in the quarrel. All his concern was to bring us food . . .'

'I hope that his friend is not like him,' said Gladys.

'The man was just upset by his friend's death. But what I am saying is that with people like that getting killed and our own boys suffering and dying at the war fronts I don't see why we should sit around throwing parties and dancing.'

'You took me there,' said she in final revolt. 'They are your friends. I don't know them before.'

'Look, my dear, I am not blaming you. I am merely telling you why I personally refuse to dance. Anyway, let's change the subject ... Do you still say you want to go back tomorrow? My driver can take you early enough on Monday morning for you to go to work. No? All right, just as you wish. You are the boss.'

She gave him a shock by the readiness with which she followed him to bed and by her language.

'You want to shell?' she asked. And without waiting for an answer said, 'Go ahead but don't pour in troops!'

He didn't want to pour in troops either and so it was all right. But she wanted visual assurance and so he showed her.

One of the ingenious economies taught by the war was that a rubber condom could be used over and over again. All you had to do was wash it out, dry it and shake a lot of talcum powder over it to prevent its sticking; and it was as good as new. It had to be the real British thing, though, not some of the cheap stuff they brought in from Lisbon which was about as strong as a dry cocoyam leaf in the harmattan.

He had his pleasure but wrote the girl off. He might just as well have slept with a prostitute, he thought. It was clear as daylight to him now that she was kept by some army officer. What a terrible transformation in the short period of less than two years! Wasn't it a miracle that she still had memories of the other life, that she even remembered her name? If the affair of the drunken Red Cross man should happen again now, he said to himself, he would stand up beside the fellow and tell the party that here was a man of truth. What a terrible fate to befall a whole generation! The mothers of tomorrow!

By morning he was feeling a little better and more generous in his judgements. Gladys, he thought, was just a mirror reflecting a society that had gone completely rotten and maggotty at the centre. The mirror itself was intact; a lot of smudge but no more. All that was needed was a clean duster. 'I have a duty to her,' he told himself, 'the little girl that once revealed to me our situation. Now she is in danger, under some terrible influence.'

He wanted to get to the bottom of this deadly influence. It was clearly not just her good-time girl friend, Augusta, or whatever her name was. There must be some man at the centre of it, perhaps one of these heartless attack-traders who traffic in foreign currencies and make their hundreds of thousands by sending young men to hazard their lives bartering looted goods for cigarettes behind enemy lines, or one of those contractors who receive piles of money daily for food they never deliver to the army. Or perhaps some vulgar and cowardly army officer full of filthy barrack talk and ficti-tious stories of heroism. He decided he had to find out. Last night he had thought of sending his driver alone to take her home. But no, he must go and see for himself where she lived. Something was bound to reveal itself there. Something on which he could anchor his saving operation. As he prepared for the trip his feeling towards her softened with every passing minute. He assembled for her half of the food he had received at the relief centre the day before. Difficult as things were, he thought, a girl who had something to eat would be spared, not all, but some of the temptation. He would arrange with his friend at the WCC to deliver something to her every fortnight.

Tears came to Gladys's eyes when she saw the gifts. Nwankwo didn't have too much cash on him but he got together twenty pounds and handed it over to her.

'I don't have foreign exchange, and I know this won't go far at all, but ...'

She just came and threw herself at him, sobbing. He kissed her lips and eyes and mumbled something about victims of circumstance, which went over her head. In deference to him, he thought with exultation, she had put away her high-tinted wig in her bag.

'I want you to promise me something,' he said.

'What?'

'Never use that expression about shelling again.'

She smiled with tears in her eyes. 'You don't like it? That's what all the girls call it.'

'Well, you are different from all the girls. Will you promise?'

'OK.'

Naturally their departure had become a little delayed. And when they got into the car it refused to start. After poking around the engine the driver decided that the battery was flat. Nwankwo was aghast. He had that very week paid thirty-four pounds to change two of the cells and the mechanic who performed it had promised him six months' service. A new battery, which was then running at two hundred and fifty pounds was simply out of the question. The driver must have been careless with something, he thought.

'It must be because of last night,' said the driver.

'What happened last night?' asked Nwankwo sharply, wondering what insolence was on the way. But none was intended.

'Because we use the head light.'

'Am I supposed not to use my light then? Go and get some people and try pushing it.' He got out again with Gladys and returned to the house while the driver went over to neighbouring houses to seek the help of other servants.

After at least half an hour of pushing it up and down the street, and a lot of noisy advice from the pushers, the car finally spluttered to life shooting out enormous clouds of black smoke from the exhaust.

It was eight-thirty by his watch when they set out. A few miles away a disabled soldier waved for a lift.

'Stop!' screamed Nwankwo. The driver jammed his foot on the brakes and then turned his head towards his master in bewilderment.

'Don't you see the soldier waving? Reverse and pick him up!'

'Sorry, sir,' said the driver. 'I don't know Master wan to pick him.'

'If you don't know you should ask. Reverse back.'

The soldier, a mere boy, in filthy khaki drenched in sweat lacked his right leg from the knee down. He seemed not only grateful that a car should stop for him but greatly surprised. He first handed in his crude wooden crutches which the driver arranged between the two front seats, then painfully he levered himself in.

'Thank sir,' he said turning his neck to look at the back and completely out of breath.

'I am very grateful. Madame, thank you.'

'The pleasure is ours,' said Nwankwo. 'Where did you get your wound?'

'At Azumini, sir. On tenth of January.'

'Never mind. Everything will be all right. We are proud of you boys and will make sure you receive your due reward when it is all over.'

'I pray God, sir.'

They drove on in silence for the next half-hour or so. Then as the car sped down a slope towards a bridge somebody screamed—perhaps the driver, perhaps the soldier—'They have come!' The screech of the brakes merged into the scream and the shattering of the sky overhead. The doors flew open even before the car had come to a stop and they were fleeing blindly to the bush. Gladys was a little ahead of Nwankwo when they heard through the drowning tumult the soldier's voice crying: 'Please come and open for me!' Vaguely he saw Gladys stop; he pushed past her shouting to her at the same time to come on. Then a high whistle descended like a spear through the chaos and exploded in a vast noise and motion that smashed up everything. A tree he had embraced flung him away through the bush. Then another terrible whistle starting high up and ending again in a monumental crash of the world; and then another, and Nwankwo heard no more.

He woke up to human voices and weeping and the smell and smoke of a charred world. He dragged himself up and staggered towards the source of the sounds.

From afar he saw his driver running towards him in tears and blood. He saw the remains of his car smoking and the entangled remains of the girl and the soldier. And he let out a piercing cry and fell down again.

From *Girls at War*, pp. 103–23.

[1, 2, 6, 8, 10, 81]

12   *Equiano on his Way to Slavery*

OLAUDAH EQUIANO

As to religion, the natives believe that there is one Creator of all things and that he lives in the sun and is girded round with a belt that he may never eat or drink; but according to some he smokes a pipe, which is our own favourite luxury. They believe he governs events, especially our deaths or captivity, but as for the doctrine of eternity, I do not remember to have ever heard of it: some however believe in the transmigration of souls in a certain degree. Those spirits which are not transmigrated, such as their dear friends or relations, they believe always attend them and guard them from the bad spirits or their foes. For this reason they always before eating, as I have observed, put some small portion of the meat and pour some of their drink, on the ground for them, and they often make oblations of the blood of beasts or fowls at their graves. I was very fond of my mother and almost constantly with her. When she went to make these oblations at her mother's tomb, which was a kind of small solitary thatched house, I sometimes attended her. There she made her libations and spent most of the night in cries and lamentations. I have been often extremely terrified on these occasions. The loneliness of the place, the darkness of the night, and the ceremony of libation, naturally awful and gloomy, were heightened by my mother's lamentations; and these, concurring with the doleful cries of birds by which these places were frequented, gave an inexpressible terror to the scene.

We compute the year from the day on which the sun crosses the line, and on its setting that evening there is a general shout throughout the land; at least I can speak from my own knowledge throughout our vicinity. The people at the same time make a great noise with rattles, not unlike the basket rattles used by children here, though much larger, and hold up their hands to heaven for a blessing. It is then the greatest offerings are made, and those children whom our wise men foretell will be fortunate are then presented to different people. I remember many used to come to see me, and I was carried about to others for that purpose. They have many offerings, particularly at full moons; generally two at harvest before the fruits are taken out of the ground, and when any young animals are killed sometimes they offer up part of them as a sacrifice. These offerings when made by one of the heads of a family serve for the whole. I remember we often had them at my father's and my uncle's, and their families have been present. Some of our offerings are eaten with bitter herbs. We had a saying among us to anyone of a cross temper, 'That if they were to be eaten, they should be eaten with bitter herbs.'

We practised circumcision like the Jews and made offerings and feasts on that occasion in the same manner as they did. Like them also, our children were named from some event, some circumstance, or fancied foreboding at the time of their birth. I was named *Olaudah*, which in our language signifies vicissitude or fortunate; also, one favoured, and having a loud voice and well spoken. [. . .]

I have before remarked that the natives of this part of Africa are extremely cleanly. This necessary habit of decency was with us a part of religion, and therefore we had many purifications and washings; indeed almost as many and used on the same occasions, if my recollection does not fail me, as the Jews. Those that touched the dead at any time were obliged to wash and purify themselves before they could enter a dwelling-house. Every woman too, at certain times, was forbidden to come into a dwelling-house or touch any person or anything we ate. I was so fond of my mother I could not keep from her or avoid touching her at some of those periods, in consequence of which I was obliged to be kept out with her in a little house made for that purpose till offering was made, and then we were purified.

Though we had no places of public worship, we had priests and magicians or wise men. I do not remember whether they had different offices or whether they were united in the same persons, but they were held in great reverence by the people. They calculated our time and foretold events, as their name imported, for we called them Ah-affoe-way-cah, which signifies calculators or yearly men, our year being called Ah-affoe. They wore their beards, and when they died they were succeeded by their sons. Most of their implements and things of value were interred along with them. Pipes and tobacco were also put into the grave with the corpse, which was always perfumed and ornamented, and animals were offered in sacrifice to them. None accompanied their funerals but those of the same profession or tribe. These buried them after sunset and always returned from the grave by a different way from that which they went.

These magicians were also our doctors or physicians. They practised bleeding by cupping, and were very successful in healing wounds and expelling poisons. They had likewise some extraordinary method of discovering jealousy, theft, and poisoning, the success of which no doubt they derived from their unbounded influence over the credulity and superstition of the people. I do not remember what those methods were, except that as to poisoning: I recollect an instance or two, which I hope it will not be deemed impertinent here to insert as it may serve as a kind of specimen of the rest and is still used by the negroes in the West Indies. A virgin had been poisoned but it was not known by whom: the doctors ordered the corpse to be taken up by some persons, and carried to the grave. As soon as the bearers had raised it on their shoulders they seemed seized with some sudden impulse, and ran to and fro unable to stop themselves. At last, after having passed through a number of thorns and prickly bushes unhurt, the corpse fell from them close to a house and defaced it in the fall, and the owner being taken up, he immediately confessed the poisoning.

The natives are extremely cautious about poison. When they buy any eatable the seller kisses it all round before the buyer to show him it is not poisoned, and the same is done when any meat or drink is presented, particularly to a stranger. We have serpents of different kinds, some of which are esteemed ominous when they appear in our houses, and these we never molest. I remember two of those ominous snakes, each of which was as thick as the calf of a man's leg and in colour resembling a dolphin in the water, crept at different times into my mother's nighthouse where I always lay with her, and coiled themselves into folds, and each time they crowed like a cock. I was desired by some of the wise men to touch these that I might be interested in the good omens, which I did, for they were quite harmless and would tamely suffer themselves to be handled; and then they were put into a large open earthen pan and set on one side of the highway. Some of our snakes, however, were poisonous. [. . .]

Kidnapped

My father, besides many slaves, had a numerous family of which seven lived to grow up, including myself and a sister who was the only daughter. As I was the youngest of the sons I became, of course, the greatest favourite with my mother and was always with her; and she used to take particular pains to form my mind. I was trained up from my earliest years in the art of war, my daily exercise was shooting and throwing javelins, and my mother adorned me with emblems after the manner of our greatest warriors. In this way I grew up till I was turned the age of 11, when an end was put to my happiness in the following manner. Generally when the grown people in the neighbourhood were gone far in the fields to labour, the children assembled together in some of the neighbours' premises to play, and commonly some of us used to get up a tree to look out for any assailant or kidnapper that might come upon us, for they sometimes took those opportunities of our parents' absence to attack and carry off as many as they could seize. One day, as I was watching at the top of a tree in our yard, I saw one of those people come into the yard of our next neighbour but one to kidnap, there being many stout young people in it. Immediately on this I gave the alarm of the rogue and he was surrounded by the stoutest of them, who entangled him with cords so that he could not escape till some of the grown people came and secured him. But alas! ere long it was my fate to be thus attacked and to be carried off when none of the grown people were nigh. One day, when all our people were gone out to their works as usual and only I and my dear sister were left to mind the house, two men and a woman got over our walls, and in a moment seized us both, and without giving us time to cry out or make resistance they stopped our mouths and ran off with us into the nearest wood. Here they tied our hands and continued to carry us as far as they could till night came on, when we reached a small house where the robbers halted for refreshment and spent the night. We were then unbound but were unable to take any food, and being quite overpowered by fatigue and grief, our only relief was some sleep, which allayed our misfortune for a short time. The next morning we left the house and continued travelling all the day. For a long time we had kept to the woods, but at last we came into a road which I believed I knew. I had now some hopes of being delivered, for we had advanced but a little way before I discovered some people at a distance, on which I began to cry out for their assistance: but my cries had no other effect than to make them tie me faster and stop my mouth, and then they put me into a large sack. They also stopped my sister's mouth and tied her hands, and in this manner we proceeded till we were out of the sight of these people. When we went to rest the following night they offered us some victuals, but we refused it, and the only comfort we had was in being in one another's arms all that night and bathing each other with our tears. But alas! we were soon deprived of even the small comfort of weeping together. The next day proved a day of greater sorrow than I had yet experienced, for my sister and I were then separated while we lay clasped in each other's arms. It was in vain that we besought them not to part us; she was torn from me and immediately carried away, while I was left in a state of distraction not to be described. I cried and grieved continually, and for several days I did not eat anything but what they forced into my mouth. At length, after many days' travelling, during which I had often changed masters, I got into the hands of a chieftain in a very pleasant country. This man had two wives and some children, and they all used me extremely well and did all they could to comfort me, particularly the first wife, who was something like my mother. Although I was a great many days' journey from my father's house, yet these people spoke exactly the same language with us. This first master of mine, as I may call him, was a smith, and my principal employment was working his bellows, which were the same kind as I had seen in my vicinity. [. . .] While I was projecting my escape, one day an unlucky event happened which quite disconcerted my plan and put an end to my hopes. I used to be sometimes employed in assisting an elderly woman slave to cook and take care of the poultry, and one morning, while I was feeding some chickens, I happened to toss a small pebble at one of them, which hit it on the middle and directly killed it. The old slave, having soon after missed the chicken, inquired after it; and on my relating the accident (for I told her the truth, because my mother would never suffer me to tell a lie) she flew into a violent passion, threatened that I should suffer for it, and, my master being out, she immediately went and told her mistress what I had done. This alarmed me very much and I expected an instant flogging, which to me was uncommonly dreadful, for I had seldom been beaten at home. I therefore resolved to fly, and accordingly I ran into a thicket that was hard by and hid myself in the bushes. Soon afterwards my mistress and the slave returned, and not seeing me they searched all the house, but not finding me, and I not making answer when they called to me, they thought I had run away and the whole neighbourhood was raised in the pursuit of me. [. . .]

I at length quitted the thicket, very faint and hungry for I had not eaten or drank anything all the day, and crept to my master's kitchen from whence I set out at first, and which was an open shed, and laid myself down in the ashes with an anxious wish for death to relieve me from all my pains. I was scarcely awake in the morning when the old woman slave, who was the first up, came to light the fire and saw me in the fireplace. She was very much surprised to see me and could scarcely believe her own eyes. She now promised to intercede for me and went for her master, who soon after came, and, having slightly reprimanded me, ordered me to be taken care of and not ill-treated.

Soon after this my master's only daughter and child by his first wife sickened and died, which affected him so much that for some time he was almost frantic, and really would have killed himself had he not been watched and prevented. However, in a small time afterwards he recovered and I was again sold. I was now carried to the left of the sun's rising, through many different countries and a number of large woods. The people I was sold to used to carry me very often when I was tired either on their shoulders or on their backs. I saw many convenient well-built sheds along the roads at proper distances, to accommodate the merchants and travellers who lay in those buildings along with their wives, who often accompany them; and they always go well armed.

From the time I left my own nation I always found somebody that understood me till I came to the sea coast. The languages of different nations did not totally differ, nor were they so copious as those of the Europeans, particularly the English. They were therefore easily learned, and while I was journeying thus through Africa I acquired two or three different tongues. In this manner I had been travelling for a considerable time, when one evening, to my great surprise, whom should I see brought to the house where I was but my dear sister! As soon as she saw me she gave a loud shriek and ran into my arms—I was quite over-powered: neither of us could speak, but for a considerable time clung to each other in mutual embraces, unable to do anything but weep. Our meeting affected all who saw us, and indeed I must acknowledge, in honour of those sable destroyers of human rights, that I never met with any ill treatment or saw any offered to their slaves except tying them, when necessary, to keep them from running away. When these people knew we were brother and sister they indulged us to be together, and the man to whom I supposed we belonged lay with us, he in the middle while she and I held one another by the hands across his breast all night; and thus for a while we forgot our misfortunes in the joy of being together: but even this small comfort was soon to have an end, for scarcely had the fatal morning appeared when she was again torn from me for ever! [. . .]

I did not long remain after my sister. I was again sold and carried through a number of places till, after travelling a considerable time, I came to a town called Timmah in the most beautiful country I had yet seen in Africa. It was extremely rich, and there were many rivulets which flowed through it and supplied a large pond in the centre of the town, where the people washed. Here I first saw and tasted coconuts, which I thought superior to any nuts I had ever tasted before; and the trees, which were loaded, were also interspersed amongst the houses, which had commodious shades adjoining and were in the same manner as ours, the insides being neatly plastered and whitewashed. Here I also saw and tasted for the first time sugar-cane. Their money consisted of little white shells the size of a finger-nail. I was sold here for 172 of them by a merchant who lived and brought me there. [. . .] The next day I was washed and perfumed, and when meal-time came I was led into the presence of my mistress, and ate and drank before her with her son. This filled me with astonishment; and I could scarce help expressing my surprise that the young gentleman should suffer me, who was bound, to eat with him who was free; and not only so, but that he would not at any time either eat or drink till I had taken first, because I was the eldest, which was agreeable to our custom. Indeed everything here, and all their treatment of me, made me forget that I was a slave. The language of these people resembled ours so nearly that we understood each other perfectly. They had also the very same customs as we. There were likewise slaves daily to attend us, while my young master and I with other boys sported with our darts and bows and arrows, as I had been used to do at home. In this resemblance to my former happy state I passed about two months; and I now began to think I was to be adopted into the family, and was beginning to be reconciled to my situation, and to forget by degrees my misfortunes, when all at once the delusion vanished; for without the least previous knowledge, one morning early, while my dear master and companion was still asleep, I was wakened out of my reverie to fresh sorrow, and hurried away even amongst the uncircumcised. [...]

All the nations and people I had hitherto passed through resembled our own in their manner, customs, and language: but I came at length to a country the inhabitants of which differed from us in all those particulars. I was very much struck with this difference, especially when I came among a people who did not circumcise and ate without washing their hands. They cooked also in iron pots and had European cutlasses and crossbows, which were unknown to us, and fought with their fists amongst themselves. Their women were not so modest as ours, for they ate and drank and slept with their men. But above all, I was amazed to see no sacrifices or offerings among them. In some of those places the people ornamented themselves with scars, and likewise filed their teeth very sharp. They wanted sometimes to ornament me in the same manner, but I would not suffer them, hoping that I might some time be among a people who did not thus disfigure themselves, as I thought they did. At last I came to the banks of a large river, which was covered with canoes in which the people appeared to live with their household utensils and provisions of all kinds. I was beyond measure astonished at this, as I had never before seen any water larger than a pond or a rivulet: and my surprise was mingled with no small fear when I was put into one of these canoes and we began to paddle and move along the river. We continued going on thus till night, and when we came to land and made fires on the banks, each family by themselves, some dragged their canoes on shore, others stayed and cooked in theirs and laid in them all night. Those on the land had mats of which they made tents, some in the shape of little houses: in these we slept, and after the morning meal we embarked again and proceeded as before. I was often very much astonished to see some of the women, as well as the men, jump into the water, dive to the bottom, come up again, and swim about. [...]

The Slave Ship

The first object which saluted my eyes when I arrived on the coast was the sea, and a slave ship which was then riding at anchor and waiting for its cargo. These filled me with astonishment, which was soon converted into terror when I was carried on board. I was immediately handled and tossed up to see if I were sound by some of the crew, and I was now persuaded that I had gotten into a world of bad spirits and that they were going to kill me. Their complexions too differing so much from ours, their long hair and the language they spoke (which was very different from any I had ever heard) united to confirm me in this belief. Indeed such were the horrors of my views and fears at the moment that, if ten thousand worlds had been my own, I would have freely parted with them all to have exchanged my condition with that of the meanest slave in my own country. When I looked round the ship too and saw a large furnace or copper boiling and a multitude of black people of every description chained together, every one of their countenances expressing dejection and sorrow, I no longer doubted of my fate; and quite overpowered with horror and anguish, I fell motionless on the deck and fainted. When I recovered a little I found some black people about me, who I believed were some of those who had brought me on board, and had been receiving their pay; they talked to me in order to cheer me, but all in vain. I asked them if we were not to be eaten by those white men with horrible looks, red faces, and loose hair. They told me I was not, and one of the crew brought me a small portion of spirituous liquor in a wine glass, but being afraid of him I would not take it out of his hand. One of the blacks therefore took it from him and gave it to me, and I took a little down my palate, which instead of reviving me, as they thought it would, threw me into the greatest consternation at the strange feeling it produced, having never tasted any such liquor before. Soon after this the blacks who brought me on board went off, and left me abandoned to despair.

I now saw myself deprived of all chance of returning to my native country or even the least glimpse of hope of gaining the shore, which I now considered as friendly; and I even wished for my former slavery in preference to my present situation, which was filled with horrors of every kind, still heightened by my ignorance of what I was to undergo. I was not long suffered to indulge my grief; I was soon put down under the decks, and there I received such a salutation in my nostrils as I had never experienced in my life: so that with the loathsomeness of the stench and crying together, I became so sick and low that I was not able to eat, nor had I the least desire to taste anything. I now wished for the last friend, death, to relieve me; but soon, to my grief, two of the white men offered me eatables, and on my refusing to eat, one of them held me fast by the hands and laid me across I think the windlass, and tied my feet while the other flogged me severely. I had never experienced anything of this kind before, and although, not being used to the water, I naturally feared that element the first time I saw it, yet nevertheless could I have got over the nettings I would have jumped over the side, but I could not; and besides, the crew used to watch us very closely who were not chained down to the decks, lest we should leap into the water: and I have seen some of these poor African prisoners most severely cut for attempting to do so, and hourly whipped for not eating. This indeed was often the case with myself. In a little time after, amongst the poor chained men I found some of my own nation, which in a small degree gave ease to my mind. I inquired of these what was to be done with us; they gave me to understand we were to be carried to these white people's country to work for them. [. . .] I had never seen among my people such instances of brutal cruelty, and this not only shewn towards us blacks but also to some of the whites themselves. One white man in particular I saw, when we were permitted to be on deck, flogged so unmercifully with a large rope near the foremast that he died in consequence of it; and they tossed him over the side as they would have done a brute. This made me fear these people the more, and I expected nothing less than to be treated in the same manner. I could not help expressing my fears and apprehensions to some of my countrymen: I asked them if these people had no country but lived in this hollow place (the ship): they told me they did not, but came from a distant one. 'Then,' said I, 'how comes it in all our country we never heard of them?' They told me because they lived so very far off. I then asked where were their women? Had they any like themselves? I was told they had: 'and why,' said I, 'do we not see them?' They answered, because they were left behind. I asked how the vessel could go? They told me they could not tell, but that there were cloths put upon the masts by the help of the ropes I saw, and then the vessel went on; and the white men had some spell or magic they put in the water when they liked in order to stop the vessel. I was exceedingly amazed at this account and really thought they were spirits. I therefore wished much to be from amongst them for I expected they would sacrifice me: but my wishes were vain, for we were so quartered that it was impossible for any of us to make our escape. While we stayed on the coast I was mostly on deck, and one day, to my great astonishment, I saw one of these vessels coming in with the sails up. As soon as the whites saw it they gave a great shout, at which we were amazed; and the more so as the vessel appeared larger by approaching nearer. At last she came to an anchor in my sight, and when the anchor was let go I and my countrymen who saw it were lost in astonishment to observe the vessel stop, and were now convinced it was done by magic. Soon after this the other ship got her boats out, and they came on board of us, and the people of both ships seemed very glad to see each other. Several of the strangers also shook hands with us black people, and made motions with their hands, signifying I suppose we were to go to their country; but we did not understand them. At last, when the ship we were in had got in all her cargo, they made ready with many fearful noises, and we were all put under deck so that we could not see how they managed the vessel. But this disappointment was the least of my sorrow. The stench of the hold while we were on the coast was so intolerably loathsome that it was dangerous to remain there for any time, and some of us had been permitted to stay on the deck for the fresh air; but now that the whole ship's cargo were confined together it became absolutely pestilential. The closeness of the place and the heat of the climate, added to the number in the ship, which was so crowded that each had scarcely room to turn himself, almost suffocated us. This produced copious perspirations, so that the air soon became unfit for respiration from a variety of loathsome smells, and brought on a sickness among the slaves, of which many died, thus falling victims to the improvident avarice, as I may call it, of their purchasers. This wretched situation was again aggravated by the galling of the chains, now become insupportable, and the filth of the necessary tubs, into which the children often fell and were almost suffocated. The shrieks of the women and the groans of the dying rendered the whole a scene of horror almost inconceivable. [. . .] One day they had taken a number of fishes, and when they had killed and satisfied themselves with as many as they thought fit, to our astonishment who were on the deck, rather than give any of them to us to eat as we expected, they tossed the remaining fish into the sea again, although we begged and prayed for some as well as we could, but in vain; and some of my countrymen, being pressed by hunger, took an opportunity when they thought no one saw them of trying to get a little privately; but they were discovered, and the attempt procured them some very severe floggings. One day, when we had a smooth sea and moderate wind, two of my wearied countrymen who were chained together (I was near them at the time), preferring death to such a life of misery, somehow made through the nettings and jumped into the sea: immediately another quite dejected fellow, who on account of his illness was suffered to be out of irons, also followed their example; [. . .] two of the wretches were drowned, but they got the other and afterwards flogged him unmercifully for thus attempting to prefer death to slavery. In this manner we continued to undergo more hardships than I can now relate, hardships which are inseparable from this accursed trade. Many a time we were near suffocation from the want of fresh air, which we were often without for whole days together. This and the stench of the necessary tubs carried off many. During our passage I first saw flying fishes, which surprised me very much: they used frequently to fly across the ship and many of them fell on the deck. I also now first saw the use of the quadrant; I had often with astonishment seen the mariners make observations with it, and I could not think what it meant. They at last took notice of my surprise, and one of them, willing to increase it as well as to gratify my curiosity, made me one day look through it. The clouds appeared to me to be land, which disappeared as they passed along. This heightened my wonder, and I was now more persuaded than ever that I was in another world and that everything about me was magic. At last we came in sight of the island of Barbados, at which the whites on board gave a great shout and made many signs of joy to us. We did not know what to think of this, but as the vessel drew nearer we plainly saw the harbour and other ships of different kinds and sizes, and we soon anchored amongst them off Bridgetown. Many merchants and planters now came on board, though it was in the evening. They put us in separate parcels and examined us attentively. They also made us jump, and pointed to the land, signifying we were to go there. We thought by this we should be eaten by these ugly men, as they appeared to us; and when soon after we were all put down under the deck again, there was much dread and trembling among us, and nothing but bitter cries to be heard all the night from these apprehensions, insomuch that at last the white people got some old slaves from the land to pacify us. They told us we were not to be eaten but to work, and were soon to go on land where we should see many of our country people. This report eased us much; and sure enough soon after we were landed there came to us Africans of all languages. We were conducted immediately to the merchant's yard, where we were all pent up together like so many sheep in a fold without regard to sex or age. As every object was new to me everything I saw filled me with surprise. What struck me first was that the houses were built with storeys, and in every other respect different from those in Africa: but I was still more astonished on seeing people on horseback. I did not know what this could mean, and indeed I thought these people were full of nothing but magical arts. While I was in this astonishment one of my fellow prisoners spoke to a countryman of his about the horses, who said they were the same kind they had in their country. I understood them though they were from a distant part of Africa, and I thought it odd I had not seen any horses there; but afterwards when I came to converse with different Africans I found they had many horses amongst them, and much larger than those I then saw. We were not many days in the merchant's custody before we were sold after their usual manner, which is this: On a signal given, (as the beat of a drum) the buyers rush at once into the yard where the slaves are confined, and make choice of that parcel they like best. The noise and clamour with which this is attended and the eagerness visible in the countenances of the buyers serve not a little to increase the apprehensions of the terrified Africans, who may well be supposed to consider them as the ministers of that destruction to which they think themselves devoted. In this manner, without scruple, are relations and friends separated, most of them never to see each other again. I remember in the vessel in which I was brought over, in the men's apartment there were several brothers who, in the sale, were sold in different lots; and it was very moving on this occasion to see and hear their cries at parting. O, ye nominal Christians! might not an African ask you, Learned you this from your God who says unto you, Do unto all men as you would men should do unto you? Is it not enough that we are torn from our country and friends to toil for your luxury and lust of gain? Must every tender feeling be likewise sacrificed to your avarice? Are the dearest friends and relations, now rendered more dear by their separation from their kindred, still to be parted from each other and thus prevented from cheering the gloom of slavery with the small comfort of being together and mingling their sufferings and sorrows? Why are parents to lose their children, brothers their sisters, or husbands their wives? Surely this is a new refinement in cruelty which, while it has no advantage to atone for it, thus aggravates distress and adds fresh horrors even to the wretchedness of slavery.

Voyage to England

I now totally lost the small remains of comfort I had enjoyed in conversing with my countrymen; the women too who used to wash and take care of me were all gone different ways, and I never saw one of them afterwards.

I stayed in this island for a few days, I believe it could not be above a fortnight, when I and some few more slaves that were not saleable amongst the rest, from very much fretting, were shipped off in a sloop for North America. On the passage we were better treated than when we were coming from Africa and we had plenty of rice and fat pork. We were landed up a river a good way from the sea, about Virgina county, where we saw few or none of our native Africans and not one soul who could talk to me. I was a few weeks weeding grass and gathering stones in a plantation, and at last all my companions were distributed different ways and only myself was left. I was now exceedingly miserable and thought myself worse off than any of the rest of my companions, for they could talk to each other, but I had no person to speak to that I could understand. In this state I was constantly grieving and pining and wishing for death rather than anything else. [. . .]

From *Equiano's Travels*, pp. 10–33

OLAUDAH EQUIANO   *Also known as Vassa Gustavus and born in 1745 or 46 in eastern Nigeria, in an area which he calls Essaka, and which Paul Edwards describes as being to the south-east of Onitsha. Equiano tells that his people, who spoke Igbo, were under the influence of Benin. He was carried off by slavers when he was ten and transported to the West Indies and to America. On being freed by his master he worked in the marine, eventually coming to England. He became an active abolitionist. He married an English woman and died in England when he was about 57. His book is truly fascinating, and represents an early achievement in a language not originally his own—an achievement which makes nonsense of both racist theories and European cultural xenophobia.*

[10, 13]

PAUL RADIN (ed.)

There was once a certain man called Hate-to-Be-Contradicted, and because of that, he built a small settlement all by himself and went to live in it. And the creature called the duiker went to visit him, and he walked with him and sat down at the foot of a palm tree. Then some of the palm nuts fell down. The duiker said, 'Father Hate-to-Be-Contradicted, your palm nuts are ripe.'

Hate-to-Be-Contradicted said, 'That is the nature of the palm nut. When they are ripe, three bunches ripen at once. When they are ripe, I cut them down; and then I boil them to extract the oil, they make three waterpots full of oil. Then I take the oil to Akase to buy an Akase old woman. The Akase old woman comes and gives birth to my grandmother who bears my mother who, in turn, bears me. When Mother bears me, I am already standing there.'

The duiker said, 'As for all that, you lie.'

And Hate-to-Be-Contradicted took a stick and hit the duiker on the head, and killed it.

Next the little abedee antelope came along. Hate-to-Be-Contradicted went off with it and sat under the palm tree, and the same thing happened. And thus it was with all the animals. Finally, Kwaku Ananse, the spider, went and fetched his cloth and his bag, slung the bag across his shoulders, and went off to visit Hate-to-Be-Contradicted's kraal. He greeted him: 'Father, good morning.'

Hate-to-Be-Contradicted replied, '*Y'aku*, and where are you going?'

He replied, 'I am coming to visit you.'

And he took his stool and placed it under the palm tree.

Hate-to-Be-Contradicted said, 'Cook food for the spider to eat.'

And while it was cooking, Ananse and Hate-to-Be-Contradicted sat under the palm tree. Some of the palm nuts fell down, and Ananse took them and placed them in his bag. This he continued to do until his bag was full. The food was brought, and Ananse ate. When he had finished eating, some of the ripe palm nuts again fell down, and Ananse said, 'Father Hate-to-Be-Contradicted, your palm nuts are ripe.'

Hate-to-Be-Contradicted said, 'It's their nature to ripen like that; when they are ripe, three bunches ripen at once. When they are ripe, I cut them down, and then I boil them to extract the oil, they make three waterpots full of oil, and I take the oil to Akase to buy an Akase old woman. The Akase old woman comes and gives birth to my grandmother who bears my mother so that she in turn may bear me. When Mother bears me, I am already standing there.'

The spider said, 'You do not lie. What you say is true. As for me, I have some okras standing in my farm. When they are ripe, I join seventy-seven long hooked poles in order to reach them to pull them down, but even then I cannot reach them. So I lie on my back, and am able to use my penis to pluck them.'

Hate-to-Be-Contradicted said, 'Oh, I understand. Tomorrow I shall come and look.'

The spider said, 'Surely.'

While the spider was going home, he chewed the palm nuts which he had

gathered and spat them out on the path. The next morning, when things began t
be visible, Hate-to-Be-Contradicted set out to go to the spider's village. Now whe
the spider had arrived home the day before, he had gone and said to his childre
'A certain man will come here who hates to be contradicted, and when he arriv
and inquires for me, you must tell him that yesterday I had said I was going o
somewhere, when my penis broke in seven places and I had to take it to a blac
smith to be repaired and, as the blacksmith could not finish it at the time, I hav
now gone to have the work finished.'

Not long afterward Hate-to-Be-Contradicted came along. He said, 'Where ha
your father gone?'

They replied, 'Alas, Father went somewhere yesterday, and his penis g
broken in seven different places. So he took it to a blacksmith, but he could n
finish the job at the time, and Father has gone to have it completed. You, Fathe
did you not see the blood on the path?'

Hate-to-Be-Contradicted said, 'Yes, I saw it.' He then asked, 'And where
your mother?'

The spider's child replied, 'Mother, too—yesterday she went to the stream, an
her waterpot would have fallen and broken had she not saved it from doing so b
just catching at it in time. But she didn't quite finish saving it from falling and ha
returned today to do so.' Hate-to-Be-Contradicted did not say anything.

Now Ananse arrived. He said, 'Cook some food that Hate-to-Be-Contradicte
may eat.' As the children were cooking the food, they used only one single litt
perch but an immense quantity of peppers. They made the soup-stew very ho
When they had finished, they set it down before Hate-to-Be-Contradicted. Hat
to-Be-Contradicted ate. Now the peppers pained him; he wanted to die. He said t
one of Ananse's sons, 'Ntikuma, where is that water?'

Ntikuma said, 'Ah, the water which we have here in our waterpot is of thre
different kinds. That belonging to Father comes first, that of my mother's co-wi
is in the middle, and that belonging to my own mother is at the bottom of the pot.
must draw for you only the water belonging to my own mother and if I do not tak
great care when drawing it, it will cause a tribal dispute.'

Hate-to-Be-Contradicted said, 'You little brat, you lie.'

Straightway Ananse said, 'Beat him so that he dies.'

Hate-to-Be-Contradicted said, 'Why should they beat me so that I may die?'

The spider said, 'You say you hate to be contradicted, and yet you have co
tradicted some one. That is why I say they must beat you so that you may die

So they beat Hate-to-Be-Contradicted until he died. Then Ananse cut up h
flesh in little pieces and scattered them all about.

That is why many persons who hate to be contradicted are to be found in t
tribe today.

From *African Folktales and Sculpture*, pp. 101–

[3, 12, 16, 25, 103]

Caribbean Prose Fiction

14 *A Morning at the Office*

EDGAR MITTELHOLZER

'... soon as I landed in the office,' Miss Henery was telling Mrs Hinckson, and Mrs Hinckson laughed again—another smothered laugh, for no one (save Mr Reynolds, the salesman, and his was a special case) ever indulged in loud laughter in the office; it would have been considered bad form.

'Before long he's going to follow you into the lunch-room.'

'Or the Ladies' Room,' said Miss Henery.

'You're right. I won't be surprised.'

Mr Waley was coming through the barrier-gate.

''Morning, Miss Henery! 'Morning, Mrs Hinckson!'

He paused, brisk and vital, gave Mrs Hinckson a brief, amused smile. 'You notice how early I am this morning. You know what that means?'

Mrs Hinckson smiled back: 'I know. I'm coming in right away.'

After he had moved on: 'I have a whole morning of dictation before me, my dear. The London mail has been piling up for the past week or more.'

'Our friend over there should take a leaf out of Mr Waley's book. If he had more work to do he wouldn't have time to be watching me on the sly.' She indulged in an obscene analogy, and Mrs Hinckson pinkened.

'Kathleen, you're the limit!'

'Isn't it the truth? Next time he rigs up any thin excuse like a fountain-pen to talk to me about, I won't hesitate to tell him just what I think is really the matter with him.'

'I can hear you telling him.'

Mrs Hinckson took the morning's mail from the *Incoming* tray, secured her notebook and pencil, and rose.

As Horace watched her vanish beyond the frosted glass door of Mr Waley's sanctum a groan moved within him. Another set-back. Another variance from the picture as he had dreamt it.

Anxiously he regarded Miss Henery to see whether she would discover the paper in the *File* tray. But she moved off and went back to her own desk.

He began to wonder whether he should not find some excuse to stroll over to Mrs Hinckson's desk and smuggle away the paper and so put an end to the whole business. But Mr Jagabir would be sure to spot him. Mr Jagabir would be curious, and would probably call out and ask him what he was doing there, what paper it was he had taken up. Nothing escaped his prying eyes. And in any case, why should his original scheme be allowed to fizzle out in this tame way? That would be failure. No. Let it remain where it was until she eventually found it. Let it stand as a kind of test. If he lost heart and cancelled the scheme, in future he would cancel greater and more important schemes.

He put aside *A Tale of Two Cities*. He saw on his blotter the blue-pencilled words and faces he had inscribed in moments of dreaming.

Chief Accountant—that was what his mother hoped he would be one day.

assistant accountant . . . *Chief Clerk* . . . *Manager* . . . He had laughed to himself when he had written that. No matter if he were the most brilliant business genius the world had ever produced, he could not hope to be Manager of this office . . . An office manager with a black skin!

assistant manager . . .

Why was it certain posts demanded initial capitals when you wrote them, and others small letters? He had seen it in circulars and letters. *Chief Clerk* but not *Assistant Accountant.* . . .

English people were too queer in their ways—

He started, and scolded himself for indulging in aimless thoughts. He took from a drawer the Pitman's textbook on shorthand and the exercise book in which he wrote the exercises set by his teacher. At five-fifteen this afternoon he had to take in two exercises, and they must be neatly and correctly done, for he wanted to keep up the reputation he had won for good work at the commercial school he attended.

It was a private school run by a coloured lady at her home, and the fees were within his means. He reckoned it as one of his minor triumphs that Mrs Brandon had accepted him as a pupil. All the other pupils were fair or olive coloured young ladies and young gentlemen; good-family people. It was only because he had heard that Mrs Brandon was a broad-minded person willing to help ambitious young people, irrespective of their class or colour, that he had had the courage to approach her. Even so, he had sensed the hesitation in her manner. But she had been very nice. She had questioned him about his job and his plans, and had seemed interested in him. He knew that he had impressed her, but had still felt a great relief when, at length, she nodded slowly and said: 'Very well, Xavier, you can come. From the first of next month.' She had spoken in a kind, friendly voice and without any patronage.

Within a minute he had switched his mind completely over to the study of the lesson, though all the while he kept on the alert for a call. He had so trained himself that he could be forever vigilant for a call or a signal from any member of the staff even when deeply engrossed in his own occupations. He was determined not to be caught napping as Mr Jagabir had caught him a little while ago.

When a moment later he heard the assistant accountant's chair scrape he glanced up, but Mr Jagabir was only moving across to Miss Henery with a sheaf of papers.

'Dese are the accounts Ah was telling you about, Miss Henery,' Mr Jagabir said to Miss Henery.

Miss Henry jabbed her thumb toward the letter-trays. 'Put them there. I'll see to them in a little.'

As always when she had to deal with him, her manner was stiff. It was not that she hated East Indians; one or two of her very good acquaintances were East Indian. Miss Bisnauth was an East Indian, and Miss Bisnauth and she got on very well; she liked Miss Bisnauth. But this man Jagabir made her sick in every way. His dissembling, his slyness and prying habits, his sycophancy, his ingratiating, yet at the same time nagging and accusatory, voice—all combined to create friction with her fearless, volatile temperament, and to breed within her a deep contempt and disgust for him.

Her upbringing, too, did not help matters. In her social sphere, a child was from an early age made to feel that the East Indians were inferior, contemptible people. They were dirty coolies, you learnt, who had come from India by the shipload to work on the sugar estates; they were a low, filthy people who wore *dhotis* and smelly rags and who walked about bare-footed; they ate nothing but rice and curried salt-fish and lived in stinking tenement barracks, hoarded their pennies in mattresses.

It was only of recent years that East Indians had begun to get rich and become somebodies. Her grandparents, Miss Henery had learnt through the remarks of adults, were ladies and gentlemen living in respectable surroundings—educated, well-bred people—when the East Indians had still, in every sense, been coolies labouring in the cane-fields.

Mr Jagabir placed the accounts in one of the trays but did not move off.

Out of the corner of her eye Miss Henery noticed that he was smiling.

'Miss, you see de paper with de love verse? Mrs Hinckson show you?'

'What's that?'

Mr Jagabir knew that Mrs Hinckson had not noticed the paper. He had watched her every movement and action from the moment she had come in. But he considered this the best way of introducing the subject to Miss Henery. Ignoring the brittleness of her manner—he was inured to it—he said: 'Somebody put a paper wid a love verse write on it in one of her letter-trays. When I come to work a lil' while ago I happen to stop by her desk to fill me pen, and Ah notice dis paper. It's somebody in dis office who put it dere, I know. A poem by Shakespeare.'

Miss Henery's curiosity so overcame her contempt that she relaxed a trifle and returned: 'No, I'm afraid I haven't seen it. How do you know it was somebody in the office who put it there? Why couldn't it have come by post?'

He shook his head and smiled mysteriously. 'No, miss, it didn't come by post. I happen to know it didn't come by post.'

Miss Henery made no comment.

'It's somebody who you would never suspeck. De person *fancy* nobody see dem, but *I* see dem when they put it there.'

She was about to tell him bluntly to stop hedging and reveal who it was, but at this point Miss Bisnauth came in and called: 'Hallo, Kathleen!' on her way to her desk.

'Hallo, Edna. How're things?'

'Not too bad, child!'

While these greetings were being exchanged Mr Jagabir took the opportunity to glide back to his desk. In any event, he would not have made any further revelations. He was satisfied that he had set to work the leaven of intrigue. Nothing delighted him more than intrigue. To be instrumental in a plot aimed at disgracing or ridiculing anyone was one of the compensations of a fear-ridden life. . . .

Horace turned his head at the quick footsteps. Without doing so he would have known it was Miss Yen Tip. She always ran up the stairs—as though her bubbly, vivacious nature could not tolerate leisurely movement.

She gave him a swift smile and an 'Ay, Xavier!' as she skipped past him so that he had to start and half-shout: ''Morning, miss!' to be sure she heard him. His cheeks went warm; it was as if her vitality, like a thin, pleasant flame, had flicked them.

She went straight to Miss Henery's desk, and Miss Henery saw that her slanting Chinese eyes were narrowed in accompaniment to the smile which revealed her white, even, but slightly projecting, teeth.

'I have some lovely news for you, Kathleen!'

'Olga, you're always with lovely news.'

'No, man, but dis is really lovely!'

'What's happened?'

In a breathless manner Miss Yen Tip told her: 'Our friend. He was there last night.'

'At the De Luxe?'

'Yes. He went wid Cynthia and her mother.'

'You don't say! Her mother went along, too!'

'Child, I nearly scream out!'

Miss Henery laughed—and Mr Murrain flicked over three leaves of the price-list in rapid succession. He called to Mr Jagabir to bring him the A–D ledger. Called in a hurried stammer.

After a few more exchanges, Miss Yen Tip said: 'Girl, lemme go and get some letters fixed up before Mr Benson come in and scold me.' (Mr Benson was the Chief Clerk, and came in at eight-thirty; Miss Yen Tip was his stenotypist.)

'I'll give you some more details,' said Miss Yen Tip, 'later on before de morning out. Ronny and I were sitting right in front of dem, and I heard her mother say somet'ing dat made me nearly die wid laughing.'

And she was off to her desk, short, slim, chic, full of little gay chortles.

Mr Jagabir gave her a disapproving glance.

Miss Henery smiled reflectively as she flicked the flannelette duster over her desk preparatory to settling down to the day's work.

The 'our friend' Miss Yen Tip had referred to as having seen at the De Luxe cinema was Herbert McGlenny, the young man who, for a long time, had been trying to persuade Miss Henery to marry him.

She was not in love with him. She liked him. Now and then she considered giving him an answer in the affirmative, for he was in every way eligible as a husband. His father's commission agency was making thousands, and his father had taken him into the business as a partner. His earnestness and persistence, too, some-times moved her—and he was a handsome fellow whom several girls were assiduously bent on capturing. He came of good class, had a light olive complexion and hair with large waves ('good' hair, Miss Henery thought of it as; as a member of the West Indian coloured middle-class, she conceived of human hair in terms of 'good' and 'bad'—sometimes 'good' and 'hard'; 'good' hair is hair that is European in appearance: 'bad' or 'hard' hair is hair of the kinky, negroid type).

Herbert's family was one of the best in Trinidad. His father's father had been a well-known barrister who had gained renown despite the disadvantages of a dark complexion and kinky hair (it was whispered that he was a pure black man). Herbert's mother was a Harrould; her brother was the late Doctor Harrould, and old Mr Harrould, her father, had been Mayor of Port of Spain on two or three occasions in the past.

Miss Henery murmured a 'Damn!' as an eraser went flying off the desk. It described grasshopper motions on the floor and came to rest not far from the iron safe against the wall.

Two chairs scraped simultaneously—Mr Lopez' (Mr Lopez' desk was just behind hers) and Mr Murrain's, the swivel-screw squeaking as well.

Mr Murrain rose and leant outward to recover the eraser, but Mr Lopez proved too athletic for him. Mr Lopez behaved as though he were fielding a ball on the cricket ground; he took one swift crab-wise stride, an arm flashed out—and the eraser was in his grasp.

Mr Murrain pinkened and laughed softly. 'I hope you'll be as fast when you play against Barbados next week.'

'He's no good in the field, sir,' grinned Mr Lorry, who had just arrived in time to witness the incident. 'He can only handle a bat.'

'That won't do in cricket,' said Mr Murrain, wagging his head. 'You've got to be an all-rounder.'

He took the opportunity of this opening to ask Mr Lopez how the Colony Eleven was shaping at practice. Next week a cricket tournament between Trinidad and Barbados commenced at the Queen's Park Oval, and Mr Lopez was one of Trinidad's best bats.

Cricket was one of Mr Murrain's weaknesses. He had never handled a bat nor bowled a ball, but he was an enthusiastic spectator, and had even allowed himself to be elected a committee member of one of the leading clubs.

Miss Henery, accustomed to these cricketing conferences in her vicinity, proceeded, unperturbed, to fix the first account form into her machine. But as she worked her thoughts kept straying back to Herbert McGlenny.

Herbert had an attractive personality, and she felt that, in time, she could coax herself into falling in love with him. At present, it would be out of the question, for she was too infatuated with her cousin's husband, Gerard Beaton.

Actually, the affair had started shortly after Miss Henery left Bishop's High School upon obtaining her Cambridge School Certificate. Confined to glances, smiles and conversational innuendoes when she and Gerard happened to be alone, the affair had not really emerged as a tangible fact until late one afternoon about three months ago. She and Gerard had met accidentally in the Rock Garden; they had sat on a grassy embankment to talk; darkness fell—and suddenly there was an explosion of feelings and an impassioned revelation. Though they had not gone beyond kissing and fondling, they had both realized that if they continued to see each other a consummation was sooner or later inevitable.

Gerard Beaton was a civil servant, efficient and zealous to the point of splitting hairs; he was an active Presbyterian. But despite these limiting factors, he had shaped for himself a fairly liberal outlook; he did not exclaim in horror at fornication; listened to and retailed smutty jokes; saw nothing wrong in getting drunk on festive occasions. He felt, however, that such things as duty, loyalty and honour were not to be treated lightly.

Kathleen Henery was approximately of the same philosophy, but sex obsessed her so much that sometimes she wondered whether it were possible for her ever to have a set code of morals. Her parents were Anglo-Catholics who went to church every Sunday and whose codes were rigid. They had trained her up to believe that fornication and adultery were grave sins which could result in catastrophic social repercussions (though not necessarily in hell-fire in the Hereafter; they were too educated to stress this).

Her cousin Rachel was one of her best chums; their friendship dated from primary school days. The thought of beguiling Rachel's husband into a sex affair and causing Rachel much unhappiness disturbed Miss Henery. She would feel wretched if her friendship with Gerard took such a turn.

Divorce was not to be thought of; Gerard looked upon marriage as a 'sacrament', and she herself would have considered the idea highly distasteful. So she had had to rule out the possibility of their ever getting married. And she knew that, above everything, she wanted to get married.

Herbert wanted to marry her—very badly—but she knew that if he found out that she had been sexually intimate with Gerard he would not want to, because Herbert, in spite of his charm and apparent worldliness, was an unsophisticated, old-fashioned young man. And, naturally, reasoned Miss Henery, she would have to be honest with him and tell him everything before they came to the point of marriage.

She took from the machine the first completed account. Removing the two carbons—for she had done it in triplicate—she saw her face, slightly distorted, reflected in the paper-release lever which was of highly polished nickel plating. She stared at it in idle contemplation, telling herself that she had no reason to be ashamed of her looks. A short, straight nose with narrow nostrils—nothing negroid about it. A mouth small and well shaped, the lips full but not thick. Her shoulders had an inclination to be round, but the shoulder-pads of her dress prevented this defect from being too apparent.

It was not so easy, however, to disguise her not-too-straight spine which gave her a slight stoop, and in order to correct this she had fallen into the habit of throwing out her chest when sitting, and being careful never to slouch when standing. Her figure was far from ideal—her breasts, apart from being too small, had sagged too early—but she made the best of it by not wearing brassières and by favouring thin dress materials.

Men found her round, fearless stare her most exciting feature. The expression of her eyes did not belie her nature; she was brave, she was spiritually adventurous; she revelled in any situation that carried with it the element of moral danger or the other sort of danger which involves social disaster. This was why she could continue her secret affair with Gerard at the risk of discovery and in the face of her scruples. It was why, too, she could accept Rachel's invitation to accompany the family to Barbados on holiday. She could visualize the many occasions when it would be convenient to whisper and exchange glances, to let Gerard kiss and fondle her. The consummation might become a *fait accompli*. A dangerous thing to picture in cold blood—dangerous and lovely—but she intended to go through with this holiday. She could face it, come whatever might.

She frowned and turned her head suddenly so that out of the corner of her eye she could see Mr Murrain. She had just remembered that he had not yet given her an answer about her leave. She must tackle him about it this very morning.

She pushed out her chest and got ready another account for the machine. She winced and uttered a lisping sound as she caught her knee a crack against the right front leg of the desk. . . .

It was an old-fashioned desk made of crabwood—the only one in the office of its kind. It had been purchased at an auction sale four years ago when a desk had been urgently needed in the office. In respect to its right front leg . . .

One night in July 1936, Wilson O'Brien, a negro cabinet-maker, was at work when he heard a sound at the door of his workshop and glanced round to see his assistant enter. 'Wha' keep you back so late, Aubrey?'

Aubrey Mowbray, his assistant, did not reply. He seemed in a surly mood, and O'Brien guessed what the trouble must be. Aubrey had been gambling and had lost. Gambling and women—especially women—were Aubrey's weaknesses.

'Wid dis kind o' life you leading, boy, you can't prosper.'

Aubrey said nothing. He was a short negro of about twenty-two.

'Your mother plead wid me and beg me to give you dis job. Ah sorry for you and tek you on—and dis is de way you carrying on.'

Without a word, Aubrey prepared to resume work. Before going home for dinner he had half completed the right front leg for the new desk (at that time it could have been right or left; only when the desk was being assembled this leg had happened to be placed on the right).

Taking up the unfinished leg from the work-bench, Aubrey turned it over contemplatively in his hands, and O'Brien heard him grunt.

Aubrey set the lathe going and was soon busy. He worked, O'Brien thought, with a steadiness unusual for him.

It was a chilly night. A thunderstorm had raged shortly after three that day, and now at half-past ten at night the air was dense with the water vapour that billowed down from the heavy-wooded hills—the hills that describe a semi-circle around Port of Spain.

A cool drift of air came in at the window over the tool-cupboard on O'Brien's right, and O'Brien decided that he had better close the window. He did not take cold easily, but suddenly the feeling possessed him that the chilly air might not be good for him; he felt uneasy about it for no particular reason.

He had pulled in the two wooden leaves of the window and slammed the bolt into place and was returning to his work-bench when he noticed that Aubrey had left the workshop. His lathe was still going, and O'Brien assumed that he must have gone outside to urinate. A pity, he told himself, the boy could not steady up. His mother was such a good woman—and his father, before he died last year, was a highly respected man in the district; one of the best carpenter-masons in the city, Aubrey's father had been made churchwarden two years ago, and he had belonged to two lodges.

Fully five minutes must have elapsed without any sign of Aubrey. The lathe was still going, and annoyed that the current should be wasted in this way, O'Brien shouted: 'Aubrey! You not coming in to work? You gone out and left de lathe on! I got to pay for de current you know.'

There was no reply from Aubrey.

O'Brien walked over to the door. He looked out on the pavement and about the street, then moved round to the side of the small building where he was certain he would find Aubrey.

But the narrow alleyway was empty. The street light illuminated it sufficiently for him to be sure no one was there. Even the street was deserted. It was a little back street, and seldom saw much traffic by day, much less by night.

Puzzled, O'Brien returned to the workshop. He paused by Aubrey's work-bench, automatically switching off the lathe. He saw the desk-leg Aubrey had been at work on—saw that it was completed. It was a good job, and O'Brien felt a little mollified.

He turned at a sound from the door.

It was Victorine—Aubrey's sister, a girl of about fourteen. She said, in a tearful voice, that her mother had sent her with a message. Aubrey was dead.

'Aubrey dead? Wha' you telling me, child?'

'Yes, Mr O'Brien, he tek sick after dinner and 'e dead.'

O'Brien laughed and told her that her mother must be joking to send him a message like this.

'Aubrey was here not five minutes ago. Look at de time. Twenty-five to eleven. And he walk out of here at half-past ten and left de lathe on. He just finish turning dis desk-leg.'

'He didn't go nowhere after dinner, Mr O'Brien. He was eating dinner and he say he got a pain in his stomach, and he fall sick and die off.'

O'Brien told her she was talking nonsense. He was a matter-of-fact man of forty-eight and entirely lacking in superstition. 'Look, child,' he told Victorine, 'spirits and *obeah* and *voodoo* don't come my way. Nor I don't know none o' my friends who believe in such things. I'm sure you' mother don't hold wid such foolishness, either. She's a sensible woman. Only de people in America and England know about de *obeah* and *voodoo* we West Indians is suppose to practise. Nobody can fool me Aubrey wasn't in dis shop working—'

A tall, slim negro entered. 'Wilson, you hear about Aubrey?'

Henry Chalmers, a mechanic, was a good friend of O'Brien's. He lived next door to the Mowbrays. He told O'Brien that shortly after nine o'clock Mrs Mowbray, Aubrey's mother, had called over to tell them that Audrey had collapsed while eating his dinner and was dead. The doctor said it was prussic acid.

A week later, O'Brien was called as a witness at the inquest, but in his evidence he stated that the last time he had seen Aubrey was just before Aubrey had left the workshop at eight o'clock to go home for dinner.

O'Brien felt that only trouble could result for the Mowbray household if he told the facts as he knew them to be, and Mrs Mowbray was too old a friend upon whom to bring unhappiness. For some reason known to the family, they were trying to make out that Aubrey had died at shortly after nine, and the Chalmers, their neighbours were conspiring to back up this story. Very well. Let it go at that. . . . Yet it did strike him as queer that the boy could have died at his home not five minutes after leaving the workshop at half-past ten. It would have taken him at least eight minutes to get home, and Victorine and Chalmers would have required another eight minutes to arrive at the workshop with the message of his death.

There was a big mystery here, thought O'Brien. He was convinced it could be explained on a physical basis, but he preferred not to make enquiries. He was not a curious man, and he had a dread of the court-house.

Often nowadays he wondered whether he had done right in using the finished desk-leg he had found on Aubrey's work-bench. Perhaps he should have put it away in the odds-and-ends cupboard and made another to replace it.

On occasion, he asked himself idly where that desk could be now. . . .

From *A Morning at the Office*, pp. 51–67.

EDGAR MITTELHOLZER *Born in 1909 in what was then British Guiana; died in England in 1965. A prolific novelist, one of the first West Indians to dedicate himself solely to writing. Much concerned with the idea that the sins of the father will be visited on his sons (and daughters), and with ethnicity and race. The multi-ethnic picture here given is in sharp contrast to the common feeling in Britain that somehow the Caribbean is really a part of Africa. The* Caribbean Sampler *in the Open University's course* U204 Third World Studies *also makes the attempt to show that although certain aspects of the culture of Africa have been important in the development of the culture of the Caribbean, many other cultures have also left their mark— not least of all through the European languages and literatures which are well known in the Caribbean—even in a sense to the illiterate through the Bible in English.*

[4, 16, 24]

GEORGE LAMMING

This was a womb which the world (meaning those other than you) was not aware of. The world passed by on the outside, intent or callous, but ignorant of the intimacy and the warmth of this house, in this corner, where those women were seated around a table, a small table with three legs and a rectangular surface, old, polished and efficient. The radio played unnecessarily, a neutral and irrelevant kind of music which interrupted no one and could be spoiled by no interruption. Background music. The morning salutation in fair or foul weather. Meaningless, but absolutely and irreversibly natural. Similarly that radio music. Turn it off and it would be missed. Leave it on and no one noticed it. But it was a link with the world, the others; and in its way it might have been a reminder that there was nothing fanciful about the others, nothing false about what was said now about that world, those who walked outside anxiously, monotonously over the surface of this corner.

There were four or five of them. One voice in four or five keys. The incidents varied in four or five ways, but the results were in essence the same. One voice that now spoke in four or five keys from this comforting corner about the others, the world, which was indeed the only reason, which could make that voice perform its proper function, the only subject which made speech possible at all.

I tell you an' I mean it she is good, an' the best o' them 'cause I try all myself in the last five years.

Good good good. Not like that one in Bayswater. Cutsie Bynoe. From down town Port-o'-Spain.

That's right. Never hear the joke 'bout her. She had a place in Marine Square long time 'fore she come up to England. In those days she ain't know nothing 'bout electric iron. The way things change, my chil'. You know the joke.

Think I heard it once. Something 'bout a coal-pot.

That's right. She use to heat up the comb on coals. And through her own stupid carelessness, she put the comb in the girl's head one day without noticing the piece o' burn charcoal between the comb teeth.

Oh Gawd!

The poor girl bawl for murder. The child head was on fire. They had to throw buckets o' cold water all over the child.

Doris Grant.

That's right. The same girl. And a lovely head o' hair she had in those days.

She never catch herself again.

She went up to be a nun.

That's right. She became a nun, and a nice, bright promisin' girl she was.

She was to marry Tom Phelps, the boy from the Customs.

So the others say he say he couldn't marry no bald-pated woman.

There was more to it than that. He wasn't the sort o' chap to leave a girl for that.

That's the girl from Warren Street?

That's right.

Soon after you pass the Savannah on your right.

Oh. She had TB.

But coming back to Miss Dorking. She know how to do your hair. She take a bit long, and, I won't like her to hear me, she don't always wash it properly, but she can press your hair good good.

She gets too much work, really.

Too much. Sometimes she gets a girl to help her, but she got to be so careful.

'Bout what?

You know you ain't suppose to do it without a licence, an' I ain't think she got any licence. 'Tis different from back home where you could set up a little place an' it ain't nobody's business. Here every damn thing is something for papers, permission, and signing here an' there, an' the income tax an' all that. You got to be so careful.

Chil' I never know so much botheration myself. Livin' here in England is like having a job, ah mean o' job apart from your work. The things yo got to remember, and look 'bout. Ration book, National Insurance card, paper for the Ministry o' this an' the Ministry o' that, an' talkin' 'bout looking for a job. The things you got to remember to answer, you tired before you start work.

Then there's the landlady. The less you say 'bout them the better. You know she went in the room one day, and see the things Miss Dorking work with, an' she nearly catch a fit. She ask more questions than what John read 'bout. An' poor Dorking had to make up one hell of a story. Say she was a dental mechanic, and these were the apparatus they use. The landlady ask where the teeth, and she say the dentist keep the teeth. She make them an' pass them on to him.

An' there's another reason, you got to be so careful.

That's right.

You can't let the Englishwomen know what you do to your hair. They malicious too bad.

That one in the office always asking me how I get my hair so straight at the top with the curls at the back.

What you tell her?

I say it was natural.

What she say. 'Cause they never stop asking questions when they get ready.

She say she see the women hair like mine and she always wonder why ours look so nice, and the men's hair stay so short with little round curls, like when you know wire.

You didn't know what to tell her.

I didn't want no quarrel. I simply say I didn't know all the facts o' nature. But it was simply a matter of the men having one kind of hair and the women a next.

They too fast, some o' these English girls.

An' that's just how the West Indian boys like them. What you think make it that none of us particularly can have a good time here.

The things they will do, no decent girl from home would ever dream of.

The boys sleep in their digs and they sleep in the boys' flats, and because our boys get on like that with them, whenever they come to take out one of us they expect to do the same thing.

And if you tell them that you not having any o' that, you never hear from them again.

That one Austin from St Vincent. He call me up the other day, ask if I'd like to come out. I say yes, when? He say any time after dinner.

The dog. You know what he mean by that?

Of course I know. He wasn't going to spend a cent on me to take me to dinner, and probably the cinema afterwards.

But he'd spend every cent o' his allowance on the English girls.

Or the Continentals.

Or the Continentals, you're right. An' simply because he knows as well as the world what an' what he can get from them he can't get from me.

Well I don't want to make him feel anyway that I want him to spend money on me. God forbid if I wait for somebody like Tony Austin to spend money on me. I say all right, after dinner. Where shall we go? He says I could come across to his digs, or we could take a walk in Hyde Park. I say no thank you. He ask why not, and I say, you're speaking to the wrong person Mr Austin, and with that I drop the telephone in his ear.

And to think that back home you won't even have given a thought 'bout Tony Austin.

And the English girls up here don't know who is who.

They pick up worse than Tony.

Not that Tony ain't a decent boy, but it's simply what happen to people in a place like this. They completely forget who they are, and they'll take you who know them for a ride at the slightest opportunity.

I hear the girls say so at the hostel, but I never really believe it.

They don't have anywhere to go, and nobody to take them.

But naturally, at home to be taken out was the thing. And what girl from respectable family would walk in a dance hall on her own. That was only for certain types.

Now if we want to go to a dance, we all have to arrange for all the girls to get a day off on the same day, and go in a bunch.

And you'll see those dogs with the English girls coming in arm in arm.

And those who don't bring will then come hoping they can pick you up.

'Tis true. I got one story to tell 'bout them when I get back, and particularly the ones who say they take back English wives.

They're a stinking lot, forgive me.

An' you'll never get an Englishman to ask out one of us.

Not that we particularly want them to, but that is the sad part of the story. You'll get our boys who come up here to study treating the English girls to everything, and you'll never find an Englishman to even look in our direction.

And if they do, you can look out, they're some queer type, thinking that it would be an experience to sleep with somebody who looks different.

An' then it ain't sleep they want.

Or if not they're perhaps a Communist or something like that who want to prove that they practise what they preach, whatever that is.

An' to tell the truth, I'm not in that. No man, English or otherwise ain't going to make me something with which he want to prove something.

An' then you got to be so careful all round. Just as we know our own people from the West Indies, and we know too that others don't know them as we know them, so we don't know the foreign people as we should. Take that African, Azi. Him.

Well he been playing up to me for only God knows how long. An' all I do I can't get the man to leave me alone. The last thing he do is to offer me marriage. And, mind you, all this on the telephone.

You met him once, wasn't it.

At one o' those hostel dances, and because I won't dance with him, he say something 'bout he going to prove to me that he can persuade me to fall in love with him, or something or the other.

He's a real pest. Every West Indian woman he sees, he wants to marry. Imagine Azi in Trinidad.

Or Barbados.

Or even St Lucia.

Why, he'd be the laughing stock of the town with all them funny marks on his face.

That is what put me off too. His face so scratched up. I wanted to ask him why he let them do that.

He say it's the mark of the tribe he was born into.

Well, I sorry, darling, but tribe or no tribe, I couldn't stand that. Some of them got marks but not so distinct.

Yes, like Belonga for example. The student at Lincoln's Inn. But Azi look like he went through a fight.

You know who he was dancin' wid the other night. A singer or something like that. Tall with long hair.

The women turned quiet when Queenie entered. Her hair was combed up from the nape into a circular mound. She wore a night blue blouse above the polka-dotted skirt which she had often used on the ship. She sat quietly in one of the far corners, and watched them shuffle through the women's magazines that were stacked on the mantelpiece.

'This is nice,' Miss Bis said, pointing to the cover design. The girl beside her nodded, and looked up secretively, feeling a definite uncertainty about their evasion.

'I like the skirt,' someone said, and Miss Bis immediately looked across at Queenie who had raised her head from the paper.

'Thank you,' said Queenie, and returned to the paper.

The Jamaican smiled, and Miss Bis did the same, turning the pages of the magazine. Miss Dorking came out through the door that separated them from the work-room. She passed the iron comb to her left hand and greeted Queenie with the other.

'Then it was you who called this morning,' she said.

'Yes,' said Queenie, withdrawing her hand.

'Well meet the girls,' said Miss Dorking.

She made the introductions briefly, thoroughly, with that professional sense of a job well done. The women were slow to make conversation, and Queenie went on playing with the edges of the paper. She felt the need for something to say, because she felt that her arrival had brought a previous conversation abruptly to an end. She wanted to restore their talk, but she didn't know any of them, and since two or three had travelled on the same ship, it seemed more difficult to make an acquaintance at this moment. Miss Dorking broke the silence by drawing their attention to a portrait which hung from one of the walls.

'A friend did it,' she said, 'years ago when I used to look like something.'

The women showed a sudden alertness, expressing their admiration for the portrait. Miss Dorking leaned against the door and talked leisurely about the past, and the women looked at her, and then at the portrait, observing the changes which had taken place in her face. She was now lean, almost rakish, with the look of someone who had survived a long and menacing illness. She had a scar on her lower jaw, and an upper row of false teeth which seemed to run around her mouth when she spoke.

'You needn't say it,' she said. 'I know just what all you thinkin'. That I change plenty.'

The women smiled, but did not commit themselves. They pretended to look at the portrait, glancing occasionally at Miss Dorking who had passed the iron comb from one hand to the other. She looked at the portrait, and the turn of her head emphasized the leanness of the neck. Ostrich-like, it crawled out from her collar, a narrow tube of flesh stringed with veins. Queenie drew her chair over to the other side of the room to get a better view of the portrait, and a more accurate assessment of that neck. But Miss Dorking had swung her head quickly to remind them that she was busy.

'So I'll leave you children to yourself,' she said, and felt for the door knob. 'But you can go in now,' she added, indicating Miss Bis. Miss Bis put the magazine on the table, and collected her things before following Miss Dorking into the other room.

Queenie closed the magazine and looked round the room with the eyes of one who is eager to strike comparisons. The others had returned to their reading, while she observed the room, low and narrow, with its faded rugs carefully placed over the floor. The distemper had peeled in patches, giving the walls a surface of flakes that rose like scales from the back of a fish. Apart from the portrait there were a few photographs in frames, and a radiogram in one corner. She could see through the window over the fence to the descent of weed on the far side. Then the view was abruptly blocked by houses which came up like a wall between two foreign territories.

There was a lavatory behind the work-room which could be entered by returning through the corridor which led to the waiting room, or through the side door of Miss Dorking's work-room. Invariably they went the way of the corridor because Miss Dorking didn't like to be interrupted, and some of the women felt uneasy about being seen when their hair was wet. The work-room was slightly larger than the lavatory with a small bench and a chair in which the person sat when the hair was being straightened. There were mirrors on the walls, and several iron combs in a small cupboard which was built into the wall.

Queenie kept looking at her watch, trying to guess how long it would be before it was her turn. She wanted to ask someone how long it would take to get to High Street, Kensington, but they were all reading, and the magazines, arranged like protective masks about them, seemed to declare their desire to be left alone. From here to High Street, Kensington. She repeated the words, wondering whether the appointment was worth the trouble, looked at the women again, and finally decided to pass the time with the magazine.

From *The Emigrants*, pp. 148–55.

GEORGE LAMMING *Born in 1927 in Barbados. After leaving high school and the special care of his remarkable mother and Frank Collymore he went to teach in Trinidad. He came to England at the beginning of the big migration from the West Indies. Lamming lived for many years in London, where he became a close friend of C. L. R. James and developed an admiration for his Marxist interpretation of history and literature. He found James's* Black

Jacobins *particularly impressive. The reissue of this book by Allison and Busby in 1980 in* paperback has an appendix well worth reading, in which the work of Walcott, Naipaul and Lamming is dealt with.

Lamming has travelled extensively: Africa, Australia, India and Scandinavia. In recent years he has taught regularly at universities in the USA. Recently he has returned to Barbados and, apparently, no longer makes his home in London. Lamming has long been one of the leading radicals of the West Indies, showing a great practical and theoretical interest in Cuba and its development under Fidel Castro.

[8, 10, 19, 21, 35]

16   The Baker's Story

V. S. NAIPAUL

Look at me. Black as the Ace of Spades, and ugly to match. Nobody looking at me would believe they looking at one of the richest men in this city of Port-of-Spain. Sometimes I find it hard to believe it myself, you know, especially when I go out on some of the holidays that I start taking the wife and children to these days, and I catch sight of the obzocky black face in one of those fancy mirrors that these expensive hotels have all over the place, as if to spite people like me.

Now everybody—particularly black people—forever asking me how this thing start, and I does always tell them I make my dough from dough. Ha! You like that one? But how it start? Well, you hearing me talk, and I don't have to tell you I didn't have no education. In Grenada, where I come from—and that is one thing these Trinidad black people don't forgive a man for being: a black Grenadian—in Grenada I was one of ten children, I believe—everything kind of mix up out there—and I don't even know who was the feller who hit my mother. I believe he hit a lot of women in all the other parishes of that island, too, because whenever I got back to Grenada for one of those holidays I tell you about, people always telling me that I remind them of this one and that one, and they always mistaking me for a shop assistant whenever I in a shop. (If this thing go on, one day I going to sell somebody something, just for spite.) And even in Trinidad, whenever I run into another Grenadian, the same thing does happen.

Well, I don't know what happen in Grenada, but Mammy bring me alone over to Trinidad when she was still young. I don't know what she do with the others, but perhaps they wasn't even she own. Anyway, she get a work with some white people in St Ann's. They give she a uniform; they give she three meals a day; and they give she a few dollars a month besides. Somehow she get another man, a real Trinidad 'rangoutang, and somehow, I don't know how, she get somebody else to look after me while she was living with this man, for the money and the food she was getting was scarcely enough to support this low-minded Trinidad rango she take up with.

It used to have a Chinee shop not far from this new aunty I was living with, and one day, when the old girl couldn't find the cash no how to buy a bread—is a hell of a thing, come to think of it now, that it have people in this island who can't lay their hands on enough of the ready to buy a bread—well, when she couldn't buy this bread she send me over to this Chinee shop to ask for trust. The Chinee woman—eh, but how these Chinee people does make children—was big like anything, and I believe I catch she at a good moment, because she say nothing doing, no trust, but if I want a little work that was different, because she want somebody to take some bread she bake for some Indian people. But how she could trust me with the bread? This was a question. And then I pull out my crucifix from under my dirty merino that was more holes than cloth and I tell she to keep it until I come back with the money for the bake bread. I don't know what sort of religion these Chinee people have, but that woman looked impressed like anything. But she was smart, though. She keep the crucifix and she send me off with the bread, which was wrap up in a big old *châle-au-pain*, just two or three floursacks sew together. I collect the money, bring it back, and she give me back the crucifix with a few cents and a bread.

And that was how this thing really begin. I always tell black people that was God give me my start in life, and don't mind these Trinidadians who does always tell you that Grenadians always praying. Is a true thing, though, because whenever I in any little business difficulty even these days I get down bam! straight on my two knees and I start praying like hell, boy.

Well, so this thing went on, until it was a regular afternoon work for me to deliver people bread. The bakery uses to bake ordinary bread—hops and pan and machine—which they uses to sell to the poorer classes. And how those Chinee people uses to work! This woman, with she big-big belly, clothes all dirty, sweating in front of the oven, making all this bread and making all this money, and I don't know what they doing with it, because all the time they living poor-poor in the back room, with only a bed, some hammocks for the young ones, and a few boxes. I couldn't talk to the husband at all. He didn't know a word of English and all the writing he uses to write uses to be in Chinee. He was a thin nashy feller, with those funny flapping khaki short pants and white merino that Chinee people always wear. He uses to work like a bitch, too. We Grenadians understand hard work, so that is why I suppose I uses to get on so well with these Chinee people, and that is why these lazy black Trinidadians so jealous of we. But was a funny thing. They uses to live so dirty. But the children, man, uses to leave that ramshackle old back room as clean as new bread, and they always had this neatness, always with their little pencil-case and their little rubbers and rulers and blotters, and they never losing anything. They leaving in the morning in one nice little line and in the afternoon they coming back in this same little line, still cool and clean, as though nothing at all touch them all day. Is something they could teach black people children.

But as I was saying this bakery uses to bake ordinary bread for the poorer classes. For the richer classes they uses to bake, too. But what they would do would be to collect the dough from those people house, bake it, and send it back as bread, hot and sweet. I uses to fetch and deliver for this class of customer. They never let me serve in the shop; it was as though they couldn't trust me selling across the counter and collecting money in that rush. Always it had this rush. You know black people: even if it only have one man in the shop he always getting on as if it have one hell of a crowd.

Well, one day when I deliver some bread in this *châle-au-pain* to a family, there was a woman, a neighbour, who start saying how nice it is to get bread which you knead with your own hands and not mix up with all sort of people sweat. And this give me the idea. A oven is a oven. It have to go on, whether it baking one bread or two. So I tell this woman, was a Potogee woman, that I would take she dough and bring it back bake for she, and that it would cost she next to nothing. I say this in a sort of way that she wouldn't know whether I was going to give the money to the Chinee people, or whether it was going to cost she next to nothing because it would be I who was going to take the money. But she give me a look which tell me right away that she wanted me to take the money. So matter fix. So. Back in the *châle-au-pain* the next few days I take some dough, hanging it in the carrier of the bakery bicycle. I take it inside, as though I just didn't bother to wrap up the *châle-au-pain*, and the next thing is that this dough mix up with the other dough, and see me kneading and baking, as though all is one. The thing is, when you go in for a thing like that, to go in brave brave. It have some people who make so much fuss when they doing one little thing that they bound to get catch. So, and I was surprise like hell, mind you, I get this stuff push in the oven, and is this said Chinee man, always with this sad and sorrowful Chinee face, who pulling it out of the oven with the long-handle shovel, looking at it, and pushing it back in.

And when I take the bread back, with some other bread, I collect the money cool-cool. The thing with a thing like this is that once you start is damn hard to stop. You start calculating this way and that way. And I have a calculating mind. I forever sitting down and working out how much say .50 a day every day for seven days, and every week for a year, coming to. And so this thing get to be a big thing with me. I wouldn't recommend this to any and everybody who want to go into business. But is what I mean when I tell people that I make my dough by dough.

The Chinee woman wasn't too well now. And the old man was getting on a little funny in a Chinee way. You know how those Chinee fellers does gamble. You drive past Marine Square in the early hours of the Sabbath and is two to one if you don't see some of those Chinee fellers sitting down outside the Treasury, as though they want to be near money, and gambling like hell. Well, the old man was gambling and the old girl was sick, and I was pretty well the only person looking after the bakery. I work damn hard for them, I could tell you. I even pick up two or three words of Chinee, and some of those rude black people start calling me Black Chinee, because at this time I was beginning to dress in short khaki pants and merino like a Chinee and I was drinking that tea Chinee people drinking all day long and I was walking and not saying much like a Chinee. And, now, don't believe what these black people say about Chinee and prejudice, eh. They have nothing at all against black people, provided they is hard-working and grateful.

But life is a funny thing. Now when it look that I all set, that everything going fine and dandy, a whole set of things happen that start me bawling. First, the Chinee lady catch a pleurisy and dead. Was a hell of a thing, but what else you expect when she was always bending down in front of that fire and then getting wet and going out in the dew and everything, and then always making these children too besides. I was sorry like hell, and a little frighten. Because I wasn't too sure how I was going to manage alone with the old man. All the time I work with him he never speak one word straight to me, but he always talking to me through his wife.

And now, look at my crosses. As soon as the woman dead, the Chinee man like he get mad. He didn't cry or anything like that, but he start gambling like a bitch, and the upshot was that one day, perhaps about a month after the old lady dead, the man tell his children to pack up and start leaving, because he gamble and lose the shop to another Chinee feller. I didn't know where I was standing, and nobody telling me nothing. They only packing. I don't know, I suppose they begin to feel that I was just part of the shop, and the old man not even saying that he sorry he lose me. And, you know, as soon as I drop to my knees and start praying, I see it was really God who right from the start put that idea of the dough in my head, because without that I would have been nowhere at all. Because the new feller who take over the shop say he don't want me. He was going to close the bakery and set up a regular grocery, and he didn't want me serving there because the grocery customers wouldn't like black people serving them. So look at me. Twenty-three years old and no work. No nothing. Only I have this Chinee-ness and I know how to bake bread and I have this extra bit of cash I save up over the years.

I slip out of the old khaki short pants and merino and I cruise around the town a little, looking for work. But nobody want bakers. I had about $700, and I see that this cruising around would do but it wouldn't pay, because the money was going fast. Now look at this. You know, it never cross my mind in those days that I could open a shop of my own. Is how it is with black people. They get so use to working for other people that they get to believe that because they black they can't do nothing else but work for other people. And I must tell you that when I start praying and God tell me to go out and open a shop for myself I feel that perhaps God did mistake or that I hadn't hear Him good. Because God only saying to me, 'Youngman, take your money and open a bakery. You could bake good bread.' He didn't say to open a parlour, which a few black fellers do, selling rock cakes and mauby and other soft drinks. No, He say open a bakery. Look at my crosses.

I had a lot of trouble borrowing the extra few hundred dollars, but I eventually get a Indian feller to lend me. And this is what I always tell young fellers. That getting credit ain't no trouble at all if you know exactly what you want to do. I didn't go round telling people to lend me money because I want to build house or buy lorry. I just did want to bake bread. Well, to cut a long story short, I buy a break-down old place near Arouca, and I spend most of what I had trying to fix the place up. Nothing extravagant, you understand, because Arouca is Arouca and you don't want to frighten off the country-bookies with anything too sharp. Too besides, I didn't have the cash. I just put in a few second-hand glass case and things like that. I write up my name on a board, and look, I in business.

Now the funny thing happen. In Laventille the people couldn't have enough of the bread I was baking—and in the last few months was me was doing the baking. But now trouble. I baking better bread than the people of Arouca ever see, and I can't get one single feller to come in like man through my rickety old front door and buy a penny hops bread. You hear all this talk about quality being its own advertisement? Don't believe it, boy. Is quality plus something else. And I didn't have this something else. I begin to wonder what the hell it could be. I say is because I new in Arouca that this thing happening. But no. I new, I get stale, and the people not flocking in their hundreds to the old shop. Day after day I baking two or three quarts good and all this just remaining and going dry and stale, and the only bread I selling is to the man from the government farm, buying stale cakes and bread for the cows or pigs or whatever they have up there. And was good bread. So I get down on the old knees and I pray as though I want to wear them out. And still I getting the same answer: 'Youngman'—was always the way I uses to get call in these prayers—'Youngman, you just bake bread.'

Pappa! This was a thing. Interest on the loan piling up every month. Some months I borrow from aunty and anybody else who kind enough to listen just to pay off the interest. And things get so low that I uses to have to go out and pretend to people that I was working for another man bakery and that I was going to bake their dough cheap-cheap. And in Arouca cheap mean cheap. And the little cash I picking up in this disgraceful way was just about enough to keep the wolf from the door, I tell you.

Jeezan. Look at confusion. The old place in Arouca so damn out of the way— was why I did buy it, too, thinking that they didn't have no bakery there and that they would be glad of the good Grenadian-baked—the place so out of the way nobody would want to buy it. It ain't even insure or anything, so it can't get in a little fire accident or anything—not that I went in for that sort of thing. And every time I go down on my knees, the answer coming straight back at me: 'Youngman, you just bake bread.'

Well, for the sake of the Lord I baking one or two quarts regular every day, though I begin to feel that the Lord want to break me, and I begin to feel too that this was His punishment for what I uses to do to the Chinee people in their bakery. I was beginning to feel bad and real ignorant. I uses to stay away from the bakery after baking those quarts for the Lord—nothing to lock up, nothing to thief—and, when any of the Levantille boys drop in on the way to Manzanilla and Balandra and those other beaches on the Sabbath, I uses to tell them, making a joke out of it, that I was 'loafiing'. They uses to laugh like hell, too. It have nothing in the whole world so funny as to see a man you know flat out on his arse and catching good hell.

The Indian feller was getting anxious about his cash, and you couldn't blame him, either, because some months now he not even seeing his interest. And this begin to get me down, too. I remember how all the man did ask me when I went to him for money was: 'You sure you want to bake bread? You feel you have a hand for baking bread?' And yes-yes, I tell him, and just like that he shell out the cash. And now he was getting anxious. So one day, after baking those loaves for the Lord, I take a Arima Bus Service bus to Port-of-Spain to see this feller. I was feeling brave enough on the way. But as soon as I see the old sea and get a whiff of South Quay and the bus touch the Railway Station terminus my belly start going pweh-pweh. I decide to roam about the city for a little.

Was a hot morning, *petit-carême* weather, and in those days a coconut uses still to cost .04. Well, it had this coconut cart in the old square and I stop by it. It was a damn funny thing to see. The seller was a black feller. And you wouldn't know how funny this was, unless you know that every coconut seller in the island is Indian. They have this way of handling a cutlass that black people don't have. Coconut in left hand; with right hand bam, bam, bam, with cutlass, and coconut cut open, ready to drink. I ain't never see a coconut seller chop his hand. And here was this black feller doing this bam-bam business on a coconut with a cutlass. It was as funny as seeing a black man wearing dhoti and turban. The sweetest part of the whole business was that this black feller was, forgetting looks, just like a Indian. He was talking Hindustani to a lot of Indian fellers, who was giving him jokes like hell, but he wasn't minding. It does happen like that some-times with black fellers who live a lot with Indians in the country. They putting away curry, talking Indian, and behaving just like Indians. Well, I take a coconut from this black man and then went on to see the feller about the money.

He was more sad than vex when I tell him, and if I was in his shoes I woulda be sad, too. Is a hell of a thing when you see your money gone and you ain't getting the sweet little kisses from the interest every month. Anyway, he say he would give me three more months' grace, but that if I didn't start shelling out at the agreed rate he would have to foreclose. 'You put me in a hell of a position,' he say. 'Look at me. You think I want a shop in Arouca?'

I was feeling a little better when I leave the feller, and who I should see when I leave but Percy. Percy was a old rango who uses to go to the Laventille elementary school with me. I never know a boy get so much cut-arse as Percy. But he grow up real hard and ignorant with it, and now he wearing fancy clothes like a saga boy, and talking about various business offers. I believe he was selling insurance—is a thing that nearly every idler doing in Trinidad, and, mark my words, the day coming when you going to see those fellers trying to sell insurance to one another. Anyway, Percy getting on real flash, and he say he want to stand me a lunch for old times' sake. He make a few of the usual ignorant Trinidadian jokes about Grenadians, and we went up to the Angostura Bar. I did never go there before, and wasn't the sort of place you would expect a rango like Percy to be welcome. But we went up there and Percy start throwing his weight around with the waiters, and, mind you, they wasn't even a quarter as black as Percy. Is a wonder they didn't abuse him, especially with all those fair people around. After the drinks Percy say, 'Where you want to have this lunch?'

Me, I don't know a thing about the city restaurants, and when Percy talk about food all I was expecting was rice and peas or a roti off a Indian stall or a mauby and rock cake in some parlour. And is a damn hard thing to have people, even people as ignorant as Percy, showing off on you, especially when you carrying two nails in your pocket to make the jingling noise. So I tell Percy we could go to a parlour or a bar. But he say, 'No, no. When I treat my friends, I don't like black people meddling with my food.'

And was only then that the thing hit me. I suppose that what Trinidadians say about the stupidness of Grenadians have a little truth, though you have to live in a place for a long time before you get to know it really well. Then the thing hit me, man.

When black people in Trinidad go to a restaurant they don't like to see black people meddling with their food. And then I see that though Trinidad have every race and every colour, every race have to do special things. But look, man. If you want to buy a snowball, who you buying it from? You wouldn't buy it from a Indian or a Chinee or a Potogee. You would buy it from a black man. And I myself, when I was getting my place in Arouca fix up, I didn't employ Indian carpenters or masons. If a Indian in Trinidad decide to go into the carpentering business the man would starve. Who ever see a Indian carpenter? I suppose the only place in the world where they have Indian carpenters and Indian masons is India. Is a damn funny thing. One of these days I must make a trip to that country, to just see this thing. And as we walking I see the names of bakers: Coelho, Pantin, Stauble. Potogee or Swiss, or something, and then all those other Chinee places. And, look at the laundries. If a black man open a laundry, you would take your clothes to it? *I* wouldn't take my clothes there. Well, I walking to this restaurant, but I jumping for joy. And then all sorts of things fit into place. You remember that the Chinee people didn't let me serve bread across the counter? I uses to think it was because they didn't trust me with the rush. But it wasn't that. It was that, if they did let me serve, they would have had no rush at all. You ever see anybody buying their bread off a black man?

I ask Percy why he didn't like black people meddling with his food in public places. The question throw him a little. He stop and think and say, 'It don't *look* nice.'

Well, you could guess the rest of the story. Before I went back to Arouca that day I make contact with a yellow boy call Macnab. This boy was half black and half Chinee, and, though he had a little brown colour and the hair a little curly, he could pass for one of those Cantonese. They a little darker than the other Chinee people, I believe. Macnab I find beating a steel pan in somebody yard—they was practising for Carnival—and I suppose the only reason that Macnab was willing to come all the way to Arouca was because he was short of the cash to buy his costume for the Carnival band.

But he went up with me. I put him in front of the shop, give him a merino and a pair of khaki short pants, and tell him to talk as Chinee as he could, if he wanted to get that Carnival bonus. I stay in the back room, and I start baking bread. I even give Macnab a old Chinee paper, not to read, because Macnab could scarcely read English, but just to leave lying around, to make it look good. And I get hold of one of those big Chinee calendars with Chinee women and flowers and waterfalls and hang it up on the wall. And when this was all ready, I went down on my knees and thank God. And still the old message coming, but friendly and happy now: 'Youngman, you just bake bread.'

And, you know, that solve another problem. I was worrying to hell about the name I should give the place. New Shanghai, Canton, Hongkong, Nanking, Yank-tse-Kiang. But when the old message come over I know right away what the name should be. I scrub off the old name—no need to tell you what that was—and I get a proper sign painter to copy a few letters from the Chinee newspaper. Below that, in big letters, I make him write:

YUNG MAN

BAKER

I never show my face in the front of the shop again. And I tell you, without boasting, that I bake damn good bread. And the people of Arouca ain't that foolish. They know a good thing. And soon I was making so much money that I was able to open a branch in Arima and then another in Port-of-Spain self. Was hard in the beginning to get real Chinee people to work for a black man. But money have it own way of talking, and when today you pass any of the Yung Man establishments all you seeing behind the counter is Chinee. Some of them ain't even know they working for a black man. My wife handling that side of the business, and the wife is Chinee. She come from down Cedros way. So look at me now, in Port-of-Spain, giving Stauble and Pantin and Coelho a run for their money. As I say, I only going in the shops from the back. But every Monday morning I walking brave brave to Marine Square and going in the bank, from the front.

From *Caribbean Rhythms*, pp. 116–28.

V. S. NAIPAUL   *Born in 1932 in Trinidad. Left high school in Trinidad for University*

College, Oxford, where he did not find literary studies particularly stimulating. He did find Chaucer's use of language and his predicament in having to choose a certain language or variety of language interesting. Chaucer's position vis-à-vis language was not unlike that of West Indian writers in modern times.

Naipaul has not returned to live in Trinidad, but has visited it often. He has travelled widely. He has a remarkable ear for the tune of language, and he gets the Trinidad flavour and usages with a remarkable and pleasing accuracy. Naipaul is certainly one of the most skilful users of the English language writing today. But his satire and refusal to be what Walcott calls 'a syntactical apologist for the Third World' and many of its corrupt politicians, has not endeared him to many. Chinua Achebe recently made a searing attack on views Naipaul expressed in New York about Third World people. Naipaul, whatever his faults, is no doubt— as far as fellow West Indians go, and radical supporters of the Third World—just too close to home for comfort!

[13, 14, 22, 23, 25]

17   *Scholarship Exam*

NEVILLE DAWES

It was a fête, a gala day, when Lucien and I went to sit the scholarship exams.

We were at Chen's shop by five in the morning waiting to ride to the Bay in the Chevrolet truck.

My father had wished me well, indirectly through God, when he said prayers early that morning and then he had gone into the Post Office to do his mystery, as Saturday was a busy day. My mother had dressed me in my first long stockings and leather shoes so that my feet didn't feel like mine at all and, walking with me to Chen's shop, she warned me about St Ann's Bay thieves who would steal even the clothes you were wearing and about Black Heart Men who enticed children with sweets and then cut their hearts out to work obeah and black magic. Like Beatrice Henry, a girl of thirteen, who had disappeared for about two weeks and then was found living with a man in a hut in Salem. But he didn't cut her heart, I said. Makes no difference, he wasn't ready yet, that's all, and listen to what ah'm telling you. Yes, mama. She warned me to be respectful to the teachers, not to skylark with Lucien in the truck for we might frighten Artie and make him turn over the truck, and not to eat from strange children because Taddeus Small got poisoning last month.

I was carrying in my satchel a pencil box, a certificate from Teacher and a ruler. I had a small shut-pan with a sweet-potato pone. I had sixpence in my pocket to buy saltfish fritters and bread at midday.

Chen had not opened the shop yet so we went into the yard where Artie was taking the green tarpaulin off the truck and Chen's yard-boys, Benjie and

Chappie, were loading on the pimento bags. Artie was polishing the bonnet. He pulled a pint bottle of rum out of the back of his overalls and took a long drink. My mother was horrified.

'But, Artie, you mean to tell me say you a-drink rum this time a' mawning?' she said.

'Clears the bowels, ma'am, clears the bowels,' Artie said cheerfully. 'You two young bway going for scholarship, don't it?' Artie said without looking at us. We could hardly make out his face in the half-light. 'Ah know whey you going. I tek you right 'pon the hill there. Government School? Don't it?' He skipped behind the truck, farted loudly and said 'Manners!' When he came back he said to us, 'Ah going move this rahted truck this morning, you see?—you frighten!' And we were in ecstasy, impatient.

When the truck was ready to go, Chen gave us each two new G-nibs, one lead pencil and a small box of crayons.

'You make good scholarship today with Chen G-nib,' he said, grinning and rubbing his fat hands. We were having a free ride, part of the goodwill-rent Chen paid to the village. We sat in front with Artie and as we moved off my mother shouted, 'Unu doan bother run wild in Sin' Ann's Bay tiday!'

Artie drove slowly and carefully while within Chen's sight and hearing. He was still going slowly at River where he reversed twice to make the bend and then changed down quickly into first gear. He did everything with a flourish.

'You hear the compression?' Artie said, jumping about in his seat as the truck moaned down River Hill, as if the engine was his personal accomplishment.

'The compression, man, the compression,' we said.

After the long winding hill past a small property called Retreat, Artie opened up and we went like a breeze. He drove with his thumb stuck to the horn button, announcing us mightily to the half-dark.

'Is how unu going scholarship an' you doan break yo' virgin-knot yet?' he laughed. 'Bi the time ah was ole like you-so, ah in an' out o' the ring-ding all-a-time.'

'Artie how ole you are?' I asked. He slowed down to put the truck gingerly over a rut across the road. The sun was rising and we began to see the landscape around us, bare hills dotted with pimento trees and covered with stones and large boulders. The close-cropped brownish grass was poor grazing-ground for the few gaunt forlorn cows that roamed there.

'I born in Bamboo,' Artie said, 'but ah never have a real cerfiticket. When I get mi licence, 1930, ah tell them say ah was twenty-one.'

'Is a hard thing to learn mechanic, Artie?' Lucien asked.

'Not so very,' he said. 'If you' nerves steady.'

'I would like be a chauffeur an' drive all over, everywhere, all the time,' Lucien said.

'You going scholarship to learn mechanic?' Artie asked angrily. 'Boy, you doan got no ambition, nuh? You t'ink eddication is a t'ing to mek joke wid an' throw 'way? You better put you' min' on lawyer or doctor or so. You doan know say life hard, you going scholarship an' a-talk 'bout learn mechanic. You t'ink say if ah did have head an' chance like you, ah woulda a-drive this rass truck? Doan get me out, you hear me sah? Doan get me out!'

He was silent for a long time and my mind drifted to the exams that would only spoil the day.

'You know Chen daughter, Irene, in the shop deh?' Artie said suddenly.

'Sometime she go h'on like she mad. Everybody jumping 'pon her like a nanny-goat—slap down to Benjie an' Chappie in the yard. Is the Chinese Blood, you know. I tell Chen 'bout it an' him beat her but she still jumping like she mad. You better mek application an' put in yo' whistle before unu go College. College tough, you know. You has to be a *man* to go College.' He leered at us and baayed like a ram-goat.

Down Llandovery Mountain, with the marl dust rising behind us and, in front of us, as the wind rustled the lush entangled stalks, were the cane fields spread out in waves on waves of green, dark and light green, blue green, and over this cool sea floated the white pennants of the blossoms. This and the plains gave us the feeling of arriving in another country. Suddenly the sea was before us, not blue and still as seen from the hills but a grey moving groaning mass, threatening the land.

Artie left us at the gates of the Government school and told us to meet him before dusk at the Hospital junction.

There were many cars in the school yard and many of the type of brown people we had seen at Cissy's funeral. The children standing around were different from those we had met at Pupil Teacher's exams in Brown's Town. They were different in dress and speech for most of them attended the special private schools, dotted all over the parish and bearing owners' names like firms, 'Thompson's' in Brown's Town, 'Minnot's' in St Ann's Bay, 'Shaw's' near Lime Hall. These schools catered for the sons and daughters of land-owners and rich lawyers and doctors, preparing them, especially in attitude, for the island's snob boarding schools. The well-dressed mothers fidgeted round their children straightening their ties, brush-ing their hair, anxiously, as if that would put their brains in order.

There were other children, from the elementary school like ourselves, standing in tense murderous little groups, whispering. There was nothing of the bustle and noise you hear before a Pupil Teachers' examination—'What's the square root of 40, again?'; 'Tell me the twelve judges of Israel, it slip mi mind clean'; or, from second or third failures (superbly nonchalant), obscene rhymes like 'Analyse and parse, chemise and drawers'. Lucien and I entered a schoolyard in which there were at least fifty healthy children but they only made a discreet murmur.

We did not have time to feel awkward; to feel, for instance, that none of the children from the special schools were wearing long stockings and leather shoes for the first time. Our attention was immediately riveted on the water-tap that Lucien and I had seen. There was one in Brown's Town Government school yard but, unfortunately, it was not working the day we were there. This one was, and we sidled towards it. What we wanted to do was quite simple—to turn it on full blast and drink from it. We stood near it for a few moments, undecided, watching it trickle and then the disappointing bell announced the start of the examination.

We wrote all we knew, for it was easy, like flying in a dream. In arithmetic, figures came together in a huge cluster, you moved them around quickly and the answer just dropped out, whole and clean. But during the English paper the insistent temptation of the water-tap became unbearable. I handed in my paper some ten minutes before time and rushed to the tap; Lucien, who had not finished his paper, joined me at once. We turned the tap on full, tried to drink from it, and nearly drowned ourselves. Lucien's white canvas shoes were masses of red wet clay and my shoes and stockings were soaked through. We took our shoes off, put them to dry on the scorching cement and walked around barefooted during the lunch recess. We were careful, in our second assault on the tap, to drink from the shut-pan.

In the afternoon we had Reading, in groups of four or five, before a white master from Victoria College. When it was Lucien's turn, he threw his head back and read in an exact imitation of Rev. John Grange reading the scriptures. I was so surprised that I laughed out loud and then pretended that I was laughing at something in the passage he was reading. Most of the other children, especially those from the private schools, read execrably, even spelling out difficult words. We read well, with no regard for meaning but with great precision of punctuation, for Teacher Sampson had taught us exactly how to pause, count one, two, or three, and how to 'change gear', as he put it, when a full stop was approaching. And a little black boy of about nine, with an enormous head and large sleepy eyes and wearing red braces, read clear and round as a bell. For days afterwards, Lucien kept reminding me of the perfection of this boy's reading.

We roamed over St Ann's Bay that afternoon and early evening, watched the miracle of sparks in a blacksmith's shop, peeped through a board fence and saw the end of a cricket match, read out the names of big shops glistening with chromium and full of remote wonderful goods, drifted through the market with its fresh fish smell and slime, and then walked the whole length of the main street, turned left at Claremont junction, passed the police grounds and were on the shore, face to face with the sea. We stepped over the nets and stood at the water's edge beside one of the canoes beached there.

'Could tek a swim, you know,' Lucien said.

'Ah doan like how it sucking in the sand so heavy. Like I hear about Blue Hole in St Mary, if you drop in there it suck you down, down, you never come up again. It doan have no bottom.'

'Mus' have bottom, man!'

'No. It would come out the other end o' the world.'

'Tha's a thing geography doan tell you, where you come out if you go right *donngh* through the groun'.'

'Like tek this sea here now, all you have is sea everywhere you look. Where it going? Where it coming from?'

'Coming from Havana-Cuba, man. Havana-Cuba right over there-so,' Lucien said, pointing beyond the black line of breakers. A large wave threw the spray over us and we tasted the warm salty water. We swam fifty yards out, halfway to the breakers, and then floated in. We were amazed at the rainbow-blue under-water and the strong urge of the tides.

Artie picked us up at the Hospital junction and whisked us off into the night. We fell asleep, exhausted, and were barely conscious that Artie stopped to change a punctured tyre. But everything was fine. We had run wild in the Bay and we had made good scholarship.

From *Interim*, pp. 44–9.

NEVILLE DAWES   *Born in 1936 in Warri, Nigeria, of Jamaican parents. He grew up in Jamaica where he went to secondary school. He took his degree at Oriel, Oxford. Taught in Jamaica then in Ghana where he was much involved in the nationalist movement. Taught at Guyana University before returning to Jamaica to be director of the Institute of Jamaica. A poet and novelist.*

[20, 21, 22, 23]

FRANK COLLYMORE

It was to be the most wonderful party ever. Something that would be talked about for many a long day, something that would take up at least a column in *Carib*, something that would make her, Maude Bush-Hall, the most envied of mothers in Barbados. For at the party there would be the announcement of her daughter's engagement—not to a mere civil service clerk, not even to one of the local big shots, but, if you please, to a member of the British aristocracy who was, incidentally, a literary celebrity, a poet whose verse had won recognition in two continents.

As a matter of fact she was at that moment holding in her plump be-ringed hand a copy of his most recently published volume of verse. Yes, no doubt of it *Rosemary for Rosencrantz*, author of *But Valour's Excrement*; and on the back of the weirdly designed jacket, in addition to the bit above the two continents, various laudatory snippets: '. . . trenchant satire . . . urgent symbolism . . . exotic imagery . . . foremost among the avant-garde . . . a young man to be watched. . . .' And she turned to the fly-leaf and read once again with a glow of proprietary pride: Ma, With love etc., Lucas T.

Sitting in the cushioned window seat and glancing across the placid fields now stripped of their screen of sugar cane to where a couple of miles away the control tower of the airport sparkled in the sun, Mrs Bush-Hall's accommodating bosom heaved in a swell of thanksgiving: her dearest ambition was on the way to fulfilment. She turned and directed her glance towards the interior of the too elaborately furnished room. At an old-fashioned desk littered with sheets of writing paper and envelopes, were bent two heads, one of them, her future son-in-law's, pure Nordic gold, the other, her daughter's—and here a transient frown ruffled her sleek brow—well, she wished it didn't remind her so much of molasses froth. But never mind that, she thought, never mind. It could pass for blonde, and it didn't seem to worry Lucas. She regarded his bowed head steadily, fondly. An English husband, no less, for her Pyrlene. Her bosom rose and fell again. This time the sigh reverberated.

The two heads were raised in enquiry.

'Was only thinkin', pet. You got down that master at the College? The one that does write poetry?'

'Lucas isn't impressed by his work, mamma. He thinks it much too derivative. He says. . . .'

'Oh stick him in, stick him in,' scowled the young man. 'He certainly won't be called upon to troll any of his tripe at the party.'

The girl giggled and the two heads were once more directed towards their task. And Mrs Bush-Hall continued to bask in the realization of her good fortune. After all, Pyrlene wasn't exactly a beauty. Not much sex appeal there either: a little too flat at whatever angle you looked at her; but, perhaps for that very reason, she was a good girl. And intelligent too, no doubt about that: she could hold her own in conversation with anyone, even with such a world-famous figure as Lucas Traherne. Their conversations were a joy to listen to—not that she could understand much of what they were saying, of course, it was all so very highbrow, but she had no reason to be ashamed of her Pyrlene in that respect; and after marriage her looks would certainly improve; she had big bones. As for Lucas, what more could she have wished for! A great poet, a handsome, though somewhat skinny, young Englishman, and a close relative of a lord. Only, she wished he would take a little more care with his dress—those dirty white pumps of his were an eyesore— and that he would mix with the people of consequence in the island, join a few clubs as befitted his status, establish himself. But he just didn't seem to care for anything like that. Why, she'd had to beseech him to get a proper suit of clothes; had to take him to town, order it, pay for it even. Not that she minded; she loved making him little presents; had already bought him an expensive wrist watch; but these modern Englishmen were so casual, so careless of their personal appearance. Ah well, she'd show them what a B'adian woman could do.

The party had been her own idea. It wasn't to be a mere get-together of personal friends of theirs. Oh no, something on a much more socially grandiose scale. She had been to a British Council party once and had never forgotten it: all sorts of people, all the really important ones—various upperclass ladies and gentle- men, politicians, literary folks, artists and so on, headmasters and their wives, a member or two of the Legislative Council, English and American visitors to the island, the Lord Bishop, even the Governor (Acting) and his wife—all standing around casually in ever-shifting groups, with waiters bustling to and fro, and all chatting with one another in as friendly a manner as you could wish for, just as though there were no class-distinctions or prejudices or anything. A real eye- opener. So she was modelling her party along similar lines. Naturally there would be her own friends and acquaintances, among them the important members of the various associations to which she belonged and in which she played so prominent a part as a devoted apostle of social welfare: the ICU and the UCME, and the RSTU and the OHO and the AHA and the INOU. And of course there would be the nice American pastor of the NCSA; for Mrs Bush-Hall although a nominal supporter of the C of E was not averse to exploring the by-ways of religion which were offered in such profusion, and the New Church of Spiritual Automation was the most recent addition to their number. And her more intimate friends, her gentlemen friends especially . . . well, nearly all, for she would most certainly have to draw the line at Willoughby Watts. Much too coarse when he 'had in' his rum, and making passes at any attractive young woman within arm's length. A sudden vision of Willoughby Watts bestowing a goodnatured smack on some upper-class bottom compelled her to question:

'You hasn't got that Willoughby on the list, has you, Pyrlie?'

'Certainly not, mamma.'

Her composure restored, Mrs Bush-Hall resumed her reflections. No, come what might, she would never neglect her old friends, all men of substance who had in various capacities played an active part in her life: Jossie Ford, Big Boy Waterford, LeRoy DaCourcey . . . his wife, Lurleen, would have to come too, the old bitch, but no matter . . . and, of course, Audible Smart. Her own dear Audible. But in any case Audible would be foremost on the list of celebrities: a member of the House, with a ministerial job in the offing, the King, as he liked to describe himself in the papers, of Real Estate. A pity he had not viewed the advent of Lucas Traherne with favour. A blasted limey, he had dubbed him. But her insistence on Lucas' aristocratic connections had brought him round eventually; in fact they got on quite well together nowadays as the frequent replenishing of her two-gallon demijean bore witness. Yes, she was so glad that little difficulty had been smoothed over; she could never afford to lose her dear Audible's friendship.

It was indeed mainly due to his good offices that she was now comfortably installed at this delightful old country house, 'The Frangipannis', away from all the noise and dust of Bridgetown. How lovely the lawn would look beneath the festoons of coloured electric bulbs! And the frangipannis all in bloom too. Her glance strayed to the biggest of them all, its girth almost matching hers, its contorted branches forming a complicated pattern against the eggshell blue of the April sky. How she wished she could keep in mind those lines Lucas had composed especially for her, composed moreover, as a special favour to her, in rhyme. She would have to make the effort and learn them, those lines . . . how did they go?

Those knubbled elbows and arthritic knees
The something something among trees

and

Tittumty tumty years flow on
O arboreal Laocoon!

What a pity she couldn't memorize things like Pyrlene. Only a line or two here and there. O arboreal Laocoon! At first she had resented the reference to what she thought was 'coon', but Lucas had explained it so nicely. It was what they called a classical adhesion. Ah, what a thing education was! And to think that a poet had written that about *her* tree. She intended showing the poem to all the really important people at the party. Not ostentatiously, but casually like, when conversation flagged. 'My Lord Bishop, has you seen this?' or 'Speaking of frangipannis, Lady Graight. . . .'
The name recalled her to a sense of the immediate.
'You write Lady Graight name yet, Pyrlene?'
'I doubt whether she'll be able to make it. She seldom goes anywhere nowadays. But we're sending her an invitation. And her secretary. Shall I tell you the invitees so far?'
Mrs Bush-Hall nodded and her daughter, scooping up a sheaf of envelopes, began:
'Mr and Mrs Pearson Porson, Major and Mrs Strokes, the Honourable and Mrs Boysie Scantlebury, Mr and Mrs Mauby Sorrell, Dr Dooms, Mr M. T. Vessle, MCP, Lady Graight, Miss Toothwaite, Mrs Fitzpitt, Mr and Mrs Celestial Barker, Miss Eurine Potts, Mrs Zimmerbloom. . . .'
'Who she is?'
'The American sculptress, mamma. Mr Talculm Fairenough, Mr and Mrs Smithbert Smith, Mr Audible Smart, MCP. . . .'
'MCP,' epeated Lucas Traherne slowly with emphasis on the C. 'A curious thing, that. Today when colonialism is equated with serfdom and slavery, a relic of the barbarous past, your members of parliament still proudly insert that derogatory letter. Can you tell me why, Ma?'
But Mrs Bush-Hall had no explanation to offer. Nor had Pyrlene. 'I suppose they'll change it in time to MWIP, or something,' she offered.
Lucas Traherne held up his hands in horror, and Pyrlene continued:
'Mr Horatio Nelson, MA, the Reverend and Mrs Chirp, Mr Hathaway Withym, Sir Charles and Lady Charles. . . .'
How proud Mrs Bush-Hall was at the recital of these notable names. She beamed.
And indeed she had every right to be proud of her achievement. She had every right to beam.

Born some forty odd years ago in the most humble surroundings imaginable, she had, after many years of privation, married a retired and ageing stevedore; had seen him, after a few years of married life, impressively buried; and had then devoted herself to the rearing and education of her only child, and to the amassing, partly by means of her late husband's investments and partly by her own shrewdness, of quite a tidy income.

Mrs Bush-Hall was, as she liked to describe herself, a 'high brown', and must have been quite attractive in her youth. Her mother had been a poor negress who made her living, or most of it, by selling fruit. Rumour had it that her father was a white man, a foreigner, and Mrs Bush-Hall had always encouraged herself to believe that he was an Englishman. How else could she account for her passion for things English, for the possession of a pair of steely grey eyes, for her absorbing interest in the doings of the royal family? Yes, she was fully convinced it was the English blood that ran in her veins that, contrary to the reaction of the boys and girls in her neighbourhood, always brought her to a stiffly erect stance whenever the Police Band struck up God Save the King.

This conviction was a source of great satisfaction to her, and if any other circumstance was needed to strengthen it, was the fact that, when she reached her teens, she always felt much more at ease with English than with American sailors when a visiting man-of-war happened to be in the harbour.

But that was in her early days. She had attended a revivalist meeting one night and by the flaming light of hell-fire had been led to seek out the less demanding profession of needle-worker. By her twenty-fifth birthday she had acquired such an aura of respectability that Mr Molly Hall, the stevedore, who was a shrewd judge of character, had, after several abortive attempts to seduce her, proposed marriage. This was a great triumph for her, for Mr Hall was quite an important personality. He was a member of the parish vestry, owned no fewer than a dozen house properties, and, even in those days, a chauffeur-driven Ford. True, he was not altogether prepossessing: he was short, stout, of very dark complexion, well on in his sixties, and was more often than not rather the worse for liquor. But what were all these defects when offset by his wealth and respectability? Besides, his age was a factor in her favour.

So she, Maude Bush, spinster, had taken Mr M. Hall to her lawful wedded husband. It was not until after his death that she had adopted the hyphenated nomenclature by which she was distinguished from the many other Hall families in the neighbourhood of Hallscourt, Mr Hall's ornate residence in Bridgetown.

Mr Hall was delighted with his bride. Until then a bachelor, and a surprisingly childless one at that, it was his ambition that she should as swiftly as possible provide him with an heir, an ambition which it was said caused him within a few months of his marriage to take to the nuptial bed permanently as the result of an apoplectic seizure. This lack of an heir was his only regret, for his wife proved a most devoted nurse and soon showed such a grasp of his financial affairs that he appointed her his attorney and was relieved of all further worldly anxiety.

A short while before he died, however, there was some slight scandal that might have embarrassed a less integrated personality than his widow-to-be.

It was her love of the English and things English that occasioned the matter. She had, in the course of her transactions with a dry goods establishment, made the acquaintance of a commercial traveller from Birmingham. This acquaintance ripened into a more intimate relationship, for exactly eight months after the departure of the gentleman in question the child Pyrlene saw the light of day.

Not unnaturally, harsh things were said, but as Mr Hall made no comment
indeed he had lost the power of speech some time previously) and as there was no
ne to dispute the child's claim to legitimacy, Mrs Hall was quite pleased with the
utcome of the affair, assuring all and sundry that the arrival of an heir, though
emale, was the long-deferred answer to her husband's prayer, and that now she
vould not be at all surprised if he departed in peace. Which he did shortly after-
vards.

One hundred and three cars followed Mr Hall's mortal remains to the cemetery,
nd everyone allowed that his widow had done all in her power to make the
ccasion a success.

She was now extremely well off. In addition to the late Mr Hall's title deeds and
ank balance there was his accumulation of old gold: the various rings, brooches
nd other bits of antique jewellery in the japanned box under his bed was worth at
east, she was assured, well over two thousand pounds.

She was not surprised therefore to find herself, after the correct time had
lapsed, besieged by a variety of suitors. She had always been led to believe that
he two essential prerequisites to happiness were love and money: having experi-
nced a surfeit of the former in her youth, she was in no mind to sacrifice her
njoyment of the latter by sharing it with any gentleman of her acquaintance. Not
hat she was averse to their attentions. A chosen few who could help her swell her
ank balance by judicious advice or assistance were encouraged to call at
Hallscourt; and these callers would often prolong their calls until the early hours
f the next day.

But even these indiscretions were abruptly terminated shortly after Pyrlene's
fth birthday. Until that time the child had been for the most part a source of
nnoyance: she suffered from almost every ailment to which young children are
rone and would frequently cause her mother to leave her bed at most inopportune
noments.

And then one morning her mother discovered her spelling out the words in the
unday Advocate. This was a revelation. She was the mother of a genius, of a
otential Barbados Scholar! All her energy must now be devoted to the education
f this prodigy. Everything must be done to ensure success. The best schools. The
est home training and influence. Those protracted calls must cease.

And so began the educational progress of Pyrlene, and, incidentally, of Mrs
Bush-Hall; for from expensive private school on to Princess Royal College the pair
vould tackle the home-work problem together; and thus the older student was
ntroduced to the hitherto unknown world of letters—*Dick Whittington, The Golden
leece, Little Women.* . . . It was unfortunate for her that Shakespeare made such an
arly appearance on the curriculum of Princess Royal: blank verse left her mind in
similar condition; so very wisely she allowed her daughter to continue on her
wn. But having acquired the habit of reading, Mrs Bush-Hall was not to be
enied: there were thrillers, romances, westerns to provide her with the entertain-
nent and excitement she craved. Besides, as she would often remark, 'Reading is
he hall mark of the truly cultured person.'

Meanwhile Pyrlene was making reasonably satisfactory progress. She was duly
romoted from form to form. But by the time she reached the upper school it was
bvious that she was not of the material of which scholars are made: in her first
nportant exam she failed in almost every subject.

Her mother was furious. Her life's work had been in vain. Poor Pyrlene's life
ecame insupportable. Her woebegone appearance and frequent uncontrolled

bursts of sobbing became a topic of comment at school. Her form mistress, Mis
Toothwaite, an Englishwoman who had become a long-established fixture a
Princess Royal, had questioned her. As a result one afternoon Miss Toothwait
had accompanied Pyrlene to Hallscourt.

'Barbados Scholarships aren't the aim and end of education, you know, Mr
Bush-Hall. In any case, despite Pyrlene's failure in certain subjects, her results i
English were outstanding.' (Miss Toothwaite had been English mistress fo
years.) 'A great future lies in store for your daughter.'

What this future was Miss Toothwaite did not choose to disclose, but in Mr
Bush-Hall's imagination the words of the gaunt grey-haired Englishwoman (a
school she was known as Duppy) were fraught with prophetic assurance. He
doubt and anger were dispelled. Hope was reborn. She embraced Miss Tooth
waite and wept unrestrainedly on her shoulder and invited her to stay on t
dinner. Mrs Bush-Hall was an excellent cook, everyone was happy, and Mis
Toothwaite spent a most rewarding evening. She was entreated to come soo
again. Entreaty was hardly necessary: she came often. Very soon she was invite
to Hallscourt for weekends, and when soon afterwards the removal to 'Th
Frangipannis' took place, she would sometimes spend the greater part of he
vacation there. The friendship proved mutually beneficial. Miss Toothwaite wa
able to add to her meagre savings and attenuated frame and Mrs Bush-Hall to he
cultural development. For Miss Toothwaite was convinced that such a dynami
personality had much to offer the community; so she encouraged her with the hel
of Mr Audible Smart's influence to enter the field of social welfare. She became
member of one of the many organizations devoted to the cause. She was congratu
lated on her ability, her zeal. She became a member of another association. An
another. Then several. She sat on various committees. Her circle of acquaintanc
widened. Her photograph appeared in the press. She gave tea parties. Her te
parties, with Miss Toothwaite always present to disseminate a modicum c
culture, were minor social events. And Pyrlene, relieved from the terrors of he
mother's now averted ambition, made satisfactory amends by obtaining passes i
no fewer than three subjects at her next public examination and left school (sh
was now nineteen) to pursue a course of study of the more esoteric modern poe
whose ranks she hoped to join some day when her mother allowed her to emigrat
to the wider literary field of London.

And then Lucas Traherne appeared on the scene. One afternoon Miss Tooth
waite's moribund two-seater wheezed up the drive at 'The Frangipannis'. A youn
man, a stranger, was driving. Miss Toothwaite dashed up the wide stone step
breathless with excitement and the young man followed at a leisurely pace. He wa
windblown and dishevelled, his clothes were far from clean, a pair of pale blue eye
glittered from a rawly-pink face; he had a lean and hungry look. In short, he migh
have been one of those merchant seamen who prowled the streets of Bridgetown.

By the time he had reached the broad verandah, Miss Toothwaite had pe
formed her act of introduction. She had gone for a sea bathe. She had met him o
the beach. They had got talking. And he was no other . . . why, they had bee
reading his *Rosemary for Rosencrantz* only last week . . . than Lucas Traherne.

Soon, stretched in a berbice chair with a tall rum and ginger at hand, he wa
relating his odyssey. He was touring the Caribbean. Writing. He liked Barbados
In fact, he liked it best of all the islands. How long was he staying? That depende
—and here he looked around appraisingly—if he could find a less expensiv
boarding-house. Poets couldn't afford the best hotels.

Next morning he moved in. A small suitcase arrived with him. That had been six months ago.

He had on more than one occasion offered to pay for his keep, that is to say, to pay when a certain cheque from his publishers arrived. But the cheque had failed to appear, and Mrs Bush-Hall had been forced to console herself with the thought that the intention was as good as the deed. Besides, it was a privilege to entertain such a distinguished guest. Moreover he was so entertaining, so companionable, so easily pleased, so useful even. He shared her enthusiasm for thrillers; regaled them with all sorts of stories—stories of the eccentricities of his illustrious family, bawdy stories of various personalities of the stage, screen, and literary world, shocking stories of political intrigue and dissimulation; pottered about in the garden and gave her invaluable hints about her roses, was delighted with the unfamiliar tropical blooms and exceedingly impressed by her collection of anthuriums (even more impressed by the collection of antique jewellery in the japanned box under the bed); often gave a hand in the kitchen; went marketing for her two or three times a week; and, when she broached the idea of a new car, saw after all the complicated business transactions and drove it home himself, a shining Jaguar. True, he would attend none of her tea parties, nor did he display the slightest interest in social welfare, but he was most affable to Miss Toothwaite despite her inability to cope with the more obscurantist and obscene of his poems, hail-fellow-well-met with the gregarious Audible, quite filial in his deportment to his dear Ma, and to Pyrlene he was most attentive. Indeed, after the arrival of the Jaguar, the couple would often disappear after dinner until the early hours of the next morning; and in spite of her daughter's repeated assurance that they spent the time discussing the problems and intricacies of modern verse, it was at this stage that Mrs Bush-Hall determined that he should state his intentions.

No matter how famous, how well-connected a young man he might be, the honour of the Bush-Halls was at stake. She wasn't going to have any monkey-business where the reputation of her only daughter was concerned.

He was watering the anthuriums when she put the pertinent question to him bluntly.

He shook a reproving finger at her. 'No wonder you are prey to these fearful imaginings, Ma, surrounded as you are' (and here he took in the tiers of lilies with a wide sweep of his arm) 'by all these travesties of floral phallism. But I can appreciate a mother's feelings and concern. My dear Ma' (approaching her and pinching her cheek) 'I thought all that was understood between us long ago. When do you propose announcing the engagement?'

And in spite of his sustaining a number of minor contusions by being propelled backwards into a nest of flowerpots by the exuberance of Mrs Bush-Hall's embrace, there was great joy at 'The Frangipannis' that day.

II

The Day broke fair and cloudless, Mrs Bush-Hall having consulted every available almanac to ensure this end. She had been up and about before dawn, and had been on her legs every moment since. All the multifarious preparations had fallen upon her, for Lucas had had to go to town in the car immediately after breakfast on important but unspecified business, Miss Toothwaite was busy at school, Audible involved in some political activity and Pyrlene hadn't been at all well lately, especially during the morning hours; but then, once the preliminaries had been accomplished in fitting style, the wedding need not be too long delayed.

It would be a quiet one: she had promised Lucas he would not have to undergo *tw*
such social trials.

A day of hard work it had been for her: arranging the floral decorations; giving
instructions to the men from the electric company about the illuminations; seeing
that the caterers had sent everything; popping in and out of the kitchen to
supervise all that was going on there; keeping a wary eye on the crisscrossing ropes
from the two marquees erected between the house and the lawn and upon all the
strange men wandering about the house and grounds, and the consequent
checking and rechecking of the knives, forks, spoons, etc., arranging the few
dozen chairs in apparently haphazard fashion about the lawn (she had wanted to
order two hundred and fifty, but Miss Toothwaite had reminded her that too
many chairs at a function of this sort would only engender a crystallization in the
circulation, and Lucas, less elegantly, that it wasn't going to be another of her
bloody tea parties); pointing out to the gardener and the boy who ran errands just
how the parking of the cars was to be controlled . . . yes, it had been a day of hard
work, not without its petty exasperations too. Major Strokes had telephoned to
state he was laid low with an attack of ptomaine poisoning; Audible had warned
her that Willoughby Watts had no intention of foregoing a freeness for lack of such
a trifle as an invitation; one of the young men from the village who had been
pressed into service had had an epileptic seizure in the W.C. and old Dr Dooms
had had to be summoned; a stray dog had made off with one of the baked turkeys
and, to cap it all, Lucas had just telephoned to say that something—nothing very
serious, he had been at pains to tell her—had gone wrong with the car and that he
would have to return by taxi.

Such a day! Nearly half-past five. Invitations had been issued for six-thirty. She
would have to wash and dress. And the question of dress had caused her some
exasperation too. She had wanted to appear in her most elaborate and expensive
gown and displaying almost every bit of jewellery she possessed; but Lucas had
been firm. 'That sort of thing just isn't done, Ma. You don't want all these people
to think you're trying to make them look insignificant. Something simple. And
just one ring and the little necklace I gave you. Remember now.'

She would certainly wear the necklace, even though it did look rather cheap; but
she had been thrilled at this unexpected gift, and she consoled herself with the
thought that one who had attended garden parties at Windsor should know best

She fingered the little gilt chain wistfully. She hadn't removed it since he had
clasped it on a week ago. For only a week ago the long-expected cheque from his
publishers had arrived. True, it was not quite what he had been counting upon
only a matter of twenty pounds, and there were so many things to be done with it
His old suitcase had completely burst asunder and he had bought one of those
lovely ones they used for air travel; he had run up quite a bill for cigarettes at the
village shop; and he had so wanted to buy that beautiful engagement ring a
Snuyder's he'd set his heart on. He'd even offered to pay what was left of the
cheque on account. But paying two pounds ten on a $500 engagement ring would
have been quite out of the question, so she had advanced the money (5 per cent of
for cash) and with the two pounds ten—or rather the better part of it—he had
purchased the necklace especially for her. She sighed tenderly at the recollection
and, as her bosom heaved, again glimpsed for a fleeting moment that delicate
token of his esteem.

Calling out last-minute instructions to everyone within earshot, she climbed the
stairs slowly. She hoped her legs would last out the night. Pyrlene in the next room

busily engaged in putting the finishing touches to a poem of hers which she hoped
Lucas might, considering the theme and the occasion, read, was routed from her
occupation and told to keep a close eye on the liquor now that the head-waiter had
arrived and to hustle Lucas into his clothes the moment he returned from town,
and then Mrs Bush-Hall made ready for her night of nights.

Her night of nights! That primary phase of her obligation as hostess
accomplished, the reception of her guests, she had withdrawn to the topmost stair
of the verandah, and from this point of vantage was contemplating with
satisfaction the pulsating scene before her.

She was dressed in a white satin gown that displayed her rounded figure perhaps
a little too bumpily, but Lucas, arriving at the very last moment, had approved.
Had approved also of the three salmon-coloured frangipanni blossoms in her hair,
and had, on second thoughts, granted her permission to wear another of her rings.
The rest she had been compelled to deposit regretfully in her jewel case. And
Lucas had whispered to her that she reminded him of a very famous duchess,
indeed, a duchess of his acquaintance.

Lucas had returned only just in time. There had been a slight accident; he had
had to leave the car in town, but it would be all right by tomorrow. He had been
unusually agitated, but her reminder that men were prone to attacks of nerves at
such crises had seemed to have restored his composure. He got dressed quickly,
joined Pyrlene and herself in greeting the early arrivals, and had been quite
charming to them.

What more could even a duchess have wished for? Everything had combined to
make the occasion astonishingly perfect. As she gazed out into the night she noted
that even the stars in their courses—and she could never remember having seen
such a profusion of them before—were obviously giving her of their best. The lawn
with its festoons of multi-coloured electric bulbs re-echoed loftier splendours, and
the lights from the airport, too, winked unqualified approval in her direction. And
all the guests, the two hundred odd of them, were so completely, so indubitably at
their ease. Their chatter and laughter were wafted up to her, a duchess upon her
dais, almost drowning the delicate drone of the scarlet-coated steel band which had
been instructed to play only the lightest of classical music until eight o'clock, when
the buffet supper would be served and the engagement announced.

How happy she was, how proud of it all—the weather, the stars, the lights, the
gay assembly! How delightful everyone had been! Everyone including Sir Charles
Charles, that paragon of the old Barbadian order about whose acceptance of the
invitation she had entertained some misgiving. How very gracious he and his wife,
Lady Emma, had been to her: 'Charmed, charmed to meet you, Mrs Bush-Hall,'
he had boomed, and had somehow managed to infuse into his greeting the fact that
he had only at that moment achieved a life-long desire. Breeding will always tell,
she thought: good old B'adian blood. She was more than ever proud of her birth-
right. Little England and Big England for ever.

Audible, very slim and very elegant in his fawn tropicals, mounted the steps and
joined her.

'Ain't it all too good to be true, Audie?' she murmured.

Audible grunted approval. 'You certainly giving them one hell of a good time,
Maudie. But why you up here all by your one? Where Pyrlene and Lucas?'

She pointed them out where they stood in the centre of a little knot of people
whom Pyrlene had previously referred to as 'the literati'. 'I going jine them now,'
she said.

The two of them walked down the steps to the lawn.

Smiles greeted her everywhere. Mrs Zimmerbloom, the American sculptress, again assured her what a wonderful time she was having and admired her cute frangipanni-coiffure, the Beethoven Smalls were effusively appreciative of the pleasantly modulated effect of the steel band, the Honourable Boysie Scantlebury congratulated her in his warmest and moistest tone on the excellence of her whisky. Mrs Orgie Wilde, the secretary of the HIYA, was moved to ecstatic ejaculations of 'Divine, my dear, too too divine' as she caught sight of her, Mr Hathaway Withym could not forbear introducing her for a second time to his most recently acquired friend, a young German, Herr Panzi, and even Lurleen DaCourcey felt it incumbent upon her to confess it was as good as an evening at Government House.

Audible wandered off in search of an elderly American who had earlier in the evening expressed a desire to purchase a property somewhere near the ocean. Mrs Bush-Hall joined the party of literati.

'All o' you still talking poetry, I suppose?'

'And what could be more essentially worth our while?' replied the eldest of the group, bowing acknowledgement. This was Mr Pearson Porson, an Englishman who had been shipped to the colonies many years ago to seek his fortune and had found it in the person of the daughter of a wealthy planter. Since that far-off time he had never done a stroke of work but was regarded as a great authority on every conceivable subject.

'That's right, Mrs Bush-Hall,' added another, a young journalist who was responsible for very occasional verse in his paper. And a third, the young schoolmaster to whose presence at the party Lucas had at first objected, chimed in, 'We're all now anxiously awaiting Mr Traherne's magnum opus, his epithalamium, to which this wonderful party,' with a sweeping wafture of his rum-and-ginger, 'would seem to be its most fitting prolegomenon.'

Not quite sure of the meaning of the intended compliment, Mrs Bush-Hall could only smile and glance at Lucas. He was scowling his darkest. 'Yes,' she ventured haltingly, 'we hope so. We hope so.'

Mr Pearson Porson came to the rescue. 'I was just saying, Mrs Bush-Hall,' he asserted in his most pontifical manner, 'that Mr Traherne can hardly have failed to observe the exquisite charm of our local place names, so English, so inspiring, so fraught with the mellow tradition of the centuries: Foursquare, Strong Hope, Mount Standfast, Providence, Venture, Boarded Hall. . . .'

'And don't forget the purely B'adian touch,' interrupted the journalist, 'Six Men's and Pie Corner and Jack-in-the-box Gully. . . .'

'And Jack-my-Nanny Gap and Penny-Hole and Cat's Castle. . . .' added the schoolmaster.

'And,' Lucas interpolated acidly, breaking his hitherto glowering silence, 'above all, don't let us forget the most inspiring of the lot, Sweet Bottom.' And, turning abruptly on his heel, he strode away followed by Pyrlene.

Mr Pearson Porson drew in his lips primly. The others, after a spell of indecision, made clucking noises of disapproval. Mrs Bush-Hall essayed a conciliatory, 'He will have his little joke, you know,' but Mr Pearson Porson's lips retained their set contour and his stare was stony. She thought it best to follow the retreating figure of Pyrlene. Lucas had gone on ahead and had disappeared indoors. 'Pyrlene!' she called. Pyrlene stopped and Mrs Bush-Hall caught up with her.

'Why Lucas had to go and make old Porson vex, na?'

'Mamma, you just won't understand. You know how Lucas hates parties and all this social fuss. You know it was only after days of persuasion we could get him to agree to this. And you know how most of these people irritate him, especially that pompous old ass, Porson. *And* that schoolmaster. Well, he has just blown up, that's all. He is in the most frightful temper. He has gone to his room and he says no one must disturb him until we're actually ready to announce the engagement.'

'But, Pyrlie, what people going say? And how I going know the exack time to send for him?'

Pyrlene shrugged her chiffon-covered shoulders. 'All I know is you'd better not trouble him when he's like this. He'll take a little time to cool off. He'll be all right. Don't hurry things. Start serving at eight as arranged. I'll go and bring him down about a quarter past. It's not even half-past seven yet.'

And Mrs Bush-Hall had to be content with that. After all, she reflected, it wasn't likely that he would be missed among all these people. Indeed, they all seemed to be enjoying themselves more than ever: the chatter and laughter had increased, the waiters were in great demand, the steel band seemed to be jazzing up some of the light classicals.

She caught sight of Miss Toothwaite. Miss Toothwaite had been delegated to entertain the strictly scholastic element, the various headmasters and head-mistresses, and she was performing her duty with distinction. She had collected them all together, and from their sustained giggles and guffaws, had apparently been plying them with drinks and a number of Lucas's bawdy stories.

The literati had dissolved into units. Mr Pearson Porson was gesticulating to two old ladies, the journalist had joined a politically inclined group, the school-master had disappeared. A withered elderly lady enmeshed in a cocoon of mauve voile approached her and seized her arm. It was Miss Twaddelle, the founder and president of the ICU. 'My dear Mrs Bush-Hall, what a beautiful party! And what a fine young man! So reserved, so well-tempered, so very English! And your dear daughter: how sweet she looks tonight! Ah, well she may to have captured the heart of so famous a person. And, just imagine: I've met every single member of our committee already!' Chirping gaily and sipping her rum-and-ginger, she melted into the crowd.

As she moved slowly across the lawn (how her legs were aching!) many others accosted her and had a few words with her. Sir Charles expressed his appreciation of the most delightful evening, the Smithbert Smiths were enchanted, Mr Gray Whitefoot was enraptured, Mr Horatio Nelson, BA, could find no words to express his ecstatic frame of mind; and all were equally congratulatory on her acquisition of so fine, so famous a son-in-law.

All this cheered her up a bit, but, God, she was tired. On her legs all day. As she moved around to a far corner of the lawn, she espied a couple of chairs which she remembered having placed in that secluded spot in the event of just such a contingency. She manoeuvered her way to them skilfully without being seen, and, flopped down and removing her shoes, she occupied both of them to best advantage.

From where she sat she could hear bits of conversation all around her. To her left, some enthusiasts were noisily selecting the next West Indian eleven, and there was great controversy. W. W. W. Pelter, himself a coming fast bowler, was main-taining stoutly that what the team needed was a spearhead attack of five fast bowlers. What did it matter if such an experiment had never yet been tried? So much the better. . . . To her right, the American pastor of the New Church of Spiritual Automation seemed to be expounding the tenets of his sect to a chosen few. She could hear '. . . for not only is the human body a machine, the soul too is a machine, if you come to think of it, a mechanical psyche motivated by the Great Mechanic. . . .' Immediately behind her, the future of the Federation was being debated. Mr Celestial Barker appeared to be voicing the consensus of opinion in stating that complete and absolute independence could be easily achieved if the hat were to be circulated among those nations who had more wealth than was morally good for them.

Hearing all these interesting points of view and not being compelled either to listen very carefully or to say anything in reply was extremely soothing. She could afford to forget Lucas and supper and everything else for a few moments. She stretched out her legs still further. . . .

Mrs Bush-Hall slept.

III

She was being rocked to and fro violently to the accompaniment of a prolonged shriek emanating from countless souls in despairing agony. As she struggled back to consciousness she became aware that the shriek was only the accustomed sound of a jet plane leaving the airport; it took her a little longer to realize that Pyrlene was responsible for the violence to her person.

'What the hell you think you doing, Pyrlene?' she enquired testily.

Pyrlene continued her shaking. 'Wake up, Mamma, wake up!'

'Stop that damn foolishness. You ain't see I wake up, girl?'

'Mamma, mamma, you know what time it is? I been looking for you for the last half-hour. We had to start supper. . . .'

Mrs Bush-Hall was wide awake now. 'What time it is?'

'Nearly half-past eight. And . . . and . . . I can't find Lucas anywhere.'

'Can't find Lucas?'

Pyrlene sank on to the chair now vacated by her mother's feet and sobbed: 'Nowhere at all, at all.'

Mrs Bush-Hall slipped on her shoes and stood up. Her fatigue had vanished. 'How you meaning you can't find Lucas?'

Pyrlene continued sobbing. 'Can't find him. Went to his room. Went to call him at quarter past eight. Wasn't there. All his clothes gone. His suitcase. Everything.'

From the far distance the sound of the retreating plane drilled a terrible thought into Mrs Bush-Hall's consciousness.

'Gone?'

'Me and Audible been searching everywhere. Didn't want to tell nobody. Couldn't find you. Why you had to go and get los' way so?'

'Come, chile,' said her mother, pulling her to her feet. It was useless reproaching herself for having dozed off. Only that terrible thought, persistent, boring its way into her brain. 'Come lewwe go and see. Where Audible is now?'

But Pyrlene did not know, and they set out across the lawn. Progress was difficult. They had to push their way through little knots of people, some of whom wanted to engage her in conversation. Willoughby Watts, who had evidently arrived late, slipped an arm around her: 'Hey, Maudie, like my invitation must be get los' in the post.' She ignored him. He could be dealt with later.

They found Audible in the hall at the telephone. He was on the point of replacing the receiver and he turned to them with a set face and much profanity. 'You know what, Maudie? That goddam limey cut and run. I now ring the airport. The son-ofabitch gone by that plane that just lef'.'

Mrs Bush-Hall did not speak. She grabbed Audible by the arm and pulled him upstairs. With that thought now in complete possession, she made straight for her bedroom. She opened her jewel case. She motioned to Audible to pull out the box from beneath the bed. Yes. Only a few bits of imitation jewellery now adorned the case; the japanned box had been rifled.

'If I could only ketch the thieving bastard,' Audible almost sobbed, 'if I could only *ketch* him. . . .'

'He have the engagement ring too?'

Pyrlene, a dumb heap on the floor, nodded assent.

For a few moments no one spoke.

Then Audible made for the door.

'Where you going, Audie?'

'To call the police.'

'You isn't doing nothing of the sort. Ring police for what? They got planes too? You keep your tail quiet, you hear, Audible Smart? This business concerning me. What I los', I los'. Nobody else. I got to think.'

A strange scene it was. Outside the music and the noise of the party louder than ever; within the room the three figures, Pyrlene sobbing, Audible blaspheming, Mrs Bush-Hall thinking. Thinking calmly, coherently, lucidly. She had been tricked, completely tricked. And in the very audacity of the trickery she found something she could, however ruefully, admire. Only Lucas could have done a thing like that. It was strange, he had made a complete fool of her, and yet . . . she bore him no malice. She had lost out. Lost maybe six or seven thousand dollars, lost the son-in-law of her dreams, everything she had planned, had hoped for, had boasted about . . . and yet. . . . She liked Lucas. She had enjoyed those months of his stay more than any other period of time she could remember. He was the only man she had really ever *liked*. If it had been her instead of Pyrlene. . . .

She glanced down at the sobbing girl on the floor. At least, all going well, there should be at 'The Frangipannis' in a few months' time a scion of English aristocracy. She would have to be content with that. And with her memories. And should she now go downstairs and announce to them all that Lucas was just a common thief and that she, Maude Bush-Hall, was the damnedest fool in Barbados? She could see the faces: the white faces, apparently sympathetic and scandalized, but smirking inwardly, old Sir Charles 'That's the sort of Englishman they export nowadays'; and the dark faces, goggle-eyed, drinking it all in, Willoughby Watts's fat grin, 'English son-in-law! Serve her damn well right, playing she is some society great dame'. She wasn't going to have *that*. Nobody was going to have the pleasure of seeing *her* spirit broken. Of course they would eventually hear the truth, but not from her. Not tonight. Not on her night of nights. What was it he had said? Like a duchess. A duchess. . . .

'Stop that snivelling, Pyrlene, and get up. Come with me. We going downstairs.'

'But what you going do?' questioned Audible.

'You go and round up the folks and tell them to gather in front the verandah. I got something to tell them.'

But something was worrying Audible. 'What I want to know is how he get the money to pay his fare. He couldn't give them no ring nor brooch nor nothing like that. And I know he didn't have a blasted blind cent.'

Pyrlene came to life. 'The Jag! The Jag! I bet he sell the Jag!'

But if Mrs Bush-Hall heard, she took no notice. She was already on her way.

For the past half-hour Miss Toothwaite had been feeling rather upset. Not only had she been steadily sipping away at far too many rum-and-gingers, but she could not understand the prolonged delay. Dear Maudie was always so efficient, so punctual. She glanced around. Everyone was becoming restless. And the wind was growing chilly. And those wretched calypsoes. Over and over. Where was Maudie? Whatever could have happened?

It was then that she observed that everyone was moving forward to the stone stairway leading up to the verandah. Mr Smart seemed to be directing operations. With the assistance of the arm of one of the headmasters, she discovered she could move forward, although not too quickly. So the announcement was to be made at last. But where was the young man? From her point of observation at the back of the crowd she could glimpse Pyrlene, all alone and almost hidden by one of the stone uprights, and Mrs Bush-Hall standing on the topmost stair. She couldn't help thinking how imposing she looked, how very dignified. Not in the least bit nervous, except that she was toying with that ridiculous little necklace Lucas had given her. What was she saying? There was a good stiff breeze blowing, and Miss Toothwaite, whose hearing was not particularly good, could catch only a few words here and there.

Mrs Bush-Hall was thanking them all for their acceptance of her invitation and for attending her party. She appreciated their presence. They all knew the object of the gathering. . . . She was speaking in her best committee voice, but was occasionally in difficulty with certain rules of concord. Dear, dear, she'd have to remind her again about the agreement of the verb with its subject. . . . What was she saying now?

'. . . one hour ago Mr Traherne receive a cable from home. It going shock all-you to hear . . . his dear mother dying . . . express a wish to see him before she pass away . . . no time to lose . . . what we could do? . . . no matter how much we want him to stay . . . a mother's dying wish . . . me and Pyrlene had to decide fast . . . Mr Smart here . . . arrangements . . . phone the airport . . . thank God . . . in time . . . plane . . . just gone. . . .'

Good gracious, what a calamity! How very unfortunate for everyone concerned. She communicated her distress to Dr Phorpous, the headmaster of St Swynetholds, on whose arm she was still depending. But Dr Phorpous replied quite unexpectedly and rather callously, she thought, 'Anyway, Miss Toothwaite, we've enjoyed a very pleasant evening. That turkey and ham was excellent.'

Mrs Bush-Hall was still speaking and Miss Toothwaite caught the last words quite clearly: '. . . and Mr Traherne beg me to say how sorry he was he didn't have the chance to wish all-you good-bye.'

Then she appeared to give a little sob and to clutch at her bosom. 'Poor Maudie,' thought Miss Toothwaite, 'I hope she doesn't go and have a stroke or something.'

But it was only the necklace that had come apart.

The broken chain was still dangling from her hand when Miss Toothwaite, with the continued assistance of Dr Phorpous's arm, struggled up the steps to wish her good-night. They were almost the last to leave. Dr Phorpous had not been able to forgo the whisky and soda he had ordered some time previously, and the band was doing its best with 'God Save the Queen' when they reached the top of the steps. She had wanted to say a few words, words of sympathy—she hardly knew what, but at that moment something had happened, something she couldn't understand, something that was to puzzle her for another few days. For Dr Phorpous, bending gallantly over Mrs Bush-Hall's proffered hand, had whispered, 'As an Englishman, I want to thank you very humbly for your magnificent gesture in defence of the Old Country,' and what had puzzled her even more was that Mrs Bush-Hall had winked, actually winked, at him, and had replied in her most gracious manner, 'Ah, Dr Phorpous, *noblesse oblige*, you know, *noblesse oblige.*'

From *BIM*, Vol. 9, No. 35, pp. 199–217.

FRANK COLLYMORE   *Born in 1893 in Barbados; died in 1980. Actor, teacher, poet, short story writer and editor. In many ways the godfather of modern West Indian literature. One of the few West Indian writers who was well established before travelling abroad. For many years the moving spirit behind BIM, the journal out of Barbados which offered so many West Indian writers their start—writers like Lamming, Selvon, Walcott, Wickham (now editor), Brathwaite, et al. Collymore was a most generous person, and many-sided; his water colour sketches are delightful, and his work on Barbadian dialect pioneering.*

[2, 6]

19   *A Wedding in Spring*

GEORGE LAMMING

London was their first lesson in cities. The solitude and hugeness of the place had joined their lives more closely than ever; but it was the force of similar childhoods which now threatened to separate them: three men and a woman, island people from the Caribbean, who waited in separate rooms of the same basement, sharing the nervousness of the night.

The wedding was only a day away.

Snooker thought he could hear the sweat spilling out of his pores. Talking to himself, old-woman-like in trouble, he started: 'Is downright, absolute stupid to make me harness myself in dis mornin' costume. . . . I ain't no Prince Philip or ever want to be. . . .'

A pause drew his attention to the morning suit he had rented. The top hat sat on its crown, almost imitating itself. It provoked Snooker. He watched it, swore at it, then stopped as though he was going to sit on it.

'Now what you think you doin'?'

Snooker was alerted. He heard the closing creak of the door and the blurred chuckle of Knickerbocker's voice redeeming the status of the top hat.

Snooker was silent. He watched Knickerbocker hold the top hat out like some extraordinary fruit in his hand.

'Is what Beresford think it is at all?' he said, turning his back on the suit to face Knickerbocker. 'My body, not to mention my face, ain't shape for dis kind o' get-up.'

'Even de beggar can be king,' said Knickerbocker, 'an' dis is de kind o' head-piece kings does wear.' He cuddled the top hat to his chest. 'An' tomorrow,' he added, lifting his head towards Snooker, 'I goin' to play king.'

'You goin' to play jackass,' Snooker said sharply.

'So what?' Knickerbocker smiled. 'Christ did ride on one.'

'Is ride these clothes goin' ride you tomorrow,' said Snooker, ''cause you ain't got no practice in wearin' them.'

'You goin' see who ride what,' said Knickerbocker, 'I sittin' in de back o' dat limousine jus' so, watch me, Snooker.' He was determined to prove his passion for formal dress. He had lowered his body on to the chair, fitting the top hat on his head at precisely the angle his imagination had shaped. He crossed his legs, and plucked at the imaginary seams of his morning trousers. The chair leaned with him while he felt the air for the leather rest which would hold his hand.

Snooker refused to look. But Knickerbocker had already entered the fantasy which the wedding would make real. His head was loud with bells and his eyes turned wild round the crowd, hilarious with praise, as they acknowledged his white gloved welcome. Even the police had removed their helmets in homage to the splendour which he had brought to a drab and enfeebled London. He was teaching the English their own tune. So he didn't hear Snooker's warning until the leather rest refused his hand and the crowd vanished into the shadows which filled the room. The chair had collapsed like a pack of cards under Knickerbocker's body. He looked like a cripple on his back.

Now he was afraid, and he really frightened Snooker too, the way he probed his hands with fearful certainty under and across his thighs. His guess was right. There was a split the size of a sword running down the leg and through the crutch of the only pair of trousers he owned.

'You break up my bes' chair,' Snooker said sadly, carrying the top hat like wet crockery across the room. It had fallen into the sink.

The crisis had begun. Knickerbocker crouched on all fours, his buttocks cocked at the mirror, to measure the damage he had done. The basement was still: Knickerbocker considering his black exposure while Snooker collected the wreckage in both hands, wondering how he could fit his chair together again. They didn't speak, but they could hear, behind the door, a quiet tumble of furniture, and after an interval of silence, the sullen ticking of the clock in Flo's room.

She was alone, twisting her hair into knotty plaits that rose like spikes out of her skull. She did not only disapprove of her brother's wedding but she also thought it a conspiracy against all they had learnt. Preoccupied and disdainful, she saw the Vaseline melt and slip like frying lard over her hands. The last plait done, she stuck the comb like a plough into the low shrub of hair at the back of her neck. She scrubbed her ears with her thumb; stretched the under lid of each eye to tell her health; and finally gave her bottom a belligerent slap with both hands. She was in a fighting mood.

'As if he ain't done born poor,' she said, caught in that whispering self-talk which filled the basement night. 'Borrowin' an' hockin' every piece o' possession to make a fool o' himself, an' worse still dat he should go sell Snooker his bicycle to rent mornin' suit an' limousine. Gran Gran. . . . Gawd res' her in de grave, would go wild if she know what Beresford doin' ... an' for what . . . for who he bringin' his own downfall?'

It was probably too late to make Beresford change his mind: what with all those West Indians he had asked to drop in after the ceremony for a drink: the Jamaican with the macaw face who arrived by chance every Sunday at supper time, and Caruso, the calypsonian, who made his living by turning every rumour into a song that could scandalize your name for life. She was afraid of Caruso, with his malicious tongue, and his sly, secretive, slanderous manner. Moreover, Caruso never travelled without his gang: Slip Disk, Toodles and Square Dick; then there were Lice-Preserver, Gunner, Crim, Clarke Gable Number Two, and the young Sir Winston. They were all from 'back home', idle, godless, and greedy. Then she reflected that they were not really idle. They worked with Beresford in the same tyre factory.

'But idle or no idle,' she frowned, 'I ain't want Beresford marry no white woman. If there goin' be any disgrace, let me disgrace him first.'

She was plotting against the wedding. She wanted to bribe Snooker and Knickerbocker into a sudden disagreement with her brother. Knickerbocker's disapproval would have been particularly damaging since it was he who had introduced the English girl to Beresford. And there was something else about Knickerbocker that Flo knew.

The door opened on Snooker who was waiting in the passage for Knickerbocker. Flo watched him in the dark and counted three before leaning her hand on his head. Her anger had given way to a superb display of weakness: a woman outraged, defenceless, and innocent of words which could tell her feeling.

'Snooker.'

'What happen now?'

'I want all you two speak to Beresford,' she said. Her voice was a whimper appropriate with grief.

'Let the man make his own bed,' said Snooker, 'is he got to lie down in it.'

'But is this Englan' turn his head an' make him lose his senses.' Flo crouched lower, tightening her hand against Snooker's neck.

'He keep his head all right,' said Snooker, 'but is the way he hearken what his mother say, like he walkin' in infancy all life long.'

'Ma wasn't ever goin' encourage him in trouble like this,' Flo said.

'Is too late to change anything,' said Snooker, 'except these kiss-me-tail mornin' clothes. Is like playin' ju-ju warrior with all that silk cravat an' fish-shape' frock they call a coat. I ain't wearin' it.'

'Forget 'bout that,' said Flo, 'is the whole thing we got to stop complete.'

Knickerbocker was slipping through the shadows, silent and massive as a wall which now rose behind Flo. The light made a white mask over his face. Flo seemed to feel her failure, sudden and complete. Knickerbocker had brought a different kind of trouble. He was fingering the safety-pins which closed the gap in his trousers. He trusted Flo's opinion in these details. He stooped forward and turned to let her judge whether he had done a good job.

'Move your tail out of my face,' she shouted, 'what the hell you take me for.'

Knickerbocker looked hurt. He raised his body to full height, bringing his hands shamefully over the safety-pins. He couldn't understand Flo's fury: the angry and unwarranted rebuke, the petulant slam of the door in his face. And Snooker wouldn't talk. They stood in the dark like dogs shut out.

Beresford was waiting in the end room. He looked tipsy and a little vacant under the light; but he had heard Flo's voice echoing down the passage, and he knew the others were near. It was his wish that they should join him for a drink. He watched the bottle making splinters with the light, sugar brown and green, over the three glasses and a cup. The label had lost its lettering; so he turned to the broken envelope on his stomach and went on talking to himself. All night that voice had made dialogue with itself about his bride. His mood was reflective, nostalgic. He needed comfort, and he turned to read his mother's letter again.

concernin the lady in question you must choose like i would have you in respect to caracter an so forth. i excuse and forgive your long silence since courtship i know takes time. pay my wellmeanin and prayerful respects to the lady in question. give flo my love and my remembrance to snooker and knick.

The light was swimming under his eyes; the words seemed to harden and slip off the page. He thought of Flo and wished she would try to share his mother's approval.

if the weddin come to pass, see that you dress proper. i mean real proper, like the folks in that land would have you. hope you keepin the bike in good condition.

The page had fallen from his hand in a moment of distraction. He was beginning to regret that he had sold the bicycle to Snooker. But his mood didn't last. He heard a knock on the door and saw Knickerbocker's head emerge through the light.

'Help yuhself, Knick.'

Beresford squeezed the letter into his pocket while he watched Knickerbocker close in on the table.

'I go take one,' Knickerbocker said, 'just one.'

'Get a next glass if the cup don't suit you.'

'Any vessel will do,' Knickerbocker said.

Knickerbocker poured rum like water as though his arm could not understand the size of a drink. They touched cup and glass, making twisted faces when the rum started its course down their throats.

'Where Snooker?'

'Puttin' up the bike,' Knickerbocker said. 'But Flo in a rage.'

'She'll come round all right,' said Beresford. 'Is just that she in two minds, one for me an' one 'gainst the wedding.'

'You fix up for the limousine?'

'Flo self do it this mornin',' said Beresford, 'they comin' for half pas' four.'

'Who goin' partner me if Flo don't come to the church?'

'Flo goin' go all right,' said Beresford.

'But you never can know with Flo.'

Beresford looked doubtful, but he had to postpone his misgivings.

Knickerbocker poured more rum to avoid further talk, and Beresford held out his glass. They understood the pause. Now they were quiet, rehearsing the day that was so near. The room in half light and liquor was preparing them for melancholy: two men of similar tastes temporarily spared the intrusion of female company. They were a club whose rules were part of their instinct.

'Snooker ask me to swap places wid him,' Knickerbocker said.

'He don't want to be my best man?' Beresford asked.

'He ain't feel friendly with the morning suit,' Knickerbocker said.

'But what is proper is proper.'

'Is what I say too,' Knickerbocker agreed. 'If you doin' a thing, you mus' do it as the done thing is doed.'

Beresford considered this change. He was open to any suggestion.

'Snooker or you, it ain't make no difference,' he said.

'Then I goin' course wid you to de altar,' Knickerbocker said.

Was it the rum or the intimacy of their talk which had dulled their senses? They hadn't heard the door open and they couldn't guess how long Flo had been standing there, rigid as wire, with hands akimbo, and her head, bull shaped, feeding on some scheme that would undo their plans.

'Get yuhself a glass, Flo,' Beresford offered.

'Not me, Berry, thanks all the same.'

'What you put your face in mournin' like that for?' Knickerbocker said. He was trying to relieve the tension with his banter. 'Those whom God join together. . . .'

'What you callin' God in this for?' Flo charged. 'It ain't God join my brother wid any hawk-nose English woman. Is his stupid excitement.'

'There ain't nothin' wrong wid the chick,' Knickerbocker parried.

'Chick, my eye!' Flo was advancing towards them. 'He let a little piece o' left-over white tail put him in heat.'

'Flo!'

Beresford's glass had fallen to the floor. He was standing, erect, wilful, his hands nervous and eager for action. Knickerbocker thought he would hit her.

'Don't you threaten me wid any look you lookin',' Flo challenged him. 'Knickerbocker, here, know what I sayin' is true. Look him in his face an' ask him why he ain't marry her.'

'Take it easy, Flo, take it easy,' Knickerbocker cautioned. 'Beresford marryin' 'cause he don't want to roam wild like a bush beast in this London jungle.'

'An' she, you know where she been roamin' all this time?' Flo answered. Knickerbocker fumbled for the cup.

'Is jus' what Seven Foot Walker tell you back in Port-o'-Spain,' Beresford threw in.

Whatever the English girl's past, Beresford felt he had to defend his woman's honour. His hands were now steady as stone watching Flo wince as she waited to hear him through.

'That man take you for a long ride, Flo, an' then he drop you like a latch key that won't fit no more. You been in mournin' ever since that mornin' he turn tail an' lef' you waitin'. An' is why you set yuh scorpion tongue on my English woman.'

'Me an' Seven Foot Walker. . . .'

'Yes, you an' Seven Foot Walker!'

'Take it easy,' Knickerbocker begged them. 'Take it easy. . . .'

'I goin' to tell you, Berry, I goin' to tell you. . . .'

'Take it easy,' Knickerbocker pleaded, 'take it easy. . . .'

Flo was equipped for this kind of war. Her eyes were points of flame and her tongue was tight and her memory like an ally demanding vengeance was ready with malice. She was going to murder them with her knowledge of what had happened between Knickerbocker and the English girl. Time, place, and circum-

stance: they were weapons which now loitered in her memory waiting for release.
She was bursting with passion and spite. Knickerbocker felt his loyalty waver. He
was worried. But Flo's words never came. The door opened and Snooker walked
in casual as a bird, making music on his old guitar. He was humming: 'Nobody
knows the trouble I've seen'. And his indifference was like a reprieve.

'The limousine man outside to see you,' he said. 'Somebody got to make some
kind o' down payment.'

The crisis had been postponed.

London had never seen anything like it before. The spring was decisive, a hard,
clear sky and the huge sun naked as a skull eating through the shadows of the
afternoon. High up on the balcony of a fifth-floor flat an elderly man with a
distressful paunch was feeding birdseed to a flock of pigeons. He hated foreigners
and noise, but the day had done something to his temper. He was feeling fine. The
pigeons soon flew away, cruising in circles above the enormous crowd which kept
watch outside the church; then closed their ranks and settled one by one over the
familiar steeple.

The weather was right; but the crowd, irreverent and forgetful in their fun, had
misjudged the meaning of the day. The legend of English reticence was stone-cold
dead. An old-age pensioner with no teeth at all couldn't stop laughing to the
chorus, a thousand times chuckled: 'Cor bli'me, look at my lads.' He would say,
''Ere comes a next in 'is tails, smashers the lot o' them,' and then: 'Cor bli'me,
look at my lads.' A contingent of Cypriots on their way to the Colonial Office had
folded their banners to pause for a moment that turned to hours outside the
church. The Irish were irrepressible with welcome. Someone burst a balloon, and
two small boys, swift and effortless as a breeze, opened their fists and watched the
firecrackers join in the gradual hysteria of the day.

Snooker wished the crowd away; yet he was beyond anger. Sullen and reluctant
as he seemed he had remained loyal to Beresford's wish. His mind alternated
between worrying and wondering why the order of events had changed. It was half
an hour since he had arrived with the bride. Her parents had refused at the last
moment to have anything to do with the wedding, and Snooker accepted to take
her father's place. He saw himself transferred from one role to another, but the
second seemed more urgent. It was the intimacy of their childhood, his and
Beresford's, which had coaxed him into wearing the morning suit. He had to make
sure that the bride would keep her promise. But Beresford had not arrived; nor
Knickerbocker, nor Flo.

Snooker remembered fragments of the argument in the basement room the
night before; and he tried to avoid any thought of Flo. He looked round the church
and the boys from 'back home' looked at him and he knew they, too, were
puzzled. They were all there: Caruso, Slip Disk, Lice-Preserver, and an incredibly
fat woman whom they called Tiny. Behind him, two rows away, he could hear
Toodles and Square Dick rehearsing in whispers what they had witnessed outside.
There had been some altercation at the door when the verger asked Caruso to
surrender his guitar. Tiny and Slip Disk had gone ahead, and the verger was
about to show his firmness when he noticed Lice-Preserver who was wearing full
evening dress and a sword. The verger suddenly changed his mind and indicated a
pew, staring in terror at the sword that hung like a frozen tail down Lice-
Preserver's side. Snooker closed his eyes and tried to pray.

But trouble was brewing outside. The West Indians had refused to share in this impromptu picnic. They had journeyed from Brixton and Camden Town, the whole borough of Paddington and the Holloway Road, to keep faith with the boys from 'back home'. One of the Irishmen had a momentary lapse into prejudice and said something shocking about the missing bridegroom. The West Indians bristled and waited for an argument. But a dog intervened, an energetic, white poodle which kicked its hind legs up and shook its ears in frenzy at them. The poodle frisked and howled as though the air and the organ music had turned its head. Another firecracker went off, and the Irishman tried to sing his way out of a fight. But the West Indians were showing signs of a different agitation. They had become curious, attentive. They narrowed the circle to whisper their secret.

'Ain't it his sister standin' over yonder?'

They were slow to believe their own recognition.

'Is Flo, all right,' a voice answered, 'but she not dress for the wedding.'

'Seems she not goin',' a man said as though he wanted to disbelieve his suspicion.

'An' they wus so close,' the other added, 'close, close, she an' that brother.'

Flo was nervous. She stood away from the crowd, half hearing the rumour of her brother's delay. She tried to avoid the faces she knew, wondering what Beresford had decided to do. Half an hour before she left the house she had cancelled the limousine and hidden his morning suit. Now she regretted her action. She didn't want the wedding to take place, but she couldn't bear the thought of humiliating her brother before this crowd. The spectacle of the crowd was like a rebuke to her own stubbornness.

She was retreating further away. Would Beresford find the morning suit? And the limousine? He had set his heart on arriving with Knickerbocker in the limousine. She knew how fixed he was in his convictions, like his grandfather whose wedding could not proceed; had, indeed, to be postponed because he would not repeat the words: *All my worldly goods I thee endow.* He had sworn never to part with his cow. He had a thing about his cow, like Beresford and the morning suit. Puzzled, indecisive, Flo looked round at the faces, eager as they for some sign of an arrival; but it seemed she had lost her memory of the London streets.

The basement rooms were nearly half a mile from the nearest tube station; and the bus strike was on. Beresford looked defeated. He had found the morning suit, but there was no way of arranging for another limousine. Each second followed like a whole season of waiting. The two men stood in front of the house, hailing cabs, pleading for lifts.

'Is to get there,' Beresford said, 'is to get there 'fore my girl leave the church.'

'I goin' deal wid Flo,' Knickerbocker swore. 'Tomorrow or a year from tomorrow I goin' deal wid Flo.'

'How long you think they will wait?'

Beresford had dashed forward again, hailing an empty cab. The driver saw them, slowed down, and suddenly changed his mind. Knickerbocker swore again. Then: a moment of revelation.

'Tell you what,' Knickerbocker said. He looked as though he had surprised himself.

'What, what!' Beresford insisted.

'Wait here,' Knickerbocker said, rushing back to the basement room. 'I don't give a goddam. We goin' make it.'

*

The crowd waited outside the church, but they looked a little bored. A clock struck the half-hour. The vicar came out to the steps and looked up at the sky. The man in the fifth-floor flat was eating pork sausages and drinking tea. The pigeons were dozing. The sun leaned away and the trees sprang shadows through the early evening.

Someone said: 'It's getting on.'

It seemed that the entire crowd had agreed on an interval of silence. It was then the woman with the frisky white poodle held her breast and gasped. She had seen them: Beresford and Knickerbocker. They were arriving. It was an odd and unpredictable appearance. Head down, his shoulders arched and harnessed in the morning coat, Knickerbocker was frantically pedalling Snooker's bicycle towards the crowd. Beresford sat on the bar, clutching both top hats to his stomach. The silk cravats sailed like flags round their necks. The crowd tried to find their reaction. At first: astonishment. Later: a state of utter incomprehension.

They made a gap through which the bicycle free-wheeled towards the church. And suddenly there was applause, loud and spontaneous as thunder. The Irishman burst into song. The whole rhythm of the day had changed. A firecracker dripped flames over the church steeple and the pigeons dispersed. But crisis was always near. Knickerbocker was trying to dismount when one tail of the coat got stuck between the spokes. The other tail dangled like a bone on a string, and the impatient white poodle charged upon them. She was barking and snapping at Knickerbocker's coat tails. Beresford fell from the bar on to his knees, and the poodle caught the end of his silk cravat. It turned to threads between her teeth.

The crowd could not determine their response. They were hysterical, sympathetic. One tail of Knickerbocker's coat had been taken. He was aiming a kick at the poodle; and immediately the crowd took sides. They didn't want harm to come to the animal. The poodle stiffened her tail and stood still. She was enjoying this exercise until she saw the woman moving in behind her. There was murder in the woman's eyes. The poodle lost heart. But the top hats were her last temptation. Stiff with fright, she leapt to one side seizing them between her teeth like loaves. And she was off. The small boys shouted: 'Come back, Satire, come back!' But the poodle hadn't got very far. Her stub of tail had been safely caught between Flo's hand. The poodle was howling for release. Flo lifted the animal by the collar and shook its head like a box of bones.

Knickerbocker was clawing his rump for the missing tail of the morning coat. Beresford hung his head, swinging the silk cravat like a kitchen rag down his side. Neither could move. Flo's rage had paralysed their speech. She had captured the top hats, and it was clear that the wedding had now lost its importance for her. It was a trifle compared with her brother's disgrace.

The vicar had come out to the steps, and all the boys from 'back home' stood round him: Toodles, Caruso, and Square Dick, Slip Disk, Clarke Gable Number Two, and the young Sir Winston. Lice-Preserver was carrying the sword in his right hand. But the poodle had disappeared.

Flo stood behind her brother, dripping with tears as she fixed the top hat on his head. Neither spoke. They were too weak to resist her. She was leading them up the steps into the church. The vicar went scarlet.

'Which is the man?' he shouted. But Flo was indifferent to his fury.

'It don't matter,' she said. 'You ju' go marry my brother.'

And she walked between Knickerbocker and her brother with the vicar and the congregation of boys from 'back home' following like a funeral procession to the altar.

Outside, the crowd were quiet. In a far corner of sunlight and leaves, the poodle sat under a tree licking her paws, while the fat man from the fifth-floor flat kept repeating like an idiot to himself: 'But how, how, how extraordinary!'

From *West Indian Stories*, pp. 28–41.

[2, 15]

20 The Red Square Just Before Spring

JOHN FIGUEROA

There are no leaves in Moscow now although Easter is very near; the few trees are gaunt; the skies are blue. A clear, light blue, lighter than the blue of Florence or Venice, further away from cobalt, as far away as possible without becoming white. But yet a more distant blue than the blue of Jamaican skies, perhaps the same shade but not quite as close, and no mountains nearby and no white fluffy clouds.

The skies are blue, the air clean, clear, crisp cold, dry. And all the while the Red Square and the tomb nothing written on it but

LENIN

STALIN

and within it nothing but the embalmed bodies. A pyramid truncated at the apex; but with the bodies no *vademecum*, no food for the journey, no boats for crossing the river to eternity. Just two sleeping corpses, unnatural in death, for all to see incorruptible (for how long?). Is it a symbol, the red pyramid? Is it a foundation stone? How does dialectical materialism rest on, or with this?

How long will they keep it open? Of course, it is in the tradition of the Greek Orthodox Church and its saints. Or is it?

Grandpa lay stretched out in his coffin, in Jamaica, Mr P flat out on his back with a false composure. And in his coffin his nose seemed so much more prominent, even as Stalin's seems somewhat hooked, slightly beaked and red.

Last night I dreamt that Grandpa had just died and Olga and I were going to bury him (Olga whom I did not meet until fifteen or seventeen years after the event; but because the time of personal experience is not sidereal time, because whatever happens in a big way to a person also happens to everything that has already happened, and will in the future happen to that person—the before and after of personal experience is not the before and after of the sun or the moon or of the shadow moving across, without marking the sundial—the death and burial of 'Mr P' taking place by sun time fifteen years before our experience entwined, cannot now, thirty-three years after the event by sun time, and an eternity after

the event by *his* time be in my experience 'before' or 'after' or 'away from' Olga.
'Before the river meets the sea—' but far up the river the salt and fish are found and
far out to sea the fresh. And the sea and the river are not knit into a time unit by
memory which does not stretch backward as we often think, but brings forward or
rather makes a moment co-extensive with all the other moments which are
somehow connected to it in the psyche.)

So in my dream, awakened by the embalmed effigies of the Red mausoleum,
Olga and I were preparing to bury Mr P. And he was being prepared and it was all
so lonely as no one seemed to know him or care that he had died.

Then he was in his coffin, his face covered with a cloth to protect it from the fly
that kept pitching on his nose—hardly bothering him, poor, lonely man, escaped
revolutionary from Cuba, growing tobacco in Jamaica, and being taken in by a
large company, and marrying and raising a family.

His going had been unexpected. Herbert, about to leave for the Scouts'
Jamboree in England, had come into the shuttered Kingston Gardens room to tell
him goodbye. I, a little boy, listened. England seemed far away then in another
world, not, certainly not, the physical place in which we subsequently lived and
from which with bag-pipes and caviar and all, we have just inaugurated the BEA
jet service to Moscow.

'Fancy, who would believe it?' Mamie (Mrs P) used to say as we sat around the
table in Jamaica, 'I was once in New Orleans; believe you me my mother took me
to live there when I was a little girl.' And then I would see the sails and rigging and
rope and decks of an old sailing ship, and would ask something about the trip and
Grandpa would suggest that I continue to eat the Sunday dinner of 'cow foot' (*not*
calves' heel) and rice that he had taught me to like.

Herbert had always lived in the house and had gone to elementary school, and
had clearly been a young man about to make something of himself. He came into
the shuttered tropical room to say goodbye to my grandfather because he was a
leading scout and had been selected to go to England and the jamboree.

There was a warm silence between them. Then something like, 'I have to say
goodbye, sir.' We all knew that, one always does. But one has to say *something*. A
gentle quiet silence.

'Be careful, behave yourself.'

'Thank you, Mr P. See you when I return.'

But Herbert was Mr P's pall bearer in three or four days' time.

And he lay stretched out in the open coffin in the front room in Kingston
Gardens. The family around. 'She kisses her father,' exclaimed a busybody as my
youngest aunt, a nun, bade farewell to the father whom, perhaps, she had not
known until then.

And we children played just outside under the palm tree where I had planted the
gungo peas—just dashing them into a small ditch, full of water, about two feet by
six inches. Overnight they had burst with the magic of life, green, quiet, self-
assured. Then tomorrow, the day after the funeral, we would transplant them.

But he was laid out, so lonely, so lonely, though people were there. And Herbert
helped to pick up the coffin looking straight ahead of him thinking of the strange
delay of the ship that had held him back for this, and of England, far away, and of
the great jamboree. . . .

Stalin and Lenin—what remains of them now—the one's nose slightly crooked,
the other's short, grey hairs glistening on what was his face—are laid out amidst
their sentinels and wondering tourists.

The children are playing in the snow beneath the blue Moscow skies, just before Easter which they do not know, but soon they will be planting seeds and wondering at the green insistence of shoots and forgetting all about this false conquest over death when the green returns to Moscow.

From *BIM*, Vol. 9, No. 35, pp. 154–6.

JOHN FIGUEROA *Born in 1920 in Kingston, Jamaica. Educated in Jamaica until going to college, on a scholarship, in the USA. Wrote and published at college. Returned home to teach in secondary schools. Then to London University for postgraduate work. On London University staff for five years before returning to Jamaica. Twenty years on staff of University of West Indies, as Professor of Education and Dean. Has also taught at University of Puerto Rico, University of Jos (Nigeria) and Indiana University. Has travelled widely in the Caribbean, Latin America, Africa and Europe. His anthology,* Caribbean Voices, *in two volumes, has been perhaps the most successful collection of West Indian verse: Vol. I has had eight reprints, Vol. II three. Edited and recorded* West Indian Authors Reading Their Own Verse *(Caedmon, No. TC 1379), which readers might find useful and interesting.*

[17, 23, 86, 93, 112]

21   *The Old Man and the City*

JOHN WICKHAM

After thirty years it seems incredible that I had been living in Port of Spain for six years when I met the old man whose personality is now inseparable in memory from the personality of the city. To be sure, I had heard stories of an old fellow living on the left bank of Dry River who had amassed, no one knew quite how, the finest collection of classical music on records on (the particular preposition is a clue to the source of the stories) the island and who was an amateur, in the original and proper sense of that often mismanaged word, of antique furniture, bric-à-brac and rare china. But the personality evoked by the stories I had heard was of a mild eccentric, a kind of legend, and since I was then still a victim of the belief that the finest spirits dwelt in the past, it was not difficult to persuade myself that the old man did not really exist in the here and now. And what gave massive support to the incredibility of the old man's actual existence was the singular provenance of the stories. For the wonders of rare pieces, cherished albums, old books and photographs and meticulously arranged records came to me, not through the native picong but through the grapevine of a number of people who used, in those days and possibly even more so now, to be referred to, with pejorative condescension, as expatriates, as if the population of the city was not itself overwhelmingly expatriate in origin. But although in time I came to see that this expatriate awareness of the old man's presence was only one of the stunning contradictions which were the city's idiom, at the time it seemed distinctly odd that it should fall to aliens to spread the gospel of a living native wonder. The fact that I know much better now is due as much to the lesson of the old man as to any other experience of life in the city.

Inevitably then, there was a mythic quality associated with the personality I encountered, in the final event not quite by accident yet haphazardly, one evening when Cecil Herbert took me, as a special treat and an earnest of his regard for me, to a house off South Quay to meet a friend of his.

Tiptoeing up the front steps of the tiny house as much in discretion as out of concern for the fragility of the floor boards, we waited for a while, then pushed a rickety half-door to the box-like verandah. Cecil knocked and shouted 'Clem!' in his deep-throated voice which had first caught my ear in its recital of some lines which spoke of far days in happy shires and goddesses caught in alabaster. An old man's voice, slightly quavering, answered: 'Who's that? Cecil?' as if Cecil's was precisely the voice which was expected.

When he appeared at the door clutching his pyjama trousers, the old man said, in a mock show of displeasure, 'Cecil, you old rogue, you wouldn't come to look for your friend all these months. What I do you?' But he was so pleased by the visit, by the token of remembrance that no one could be fooled by his tone into thinking that he was angry. Cecil was, of course, delighted and flattered (how could he not be?) by the tribute and I, whose affection for him swung between despair at the waste of his gift that he allowed and rage at the poseur that possessed him, was touched by the fondness in the old man's voice for 'the old rogue'.

Cecil introduced me and Clem slapped me on the shoulder in the off-hand gesture which, during the years I had lived in Port of Spain, I had come to recognize as not slighting or rude but as an invitation, an acceptance into a relationship of intimacy. For one brought up in the less casual environment of Barbados where manners were more formal, that first encounter was unforgettable.

'But I don't see you, Cecil. I ask for you, I don't hear a word. What's happening?'

The concern was patent, anxious, but Cecil shrugged his shoulders, took a cigarette from a package, tapped it tight, lit it and blew the smoke through his teeth. The old man made a waving gesture to tell me that I had the freedom of the room and could sit where I wished and I sat on an old mahogany sofa with a carved back of the period which I thought of as Barbados plantation. Cecil settled in an armchair next to a glass-fronted bookcase and the old man sat in what was clearly his favourite chair with his back to the door which led to the yard. Between us, no more than an arm's length from either of us, in the centre of the triangle was the record player, its connecting wires hanging from a socket which swung from the roof, the focal point of the room, like the fireplace in a cold climate, the spot which engages the attention of all the eyes.

The room was small and so crowded with bits and pieces that it was clear that movement about it was neither intended nor encouraged. How to describe it now, thirty years after that first impression? But the impression has faded very little. It was an old curiosity shop, cluttered with an accumulation of bijouterie and furniture, faded photographs in old but still elegant frames, a stately epergne, a crystal punch bowl and, locked behind another glass-fronted cupboard, several china cups and saucers; wine glasses on long stems as graceful as the necks of swans, silver teaspoons, a brass gong, four handsome pewter mugs, a gold snuff box, a crimson flower vase shot with mauve and indigo, a hand mirror with an embroidered back, a lady's sewing box, thimble and all, several pieces of jade, a glass egg. A trinity of candlesticks stood on top of the bookcase, flanked by an assortment of miniature china figures: little pigs, the Mad Hatter, Humpty Dumpty, Mr Pickwick, John Bull. In one corner of the room, alone on a triangular shelf, stood a handsome oil lamp with a brass bowl and a flowered chimney and a milk-white shade.

But I did not see all of this on that first visit. The whole display was so unexpected that it was impossible to take it in at once, especially as there was only a dim light—Clem did not like bright lights, they hurt his eyes—which shone over the record player and left the room in dark shadow outside the edge of the circle of light. But there was enough light to see the outlines of photographs, hundreds of them on the walls, of artists and musicians and politicians and philanthropists. I could make out the rugged outlines of Albert Schweitzer's face, Ralph Bunche, Eve Curie. Over the doorway, presiding, there was a full length of Paul Robeson. There was Haile Selassie as well as George Washington Carver, Booker T. Washington, George Headley, Ella Fitzgerald, Menuhin, the plaster cast of Paderewski's hands, Gershwin, Joe Louis, a wild-haired Albert Einstein. Clem saw me looking around the room and said: 'You must come again whenever you like now that you know the place. I am here all the time, too old to move around now much, eh Cecil?' And he chuckled hoarsely as if he and Cecil had shared the escapades of youth and as if the loss of that youth was the most amusing thing in the world. He spoke again in the unpretentious, easy-going manner that I was to come to know very well, which made the most generous act of hospitality, the most thoughtful kindness seem to be of no account, to be one of those everyday things that just happen.

'You boys would like a drink? I have some red wine there, had it since Christmas, keeping it for an occasion. And what is the use of a bottle of wine if you can't share it with your friends? But I can't vouch for it, so don't blame me if it tastes like vinegar.'

He chuckled again, this time at the monstrosity of the idea of wine tasting like vinegar, like a child, hugely and with a child's innocent delight. He brought out the wine, a dust-covered unlabelled bottle, uncorked it with a fancy corkscrew and took three glasses from the cupboard. He wiped the glasses with a piece of toilet paper, pinged each one on its rim with the nail of his forefinger to show the quality and handed one to each of us.

'Your health, gentlemen,' he said, with a hint of a bow in our direction as he sat back in his chair. We sipped. He said, 'Chambre,' chuckling again so warmly that I felt a glow of pleasure from his being so pleased. In the dimness of the room I could not see his face but it was impossible not to feel the cosy, warm-hearted welcome of his expression. We sipped in silence in the shadowed darkness of the room, the glow of the single bulb just enough to pick out the record player.

After a while, Clem asked, 'What about some music?' He sounded solicitous, eager to atone for having omitted so essential an element of hospitality. But, as I came to understand him later in our friendship, he was also showing off a little. He wished to offer his passion for our admiration, for if there was the slightest conceit in him, if he had the tiniest shred of vanity in his character, it lay in his collection of gramophone records.

'What about some music?'

Cecil turned and nodded, conceding to me, as new boy, the privilege of choosing.

The albums, hundreds, perhaps thousands of them, rested neatly on shelves around the room. I was at a loss to make a choice, like a child in the treasure house of a toy shop, surrounded by too many possibilities, too many realizable dreams. And, like a child, I tried to shift the onus of choice somewhere else.

'What have you got?' I asked stupidly.

'What would you like to hear, man?' Clem's tone was a trifle sharp, I thought. I was being put on my mettle. In the gentlest manner I was being asked how I dared to insult the occasion by not having an immediate preference. What kind of person was this that Cecil had inflicted on him? A man who did not even know what music he liked? I began to feel uncomfortable and made a pretence of racking my brain for the piece of music that would be appropriate to the evening's mood, my own first visit, and at the same time convey the subtlest of suggestions that I did have a confident and developed taste in music. And, as it often happens when make-believe exerts its demanding influence on our imaginations that we discover in the farthest recesses of memory, hidden under layers of litter which is worthless but is hoarded against the possibility of its coming in handy some day, some unsuspected semblance of truth or reality, a forgotten experience came to my rescue.

A few years before, at a concert in Port of Spain, I had heard a visiting pianist play Debussy's *L'après-midi d'un faune.* More by instinct than through any refinement of musical appreciation I had enjoyed what I could only think of as the chordal assembly which seemed to me to convey exquisitely the suggestion of the title which itself had caught my fancy. I had never heard this music before nor had I heard it since that evening but, suddenly, its sound came welling up on a wave of memory and I found myself asking a self-conscious question.

'Do you have *L'après-midi d'un faune?*'

Clem laughed out loud in ridicule but not unkindly for it was the kind of naive question which gave him just the chance he wished to display the richness of his collection. He did so as modestly as his pride in his possessions would let him.

'Played by?' he asked.

He had me there. My ignorance lay exposed. But I dodged behind a façade of polite concession to the host.

'Who is your favourite?'

'Come on, the choice is yours. Say.'

Again the surge of a faint recollection: of Claudio Arrau playing Chopin, a brilliant tone. Perhaps he had played Debussy. I took a chance. 'Claudio Arrau,' I said, with a little smugness at the fact that I knew the name of at least one famous pianist.

Without a word Clem rose from his chair, went to a shelf and, feeling with his fingers in the light that was too dark to see by, put his hand on the jacket of a record. He pulled out the record, puffed his cheeks and blew away the unseen dust and put the record on the player. He touched a switch and Debussy by Arrau poured into the room. No word passed until the end of the playing and then Clem laughed in satisfaction. I murmured a word of unnecessary thanks.

We left the house that night about midnight. I was drunk as much with wine as with the elation of discovery and as I was going through the door, thinking how to say that I would be back for sure, Clem said, 'Eh, eh, but John, you have to sign the book. You know when you go to Government House, you have to sign the book, what makes you think you don't have to sign the book here too?'

And he pushed a heavy leather-bound book into my hand, made me find the page appropriate to my birthdate and sign of the zodiac and write my name to record that I was there.

The affection which came to life between Clem and me on and after that first visit was possible, I fancy, only because I had, by the time of its occurrence, already become familiar with the accent and idiom of the conundrum of the city which was Port of Spain. That instantaneous affection, I have come to see, was itself a catalytic factor in any further understanding of the city that I may have achieved and so, old man and city stand in a relation to each other of mutual revelation and dependence. The idea of neither exists for me separately from the other, each of the two personalities promotes and illuminates the other precisely through the improbabilities of their association. Their co-existence within the same context of time could not have been imagined but I came to see that the coincidence was of the same order of magnificence as those accidents which our hindsight eventually discerns to have been inevitable.

It was very near to where Clem lived, only across the road, in fact, that I had my first impression of Port of Spain. The bustle of the railway station, taxi drivers bawling invitations to travel to San Fernando, the dazzle of the bright lights of South Quay were more than the wartime economies of Bridgetown, from which I had only an hour or so before arrived, and the rural somnolence of Grenville, the only other town with which I had up to then achieved any measure of familiarity, had prepared me for. Port of Spain, Trinidad. Trinidad, Trickidad. Trinidad is a very nice place but fire down dey. A schoolfellow, having followed the trail laid by the Yankee dollar during the war, had returned and whispered into my uneasy ear that you could get anything in Trinidad. Anything, he had said ominously and had then added the rider, 'To buy!' It was enough to frighten my timid spirit. And shortly before I had left my small island a man who had studied these things told me that Port of Spain had for the Bajan the same combination of horror and fascination that a snake has for most people: it terrifies you but you can't take yours eyes off it.

And yet, the reality of the place turned out to be less than frightening. Congenial, easy-going, undemanding, purposeless (the most popular reason for any action or gesture seemed to be 'for so') the atmosphere was the most accommodating it was possible to imagine. There was something for everyone. Although the Yankees had surrendered the freedom of the city to the then fledgeling Sparrow and the streets swarmed with their stranded 'sufferers', there was more money around than there had ever been in Bridgetown and there was little evidence of any reluctance to spend it, so that, compared to the town I had just left, Port of Spain had the appearance of an unbelievable bazaar, a big city *en fête*. And even in places where there was no money, for there were pockets of poverty, the atmosphere of the city had bred a style which was indistinguishable from the style of high living. People greeted each other with shouts across the street in terms of a picong which came perilously near to the edge of insult. But all was good-natured fun which only a solemn, humourless Bajan would take exception to and if you were not disposed to look hard or listen carefully you would have very little difficulty in persuading yourself that all was well. It was impossible to resist the appeal to jettison sobriety and to put an end to wartime self-denial.

And then there was the phenomenon of Carnival for which there could have been no adequate preparation or apprenticeship. All that colour and explosion of high spirits, that abandon, that magnificent casting out of inhibitions, were, in a jargon that had not yet been invented, something else. The world that was revealed was wonderful. There was a naked honesty about the expression that was refreshing and could not fail to capture the imagination, that was so attractive that it tended to assume a significance which a more sophisticated articulation would have denied. 'For so' did not seem to be a satisfactory explanation.

And so it happened that what made the city infinitely more affecting was the transparency of the façade of sophistication. Pretty girls stepped smartly, primly sometimes, along Frederick Street pavements wearing their modish clothes with Parisian elegance and with just that touch of carelessness and nonchalance which, however natural it looked, was the result of a careful strategy to make sure that attention was never distracted by the clothes from the figure that they clothed. The picture of one of them, a Junoesque beauty, à peau cannelle, walking down Marine Square licking an ice cream cone refuses to take leave of my memory. Saga boys exaggerated the zoot suit styles, eager to make a pappy show of themselves in the name of fashion. It was when they came to speak, these boys and girls, that the innocent stranger felt that he had been taken. An English visitor, a painter who lived in Barbados, described some of the girls as frothy. Extensive quotation of the Fitzgerald translation of Omar Khayyám was taken as the height of erudition. The words of the serious calypsos were of a surprising banality. It was disappointing. Style was everything. You had to have it. I had seen for years the visiting Trinidad cricketers display the kind of style in Barbados that was now around me in Port of Spain. Bright, flamboyant blazers and accents, a loose-limbed swaggering gait were the features of their promenades along Broad Street. Only our own Derek Sealy, with his knotted neckerchief and his cap daringly askew could match them for panache and it wasn't very long before he too went to live among them.

And yet, it was undeniable that the place was a joy. The girls were decorous as well as decorative, the tram car clanged along Frederick Street and around the Savannah up to St Ann's and Bridgetown offered nothing as appealing as the pastime of sucking oranges and oysters on the pitch or as delicious as hot roti from the wayside trays at the corner of Park and Charlotte or as subtly flavoured as pow from the Chinaman at the top of Queen Street. And shallow as the talk might be, it was sharp and new every morning. A tess was smoke or full of flash and grand charge if he was not to be taken seriously and if you tried to stop a Trinidadian from playing mask you would be spinning top in mud. You greeted your friend in the street by giving him a right or giving him tone but if you wanted to cut him dead you passed him like a full trolley bus. It was exciting and who cared if it was not profound. Life itself lasted very little longer than the Red House fire and solemnity would not change the price of cocoa. Every year new kings and queens and knaves took over a new carnival in a new profusion of colour. You could never grow tired of the songs and the costumes and the picong. Until Killer and Attila [. . .] died and carried their styles with them. And one Carnival Tuesday evening, after the city had lost its life, in the dust and torn tinsel and the litter of broken bottles, a pretty girl, unmasked, her costume in tatters and she in tears that made channels through the paint on her face, cried as she scraped along St Vincent Street, barely able to lift her feet from the ground now that there was not a ping-pong of steel within earshot, cried to break her heart, 'O God, never again, never again!'

Suddenly Carnival stopped being the bright novelty it was trumped up to be and became the most traditional, the most conservative of fêtes, an annual redeployment of old ideas and conventions that had happened before and would happen again.

Precisely at this time of revelation Clem entered my Port of Spain and I made my first entry into the unlikely world of his house at South Quay and through it into a fuller understanding of the city. Given the happiness of that coincidence, it was no wonder that Clem, the man and his house and interest, assumed the dimension of a miracle. And even now, so long after the event, the sense of miracle persists, for it is clear that if I had not met Clem, and at that time, I should have been restricted to only the barest minimum of comprehension of the city and that my appreciation of it would have been unable to withstand the assaults which time and events have made on its image. As it is, thanks to Clem, the place achieved a hard core of meaning which the Federation collapse, the politics of the post-1956 years, the revolution of 1970 and the oil boom have not been able to disfigure. In fact, much that has happened since our meeting has served merely to confirm the meaning of Port of Spain as Clem led me to discover it. One incident which occurred at that time became part of the same package of experience which helped to make the picture of the city whole. It seemed at the time to be a duplicate of the meeting with Clem with which it combines to make a statement of the place where both occurred.

Paramin is a small village on the slope of the hill behind the trees you can see across the Maraval valley to your left when you are on the road to Maracas. It has managed, partly because the terrain makes it difficult to reach and partly because its attractions are not blatant, to escape the depredations of the now-for-now developers. The village centre comprises the wooden building which serves as school during the week and as church on Sunday, a shop and parlour and a standpipe and from this huddle of communal elements houses straggle up the hillside on one side of a beaten path which runs through the abandoned cocoa. Behind the houses the hill slopes sharply down to a wide valley but not too sharply to accommodate the beds of succulent chives for which the district is renowned.

We had heard that Paramin was one of the few villages in Trinidad remaining unspoilt and that we should still find there remnants of the charm and character which were so fascinating a feature of the old folks' stories. We had heard, in fact, that in Paramin we should hear very little English and even that little would carry the old time accent of the French patois which was the mother tongue of the village. But if we wanted to catch some of this old flavour we should have to hurry for no one knew how much time was left to the old customs and manners before they were taken over by galloping progress. And so, four of us set out one Sunday morning just before the rainy season began, when the pouis were still in flower, to make an expedition to the heights of Paramin.

When we arrived at the foot of the hill mass had just ended and the villagers were coming out of the church and beginning to make their way back to their houses up the hill. Girls and boys, shy and eager, stared at us and returned our hellos with radiant smiles. Father greeted us from the door of the church when we parked the car. Port of Spain was barely twenty minutes away but already we were in another world of bare feet, rustic courtesy and modest manners, a far, far cry from the strident brashness of Woodbrook and St James.

We set off up the hill along the path under the cocoa and the shading mango. Over to the right the tree-filled valley stretched to the main road to Maracas and the hills which framed the landscape were tinted with a soft blue mist. A mango scent mingled with the perfume of over-ripe cocoa. Every few yards a gap in the growth offered a glimpse of a garden path sloping down the hillside in rows of chives and thyme. From time to time we came upon a clearing with a row of cottages with slanting roofs and tiny outhouses and, on either side of each set of front steps, a flaming ixora bush or a scatter of periwinkles to affirm the difference between a front garden and a back one. A few fowls scrabbled and clucked at the sides of the houses. We met young men and women coming down the hill on their way to the standpipe and they greeted us so pleasantly that I remembered how an old woman I met one morning as I walked up one of the Bathsheba hills told me that nothing pleased her more than to see strangers enjoying her little village. 'I does feel too nice,' she said, which was more eloquent and certainly more refined a welcome than the screaming banners and posters of the tourist agencies.

It began to rain, drip-drip on the leaves overhead, when we had walked for about half an hour. At first the fall was too light to pay any attention to it, no more than a staccato accompaniment to the scuffling sound of our feet among the dead leaves, and we went merrily along trying to think what life must have been like when cocoa was king. One of us wondered how long it would be before we reached the end of the track and won a view of the sea from the top of the hill near Saut d'Eau. The track wound through the cocoa, the Sunday sun came through the thick canopy of foliage and dappled the ground at our feet, all sweetness and filtered light. Then, all of a sudden, in a cloudburst of decision, the rain came down bucket a drop. The sight of a house standing by itself near the edge of the path made us decide that we were getting too wet for comfort and that the slight overhang of its roof would be a convenient shelter.

We lined ourselves off under the eaves, instinctively muting our voices so as not to draw attention to our presence. One of us had been provident enough to pack a flask of Mount Gay in his satchel and he passed it around to forestall any possible chill. As we drank, a woman called out to us to come in out of the rain. The sweetness of the patois in the voice made the invitation irresistible and we went inside the house and were given chairs in a bare room in which a table with cups and plates under a coloured oilcloth and a tall wooden cupboard were the only other pieces of furniture and a print of the Sacred Heart the only decoration on the walls. The woman's skin was the colour of copper but from under a bright head-tie her hair escaped in springy coils of grey. Her tired face brightened as she wished us good morning and reassured us that it was only a passing shower and then she went to the window which looked out on the back yard and began to help a young man, who had his back to us and who hadn't even looked around when we entered the house, wash some dishes.

The young man was of indeterminate age. He had an oversized head which, seen from the back, had a grotesque look. He washed some tin cups and a saucepan blackened with soot and turned them down to drain on a ledge in the window. A young girl, on the brink of nubility, passed through the room, smiled shyly and went out through the back door. We could hear her voice talking to the young man from outside. The woman whispered something to the young man after he had finished washing the cups and he poured some clean water from a bucket into the saucepan. I took the woman to be his mother from the way she let her eyes rest on him. When he turned to face us, with his large head he had that gentle innocent calf look which retarded children frequently have. The woman went to the wooden cupboard and took out four coffee cups and saucers decorated with a blue floral pattern and put them on the table. When the water in the saucepan began to boil she said, 'How do the gentlemen like coffee, black?' The patois accent sang in her voice.

While the woman was making the coffee one of us asked her whether many people went walking up the hill but she did not catch the meaning of the question and said that we were the first she had seen that morning. No one bothered to pursue the academic question because the coffee was ready and each of us murmured thanks as the woman handed him a demi-tasse. The flask of Mount Gay passed around again and we strengthened our cups.

We drank the strong black coffee very cosily with the rain drumming on the roof but no sooner had we finished than the rain stopped. The young man grinned at us at last when he took our cups from us. We shook hands with the woman and said goodbye. She wished us well and told us to go safely.

I cannot remember any details of the rest of that Sunday morning's events except that we walked over damp leaves and that occasionally a water droplet, suspended on the tip of a cocoa or mango leaf or on the frond of a heliconia, caught the sunlight and sparkled like a jewel. I can summon up no recollection of how far up the hill we reached, whether we persevered to the top or whether we ever set eyes on the sea on the other side of the hill. The journey back down to the village centre where we had left the car has left not the faintest mark on my mind. But I have not been able these many years to put away the memory of the most aristocratic, most graceful gesture of hospitality I have known. It was the very essence of hospitality, unobtrusive, expressed not in insistent invitation but in the gentlest confidence that we would have a cup of coffee with our host. The superb style of the gesture was prompted by the simple instinctive assumption that as guests we were bound by the same primitive convention that bound her who was our host and that though the group of us might never collide again, for a few moments we had been caught in a context of mutual awareness, the same web of time, the bonds of a common humanity.

I cannot help thinking that Clem's welcome and the hospitality of the nameless woman of Paramin belong to the same family of behaviour and are, both of them, vivid articulations of the spirit which defined the city and provided me with a distinct clue to its personality.

The first meeting with Clem left a haunting impression. It was clear that I could not be content with that single visit and I was certainly not prepared to wait for Cecil to take me round again. The more I thought about the house and the collection and the man, the less credible their existence became. The whole experience of that first visit, the Debussy in the dim light, the pinging of the wine glass, the hoarse chuckle and the pervasive smell of old furniture and books seemed like a dream. I could have been persuaded that it had never happened. But I spoke to no one and prepared to find Clem again by myself.

One Saturday morning with the taxi drivers crying for fares and the whole length of Marine Square crowded with shoppers and con-men and limers, I made my way past the Cathedral of the Immaculate Conception in an attempt to find Clem's house, not from South Quay but from the Piccadilly Street—Old St Joseph Road side. I had some odd idea that the house would be more easily spotted from the back. The bustle thinned out quickly beyond the statue of Columbus in Tamarind Square and the small neighbourhood shops and parlours became more ramshackle but more intimate the further east I went. I asked a woman with her grandchild in her arms if she knew where Clem Philips lived, explaining that I would know the house if I saw it.

'Clem Philips? Clem Philips? A old man? He was a postman?'

I couldn't tell her. I didn't know. I could only describe an old man with a bald pate, very few teeth and a passion for classical music. I told her that he had a lot of records.

'Oh, I know who you mean. You have to go round the other side.' That was how I found that there was only one entry to Clem's street—a cul-de-sac.

I knocked and knocked and shouted but no one was at home. The houses in the narrow street were very much alike and I marked Clem's by the jacaranda bush in the tiny front garden and a slanting coconut tree in the back garden whose top branches were visible over the roof, the only features to distinguish it from the other grey-painted houses which made an enclave of the area.

Eventually, I did find Clem at home one evening and he greeted me as if we were old friends with a casualness and absence of surprise that was very touching. I said that I was sorry that I was calling without warning and he laughed at my formal manners.

'You don't have to give me any warning except to save yourself the trouble of coming and not finding me here. Warning? Fie upon you!' He put me in my place and at ease at the same time. He explained that he went out every day (I got the impression that it was to a son in Belmont) for his meal and in the afternoon he collected food for his ducks but I should normally find him at home in the evening and I was welcome whenever I felt like dropping in. I did not let him know that I had made a couple of attempts to see him since my first visit.

In the years that followed I visited Clem regularly and came to know him well. I took a few of my friends to meet him but I was always careful whom I introduced to the house and the ambience because the better I came to know him the more clearly I saw how easy it was for people to misread him and once or twice I was embarrassed by the condescending manner which someone considered appropriate. And yet, although, as I say, I knew him well, it was remarkable how little I knew of him. Knowing him and being his friend did not at all depend on any familiarity with the circumstances of his life. I went abroad from time to time for longish periods: I would write him, send him a card and when I returned to Port of Spain would tell him what I had seen and enjoyed. And he would tell me what he had done, what new piece he had acquired. But he said very little about himself. The details of his life which he chose to share with me were enough, he judged cannily, to satisfy the claims of the particular relationship which he had decided was warranted and that judgement remains one of the most astute and perceptive insights into the nature of friendship that I know. Enough is enough. He understood through his instinct and his experience, for he had little formal schooling, that there is an area of mutual interest, affection and concern which is available for exploration but beyond which lies a dominion where trespassing is forbidden and whose privacy must be kept inviolable.

Not that he was secretive. Not by any means. What I learned of him I had from his own lips. But I learned from him too that the most certain way to be misinformed is to seek information by direct question. Ask no question, he said, hear no lies, put down no molasses, catch no flies.

We sat in the dark listening to music and Clem told me how he came to start collecting classical records. One of the department stores on Frederick Street was going out of business and offered a sale of a large stock of records, mainly of classical music on the old seventy-eights. They were virtually giving them away at twelve cents each and he, a poor postman, was attracted. He bought one of the old orn gramophones at a sale for next to nothing and began week by week, one at a time, to acquire what was to become his passion. Imagine, he said, a record a week, twelve cents a week, and yet there were some weeks when he couldn't afford to buy. But old Mr Whoever was indulgent and would save his choices for him. In any case, how many people were interested in classical music? He had some of the best: Roland Hayes, the young Robeson, Caruso, some early jazz—*Ain't She Sweet?*, *Mean to Me*. People thought he was mad, a postman buying records. They couldn't understand. But, you know, he said, it's funny, they would have understood, if he was buying rum. The joke of it amused him. And when the electric players came, he went straight up to Mr So and So and told him, as man to man, 'Look, I must have something decent to play my records on and I don't have any money.' Mr So and So was flabbergasted at the cheekiness of it. 'No, Clem,' he said. 'You won't be able to afford one of these.' Clem said, 'Try me and see.' And just by being bold-faced he got what he wanted. 'And I paid for it too, every cent. That's a good one, eh? But I have a better one for you. Your humble servant don't know a note of music. If you put a sheet of music before him as big as the Red House, he wouldn't be able to tell one note from another. He couldn't make a note. That's a joke for you eh, eh?' And he collapsed into huckle of laughter at his disability that left him weak.

But he loved music. 'I have heard every single visiting artist since I was eighteen. Marian Anderson had water coming from my eye. Bruce Wendell, Odnoposoff, Robeson, I went to hear him three times, and have his autograph too. I can't complain, I have heard the best of them and those I haven't heard in person, I have heard on records. You can't beat that. Music, man, the language of the gods.'

And another time: 'Listen, man what I want with money? Money to do what with? Die and leave for somebody else to spend? Not me. You see that set of candlesticks? It was in a sale in St Clair and I say I want it. I went before the sale started to the auctioneer and I say, "Look, I am interested in those candlesticks." He ask me, "Clem, what you going to do with them old things?" He knew me well, I could have told him anything. I say, "That's none of your blasted business. I want them and I must have them." This time the things old and looking dirty too bad and the old stupid man saying, "Clem, what you want with candlesticks and they have so much electric light all over the place?" The bidding start low, low, a few dollars. I didn't open my mouth. When it reached twenty dollars, hear Clem! I shout, "Thirty" and I had them bouleverse. People looking around to see who the madman was. Before you could say Jack Robinson the auctioneer say, "Going, going, gone," and I have my candlesticks. Easy so. And you know something? Who tell you that one of them white people didn't come running behind me asking if I would take a hundred dollars for the set? I tell her, "No, thank you, lady!" and I come home.

'And you see all them books inside there? I bought them at sales too, some at six cents, some at four cents, with lagniappe too, you know. Believe that. Oscar Wilde, Thackeray, Sir Walter Scott, James Boswell, all them giants for a bob!'

In his bedroom, all round the high four poster with its old style tester, piles of books reached nearly to the ceiling, copies of the Koran, scholarly Hebrew volumes, the Kama Sutra, medical encyclopedias, whatever came in the rag bag of jumble and auction. He entertained me in this room one evening when he was feeling ill with the 'flu and looking more gnome-like and mischievous than ever in his pyjamas among the bedclothes. He made me search in the bottom drawer of a high chest of drawers until I found a bottle of rum and there was a monkey of water in the kitchen. We passed the time very companionably and it was that evening that he told me about the ducks.

The subject came up when I asked him who was looking after him. His reply was that he didn't need anyone to look after him, but that his ducks were a bother. Had been for a long time. He kept a flock of ducks in his yard and every evening, by arrangement, he went to a Chinese restaurant near Park Street to collect the scraps which the Chinaman allowed him from the kitchen for their food. I could not be sure, and I never asked, but it was possible that the arrangement involved the supply of ducks to the restaurant. However, there was some kind of falling out and Clem was determined to put an end to the arrangement. He wasn't going to sell the ducks, eighty-four of them. He had a more direct solution, absolutely elegant in its simplicity. He was going to eat them.

'But they are eighty-four ducks, Clem. You can't eat eighty-four ducks.' I said that I thought that was going a trifle far.

'Not one time,' he said. 'But a duck a day, curried duck, duck soup, roast duck, duck in all ways. A duck a day till all gone.'

It was beautifully simple. It was impossible not to admire Clem.

I never knew, never bothered to try to know whether Clem had ever married or what his marital state was. Whatever it may have been it was quite irrelevant to our friendship. He used once in a way to mention 'the boy' but this was not often nor obsessive and when he did it was to say, without any undertone of regret, that the boy was not much interested in any of the things he had collected. It seemed a pity, I said once, that something so lovingly and patiently created, should be destroyed. But he would have none of that talk. He said that he had had his pleasure, the collection was his and any meaning it had came from the fact that he had made it and it was his creation. When he was gone, its relevance and its value would, by definition, come to end. He spoke without reproach or self-pity. It was impossible not to admire him.

But, so long as he was alive, he guarded his collection with jealous care. One of the first things he told me was that he was not a lender.

'You can come here as often as you like and listen and look as long as you like but don't ask me to lend you anything.' He told me what happened when he was persuaded against all his principles to lend—his only recording of Handel's *Harmonious Blacksmith*, one of the old seventy-eights in perfect condition.

The man whose name he mentioned was a well known Port of Spain figure busy on committees, picture always in the newspapers, a culture vulture. He was organizing some kind of soirée, Clem said, for which, for some reason, the Handel suite was essential. The man had asked all over the town and no one could help him with a recording of the music. Inevitably, he finally arrived at Clem's front door. Clem, of course, said quite bluntly that he never lent any of his records and he had no intention of doing so on this occasion. Days of pleading followed. The man was not only importunate himself but he induced his friends to intercede on his behalf. 'Man, he all but cried,' Clem said. 'And he got his friends to cry too, until I was the most selfish person in the world because I wouldn't lend him my record.'

In the end, Clem weakened and the man took the record, promising to guard it with the equivalent of his life and return it promptly. Clem came as close to tears as he ever did in my presence when he told the story, for he never saw the record again.

'Can you believe, John, what that man had the face to tell me when I rang him, I rang him, to ask for my record? Guess!'

'That man said that he had the record on a chair and one of the children sat on it. I could have killed him, I tell you. I could have killed him easy, easy so.'

It was a feeling with which most people would have had an instant sympathy. I believe that for Clem Port of Spain was the world. In his back yard he grew a few anthuriums and some roses. He once kept pigeons, he told me. In his house he had music to fill all his days. He had a few, not many, faithful friends and all those he met remembered him and were fond of him. He did not want a great deal. I asked him once why he had never wanted to travel. Did he ever have the opportunity? Yes, he had, but he was never fussy about it. For why does a man travel? He asked the question and answered it himself. To taste the food and the women of another country. 'And I have had my belly full of both right here in Port of Spain.'

When I heard that Clem had died I tried to remember the last time I had seen him. It was latish one evening just before Carnival. I was visiting Port of Spain for a few days and dropped in on him unannounced with a friend. He was delighted to see me—he hadn't seen me for years—he gave us a drink of Dubonnet and offered some music. His sight was going and as he put the Chopin on the player I remembered how he had impressed me several years before, the first time I had met him, with the uncanny accuracy of his fingers' selection of the Debussy record. I remembered that it had crossed my mind then that if blindness came, it would be no handicap for he didn't need eyes to see what he loved. It was as if even then he was preparing himself to deal with what would otherwise have been a calamity.

There can never have been anyone whom it was more pleasure to visit, for no one I have known was ever so pleased to see his friends. He chuckled, he showed off, he offered his wine, his music, the whole fabric of his life for your enjoyment. To say that his friends are the richer for having known him is, for once, an absolute truth.

As we were about to say goodbye to him that last time, he remembered to ask my friend to sign the book. When he brought it, for some unaccountable reason, I could not remember whether I had myself signed it or whether I merely thought I had done so. But I had. There, on the appropriate page, was my autograph—a confirmation which amused Clem to his happiest chuckles.

From *BIM*, Vol. 16, No. 16, pp. 18–33.

JOHN WICKHAM   *Born in Barbados in 1923. Now editor of* BIM, *the remarkable Barbados and West Indian journal, so long edited by Frank Collymore. Wickham worked in Trinidad, France, England and Switzerland; a close observer of the social and political scene. He also worked for some time at the World Meteorological Organization in Geneva.*

[3, 8, 15, 17, 23]

V. S. NAIPAUL

Three beggars called punctually every day at the hospitable houses in Miguel Street. At about ten an Indian came in his dhoti and white jacket, and we poured a tin of rice into the sack he carried on his back. At twelve an old woman smoking a clay pipe came and she got a cent. At two a blind man led by a boy called for his penny.
Sometimes we had a rogue. One day a man called and said he was hungry. We gave him a meal. He asked for a cigarette and wouldn't go until we had lit it for him. That man never came again.
The strangest caller came one afternoon at about four o'clock. I had come back from school and was in my home-clothes. The man said to me, 'Sonny, may I come inside your yard?'
He was a small man and he was tidily dressed. He wore a hat, a white shirt and black trousers.
I asked, 'What you want?'
He said, 'I want to watch your bees.'
We had four small gru-gru palm trees and they were full of uninvited bees.
I ran up the steps and shouted, 'Ma, it have a man outside here. He say he want to watch the bees.'
My mother came out, looked at the man and asked in an unfriendly way, 'What you want?'
The man said, 'I want to watch your bees.'
His English was so good, it didn't sound natural, and I could see my mother was worried.
She said to me, 'Stay here and watch him while he watch the bees.'
The man said, 'Thank you, madam. You have done a good deed today.'
He spoke very slowly and very correctly as though every word was costing him money.
We watched the bees, this man and I, for about an hour, squatting near the palm trees.
The man said, 'I like watching bees. Sonny, do you like watching bees?'
I said, 'I ain't have the time.'
He shook his head sadly. He said, 'That's what I do, I just watch. I can watch ants for days. Have you ever watched ants? And scorpions, and centipedes, and *congorees*—have you watched those?'
I shook my head.
I said, 'What you does do, mister?'
He got up and said, 'I am a poet.'
I said, 'A good poet?'
He said, 'The greatest in the world.'
'What your name, mister?'
'B. Wordsworth.'
'B for Bill?'
'Black. Black Wordsworth. White Wordsworth was my brother. We share one heart. I can watch a small flower like the morning glory and cry.'

I said, 'Why you does cry?'

'Why, boy? Why? You will know when you grow up. You're a poet, too, you know. And when you're a poet you can cry for everything.'

I couldn't laugh.

He said, 'You like your mother?'

'When she not beating me.'

He pulled out a printed sheet from his hip-pocket and said, 'On this paper is the greatest poem about mothers and I'm going to sell it to you at a bargain price. For four cents.'

I went inside and I said, 'Ma, you want to buy a poetry for four cents?'

My mother said, 'Tell that blasted man to haul his tail away from my yard, you hear.'

I said to B. Wordsworth, 'My mother say she ain't have four cents.'

B. Wordsworth said, 'It is the poet's tragedy.'

And he put the paper back in his pocket. He didn't seem to mind.

I said, 'Is a funny way to go round selling poetry like that. Only calypsonians do that sort of thing. A lot of people does buy?'

He said, 'No one has yet bought a single copy.'

'But why you does keep on going round, then?'

He said, 'In this way I watch many things, and I always hope to meet poets.'

I said, 'You really think I is a poet?'

'You're as good as me,' he said.

And when B. Wordsworth left, I prayed I would see him again.

About a week later, coming back from school one afternoon, I met him at the corner of Miguel Street.

He said, 'I have been waiting for you for a long time.'

I said, 'You sell any poetry yet?'

He shook his head.

He said, 'In my yard I have the best mango tree in Port of Spain. And now the mangoes are ripe and red and very sweet and juicy. I have waited here for you to tell you this and to invite you to come and eat some of my mangoes.'

He lived in Alberto Street in a one-roomed hut placed right in the centre of the lot. The yard seemed all green. There was the big mango tree. There was a coconut tree and there was a plum tree. The place looked wild, as though it wasn't in the city at all. You couldn't see all the big concrete houses in the street.

He was right. The mangoes were sweet and juicy. I ate about six, and the yellow mango juice ran down my arms to my elbows and down my mouth to my chin and my shirt was stained.

My mother said when I got home, 'Where was you? You think you is a man now and could go all over the place? Go cut a whip for me.'

She beat me rather badly, and I ran out of the house swearing that I would never come back. I went to B. Wordsworth's house. I was so angry, my nose was bleeding.

B. Wordsworth said, 'Stop crying, and we will go for a walk.'

I stopped crying, but I was breathing short. We went for a walk. We walked down St Clair Avenue to the Savannah and we walked to the race-course.

B. Wordsworth said, 'Now, let us lie on the grass and look up at the sky, and I want you to think how far those stars are from us.'

I did as he told me, and I saw what he meant. I felt like nothing, and at the same time I had never felt so big and great in all my life. I forgot all my anger and all my tears and all the blows.

When I said I was better, he began telling me the names of the stars, and I particularly remembered the constellation of Orion the Hunter, though I don't really know why. I can spot Orion even today, but I have forgotten the rest.

Then a light was flashed into our faces, and we saw a policeman. We got up from the grass.

The policeman said, 'What you doing here?'

B. Wordsworth said, 'I have been asking myself the same question for forty years.'

We became friends, B. Wordsworth and I. He told me, 'You must never tell anybody about me and about the mango tree and the coconut tree and the plum tree. You must keep that a secret. If you tell anybody, I will know, because I am a poet.'

I gave him my word and I kept it.

I liked his little room. It had no more furniture than George's front room, but it looked cleaner and healthier. But it also looked lonely.

One day I asked him, 'Mister Wordsworth, why you does keep all this bush in your yard? Ain't it does make the place damp?'

He said, 'Listen, and I will tell you a story. Once upon a time a boy and girl met each other and they fell in love. They loved each other so much they got married. They were both poets. He loved words. She loved grass and flowers and trees. They lived happily in a single room, and then one day, the girl poet said to the boy poet, "We are going to have another poet in the family." But this poet was never born, because the girl died, and the young poet died with her, inside her. And the girl's husband was very sad, and he said he would never touch a thing in the girl's garden. And so the garden remained, and grew high and wild.'

I looked at B. Wordsworth, and as he told me this lovely story, he seemed to grow older. I understood his story.

We went for long walks together. We went to the Botanical Gardens and the Rock Gardens. We climbed Chancellor Hill in the late afternoon and watched the darkness fall on Port of Spain, and watched the lights go on in the city and on the ships in the harbour.

He did everything as though he were doing it for the first time in his life. He did everything as though he were doing some church rite.

He would say to me, 'Now, how about having some ice-cream?'

And when I said yes, he would grow very serious and say, 'Now, which café shall we patronize?' As though it were a very important thing. He would think for some time about it, and finally say, 'I think I will go and negotiate the purchase with that shop.'

The world became a most exciting place.

One day, when I was in his yard, he said to me, 'I have a great secret which I am now going to tell you.'

I said, 'It really secret?'

'At the moment, yes.'

I looked at him, and he looked at me. He said, 'This is just between you and me, remember. I am writing a poem.'

'Oh.' I was disappointed.

He said, 'But this is a different sort of poem. This is the greatest poem in the world.'

I whistled.

He said, 'I have been working on it for more than five years now. I will finish it in about twenty-two years from now, that is, if I keep on writing at the present rate.'

'You does write a lot, then?'

He said, 'Not any more. I just write one line a month. But I make sure it is a good line.'

I asked, 'What was last month's good line?'

He looked up at the sky, and said, '*The past is deep.*'

I said, 'It is a beautiful line.'

B. Wordsworth said, 'I hope to distil the experiences of a whole month into that single line of poetry. So, in twenty-two years, I shall have written a poem that will sing to all humanity.'

I was filled with wonder.

Our walks continued. We walked along the sea-wall at Docksite one day, and I said, 'Mr Wordsworth, if I drop this pin in the water, you think it will float?'

He said, 'This is a strange world. Drop your pin, and let us see what will happen.'

The pin sank.

I said, 'How is the poem this month?'

But he never told me any other line. He merely said, 'Oh, it comes, you know. It comes.'

Or we would sit on the sea-wall and watch the liners come into the harbour.

But of the greatest poem in the world I heard no more.

I felt he was growing older.

'How you does live, Mr Wordsworth?' I asked him one day.

He said, 'You mean how I get money?'

When I nodded, he laughed in a crooked way.

He said, 'I sing calypsoes in the calypso season.'

'And that last you the rest of the year?'

'It is enough.'

'But you will be the richest man in the world when you write the greatest poem?'

He didn't reply.

One day when I went to see him in his little house, I found him lying on his little bed. He looked so old and so weak, that I found myself wanting to cry.

He said, 'The poem is not going well.'

He wasn't looking at me. He was looking through the window at the coconut tree, and he was speaking as though I wasn't there. He said, 'When I was twenty I felt the power within myself.' Then, almost in front of my eyes, I could see his face growing older and more tired. He said, 'But that—that was a long time ago.'

And then—I felt it so keenly, it was as though I had been slapped by my mother. I could see it clearly on his face. It was there for everyone to see. Death on the shrinking face.

He looked at me, and saw my tears and sat up.

He said, 'Come.' I went and sat on his knees.

He looked into my eyes, and he said, 'Oh, you can see it, too. I always knew you had the poet's eye.'
He didn't even look sad, and that made me burst out crying loudly.
He pulled me to his thin chest, and said, 'Do you want me to tell you a funny story?' and he smiled encouragingly at me.
But I couldn't reply.
He said, 'When I have finished this story, I want you to promise that you will go away and never come back to see me. Do you promise?'
I nodded.
He said, 'Good. Well, listen. That story I told you about the boy poet and the girl poet, do you remember that? That wasn't true. It was something I just made up. All this talk about poetry and the greatest poem in the world, that wasn't true, either. Isn't that the funniest thing you have heard?'
But his voice broke.
I left the house, and ran home crying, like a poet, for everything I saw.

I walked along Alberto Street a year later, but I could find no sign of the poet's house. It hadn't vanished, just like that. It had been pulled down, and a big, two-storeyed building had taken its place. The mango tree and the plum tree and the coconut tree had all been cut down, and there was brick and concrete everywhere. It was just as though B. Wordsworth had never existed.

From *Miguel Street,* pp. 56–65.

[8, 16, 17, 23]

23   *I Meet an English Gentleman*

CLAUDE McKAY

Meanwhile I continued writing poetry. I had started way back in elementary school and was very pleased when my brother used some of my acrostics for graduation exercises. One of my dearest friends had said that I was an infant Shakespeare but I hadn't taken that seriously. Thank God, I was never a child of vanity, even when I had a real literary success. I always used to say to myself, 'I wonder how long it will last?' However, poetry was my real love and I did want to get some critical opinions on the stuff that I had written.
Soon after my mother died, I met Mr Walter Jekyll again. He was a highly-educated Englishman who knew many languages. He was also an excellent judge of poetry, prose and painting. He had been living quietly in the island for some years.

I had first met him in Brown's Town where he had dropped in coming from Moneague where there is a hotel for English tourists. He was brought to the man I was apprenticed to, by one of his customers. He came in to get the spokes of a wheel on his carriage fixed. My boss, who also knew that I wrote poetry and knew that this man was a writer, made a remark, 'Here I have an apprentice who writes poetry.' Mr Jekyll was interested and asked me to let him see what I had written. I told him that they were all at home, but I could send them to him. He gave me his address in St Andrew and we started to correspond.

I can still remember the look on old 'Brenga', as we called my boss. He thought he was being funny, but Mr Jekyll was quite serious and thought it was so interesting to meet a Negro who was writing poetry.

In Jamaica the older peasants had a store of wonderful African stories which we called Annancy stories. This Englishman was very much interested in these stories and thought they formed the basis of the island's culture. He had collected some of them into a book which he published in London under the title of *Jamaica Song and Story*. He was still collecting when I met him.

We liked each other immediately. He was about fifty-odd years old, I was eighteen. He read my poetry one day. Then he laughed a lot, and I became angry at the laughing because I thought he was laughing at me. All these poems that I gave him to read had been done in straight English, but there was one short one about an ass that was laden for the market—laden with native vegetables—who had suddenly sat down in the middle of the road and wouldn't get up. Its owner was talking to it in the Jamaican dialect, telling it to get up. That was the poem that Mr Jekyll was laughing about. He then told me that he did not like my poems in straight English—they were repetitious. 'But this,' said he, holding up the donkey poem, 'this is the real thing. The Jamaican dialect has never been put into literary form except in my Annancy stories. Now is your chance as a native boy to put the Jamaica dialect into literary language. I am sure that your poems will sell.'

I was not very enthusiastic about this statement, because to us who were getting an education in the English schools the Jamaican dialect was considered a vulgar tongue. It was the language of the peasants. All cultivated people spoke English, straight English.

However, later on I began thinking seriously of what Mr Jekyll had proposed and as I knew so many pieces in the dialect which were based on our local songs of the draymen, the sugar mills, and the farm land, I decided to do some poems in dialect. They were so much easier to write than poems in straight English. While I was doing these poems, Mr Jekyll often invited me to visit him, but he lived far away on the other side of the island, up in the Blue Mountains.

Once I did visit him and was enchanted with his cottage, the wild tropical flowers that grew around it and the simple way in which he lived. When I returned home I was soon haunted by the idea of going to Kingston again because it was near to where Mr Jekyll lived in the Blue Mountains.

One day I packed my few things in a battered old suitcase and went off to Kingston. This time I had no special objectives there and I didn't want to tell Mr Jekyll that I had run away from home to be near him.

In Kingston I made some new friends who were quite different from the types of people I had known before. They were chiefly waiters in the big hotels and cabarets and lived very fast lives.

When I had gone through all my money, I went to work in a match factory, but the hours were long and there was no fun in it. One night I met a new friend who had been kept a long time by the most beautiful prostitute in the city. Now he was fed up, too, and wanted to get away from it all. We both decided to go to Spanish Town and join the Jamaica Constabulary. When we got there we found we were a little too short, but the officials in the office liked us and passed us through.

I continued to write my poems for I was happy with my new friend. Almost every week-end, now, I went up to the Blue Mountains to visit Mr Jekyll. It was a new life. He knew so much more about books than my brother and seeing that I had possessed a keen mind, he desired to educate me.

Now to be educated by Mr Jekyll we had to be together often, but I did not know how to approach any of the officials on such a delicate subject. Then, one morning, when the lieutenant-colonel, who was the head of the Constabulary was there and we fellows were out on the commons drilling, we suddenly noticed a strange little white man at the big gate. I must say strange because Mr Jekyll never dressed up. He either wore white ducks or brown crash and they were loosely fitted. He always said that he did not leave the terror of dressing up in England to come to a tropical island like Jamaica to repeat the performance. One of the strangest things I remember about his attire was that he used to wear gaiters over his brown shoes.

Well, Mr Jekyll demanded to see our lieutenant-colonel and soon he was ushered into the presence. We boys were terribly awed whenever the lieutenant-colonel visited the depot for he was the head of His Majesty's Constabulary. Under him there were two captains with whom we were familiar and a high-ranking sergeant-major.

The amazement of my comrades was even greater when the news got around that the strangely dressed little white man had come to see the lieutenant-colonel about me, for I had kept a very close mouth about the relationship between Mr Jekyll and myself. When I had gone up to Kingston for the week-end, the boys always thought that I had gone to see friends or girls. I never told them of my trips up to the Blue Mountains. Now the cat was out of the bag because Mr Jekyll was a very blunt Englishman and one couldn't imagine him hedging around. Now the men and officers were aware that I was a poet. They all wanted to see my stuff. They also wanted me to read for them which I did; but it was all very embarrassing. I had to do my regular work like any man in the depot. Now there was, added to that, the extra business of being a little personage.

Meantime I continued writing poems in the dialect. My association with my comrades seemed to help inspire the writing. Sometimes in the evening as I walked with some companions along the banks of the Rio Cobre, a new poem would pop into my head. Poems seemed to flow from my heart, my head and my hands. I just could not restrain myself from writing. When I sent them on to Mr Jekyll, he wrote back to say that each new one was more beautiful than the last. Beauty! A short while before I never thought that any beauty could be found in the Jamaican dialect. Now this Englishman had discovered beauty and I too could see where my poems were beautiful. Also my comrades and sometimes the peasants going to market, to whom I would read some of them, liked them. They used to exclaim, 'Why they're just like that, they're so natural.' Then I felt that I was fully rewarded for my efforts.

Mr Jekyll lived very quietly and simply up there in the hills. At first when he arrived in Jamaica, he had built a large house. Later on he gave it away to some of his trusted servants and was now living in a rented cottage. His cottage consisted of two bedrooms, a dining room which also served as a sitting room, a library, and a little porch. It was in the library that I did most of my studying. Mr Jekyll knew about six different languages. When he asked me which I wanted to learn first, I said, 'French.' So he took down a book of French prose and started to read it and told me that I should read it with him. I was astonished because I thought that I should start in with grammar first. But he said, no, that was the way he had learned and he thought that was the best way for me to learn.

He was also a free thinker and had translated some books of Schopenhauer. He then started me to reading German philosophy—Schopenhauer, Kant, Neitzsche, and Hegel. Besides these he had translated some poems from Goethe, Schiller and Heine. I have never forgotten the famous lines from Goethe:

Who never ate his bread in sorrow,
Who never spent the midnight hours
Watching and waiting for the morrow,
He knows you not, ye unseen powers.

I loved German poetry. Mr Jekyll always read the German, deep and sonorous before he translated it into English for me.

Later we read some of the English philosophers such as Berkeley, Hume and Herbert Spencer whom I especially liked because he was so in tune with the British Empire at that time. Of course, Mr Jekyll hated the British Empire but he used to say, 'What is there to take its place, Claude? The Germans are still too young and arrogant; they will never do.'

He was disillusioned with British liberalism, yet he did not believe in socialism or any of the radical parties of the day. He always said to me that the British upper class would know how to handle radicals and that Lloyd George who was the famous liberal radical then, would finish up as a lord. Mr Jekyll was also something of a Buddhist and did not think that the world could be reformed. He used to say that the politicians fool the people all the time, until the end of time. He was a member of the English upper class and knew that class thoroughly.

His best friend in London was the private secretary of King Edward VII. His eldest brother was a governor in India and many of his other relatives were members of the British Government and closely associated with the great banks in England. He, however, had chosen to give up all of this and come out to Jamaica to live like a peasant except for his books.

In spite of his gentleness and otherworldliness, he possessed a curious kind of class pride. In fact he was strangely proud of his class. I remember one week-end when I went up to visit him, I met our Governor, Lord Olivier, there. Of course, in my eyes, the Governor was the biggest man in the island, for he was the appointed representative of the King. We had dinner together; it was very simple. Then in the course of the after-dinner conversation, to which I listened but hardly spoke a word, Lord Olivier suggested that he would like to stay at Mr Jekyll's for the night. Lord Olivier was a very handsome man, tall and always well-dressed. He was supposed to be the handsomest of the British governors. Evidently he relished the simplicity of Mr Jekyll's surroundings and wanted to stay for a night instead of returning to King's House (the Governor's residence), or perhaps staying in some hotel in the Blue Mountains with its large retinue of servants. But Mr Jekyll said to him quite sharply: 'There is no place for you to stay.' The Governor nodded towards me and said: 'But he stays here.' Mr Jekyll replied: 'But he is my special friend.'

Later, when the Governor had left, Mr Jekyll raved. I had never seen him in such a temper. Said he: 'That's English middle-class bad manners. No person of my class would ever say that to me. We just cannot stand them because they never know when to say the right thing.' So I said to him: 'But Mr Jekyll, how can you tolerate me? I am merely the son of a peasant.' 'Oh,' said he, 'English gentlemen have always liked their peasants, it's the ambitious middle class that we cannot tolerate.'

I guess that I was a little snobbish myself, because I admired Mr Jekyll for pulling the Governor down a step. The people of Jamaica were a curious lot—as if God had planted a lovely garden of humanity there. The greatest drawback in the island was its extreme poverty. Otherwise the different races of people lived very happily together.

The Negroes, that is the blacks and dark browns, were about ninety per cent of the population. Next to them we had the landed mulattoes, that is the light browns. They were the middle class of the island, possessing most of its wealth.

Then we had the English officials and Scotch, Irish and our missionaries who were mostly English, Scotch and Irish.

We also had the Jews, who owned large stores in Kingston, but there was never any feeling against them. I never heard the word 'Christ-killer' until I came to America. Later I learned from an English friend that they were Sephardic Jews who had come to the island from Spain and Portugal during the Inquisition. He told me that they were a different type of Jew from the Ashkenazi Jews who came from Russia and Germany. To the people of the island they were very romantic and we all spoke of them as the 'chosen people of God'. They were very beautiful with their black hair and extremely white skin—something like what we usually imagine the Spanish people look like. They participated in the life of the island exactly as the other whites did.

Then we also had Chinese and Indians, Hindus and Mohammedans, who married our native women and had beautiful children. As I have said, the people of Jamaica were like an exotic garden planted by God.

From *My Green Hills of Jamaica*, pp. 65–72.

CLAUDE McKAY   *Born in Jamaica in 1889, died in the USA in 1948 (buried at Queens, New York). Known mainly as a lyric poet writing out of Harlem, he was also a novelist of quality: Banjo; Banana Bottom, etc. Also a world traveller, as his letters show; visited and lived in the USSR; also lived in the South of France and, for many years, in the USA. Despite his nostalgic poems about Jamaica he never did return to his native land, having once left it to attend a Negro College which he much disliked. Perhaps Wayne Cooper's* The Passion of Claude McKay: Selected Prose and Poetry 1912–1948 *(New York, Shocken Books, 1973), gives the best introduction to his work. Interesting from the point of Third World studies is Mervyn Morris' statement: 'Physically he never came home. But, psychologically, he was always ours, i.e. Jamaican.'*

[16, 17, 20, 21, 22, 114]

JOHN HEARNE

'Dis one is no boss fe' we, Dunnie,' Son-Son say. 'I don' like how him stay. Dis one is boss fe' messenger an' women in department office, but not fe' we.'

'Shut your mout',' I tell him. 'Since when a stupid, black nigger can like and don't like a boss in New Holland? What you goin' do? Retire an' live 'pon your estate?' But I know say that Son-Son is right.

The two of we talk so at the back of the line; Son-Son carrying the chain, me with the level on the tripod. The grass stay high, and the ground hard with sun. It is three mile to where the Catacuma run black past the *stelling*, and even the long light down the sky can't strike a shine from Catacuma water. You can smell Rooi Swamp, dark and sweet and wicked like a woman in a bad house back in Zuyder Town. Nothing live in Rooi Swamp except snake; like nothing live in a bad woman. In all South America there is no swamp like the Rooi; not even in Brazil; not even in Cayenne. The new boss, Mister Cockburn, walk far ahead with the little assistant man, Mister Bailey. Nobody count the assistant. Him only come down to the Catacuma to learn. John stay close behind them, near to the rifle. The other rest of the gang file out upon the trail between them three and me and Son-Son. Mister Cockburn is brand-new from head to foot. New hat, new bush-shirt, new denim pant, new boot. Him walk new.

'Mister Cockburn!' John call, quick and sharp. 'Look!'

I follow the point of John's finger and see the deer. It fat and promise tender and it turn on the hoof-tip like deer always do, with the four tip standing in a nickel and leaving enough bare to make a cent change, before the spring into high grass. Mister Cockburn unship the rifle, and *pow*, if was all cow then him shoot plenty grass for us to eat.

'Why him don't give John de rifle?' Son-Son say.

'Because de rifle is Government,' I tell him, 'and Mister Cockburn is Government. So it is him have a right to de rifle.'

Mister Cockburn turn and walk back. He is a tall, high mulatto man, young and full in body, with eyes not blue and not green, but coloured like the glass of a beer bottle. The big hat make him look like a soldier in the moving pictures.

'Blast this sun,' he say, loud, to John. 'I can't see a damn' thing in the glare; it's right in my eyes.'

The sun is falling down the sky behind us but maybe him think we can't see that too.

John don't answer but only nod once, and Mister Cockburn turn and walk on, and I know say that if I could see John's face it would be all Carib buck. Sometimes you can see where the Indian lap with it, but other times it is all Indian and closed like a prison gate; and I knew say, too, that it was this face Mister Cockburn did just see.

'Trouble dere, soon,' Son-Son say, and him chin point to John and then to Mister Cockburn. 'Why Mister Hamilton did have to get sick, eh, Dunnie? Dat was a boss to have.'

'Whatever trouble to happen is John's trouble,' I tell him. 'John's trouble and

Mister Cockburn's. Leave it. You is a poor naygur wid no schooling, five *pickney* and a sick woman. Dat is trouble enough for you.'

But in my heart I find agreement for what stupid Son-Son have to say. If I have only known what trouble. . . .

No. Life don't come so. It only come one day at a time. Like it had come every day since we lose Mister Hamilton and Mister Cockburn take we up to survey the Catacuma drainage area in Mister Hamilton's stead.

The first day we go on the savannah beyond the *stelling*, I know say that Mister Cockburn is frighten. Frighten, and hiding his frighten from himself. The worst kind of frighten. You hear frighten in him voice when he shout at we to keep the chain straight and plant the markers where him tell us. You see frighten when him try to work us, and himself, one hour after midday, when even the alligators hide in the water. And you understand frighten when him try to run the camp at the *stelling* as if we was soldier and him was a general. But all that is because he is new and it would pass but for John. Because of John everything remain bad. From the first day when John try to treat him as he treat Mister Hamilton.

You see, John and Mister Hamilton was like one thing except that Mister Hamilton have schooling and come from a big family in Zuyder Town. But they each suck from a Carib woman and from the first both their spirit take. When we have Mister Hamilton as boss whatever John say we do as if it was Mister Hamilton say it, and at night when Mister Hamilton lie off in the big Berbice chair on the veranda and him and John talk it sound like one mind with two tongue. That's how it sound to the rest of we when we sit down the steps and listen to them talk. Only when Mister Cockburn come back up the river with me, after Mister Hamilton take sick, we know say all that is change. For Mister Cockburn is frighten and must reduce John's pride, and from that day John don't touch the rifle and don't come to the veranda except to take orders and for Mister Cockburn to show that gang foreman is only gang foreman and that boss is always boss.

Son-Son say true, I think. Trouble is to come between John and Mister Cockburn. Poor John. Here, in the bush, him is a king, but in New Zuyder him is just another poor half-buck without a job and Mister Cockburn is boss and some he cast down and some he raiseth up.

Ahead of we, I see Mister Cockburn trying to step easy and smooth, as if we didn't just spend seven hours on the savannah. Him is trying hard but very often the new boot kick black dirt from the trail. That is all right I think. Him will learn. Him don't know say that even John hold respect for the sun on the Catacuma. The sun down here on the savannah is like the centurion in the Bible who say to one man, Come, and he cometh, and to another, Go, and he goeth. Like it say go, to Mister Hamilton. For it was a man sick bad we take down to the mouth of the river that day after he fall down on the wharf at the *stelling*. And it was nearly a dead man we drive up the coast road one hundred mile to Zuyder Town. We did want to stop in Hendrikstadt with him that night, but he think him was dying—we think so too—and him would not stop for fear he die away from his wife. And afterwards the Government doctor tell Survey that he must stay in the office forevermore and even Mister Hamilton who think him love the bush and the swamp and the forest more than life itself was grateful to the doctor for those words.

So it was it did happen with Mister Hamilton, and so it was Mister Cockburn come to we.

Three weeks we is on the Catacuma with Mister Cockburn, and every new day things stay worse than the last.

In the morning, when him come out with the rifle, him shout: 'Dunnie! Take the *corial* across the river and put up these bottles.' And he fling the empty rum and beer bottle down the slope to me and I get into the *corial* and paddle across the river, and put the necks over seven sticks on the other bank. Then him and the little assistant, Mister Bailey, stay on the veranda and fire across the river, each spelling each, until the bottle is all broken.

And John, down by the river, in the soft morning light, standing in the *corial* we have half-buried in the water, half-drawn upon the bank, washing himself all over careful like an Indian and not looking to the veranda.

'John!' Mister Cockburn shout, and laugh bad. 'Careful, eh, man. Mind a *perai* don't cut off your balls.'

We have to stand in the *corial* because *perai* is bad on the Catacuma and will take off your heel and your toe if you stand in the river six inches from the bank. We always joke each other about it, but not the way Mister Cockburn joke John. That man know what him is doing and it is not nice to hear.

John say nothing. Him stand in the still water catch of the *corial* we half-sink and wash him whole body like an Indian and wash him mouth out and listen to Mister Cockburn fire at the bottle across the river. Only we know how John need to hold that rifle. When it come to rifle and gun him is all Indian, no African in it at all. Rifle to him is like woman to we. Him don't really hold a rifle, him make love with it. And I think how things go in Mister Hamilton's time when him and John stand on the veranda in the morning and take seven shots break seven bottle, and out in the bush they feel shame if four shot fire and only three piece of game come back. Although, I don't talk truth, if I don't say how sometimes Mister Hamilton miss a shot on the bottle. When that happen you know him is thinking. He is a man think hard all the time. And the question he ask! 'Dunnie,' he asked, 'what do you see in your looking-glass?' or, 'Do you know, Dunnie, that this country has had its images broken on the wheels of false assumptions? Arrogance and servility. Twin criminals pleading for the mercy of an early death.' That is how Mister Hamilton talk late at night when him lie off in the big Berbice chair and share him mind with we.

After three weeks on the Catacuma, Mister Cockburn and most of we go down the river. Mister Cockburn to take him plans to the Department and the rest of we because nothing to do when him is gone. All the way down the river John don't say a word. Him sit in the boat bows and stare down the black water as if it is a book giving him secret to remember. Mister Cockburn is loud and happy, for him feel, we know say, now, who is boss and him begin to lose him frighten spirit. Him is better now the frighten gone and confidence begin to come.

'Remember, now,' him say in the Department yard at Zuyder Town. 'Eight o'clock sharp on Tuesday morning. If one of you is five minutes late, the truck leaves without you. Plenty of men between here and the Catacuma glad to get work.' We laugh and say, 'Sure, boss, sure,' because we know say that already him is not so new as him was and that him is only joking. Only John don't laugh but walk out of the yard and down the street.

Monday night, John come to my house; I is living in a little place between the coolie cinema and the dockyard.

'Dunnie,' he say, 'Dunnie, you have fifteen dollar?'

'Jesus,' I say, 'what you need fifteen dollar for, man? Dat is plenty, you know?'

'All right,' he say. 'You don't have it. I only ask.'

Him turn, as if it was the time him ask and I don't have no watch.

'Hold on, hold on,' I tell him. 'I never say I don't have fifteen dollar. I just say what you want it for?'

'Lend me. I don't have enough for what I want. As we pay off next month, you get it back. My word to God.'

I go into the house.

'Where de money?' I ask the woman.

'What you want it for?' she ask. 'You promise say we don't spend dat money until we marry and buy furnitures. What you want tek it now for?'

'Just tell me where it stay,' I tell her. 'Just tell me. Don't mek me have to find it, eh?'

'Thank you, Dunnie,' John say when I bring him the fifteen dollar. 'One day you will want something bad. Come to me then.'

And him gone up the street so quick you scarcely see him pass under the light.

The next morning, in the truck going down to the boat at the Catacuma mouth, we see what John did want fifteen dollar for.

'You have a licence for that?' Mister Cockburn ask him, hard and quick, when he see it.

'Yes,' John say, and stow the new Ivor-Johnson repeater with his gear up in the boat bows.

'All right,' Mister Cockburn say. 'I hope you do. I don't want any unlicensed guns on my camp.'

Him and John was never born to get on.

We reach the *stelling* late afternoon. The bungalow stand on the bluff above the big tent where we sleep and Zacchy, who we did leave to look to the camp, wait on the wharf waving to us.

When we passing the gear from the boat, John grab his bundle by the string and swing it up. The string break and shirt, pant and handkerchief fly out to float on the water. Them float but the new carton of .32 ammunition fall out too and we see it for a second, green in the black water as it slide to the bottom and the mud and the *perai*.

Mister Bailey, the little assistant, look sorry, John look sick, and Mister Cockburn laugh a little up in the back of him nose.

'Is that all you had?' him ask.

'Yes,' John say. 'I don't need no more than that for three weeks.'

'Too bad,' Mister Cockburn reply. 'Too bad. Rotten luck. I might be able to spare you a few from stores.'

Funny how a man who can stay decent with everybody always find one other who turn him bad.

Is another three weeks we stay up on the survey. We triangulate all the stretch between the Rooi Swamp and the first forest. Things is better this time. Mister Cockburn don't feel so rampageous to show what a hard boss him is. Everything is better except him and John. Whenever him and John speak, one voice is sharp and empty and the other voice is dead, and empty too. Every few days him give John two-three cartridge, and John go out and come back with two-three piece of game. A deer and a *labba*, maybe. Or a bush pig and an *agouti*. Whatever ammunition John get him bring back meat to match. And, you know, I think that rowel Mister Cockburn's spirit worse than anything else John do. Mister Cockburn is shooting good, too, and we is eating plenty meat, but him don't walk with the gun like John. Who could ever. Not even Mister Hamilton.

The last Saturday before we leave, John come to Mister Cockburn. It is afternoon and work done till Monday. Son-Son and me is getting the gears ready for a little cricket on the flat piece under the *kookorit* palms. The cricket gears keep in the big room with the other rest of stores and we hear every word John and Mister Cockburn say.

'No, John,' Mister Cockburn tell him. 'We don't need any meat. We're leaving Tuesday morning. We have more than enough now.'

Him voice sleepy and deep from the Berbice chair.

'Sell me a few rounds, Mister Cockburn,' John say. 'I will give you store price for a few rounds of .32.'

'They're not mine to sell,' Mister Cockburn say, and him is liking the whole business so damn' much his voice don't even hold malice as it always do for John. 'You know every round of ammunition here belongs to Survey. I have to indent and account for every shot fired.'

Him know, like we know, that Survey don't give a lime how much shot fire up in the bush so long as the men stay happy and get meat.

'You can't give three shot, Mister Cockburn?' John say. You know how bad John want to use the new repeater when you hear him beg.

'Sorry, John,' Mister Cockburn say. 'Have you checked the caulking on the boat? I don't want us shipping any water when we're going down on Tuesday.'

A little later all of we except John go out to play cricket. Mister Cockburn and Mister Bailey come too and each take captain of a side. We play till the parrots come talking across the river to the *kookorits* and the sky turn to green and fire out on the savannah. When we come back to the camp John is gone. Him take the *corial* and gone.

'That damn' buck,' Mister Cockburn say to Mister Bailey. 'Gone up the river to his cousin, I suppose. We won't see him until Monday morning now. You can take an Indian out of the bush, but God Almighty himself can't take the bush out of the Indian.'

Monday morning, we get up and John is there. Him is seated on the *stelling* and all you can see of him face is the teeth as him grin and the cheeks swell up and shiny with pleasure. Lay out on the *stelling* before him is seven piece of game. Three deer, a *labba* and three bush pig. None of we ever see John look so. Him tired till him thin and grey, but happy and proud till him can't speak.

'Seven,' him say at last and hold up him finger. 'Seven shots, Dunnie. That's all I take. One day and seven shot.'

Who can stay like an Indian with him game and no shot gone wide?

'What's this?' a voice call from up the veranda and we look and see Mister Cockburn in the soft, white-man pyjamas lean over to look at we on the *stelling*. 'Is that you, John? Where the devil have you been?'

'I make a little trip, Mister Cockburn,' John say. Him is so proud and feel so damn' sweet him like even Mister Cockburn. 'I make a little trip. I bring back something for you to take back to town. Come and make your choice, sir.'

Mister Cockburn is off the veranda before the eye can blink, and we hear the fine red slipper go slap-slap on the patch down the bluff. Him come to the wharf and stop short when him see the game. Then him look at John for a long time and turn away slow and make water over the *stelling* edge and come back, slow and steady.

'All right,' him say, and him voice soft and feel bad in your ears, like you did stumble in the dark and put your hand into something you would walk round. 'All right, John. Where did you get the ammunition? Who gave it you, eh?'

Him voice go up and break like a boy's voice when the first hairs begin to grow low down on him belly.

'Mister Cockburn,' John say, so crazy proud that even now him want to like the man and share pride with him. 'I did take the rounds, sir. From your room. Seven shot I take, Mister Cockburn, and look what I bring you back. Take that deer, sir, for yourself and your family. Town people never taste meat like that.'

'You son of a bitch,' Mister Cockburn reply. 'You damned impertinent, thieving son of a bitch. Bailey!' and him voice scream until Mister Bailey come out to the veranda. 'Bailey! Listen to this. We have a thief in the camp. This beauty here feels that the government owes him his ammunition. What else did you take?'

Him voice sound as if a rope tie round him throat.

'What else I take?' John look as if him try to kiss a woman and she slap him face. 'How I could take anything, Mister Cockburn? As if I am a thief. Seven little shot I take from the carton. You don't even remember how many rounds you did have left. How many you did have leave, eh? Tell me that.'

'Don't back chat me, you bloody thief!' Mister Cockburn yell. 'This is your last job with Survey, you hear me? I'm going to fire your arse as soon as we get to the river mouth. And don't think this game is yours to give away. You shot it with government ammunition. With *stolen* government ammunition. Here! Dunnie! Son-Son! Zacchy! Get that stuff up to the house. Zacchy gut them and hang 'em. I'll decide what to do with them later.'

John stay as still as if him was dead. Only when we gather up the game and a kid deer drop one splash of dark stomach blood onto the boards him draw one long breath and shiver.

'Now,' Mister Cockburn say, 'get to hell out of here! Up to the tent. You don't work for me any more. I'll take you down river on Tuesday and that's all. And if I find one dollar missing from my wallet I'm going to see you behind bars.'

It is that day I know say how nothing so bad before but corruption and rottenness come worse after. None of we could forget John's face when we pick up him game. For we Negro, and for the white man, and for the mulatto man, game is to eat sometimes, or it is play to shoot. But for the Indian, oh God, game that him kill true is life everlasting. It is manhood.

When we come back early in the afternoon, with work done, we don't see John. But the *corial* still there, and the engine boat, and we know that him not far. Little later, when Zacchy cook, I fill a billy pot and go out to the *kookorits*. I find him there, in the grass.

'John,' I say. 'Don't tek it so. Mister Cockburn young and foolish and don't mean harm. Eat, John. By the time we reach river mouth tomorrow everyt'ing will be well again. Do, John. Eat dis.'

John look at me and it is one black Indian Carib face stare like statue into mine. All of him still, except the hands that hold the new rifle and polish, polish, polish with a rag until the barrel shine blue like a Chinee whore hair.

I come back to the *stelling*. Mister Cockburn and Mister Bailey lie into two deckchair under the tarpaulin, enjoying the afternoon breeze off the river. Work done and they hold celebration with a bottle. The rest of the gang sit on the boards and drink too. Nothing sweeter than rum and river water.

'Mister Cockburn,' I tell him, 'I don't like how John stay. Him is hit hard, sah.'

'Oh, sit down, Dunnie,' him say. 'Have a drink. That damned buck needs a lesson. I'll take him back when we reach Zuyder Town. It won't do him any harm to miss two days' pay.'

So I sit, although I know say I shouldn't. I sit and I have one drink, and then two, and then one more. And the Catacuma run soft music round the piles of the *stelling*. All anybody can feel is that work done and we have one week in Zuyder Town before money need call we to the bush again.

Then as I go to the *stelling* edge to dip water in the mug I look up and see John. He is coming down from the house, gliding on the path like Jesus across the Sea of Galilee, and I say, 'Oh God, Mister Cockburn! Where you leave the ammunition, eh?'

But already it is too late to say that.

The first shot catch Mister Cockburn in the forehead and him drop back in the deck-chair, peaceful and easy, like a man call gently from sleep who only half wake. And I shout, 'Dive-oh, Mister Bailey!' and as I drop from the *stelling* into black Catacuma water, I feel something like a *marabunta* wasp sting between my legs and know say I must be the first thing John ever shoot to kill that him only wound.

I sink far down in that river and already, before it happen, I can feel *perai* chew at my fly button and tear off my cod, or alligator grab my leg to drag me to drowning. But God is good. When I come up the sun is still there and I strike out for the little island in the river opposite the *stelling*. The river is full of death that pass you by, but the *stelling* holds a walking death like the destruction of Apocalypse.

I make ground at the island and draw myself into the mud and the bush and blood draw after me from between my legs. And when I look back at the *stelling*, I see Mister Cockburn lie down in him deck-chair, as if fast asleep, and Mister Bailey lying on him face upon the boards, with him hands under him stomach, and Zacchy on him back with him arms flung wide like a baby, and three more of the gang, Will, Benjie and Sim, all sprawl off on the boards, too, and a man more, the one we call 'Venezuela', fallen into the grass, and a last one, Christopher, walking like a chicken without a head until him drop close to Mister Bailey and cry out once before death hold him. The other seven gone. Them vanish. All except Son-Son, poor foolish Son-Son, who make across the flat where we play cricket, under the *kookorits* and straight to Rooi Swamp.

'Oh Jesus, John!' him bawl as him run. 'Don't kill me, John! Don't kill me, John!'

And John standing on the path, with the repeater still as the finger of God in him hands, aim once at Son-Son, and I know say how, even at that distance, him could break Son-Son's back clean in the middle. But him lower the gun, and shrug and watch Son-Son into the long grass of the savannah and into the swamp. Then him come down the path and look at the eight dead men.

'Dunnie!' him call. 'I know you is over there. How you stay?'

I dig a grave for the living into the mud.

'Dunnie!' him call again. 'You hurt bad? Answer me, man, I see you, you know? Look!'

A bullet bury itself one inch from my face and mud smack into my eye.

'Don't shoot me, John,' I beg. 'I lend you fifteen dollar, remember?'

'I finish shooting, Dunnie,' him say. 'You hurt bad?'

'No,' I tell him the lie. 'I all right.'

'Good,' him say from the *stelling*. 'I will bring the *corial* come fetch you.'

'No, John!' I plead with him. 'Stay where you is. Stay there! You don't want to kill me now.' But I know say how demon guide a Carib hand sometimes and make that hand cut throats. 'Stay there, John!'

Him shrug again and squat beside Mister Cockburn's chair, and lift the fallen head and look at it and let the head fall again. And I wait. I wait and bleed and suffer, and think how plenty women will cry and plenty children bawl for them daddy when John's work is known in Zuyder Town. I think these things and watch John the way I would watch a bushmaster snake and bleed in suffering until dark fall. All night I lie there until God take pity and close my eye and mind.

When my mind come back to me, it is full day. John gone from the *stelling* and I can see him sit on the steps up at the house, watching the river. The dead stay same place where he drop them. Fever burn in me, but the leg stop bleed and I dip water from the river and drink.

The day turn above my head until I hear a boat engine on the far side of the bend, and in a little bit a police launch come up mid-stream and make for the *stelling*. When they draw near, one man step to the bows with a boat-hook, and then the rifle talk from the steps and the man yell, hold him wrist and drop to the deck. Him twist and wriggle behind the cabin quicker than a lizard. I hear an Englishman's voice yell in the cabin and the man at the wheel find reverse before the yell come back from the savannah. The boat go down-stream a little then nose into the overhang of the bank where John's rifle can't find them. I call out once and they come across to the island and take me off on the other side, away from the house. And is when I come on board that I see how police know so quick about what happen. For Son-Son, poor foolish old Son-Son, who I think still hide out in the swamp is there. Him have on clothes not him own, and him is scratched and torn as if him had try to wrestle a jaguar.

'Man,' the police sergeant tell me. 'You should have seen him when they did bring to us. Swamp tear off him clothes clean. Nearly tear off him skin.'

As is so I learn that Son-Son did run straight as a *peccary* pig, all night, twenty mile across Rooi Swamp where never any man had even put him foot before. Him did run until him drop down in the camp of a coolie rancher bringing cattle down to the coast, and they did take him from there down to the nearest police post. When him tell police the story, they put him in the jeep and drive like hell for the river mouth and the main station.

'Lord witness, Son-Son,' I say, 'you was born to hang. How you didn't meet death in Rooi Swamp, eh?'

Him just look frighten and tremble, and the sergeant laugh.

'Him didn't want to come up river with we,' he say. 'Superintendent nearly have to tie him before him would step on the boat.'

'Sergeant,' the Superintendent say. Him was the Englishman I hear call out when John wound the policeman. 'Sergeant, you take three men and move in on him from behind the house. Spread out well. I'll take the front approach with the rest. Keep low, you understand. Take your time.'

'Don't do it, Super,' I beg him. 'Look how John stay in that house up there. River behind him and clear view before. Him will see you as you move one step. Don't do it.'

Him look at me angry and the white eyebrow draw together in him red face.

'Do you think I'm going to leave him up there?' he say. 'He's killed eight and already tried to kill one of my men.'

Him is bad angry for the constable who sit on the bunk and holding him wrist in the red bandage.

'No, Super,' I tell him. 'John don't *try* to kill you. If him did try then you would have take one dead man out of the river. Him only want to show that him can sting.'

But what use a poor black man talk to police. The sergeant and him three stand on the cabin roof, hold onto the bank and drag themself over. Then the Super with him five do the same. I can hear them through the grass like snakes on them stomach. John let them come a little way to the house, and then, with him first shot, him knock the Super's black cap off, and with him second, him plug the sergeant in the shoulder. The police rifles talk back for a while, and Son-Son look at me.

When the police come back, I take care to say no word. The sergeant curse when the Super pour Dettol on the wound and beg the Super to let him go back and bring John down.

'We'll get him,' the Super say. 'He knows it. He knows he doesn't stand a chance.'

But him voice can't reach John to tell him that, and when them try again one man come back with him big toe flat and bloody in the police boot. When I go out, though, and walk along the bank to the *stelling* and lay out the bodies decent and cover them with canvas from the launch, it could have been an empty house up there on the bluff.

Another hour pass and the police begin to fret, and I know say that them is going to try once more. I want to tell them don't go, but them is police and police don't like hear other men talk.

And is then, as we wait, that we hear a next engine, an outboard, and round the bend come a Survey boat, and long before it draw up beside the overhang, my eye know Mister Hamilton as him sit straight and calm in the bows.

'Dunnie, you old fool,' him say and hold me by the shoulders. 'Why didn't you stop it? D'you mean to say you couldn't see it coming?'

Him smile to show me that the words is to hide sorrow. Him is the same Mister Hamilton. Dress off in the white shirt and white stocking him always wear, with the big linen handkerchief spread upon him head under the hat and hanging down the neck back to guard him from sun.

'I came as soon as I could,' him say to the Super. 'As soon as the police in Zuyder rang Survey and told us what you had 'phoned through.'

You can see the Super is glad to have one of him own sort to talk with. More glad, though, because it is Mister Hamilton and Mister Hamilton's spirit make all trouble seem less.

'We might have to bomb him out,' Super say. 'I've never seen a man to shoot like that. He must be a devil. Do you think he's sane, Hamilton?'

Mister Hamilton give a little smile that is not a smile.

'He's sane now,' he say. 'If he wasn't he'd have blown your head off.'

'What's he going to do?' Super ask.

Mister Hamilton lift him shoulder and shake him head. Then him go up to the cabin top and jump on the bank and walk to the *stelling*. Not a sign from the house.

I follow him and move the canvas from all the staring dead faces and him look and look and pass him hand, tired and slow, across him face.

'How did it go, Dunnie?' him ask.

I tell him.

'You couldn't have stopped him?'

'No,' I say. 'Him did have pride to restore. Who could have stopped that? You, maybe, Mister Hamilton. But I doubt me if even you.'

'All right,' him say. 'All right.'

Him turn and start to walk to the house.

'Come back, man,' Super shout from where him lie in the grass on the bank. Mister Hamilton just walk on regular and gentle.

John's first bullet open a white wound in the boards by Mister Hamilton's left foot. The next one do the same by the right. Him never look or pause; even him back, as I watch, don't stiffen. The third shot strike earth before him and kick dirt onto him shoe.

'John!' him call, and Mister Hamilton have a voice like a howler monkey when him want. 'John, if you make a ricochet and kill me, I'm going to come up there and break your ——ing neck.'

Then I know say how this Mister Hamilton is the same Mister Hamilton that left we.

Him walk on, easy and slow, up the path, up the steps, and into the house. I sit by the dead and wait.

Little bit pass and Mister Hamilton come back. Him is alone, with a basket in him hand. Him face still. Like the face of a mountain lake, back in the Interior, where you feel but can't see the current and the fullness of water below.

'Shirley,' him call to the Super, 'bring the launch up to the *stelling*. You'll be more comfortable here than where you are. It's quite safe. He won't shoot if you don't rush him.'

I look into the basket him bring down from the house. It full of well-cooked *labba*. Enough there to feed five times the men that begin to gather on the *stelling*.

The Super look into the basket also, and I see a great bewilderment come into his face.

'Good God!' him say. 'What's all this? What's he doing?'

'Dunnie,' Mister Hamilton say to me. 'There's a bottle of rum in my boat. And some bread and a packet of butter. Bring them over for me, will you? Go on,' him tell Super. 'Have some. John thought you might be getting hungry.'

Him draw up the deck-chair in which Mister Cockburn did die. I go to the Survey boat and fetch out the rum and the bread and the butter. The butter wrap into grease paper and sink in a closed billy pot of water to keep it from the sun. I bring knife, also, and a plate and a mug for Mister Hamilton, and a billyful of river water for put into the rum. When everything come, him cut bread and butter it and pour rum for Super and himself, and take a leg of *labba*. When him chew the food, him eat like John. The jaws of him mouth move sideways and not a crumb drop to waste. The rest of we watch him and Super, and then we cut into the *labba* too, and pour liquor from the bottle. The tarpaulin stretch above we and the tall day is beginning to die over the western savannah.

'Why did he do it?' Super say and look at the eight dead lay out under the canvas. 'I don't understand it, Hamilton. Christ! He *must* be mad.'

Him lean over beside Mister Hamilton and cut another piece of *labba* from the basket.

'What does he think he can do?' him ask again. 'If he doesn't come down I'm going to send down river for grenades. We'll have to get him out somehow.'

Mister Hamilton sit and eat and say nothing. Him signal to me and I pass him the bottle. Not much left into it, for we all take a drink. Mister Hamilton tilt out the last drop and I take the billy and go to the *stelling* edge and draw a little water for Mister Hamilton and bring it back. Him draw the drink and put the mug beside him. Then him step from under the tarpaulin and fling the empty bottle high over Catacuma water. And as the bottle turn and flash against the dying sun, I see it fall apart in the middle and broken glass falling like raindrops as John's bullet strike.

We all watch and wait, for now the whole world stand still and wait with me. Only the water make soft music round the *stelling*.

Then from up the house there is the sound of one shot. It come to us sudden and short and distant, as if something close it round.

'All right,' Mister Hamilton say to the Super. 'You better go and bring him down now.'

From *West Indian Stories*, pp. 51–68.

JOHN HEARNE   *Born in Montreal, Canada in 1926 of Jamaican parents. Educated in Jamaica and England, he knows the Caribbean well as his story* At the Stelling *shows. Novelist, teacher, journalist and academic, he is now in charge of the Creative Arts Centre, University of the West Indies, Mona, Jamaica. Recently he has been much involved in political journalism. He lives in Jamaica.*

[4, 14, 79, 98, 102, 104, 114]

25   *Bouki and Ti Malice Go Fishing*

HAROLD COURLANDER (ed.)

In the Ashanti version of this story, the antagonists are Anansi, the spider trickster, and Anene, the crow.

Anansi invited Anene to work with him at setting fish traps. Anene agreed. They went together to the bush to cut palm branches to make their fish traps. Arriving there, Anansi said, 'Give me the knife. I will cut the palm leaves and weave the traps. You, sit over there and get tired for me.' Anene replied, 'I do not want to get tired. Therefore I shall do the cutting and weaving. I will make the traps. You, go over there in that place and sit. You, you get tired. That is your part.' So Anansi sat in the shade and dozed while Anene did the work. Sometimes he moaned, saying, 'Oh, but the sun is hot! Oh, but the arms are weary!'

When the traps were finished, Anansi said, 'Now I will carry the traps to the water. Come behind and feel the weariness for me.' Anene said, 'No, on the contrary, I will carry them. You may take the weariness.' Anene carried the traps to the water, Anansi walking behind and groaning. Arriving at the water, Anansi said, 'Well, I will go into the water and set the traps. If I should be bitten by a great fish, you can die for me.' Anene replied, 'No, no. It is I who shall set the traps.' Anene set the traps. The two of them went home, each to his own house.

The next morning they returned to the water. They found fish in the traps.

They started to divide the catch. Anansi said, 'Oh, but the fish are small. You take all the small ones today, and I will take all the large ones tomorrow.' Anene answered, 'Anansi, I perceive your intention. Why should not I take the larger ones? No, you take all the small ones today, tomorrow I shall take the larger.' They went home, Anansi with the fish, Anene with nothing.

They came again the next day. Anansi said, 'The fish are somewhat larger. They are yours. But there are only a few. Tomorrow will be my turn. There will be more.' Anene said, 'Why should I take only a few and you many? You are exploiting me. You, Anansi, take the fish today and I will take my share tomorrow.' Anansi took the fish. They went home.

Again they returned to the traps. They took out the fish. 'A bad day,' Anansi said, 'small fish again. Take them, it is your turn. Tomorrow surely will be better.' Anene protested, 'No, indeed, the small fish are yours. Tomorrow I will take the larger ones.'

It went on this way. Anansi took all the fish, while Anene took none. At last the traps began to rot. Anene said to himself, 'Now I perceive it. Anansi has been getting everything, I have been getting nothing. It is time to bring this affair to an end.' When they went again to the water, Anene said, 'The traps are rotten. We can not catch with them any more. I will take them into town and sell them. That way I will get something for my work.' Anansi answered, 'Why should it be you? If the traps must be sold, it is I who will sell them.' He pulled the rotten traps out of the water. He carried them to town. Anansi went through the market place calling out, 'Here are rotten fish traps! I am selling rotten fish traps!' People in the market laughed at Anansi. But afterwards they became angry, saying, 'He acts as though we were fools.' Anansi continued to call out, 'Get your rotten traps here!' The chief of the town heard about it. He sent for Anansi.

The chief said, 'You with the rotten fish traps, what do you take the people for? Are you yourself a fool, or do you consider this to be a town of fools? No man wants a rotten trap. But you, vendor of rotten traps, you persist in insulting us.' The chief called his guards. He instructed them. They took Anansi to the gates of the town. They whipped him and sent him away. He was ashamed. He hid in dark corners where people would not see him. So it is until now that the spider is found hiding in places where other people do not go.

From *Treasury of Afro-American Folklore*, pp. 584–5.

[3, 13, 16]

African Poetry

26   *In Memory of a Poet*

JOE DE GRAFT

And what shall we remember him by?
    Not by the high throne of office
        he sat on,
    Not his golden mention in the scrolls
        of the nation's great,
    Neither power, which he never knew,
        to summon or dismiss,
    Nor his quarried likeness set
        in the centre of the Square.

What then shall we remember him by?
    Children sleep-drunk around the dying fire,
    Old folk weary with their life,
    Workmen home from days of dusty toil, and
    Lovers cloistered in the stillness
        of moonlit shadows—
    All who listened to his voice,
        Spell-bound

We shall remember him
    By the truths he dared to speak,
    The songs of hope he gave us
        To sing.

Legon, 22 September 1967

From *Beneath the Jazz and Brass*, p. 98.

JOE DE GRAFT   *Born in 1924 in Cape Coast, Ghana. Poet, actor and playwright. Has lived in both East and West Africa.*

27 *Letter to Mamma*

I. CHOONARA

Do not ask me
why we are here, mamma.
That is an irrelevancy.
We cannot tell
the difference
between the North,
the South.
Neither could grand-pa back home
A hundred years ago
when he was a child.
If it moves
we shoot
straight between the
slanty eyes.
That it is the enemy
of the ideal we are defending.
Do not ask me why.

Fred. You know Fred, mom.
Remember Fred. He is dead.
And Bill was killed on the hill.
Some others you know mom
are gone.
But we go on, and on, and on.
We are defending an ideal.
We know it does not sound real,
but here we see clear
the yellow peril in the green jungle
and the red peril in the green jungle,
the flies besides, and the mosquitoes,
the swamps, and the riverboats.
Then there are the bombs, booby traps, bazookas
and a sniper's bullet to stop you dead
in your tracks, mom. Remember Fred.
But we still stick fast, mamma
because we are defending
the Great Ideal.
But it is so far away from home, mamma,
so far from ideal.

From *Seven South African Poets*, pp. 42–3.

I. CHOONARA   *Born in Transvaal, South Africa. Has published both short stories and poems. A graduate of London University and a research chemist.*

28 *After a War*

CHINUA ACHEBE

After a war life catches
desperately at passing
hints of normalcy like
vines entwining a hollow
twig; its famished roots
close on rubble and every
piece of broken glass.

Irritations we used
to curse return to joyous
tables like prodigals home
from the city ... The metre-man
serving my maiden bill bore
the first friendly face to my circle
of sullen strangers and brought me
smiling gratefully
to the door.

After a war
we clutch at watery
scum pulsating on listless
eddies of our spent
deluge . . . Convalescent
dancers rising too soon
to rejoin their circle dance
our powerless feet intent
as before but no longer
adept contrive only
half-remembered
eccentric steps.

After years
of pressing death
and dizzy last-hour reprieves
we're glad to dump our fears
and our perilous gains together
in one shallow grave and flee
the same rueful way we came
straight home to haunted revelry.

Christmas 1971

From *Beware, Soul Brother*, pp. 20–1.

29 *Red Our Colour*

A. N. C. KUMALO

Let's have poems
blood-red in colour
ringing like damn bells.

Poems
that tear at the oppressor's face
and smash his grip.

Poems that awaken man:

Life not death
Hope not despair
Dawn not dusk
New not old
Struggle not submission.

Poet
let the people know
that dreams can become
reality.

Talk of freedom
and let the plutocrat
decorate his parlour walls
with the perfumed scrawls of dilettantes.

Talk of freedom
and touch people's eyes
with the knowledge of the power
of multitudes
that twists prison bars like grass
and flattens granite walls like putty.

Poet
find the people
help forge the key
before the decade
     eats the decade
        eats the decade

From *Poets to the People*, p. 58.

A. N. C. KUMALO *Born in 1938 in Johannesburg. The name is a pseudonym. Has published both short stories and poems in many African journals. A member of the military wing of The African National Congress.*

30 *April 1978, the Prisoners Quietly Back*

JACK MAPANJE

For goodness sake Sweetie, let's stop fretting
About turbid top cockroaches without the brains
To penetrate even their own images. Let us
For once when the prisoners are quietly home
Enjoy the fruits of the evergreen landscape of
Zomba plateau. Let us walk up this Colossus
When the winding avenues are littered with
The purple of jacarandas and the tongues of
Flames-of-the-forests.
                              At the sawmill let us
Pause to greet plateau boys buying their fresh
Luscious granadilla and gorgeous strawberries
And up Mlungusi fountain let us select a rock
To sit down on and as the sparrows hop about
The tree branches twittering, let us chew our
Chambo sandwiches to the welling crests splattering
Nervously down the river. Or let us fondle our
Released hope hurtling down the turf in a strange
Joy today when the prisoners are quietly back.

From *Of Chameleons and Gods*, p. 71.

JACK MAPANJE   *Comes from Malawi. Clearly a poet who works at his art, developing
the craft side of his work. While his poetry is not removed from his home culture it has a kind of
universality not always present in Caribbean and African poetry. Mapanje is currently working
on a PhD in Linguistics at London University.*

31 *Letter from Pretoria Central Prison*

ARTHUR NORTJE

The bell wakes me at 6 in the pale spring dawn
with the familiar rumble of the guts negotiating
murky corridors that smell of bodies. My eyes
find salutary the insurgent light of distances.
Waterdrops rain crystal cold, my wet
face in ascent from an iron basin
greets its rifled shadow in the doorway.

They walk us to the workshop. I am eminent,
the blacksmith of the block: these active hours
fly like sparks in the furnace, I hammer metals
with zest letting the sweating muscles
forge a forgetfulness of worlds more magnetic.
The heart, being at rest, life peaceable,
your words filter softly through my fibres.

Taken care of, in no way am I unhappy,
being changed to neutral. You must decide
today, tomorrow, bear responsibility,
take gaps in pavement crowds, refine ideas.
Our food we get on time. Most evenings
I read books, Jane Austen
for elegance, agreeableness (Persuasion).

Trees are green beyond the wall, leaves through the mesh
are cool in sunshine
among the monastic white flowers of spring that floats
prematurely across the exercise yard, a square
of the cleanest stone I have ever walked on.
Sentinels smoke in their boxes, the wisps
curling lovely through the barbed wire.

Also music and cinema, yesterday double feature.
At 4 p.m. it's back to the cell, don't laugh
to hear how accustomed one becomes. You spoke
of hospital treatment—I see the smart nurses
bringing you grapefruit and tea—good
luck to the troublesome kidney.
Sorry there's no more space. But date your reply.

August 1966

From *Poems of Black Africa*, pp. 106–7.

ARTHUR NORTJE   *Born in 1942 in Port Elizabeth, South Africa. Died in England in 1970. An outstanding South African poet. BA, Belleville College; BA, Oxford, he had also taught in Canada and South Africa. Was taught at school by Dennis Brutus who encouraged him and admired his work.*

32   *The Motoka*

THEO LUZUKA

You see that Benz sitting at the rich's end?
Ha! That motoka is motoka
It belongs to the Minister for Fairness
Who yesterday was loaded with a doctorate
At Makerere with whisky and I don't know what
Plus I hear the literate thighs of an undergraduate.

You see those market women gaping their mouths?
The glory of its inside has robbed them of words,
I tell you the feather seats the gold steering
The TV the radio station the gear!
He can converse with all world presidents
While driving in the back seat with his darly
Between his legs without the driver seeing a thing! ha! ha! ha!
Look at the driver chasing the children away
They want to see the pistol in the door pocket
Or the button that lets out bullets from the machine
Through the eyes of the car—sshhhhhhhhhhhhhhhhhh!
Let's not talk about it.

But I tell you that motoka can run
It sails like a lyato, speeds like a swallow
And doesn't know anyone stupid on its way
The other day I heard—
But look at its behind, that mother of twins!
A-ah! That motoka is motoka
You just wait, I'll tell you more
But let me first sell my tomatoes.

From *Poems of Black Africa*, pp. 118–19.

THEO LUZUKA   *Editor of* Dhna. *Works in the English Department of the University of Singapore.*

33   *City Johannesburg*

MONGANE WALLY SEROTE

This way I salute you:
My hand pulses to my back trousers pocket
Or into my inner jacket pocket
For my pass,[1] my life.
Jo'burg City.
My hand like a starved snake rears my pockets
For my thin, ever lean wallet,
While my stomach groans a friendly smile to hunger,
Jo'burg City.
My stomach also devours coppers and papers
Don't you know?
Jo'burg City, I salute you;
When I run out, or roar in a bus to you,
I leave behind me, my love.
My comic houses and people, my dongas[2] and my ever whirling dust,
My death,
That's so related to me as a wink to the eye.
Jo'burg City
I travel on your black and white and roboted[3] roads,
Through your thick iron breath that you inhale,
At six in the morning and exhale from five noon.
Jo'burg City
That is the time when I come to you,
When your neon flowers flaunt from your electrical wind,
That is the time when I leave you,
When your neon flowers flaunt their way through the falling darkness
On your cement trees.
And as I go back, to my love,
My dongas, my dust, my people, my death,
Where death lurks in the dark like a blade in the flesh,
I can feel your roots, anchoring your might, my feebleness
In my flesh, in my mind, in my blood,
And everything about you says it,
That, that is all you need of me.
Jo'burg City, Johannesburg,
Listen when I tell you,
There is no fun, nothing, in it,
When you leave the women and men with such frozen expressions,
Expressions that have tears like furrows of soil erosion,
Jo'burg City, you are dry like death,
Jo'burg City, Johannesburg, Jo'burg City.

From *Poets to the People*, pp. 162–3.

MONGANE WALLY SEROTE   *Born in 1944 in Johannesburg. A powerful poet,*
imprisoned in 1964 under the Terrorism Act, South Africa.

[1] Pass—identification document which Africans are forced to carry at all times.
Failure to produce a pass on demand means certain imprisonment.
[2] Dongas—ditches.
[3] Robots—traffic lights.

34   *Song of Malaya*

OKOT p'BITEK

Sister Prostitutes
Wherever you are

I salute you

Wealth and Health
To us all

1 Karibu
Welcome ashore
You vigorous young sailor,
I see you scanning the horizon
In search of dry land

I hear your heart drumming
tum-tum-tu-tu-tum . . .

That time bomb
Pulsating in your loin
Surely weighs you down!
Oh . . . oh!

                *   *   *

You soldier
Home bound,
I hear your song . . .
I see the girls
On the platform
Waving a farewell . . .

You reprieved murderer
You prisoner and detainee
About to be released,
Your granaries full
To overflow . . .

Welcome home!

*   *   *

You drunken Sikhs
The night club
Your battle ground,
Turbans, broken heads
And broken glass
Strewn on the floor . . .

Are your wives here?

*   *   *

And you skinny
Indian vegetarian
Your wife breeding
Like a rat,
Welcome to my table too,
I have cooked red meat
With spices . . .
You hairy
Thick-skinned white miner
At Kilembe, at Kitwe . . .

You sweating engineer
Building roads and bridges,
I see the cloud of dust
Raised by your bumping Land Rover
Heading for the City.

Karibu, Come in,
Enter . . .

*   *   *

All my thanks
To you
Schoolboy lover,
I charge you
No fee . . .
That shy smile
On your face,
And . . .

Oh!
I feel ten years
Younger . . .

Hey! Listen . . .
Do not let the
Teacher know . . .
Mm . . . mmm?
He was there
Last night . . .!

          *   *   *

Welcome you teachers
Teaching in bush schools,
I see you in buses
And on bicycles
Coming into the City
Your trouser pockets
Bulging with wallets . . .

Chieftain,
I see your gold watch
Glittering on your wrist,
You are holding
Your wife's waist
And kissing her
Goodbye.

Your shimmering briefcase
Is pregnant . . .

How long
Will your Conference last?
You bus drivers
and you taxi men
Driving away from your home towns,
Will you be back
Tonight?

          *   *   *

You factory workers
Do you not hear
The bells?
Is that not the end
Of your shift?

You shop assistants
Standing there all day
Displaying your wares
And persuading the customers
With false smiles

When do you close?

*　　*　　*

Brother,
You leader of the People,
How is our Party doing?
How many rallies
Have you addressed today?
How many hands
Have you shaken?

Oh—oh . . .
Your blue shirt
Is dripping wet with sweat,
Your voice is hoarse,
You look a bit tired
Friend . . .

I have cold beer
In the house,
I have hot water
And cold water,
You must rest
A little,
Drink and eat
Something . . .

Brother,
Come!

*　　*　　*

Sister Harlots
Wherever you are,
Wake up
Wash up
Brighten up

Go gay and clean,
Lay
Your tables
Bring in fresh flowers . . .

Load your trays
With fresh fruits
Fresh vegetables
And plenty of fresh meat . . .
The hungry lions
Of the World
Are prowling around . . .
Hunting!

From *Poems of Black Africa*, pp. 137–41.

OKOT p'BITEK *Born in 1931 in northern Uganda. One of the pioneers of Ugandan literature. Has written a novel in his mother tongue, Lwo. Was Director of the Uganda National Theatre in the 1960s, and is currently Professor of Creative Writing at Makerere University, Kampala.*

35 *The Cheerful Girls at Smiller's Bar, 1971*

JACK MAPANJE

The prostitutes at Smiller's Bar beside the dusty road
Were only girls once in tremulous mini-skirts and oriental
Beads, cheerfully swigging Carlsbergs and bouncing to
Rusty simanje-manje and rumba booming in the juke-box.
They were striking virgins bored by our Presbyterian
Prudes until a true Presbyterian came one night. And like
To us all the girls offered him a seat on cheap planks
In the dark backyard room choked with diesel-oil clouds
From a tin-can lamp. Touched the official rolled his eyes
To one in style. She said no. Most girls only wanted
A husband to hook or the fruits of Independence to taste
But since then mini-skirts were banned and the girls
Of Smiller's Bar became 'ugly prostitutes to boot!'

Today the girls still giggle about what came through
The megaphones: the preservation of our traditional
et cetera

From *Of Chameleons and Gods*, p. 22.

36   *The People of Darkness*

C. J. DRIVER

For Harry Cohen

All this is guesswork, an order based on small fact
And word-lust. It will not break one bone of exile.

It is an easy way to disguise the flesh of despair
As a hesitation in the voice, a small diffidence,
When it would cry out, 'God save us, save us'—
For my gods are only words dressed up like poems.

Various marks stumble darkly on a white page.
They go, my brave explorers, across their continents
Into the green, green summer.
                              There they shall rest.

Proudly my gods blow and puff their poor feathers.

From *Seven South African Poets*, p. 61.

C. J. DRIVER   *Born in Transvaal. Did degree at University of Cape Town and then a BPhil at Trinity College, Oxford. Has published two novels.*

37   *Christmas 1965*

DENNIS BRUTUS

Through the bruises and the spittle
the miasma of invective
and the scaled refractions of our prejudice
painfully man emerges.

Straw, shavings, hay
and the mist of the cows' cloudbreath:
and through it flickered the lambence
of man's inherent divinity.

From *Seven South African Poets*, p. 28.

DENNIS BRUTUS   *Born in 1924 in Zimbabwe (then Southern Rhodesia) in Harare (formerly Salisbury) of Coloured South African parents. Grew up and educated in Port Elizabeth, South Africa. BA in English at Fort Hare, 1946, and studied law at Witwatersrand 1962–3. Taught English and Afrikaans in South African high schools.*

Because of his opposition to apartheid he was fired from his teaching post, then banned from writing and political activity. Eventually, after many trials and being wounded, he served 18 months of hard labour on Robben Island, and was then permitted to leave South Africa with his wife and family.

He has been active in the International Campaign Against racism in Sport. His poems have been widely published and translated. Now lives in the USA where he has been helping to build up the university study of African Literature.

38   'Franvenkirche' (Our Lady's Cathedral, Munich)

GABRIEL OKARA

I am standing on an age which is now
an object of curiosity and wonder
and which has withstood centuries
and perfected means of destruction.

I am indeed standing on Faith
absolute Faith, twin-towered Faith
in which echoes of whispered prayers
clinging to the walls give one a feeling
strange yet not strange. A feeling
which knows no language no creed
and running through my inside
to my hands made them one
with those that set brick upon brick
to build this memorial, this symbol of Faith
and landmark to this city of Munich.

Munich, 1963

From *The Fisherman's Invocation*, p. 35.

39   *Being the Mother of God*

DENNIS BRUTUS

Being the mother of God
you need not overly concern
yourself with such a churlish child
—indeed might well dispense
with such a bad-mannered son:

So I must beg you to excuse
any inattention and neglect of you
in the midst of what is really your event
and hope that you will accept my anxious thought
and planning for the joy of others
as something which is really yours.

From *Seven South African Poets*, p. 29.

40   *Martin Luther King*

AMIN KASSAM

under abraham's vacant eyes
he proclaimed a dream
a dream
that blossomed a sun
where darkness had reigned
a dream
that bestrode the eagle
with ringing heart
wheeling high above
flailing truncheons thudding
on bare flesh
from rocky desert
he carved a green valley
where soil and clouds
embraced and fused
with the voice of man
tearing into his neck . . .

From *Poems of Black Africa*, pp. 316–17

AMIN KASSAM   *Born in 1948 in Mombasa, Kenya.*

41 *Letters to Martha, Nos 2 and 4*

DENNIS BRUTUS

2
One learns quite soon
that nails and screws
and other sizeable bits of metal
must be handed in;

and seeing them shaped and sharpened
one is chilled, appalled
to see how vicious it can be
—this simple, useful bit of steel:

and when these knives suddenly flash
—produced perhaps from some disciplined anus—
one grasps at once the steel-bright horror
in the morning air
and how soft and vulnerable is naked flesh.

4
Particularly in a single cell
but even in sections
the religious sense asserts itself;

perhaps a childhood habit of nightly prayers
the accessibility of Bibles,
or awareness of the proximity of death:

and of course, it is a currency—
pietistic expressions can purchase favours
and it is a way of suggesting reformation
(which can procure promotion);

and the resort of the weak
is to invoke divine revenge
against a rampaging injustice;

but in the grey silence of the empty afternoons
it is not uncommon
to find oneself talking to God.

From *Poems of Black Africa*, pp. 104–5.

42   *B's Letters*

MBELLA SONNE DIPOKO

B wrote the other day
From the States;
Included the Tennyson song
I sang to the winds of Aguilas
On our way to Malaga.
She writes every once in a while
Talking of San Francisco
And hoping we meet again,
And of her father
Whose wagon still rolls
In the West;
And when I was in Tangier
After I had quarrelled
With the only white liberal acquaintance I had made
In that city
Over a matter of my pride
Which I will let no one fool around with
And I was bitter against those white liberals
Who never really accept the coloured man
As their equal
In spite of instant first name civilities
And stiff upper lip friendship
It was B's letters that helped mitigate
My bitterness.
By the constancy of her tenderness
Etched against the fickle frivolity of my African girl-friend's
I told myself that we were all individuals
And the failings of one
Should never be blamed on a whole people.
Still I know
There is no charity in the West
And when B writes those letters
And sends me money
As she did again the other day
Knowing I am still broke,
I am worried
And feel I have to show her some kindness in return
Some happy day
When we are together as we were
Two years ago;
But hopes of a reunion grow dim
With the ageing of time.
With one of her letters she sent candles, incense
And a Crowley book
On the eight limbs of the Yoga

And with the candles lit
And the incense burning
I relived our friendship
And saw ourselves doing yoga exercises
By the Seine at midnight
Before we left for Spain,
While far away,
In the sunny distance of Africa,
My father was wondering
What I was doing abroad
All these years—
Just being myself, daddy,
Kissing across the colourline
Falling in and out of love
While dreaming of a black woman of home
And writing stories well into the night.

February 1971

From *Black and White in Love*, pp. 63–4.

MBELLA SONNE DIPOKO   *Born in 1936 in Douala, Cameroun. Grew up in Nigeria. Has lived for a long time in France.*

43   *In the Friendly Dark*

DENNIS BRUTUS

In the friendly dark, I wheel
as a bird checks in flight
to glide down streams
and planes of slanting air

so I turn, worn by work
and the dull teeth of care
to find your face, your throat
and the soft dark of your hair;

flesh lies snugged in sheets
the brain, wrapped close in folds
of the still-blanketing night,
awaits the easy balm of dreams,

but my heart soars and wheels
hurtling through the friendly dark
to find your mouth and your heart
and nest quietly there.

From *Poems of Black Africa*, pp. 253–4.

44   *And All Our Lights Were Burning Bright*

JOE DE GRAFT

That evening
Mumbi came and sat at my feet
Fear in her distant eyes.
   My husband,
   They have been on the air again,
      She said;
   They say you have been talking.

Power reared on treason shall not last,
   I said;
This well they know
And all the people they would rule.
But woe the man who dares
To speak it out aloud,
   I said;
Silence in our time is more than golden.

That middle of the night later
No heavy knocking on the door
Presaged their coming—
Our faithful servant-man had seen to that:
Sudden from my dazed pillow
Only the men's faces towering grim,
And their officer's stern voice
Which said:
   You are to come with us, sir.

Mumbi was brave
That morning past midnight
As I stepped into the Land-Rover,
The men's bayonets at my back.
Last view
From the cramped interior of my bristling cage
As we drove into the darkness:
      The front-room door was still wide open
      Mumbi was standing on the stoep outside
      And all our lights were burning bright.

Nairobi, 17 December 1973

From *Beneath the Jazz and Brass*, pp. 78–9.

45   *The Vision:* Ad Gloriam Africanam

JOE DE GRAFT

One fateful midnight hour
In a vision
  Across a stately sky all black, serene,
He saw—
    A shooting star,
    Himself riding
    Astride its incandescent tail
     Ad gloriam Africanam.
The seventh day to the minute
  A coup flashed across the land:
    The newest head of state was born.

    Mar the pattern
    Snarl the thread:
  What the goat can weave
  The colobus too can weave—
    And better!

The thunder that announced his birth
Still echoes
Down the hushed corridors of ousted power.

    Seize the shuttle
    Break the loom:
  What the goat can weave
  The colobus too can weave—
    No better!

Seven promised years
Of plenty for all. . . .
  We not his tribesmen
  Still gaze
    At his bemedalled image on the wall;
  Groaning stomachs
  Severed hands
  Tongues tied
    But still in hope:
     Manna from the louring skies?

Nairobi, 17 May 1972

From *Beneath the Jazz and Brass*, pp. 76–7.

46 *African Prometheus*

DAVID EVANS

For Bram Fischer, Nelson Mandela and other South African fighters against apartheid

High
upon the krantz[1]
smeared with blood and gore and shit
Prometheus
is chained.
Handcuffs rasp his aching wrists
the ridge knife-cuts his bleeding back
King Zeus
holds a blowtorch to his blistered face.

Nightfall
brings the eagles
like hunger lust and fear
to rip
with beaks and talons
at his gut
his groin
and then it all begins again.
He prays
for death—and cannot die
cursed with endless life.

Girls
come in their mini skirts
their smooth thighs moist for love;
he feels paps soft upon his chest
the sweet sap swell his horn
hears the whispers in his ear. . . .
Recant.

Zeus
stubs his fat cigar
his voice too is soft:
you stole the sacred flame for men
joined the mob behind my back
led revolt against the gods
tried to turn my world to ash
and build a new. But
I forgive.
forget that rabble.
Recant.

[1] Krantz is Afrikaans for crag.

Hermes
comes
the messenger
soft-footed in his brown-suede shoes
exit permit in his hand:
We drank together at the club
you've only got to say the word
sign here on the dotted line.
Recant.

Prometheus
writhes against the rock
teeth-torn lips spit out a groan
I can't.

Zeus
in his car below
tells the chauffeur to drive on
Eagle-wings
blot out the sun
eagle-beaks tear out the gut
again.

Heracles
is far away
beyond the reach of telegram
while silent on the folded plains
the unseen people
seem to sleep.

But
smouldering in a sullen town
a hut fire gleams
flares
disappears.
Prometheus
endures.

From *Poets to the People*, pp. 12–14.

DAVID EVANS   *Born in 1935 in Cape Province, South Africa. Did postgraduate work at Oxford. Was imprisoned for five years in South Africa.*

47   *The Passage*

CHRISTOPHER OKIGBO

BEFORE YOU, mother Idoto,[1]
   naked I stand;
before your watery presence,
   a prodigal

leaning on an oilbean,
lost in your legend.

Under your power wait I
   on barefoot,
watchman for the watchword
   at *Heavensgate*;

out of the depths my cry:
give ear and hearken. . . .

DARK WATERS of the beginning.

Rays, violet and short, piercing the gloom,
foreshadow the fire that is dreamed of.

Rainbow on far side, arched like boa bent to kill,
foreshadows the rain that is dreamed of.

Me to the orangery
solitude invites,
a wagtail, to tell
the tangled-wood-tale;
a sunbird, to mourn
a mother on a spray.

Rain and sun in single combat;
on one leg standing,
in silence at the passage,
the young bird at the passage.

SILENT FACES at crossroads:
   festivity in black. . . .

Faces of black like long black
   column of ants,

behind the bell tower,
into the hot garden
where all roads meet:
festivity in black. . . .

O Anna at the knobs of the panel oblong,
hear us at crossroads at the great hinges
where the players of loft pipe organs
rehearse old lovely fragments, alone—

strains of pressed orange leaves on pages,
bleach of the light of years held in leather:

For we are listening in cornfields
    among the windplayers,
listening to the wind leaning over
    its loveliest fragment. . . .

From *Labyrinths with Path of Thunder*, pp. 3–5.

CHRISTOPHER OKIGBO *Born in 1932 near Onitsha, eastern Nigeria. Died in 1967. One of the outstanding Nigerian poets, unfortunately killed in the Civil War. In 1967 he had started a publishing company in partnership with Chinua Achebe. He had read Classics at Ibadan and played jazz as his* Elegy for Alto *shows.*

[1] A village stream. The oilbean, the tortoise and the python are totems for her worship.

48 *Immigrant*

ARTHUR NORTJE

Don't travel beyond
Acton at noon in the intimate summer light
of England

to Tuskaloosa, Medicine Hat, preparing
for flight

dismissing the blond aura of the past
at Durban or Johannesburg
no more chewing roots or brewing riots

Bitter costs exorbitantly at London
airport in the neon heat
waiting for the gates to open

Big boy breaking out of the masturbatory
era goes
like eros over atlantis (sunk
in the time-repeating seas, admire our
tenacity)
jetting into the bulldozer civilization
of Fraser and Mackenzie
which is the furthest west that man has gone

A maple leaf is in my pocket.
X-rayed, doctored at Immigration
weighed in at the Embassy
measured as to passport, smallpox, visa
at last the efficient official informs me
I am an acceptable soldier of fortune, don't

tell the Commissioner
I have Oxford poetry in the satchel
propped between my army surplus boots
for as I consider Western Arrow's
pumpkin pancake buttered peas and chicken canadian style
in my mind's customs office
questions fester that turn the menu
into a visceral whirlpool. You can see
that sick bags are supplied.

Out portholes beyond the invisible propellers
snow mantles the ground peaks over Greenland.
What ice island of the heart has weaned
you away from the known white kingdom
first encountered at Giant's Castle?
You walked through the proteas nooked in the sun rocks
I approached you under the silver trees.
I was cauterized in the granite glare
on the slopes of Table Mountain, I was baffled
by the gold dumps of the vast Witwatersrand
when you dredged me from the sea like a recent fossil.

Where are the mineworkers, the compound Africans,
your Zulu ancestors, where are
the root-eating, bead-charmed Bushmen, the Hottentot sufferers?
Where are the governors and sailors of the
Dutch East India Company, where are
Eva and the women who laboured in the castle?
You are required as an explanation.

Glaciers sprawl in their jagged valleys,
cool in the heights, there are mountains and mountains.
My prairie beloved, you whose eyes are
less forgetful, whose fingers are less oblivious
must write out chits for the physiotherapy customers
must fill out forms for federal tax.

Consolatory, the air whiskies my veins.
The metal engines beetle on to further destinations.
Pilot's voice reports over Saskatchewan
the safety of this route, the use of exits,
facility of gas masks, Western Arrow's
miraculous record. The flat sea washes
in Vancouver bay. As we taxi in
I find I can read the road signs.

Maybe she is like you, maybe most women
deeply resemble you, all of them are
all things to all poets: the cigarette girl
in velvet with mink nipples, fishnet thighs,
whose womb is full of tobacco.
Have a B.C. apple in the A.D. city of the saviour,
and sing the centennial song.

From *Seven South African Poets*, pp. 127–9.

49   *To the Dark, Singing*

C. J. DRIVER

In memory of John Harris, who was executed in 1965, for sabotage and murder, and who went to his execution singing, 'We Shall Overcome'.

This man's no hero; mad, perhaps,
Killed an old woman and burned
A child's face to a white skull
So he might make a god out of pain
To free his country from the praise
Of a golden beast. But we are fools
Who dose our disease with hate,

Though we sing when we die.

No praise then; and no prayer either—
For we are past the praying stage.
All prayers shout out too loudly
When one man goes alone to die
In a short falling, a short way
Through his little dark to the dark,

Though he sings when he dies.

Each of us makes a separate peace
With the dark; he made his cruelly
Both ways, that his beast of fire
Might gobble the other golden beast
And that the sweet smell of flesh
Burning, burning, might crowd the gate
Where his country waits, unspeaking,

Though it sang when he died.

I can see no beauty in this
Except that a man should sing
To his dark
Till the rope breaks his voice—

The flames burn white in his skull
And no one death repeats another,

Though he sang when he died.

From *Seven South African Poets*, pp. 64–5.

50   *Conceit*

TIMOTHY HOLMES

With a memory for sights and sounds
Which men and even elephants lack
The tiny eyelet bird which perches
Singing on the traveller's back
Casts his glance to left and right
To take the shifting landscape in
Absorbing, noting, knowing too well
Each detail missed a mortal sin:

His task is set by the Eagle, Vee'd
Sky dolphin: and should he dare
To close his eyelid, rest the eye
He would be the eagle's fare.

At journey's end, and one by one,
He sings his observations out
In music so sweet, so shrill and clear
It puts to shame the Eagle's shout.

From *Seven South African Poets*, p. 71.

TIMOTHY HOLMES   *Born in 1936 in Johannesburg, South Africa. Did his degree at Trinity College, Oxford, before going to teach in Zambia.*

51   *Conquest*

TIMOTHY HOLMES

One throw cutting the evening air,
A broken scream, a silent fall,
A bounce from scrub to rock and bush,
Finished a generation, left clear
For newcomer with plough and gun
The dew-bejewelled country, rich
In soil, trees, birds, red meat,
Rivers, the bounty of a kingly sun.

Three days before, the last tired clan
Of a lost people, four generations,
Were hunted from their eyrie; and ran
Up mountain slopes that quailed the kite—
Were followed by shouts and voices born
Six thousand miles away.

　　　　　Shot after shot
Felled ancestor, father, uncle, husband. Fright
Sent mother-wife to scale the highest bluff.

There two final deaths gave the country over
To strangers.

From *Seven South African Poets*, p. 79.

52 *Just a Passerby*

OSWALD M. MTSHALI

I saw them clobber him with kieries,
I heard him scream with pain
like a victim of slaughter;
I smelt fresh blood gush
from his nostrils,
and flow on the street.

I walked into the church,
and knelt in the pew
'Lord! I love you,
I also love my neighbour. Amen.'

I came out
my heart as light as an angel's kiss
on the cheek of a saintly soul.

Back home I strutted
past a crowd of onlookers.
Then she came in—
my woman neighbour:
'Have you heard? They've killed your brother.'
'O! No! I heard nothing. I've been to church.'

From *Poems of Black Africa*, pp. 317–18.

OSWALD M. MTSHALI   *Born in 1940 in Natal, South Africa. Now living in the USA.*

53   *The New Platform Dances*

JACK MAPANJE

Haven't I danced the big dance
Compelled the rains so dust could
Soar high above like when animals
Stampede? Haven't I in animal
Skins wriggled with amulets
Rattled with anklets
Scattered nervous women
With snakes around my neck
With spears in these hands
Then enticed them back
With flywhisk's magic?
Haven't I moved with all
Concentric in the arena
To the mystic drums
Dancing the half-nude
Lomwe dance
Haven't I?

Haven't my wives at mortars sang
Me songs of praise, of glory,
How I quaked the earth
How my skin trembled
How my neck peaked
Above all dancers
How my voice throbbed
Like the father-drum
I danced to
Haven't they?

Now, when I see my daughters writhe
Under cheating abstract
Voices of slack drums, ululate
To babble-idea-men-masks
Without amulets or anklets,
Why don't I stand up
To show them how we danced
Chopa, how IT was born?
Why do I sit still
Why does my speech choke
Like I have not danced
Before? Haven't I
Danced the bigger dance?
Haven't I?

From *Of Chameleons and Gods*, pp. 12–13.

54   *Whistle for Pennies*

KEORAPETSE KGOSITSILE

Haartebeesport Dam! And song and dance would pierce
the air celebrating the birth of a new year, the lyrics, with
poetic precision, caressing, describing, exploring this experience
with the robustness of released township passions. Happy New
Year.... Happy New Year! Kwa se kusuk'amaphepha ...
and the papers flew ... isitimela siy'eOrlando ... the train
going to Orlando. Yes. Mbaqanga dubbed kwela by white
critics who hear the music as nothing more than an expression
of the noisy happiness of simple-minded township natives and
a gold mine for recording companies. Fuduwa ousi ...
Grind sister. Girl's loins right in there. Kwa suk'amaphepha.
Colossal sounds would leap out of those tiny pennywhistles
to bathe our passions in the spirit of this moment far away
from the slime of narrow, very rarely paved township streets.

From *Seven South African Poets*, p. 98.

KEORAPETSE KGOSITSILE   Born in 1938 in Johannesburg, South Africa. Since 1961
has been living in exile. Teaches at the University of Tanzania.

55   *Public Execution in Pictures*

CHINUA ACHEBE

PUBLIC EXECUTION IN PICTURES

The caption did not overlook
the smart attire of the squad. Certainly
there was impressive swagger in that
ready, high-elbowed stance; belted
and sashed in threaded dragon teeth
they waited in self-imposed restraint—
fine ornament on power unassailable—
for their cue

at the crucial time
this pretty close-up lady in fine lace
proved unequal to it, her first no doubt,
and quickly turned away. But not
this other—her face, rigid
in pain, firmly held between her palms;
though not perfect yet, it seems
clear she has put the worst
behind her today

in my home
far from the crowded live-show
on the hot, bleached sands of Victoria
Beach my little kids will crowd
round our Sunday paper and debate
hotly why the heads of dead
robbers always slump forwards
or sideways.

From *Beware, Soul Brother*, p. 41.

---

56   *The Sun has Paled*

LENRIE PETERS

The sun has paled and turned away
  till after the Referendum

the moon holds portents great
  till after the Referendum

all fold their hearts and cross their breasts
  till after the Referendum

men scamper to a Lamprey's death
  after the Referendum

the morning glory blooms and blazes
  till after the Referendum

how about une nuit d'amour ma chère?
After the Referendum!

From *Poems of Black Africa*, p. 127.

LENRIE PETERS   *Born in 1932 in the Gambia. Leading West African poet. He is also a novelist and a physician.*

57   *Grass will Grow*

JONATHAN KARIARA

If you should take my child Lord
Give my hands strength to dig his grave
Cover him with earth
Lord send a little rain
For grass will grow.

If my house should burn down
So that the ashes sting the nostrils
Making the eyes weep
Then Lord send a little rain
For grass will grow.

But Lord do not send me
Madness
I ask for tears
Do not send me moon-hard madness
To lodge snug in my skull
I would you sent me hordes of horses
Galloping
Crushing
But do not break
The yolk of the moon on me.

From *Poems of Black Africa*, p. 336.

JONATHAN KARIARA   *Works as an editor in Nairobi. He has also worked as an editor for Oxford University Press.*

58   *The Spectacle of Youth*

MAZISI KUNENE

I loved the children of the lion
When their manes were beginning to grow,
Simulating the ancient heroes.
I knew the greatness of their future
When they leapt on the tender necks of antelopes
Which so long prided themselves on their fleetness.
I praised the skilfulness of their power,
Knowing how soon they will be killing buffaloes.

From *Poems of Black Africa*, p. 156.

MAZISI KUNENE   *Born in 1930 in Durban, South Africa. Has lived in exile since 1959. He is Professor of African Literature at the University of California, Los Angeles, USA.*

59   *Ibadan*

J. P. CLARK

Ibadan,
          running splash of rust
and gold—flung and scattered
among seven hills like broken
china in the sun.

From *Poems of Black Africa*, p. 142.

J. P. CLARK   *Born in 1935 in the Ijaw section of Nigeria. Did his degree at University College, Ibadan. Has published many collections of poems.*

60   *The Snowflakes Sail Gently Down*

GABRIEL OKARA

The snowflakes sail gently
down from the misty eye of the sky
and fall lightly on the
winter-weary elms. And the branches
winter-stripped and nude, slowly
with the weight of the weightless snow
bow like grief-stricken mourners
as white funeral cloth is slowly
unrolled over deathless earth.
And dead sleep stealthily from the
heater rose and closed my eyes with
the touch of silk cotton on water falling.

Then I dreamed a dream
in my dead sleep. But I dreamed
not of earth dying and elms a vigil
keeping. I dreamed of birds, black
birds flying in my inside, nesting
and hatching on oil palms bearing suns
for fruits and with roots denting the
uprooters' spades. And I dreamed the
uprooters tired and limp, leaning on my roots—
their abandoned roots
and the oil palms gave them each a sun.

But on their palms
they balanced the blinding orbs
and frowned with schisms on their
brows—for the suns reached not
the brightness of gold!
Then I awoke. I awoke
to the silently falling snow
and bent-backed elms bowing and
swaying to the winter wind like
white-robed Moslems salaaming at evening
prayer, and the earth lying inscrutable
like the face of a god in a shrine.

From *The Fisherman's Invocation*, pp. 30–1.

61   *Turning the Pages*

LENRIE PETERS

Turning the pages of my diary slowly
But rationally under candle light
Halting over entries of bare folly
And the many words I did not write

The sudden shock of scattered references
And 'to be developed' signs
Jotted with unwholesome sentences
And ill-developed rhymes

Pages fastened with candle grease and ink
Remind me I was at least awake
The many evenings when I could not think
But sat enjoying my pulse till daybreak

Turning the chained and fated pages
Was like fumbling with soft life
Melted years mouthed into the ocean
Of pages clouded and wet with tears

But one more page—tomorrow's page
Misty like a reflecting mirror
Showing the shimmering wrinkles of age
And the trenched islands of horror.

The time when sensation goes out of my fingertips
I must distinguish hot and cold by instinct
The time when I must know myself Controller of events
Which have been governed only by the sense

What if I am a recessive mutation
Destined to give way in time
To the surge of biological motion
Which raised the mammal from the reptile?

Then the candle grease and ink
Insomnia and drink
Would be just another link
When I have gone over the brink.

From *Poems of Black Africa*, pp. 299–300.

62 *Ulysses*

WOLE SOYINKA

Notes from here to my Joyce class

Haunting the music of the mind, I watched
Once, through sun slats a raindrop
Lengthen out to rivers on a window-pane
And on this painless rack of time, stretched
I was, heritage of thought, clay and voices
Passing easily to wind and rain-becoming
And, lest I lose the landmarks of my being
Pocked the air with terse, echoing rounds
Drumtap feelers on the growth of leaves.

This storm has cold wings, and they beat
An interchange in time to death and birth
The rain's harrowing passion, midwife love
Winds newcomer-wanderer in its toils.
Lodged in barrenness of ante-rooms
To manger-haven, I, sleep-walker through
The weary cycle of the season's womb
Labouring to give birth to her deathless self,
One more reveller at the rites, I watch
The years re-lay their yeasting dregs
Beneath the froth, hard soles travel pressed
In poultice of new loam. We embrace,
The world and I in great infinitudes.
I grow into that portion of the world
Lapping my feet, yet bear the rain of nails
That drill within to the archetypal heart
Of all lone wanderers.

How pleasant to have toyed with concepts.
Time—we touched upon it—Time I hold
Beyond my hands, a febrile heart slowing
To the calm of death. It weighs all and nothing,
Ceased with rain and ran between my fingers.
It was a crystal cover on the world
A rake of thunders showered its fragments
To a slow dissolve in hailstones, and I was
Held awhile to its truthfulness of transience.
But not for long. It flowed to raise a flotsam from
Tobacco shreds, weaving space inflated
To a swell of dancing seas and pygmy fountains—
Detritus of change, warts on continuity

Drowned steeples of the broken sees, tossed thorn
In matriseas—mud consummation. I trail
A sea-weed cord to hold your breaths to mine
Prime turd among a sea of faeces—oh how
We surf-wrestle to manure the land at ebb!
How golden finally is the recovered fleece?
A question we refuse to ask the Bard.

It turns on quest cycles, to track a skein
Of self through eyeless veils, stumble on warps
Endure the blinds of spidery distortions, till
Swine-scented folds and caressing tunnels
Come to crossroads at the straits, between
Vaginal rocks. Here, the moment of time's
Overlap, forfeiture of flesh, we shed
Our question here, turn from bridging
Passes of eroded runs, from scratching
Upon the calloused skin of blind redemptive
Doors. On minds grown hoary from the quest
Rest, rooted even in the turmoil agency
A boulder solitude amidst wine-centred waves
And hold, in paradox of lighthouse windows
On dark-fallen seas, our lighted beings
Suspended as mirages on the world's reality.

From *Poems of Black Africa*, pp. 302–3.

WOLE SOYINKA *Born in 1934, near Abeokuta, in Yoruba country (Nigeria). Best known as a dramatist and for his political stance on freedom and against corruption. Head of the Drama Department, Ife University. Well aware of both his own religious heritage and that of the West, he explores interestingly traditional beliefs and their relationship with modern Nigeria in two of his plays,* The Lion and the Jewel, *and* The Road.

63 *Lost Friends*

LENRIE PETERS

They are imprisoned
In dark suits and air-conditioned offices
Alsatians ready at the door
On the saliva carpeted floor

They spend their nights
In jet airlines—
Would change them in mid-air
To show how much they dare

Drunk from the vertigo
Of never catching their tails
They never seem to know
When not to bite their nails

Their new addiction
Fortifies their livers
They are getting there
While the going's good
They have no time for dreamers.

From *Poems of Black Africa*, p. 322.

64 *You Laughed and Laughed and Laughed*

GABRIEL OKARA

In your ears my song
is motor car misfiring
stopping with a choking cough;
and you laughed and laughed and laughed.

In your eyes my ante-
natal walk was inhuman, passing
your 'omnivorous understanding'
and you laughed and laughed and laughed.

You laughed at my song,
you laughed at my walk.

Then I danced my magic dance
to the rhythm of talking drums pleading, but you shut your
eyes and laughed and laughed and laughed.

And then I opened my mystic
inside wide like
the sky, instead you entered your
car and laughed and laughed and laughed.

You laughed at my dance,
you laughed at my inside.

You laughed and laughed and laughed.
But your laughter was ice-block
laughter and it froze your inside froze
your voice froze your ears
froze your eyes and froze your tongue.

And now it's my turn to laugh;
but my laughter is not
ice-block laughter. For I
know not cars, know not ice-blocks.

My laughter is the fire
of the eye of the sky, the fire
of the earth, the fire of the air,
the fire of the seas and the
rivers fishes animals trees
and it thawed your inside,
thawed your voice, thawed your
ears, thawed your eyes and
thawed your tongue.

So a meek wonder held
your shadow and you whispered:
'Why so?'
And I answered:
'Because my fathers and I
are owned by the living
warmth of the earth
through our naked feet.'

From *The Fisherman's Invocation*, pp. 24–5.

65   *Gently Fall the Leaves*

JOE DE GRAFT

To Yaa-Jo, Cobbie and Kweku.

Echoes from the sea and the stars
And children's voices singing. . . .

If I reach forward
    My roosters die;
Behind me
    Roosters upon rafters
    My roosters strangled,
    Cobwebs between rafters.

Let my eyes be filled with cowries
Let my sleep be sound and endless;
Peace to them gone into the mists
Peace to them that arrive
    Upon the waves and sands.

My young ones,
If you hear talk of
    Torture in the morning,
    Men tortured at seed-time
        that would not yield to expediency,
Do not bend double
Do not bend backwards:
    The evening shall be yours, its song,
    And harvest-time laughter—
        So your courage keeps blazing pure!

Echoes from the sea and the stars
And children's voices singing. . . .

    Gently fall the leaves
    Silently the dust.

Legon, 20 March 1968

From *Beneath the Jazz and Brass*, p. 80.

66   *Once Upon a Time*

GABRIEL OKARA

Once upon a time, son,
they used to laugh with their hearts
and laugh with their eyes;
but now they only laugh with their teeth,
while their ice-block-cold eyes
search behind my shadow.

There was a time indeed
they used to shake hands with their hearts;
but that's gone, son.
Now they shake hands without hearts
while their left hands search
my empty pockets.

'Feel at home'! 'Come again',
they say, and when I come
again and feel
at home, once, twice,
there will be no thrice—
for then I find doors shut on me.

So I have learned many things, son.
I have learned to wear many faces
like dresses—homeface,
officeface, streetface, hostface,
cocktailface, with all their comforming smiles
like a fixed portrait smile.

And I have learned, too,
to laugh with only my teeth
and shake hands without my heart.
I have also learned to say, 'Goodbye',
when I mean 'Good-riddance',
to say 'Glad to meet you',
without being glad; and to say 'It's been
nice talking to you', after being bored.

But believe me, son.
I want to be what I used to be
when I was like you. I want
to unlearn all these muting things.
Most of all, I want to relearn
how to laugh, for my laugh in the mirror
shows only my teeth like a snake's bare fangs!

So show me, son,
how to laugh; show me how
I used to laugh and smile
once upon a time when I was like you.

From *The Fisherman's Invocation*, pp. 18–19.

67   *A Parting of the Ways*

MBELLA SONNE DIPOKO

To P.A.

When a few years ago I resigned from the staff of your pages
I was wrong to have continued all the same writing for you
Lending to you my bitterness
Against the oppressors
And my hopes for a change,
Loading my messages on the band-wagon of our ideas
Cluttered with records of ancient ways, masks and fetishes
And manned by phrase-coiners of culture in the head
Who hum laments of the ceremonial times of the aristocrats
And feudal lords of the Congo and the Senegal.
But ten years have proved
That the black colour of our skins
And a common ancestry are not enough
To hold us together
For in Africa today
The class struggle is real indeed
And I have comrades beyond the colourline
And there are black oppressors who need interminable elegies to the past;
And there are black oppressed and exploited who need the future.
I stand by the latter against the former
And out of the past I want
Only the popular dances
The arts and crafts and Swahili and a few other languages
Of our ancestors
Whom, in the cult of *griots*,
You try so hard to resurrect
When so far we have very little to show them
On this side of the day;
And so I say goodbye
As the only way out of our quarrels.
After this explanation
And a story of the river of home
Not another note of mine
Near the wings of your choirs sung
To a Timbuctoo that is no more.

March 1971

From *Black and White in Love*, pp. 67–8.

68 *When this Carnival Finally Closes*

JACK MAPANJE

When this frothful carnival finally closes, brother
When your drumming veins dry, these very officers
Will burn the scripts of the praises we sang to you
And shatter the calabashes you drank from. Your
Charms, these drums, and the effigies blazing will
Become the accomplices to your lie-achieved world!
Your bamboo hut on the beach they'll make a bonfire
Under the cover of giving their hero a true traditional
Burial, though in truth to rid themselves of another
Deadly spirit that might otherwise have haunted them,
And at the wake new mask dancers will quickly leap
Into the arena dancing to tighter skins, boasting
Other clans of calabashes as the undertakers jest:
What did he think he would become, a God? The devil!

From *Of Chameleons and Gods*, p. 61.

69   *Were I to Choose*

GABRIEL OKARA

When Adam broke the stone
and red streams raged down to
gather in the womb,
an angel calmed the storm;

And, I, the breath mewed
in Cain, unblinking gaze
at the world without
from the brink of an age

That draws from the groping lips
a breast-muted cry
to thread the years
(O were I to choose)

And now the close of one
and thirty turns, the world
of bones is Babel, and
the different tongues within
are flames the head
continually burning.

And O of this dark halo
were the tired head free.

And when the harmattan
of days has parched the throat
and skin, and sucked the fever
of the head away,

Then the massive dark
descends, and flesh and bone
are razed. And (O were I to choose) I'd cheat the worms
and silence seek in stone.

From *The Fisherman's Invocation*, p. 21.

70   *Black and White in Love, Part I*

MBELLA SONNE DIPOKO

For B in San Francisco.

There is a city in Yorkshire, I will not name
I'll leave it to friends to whisper
The five letters which suggest
The eternity of metal
More than the metaphysics of love.
I remember it by the colour of autumn
And the laments of the winds on the moors
And me calling on you
In your room
Where, cross-legged,
You were yoga-ing the evening away
And all the after-holiday talk of Cuba
And of the beaches of Havana
Which I didn't know
And which those days only meant
Your girlfriend S whose lover I was
And because of whom we met
And my sadness when you left for Oslo
With only a few lines on you
To link your past and my past
With a future I hoped would be made
Of a lasting friendship.

Now, there's no need for you to feel jealous
Because of the scooter trip with S to Gosforth
The day you saw me in bed with her
And you left for Oslo
Although sometimes
Tears run down
Certain corners of my memory
Whenever I recall the beauty
Of the Cumbrian mountains
And of the Irish Sea at Seascale
And an old love on the rocks
Because of you and me.
Rydal Water
Windermere
And Derwent Water
Were mirrors reflecting you
And your brown eyes
As we talked for the first time
Sitting by the fireplace
And the music on records was of a home
Just north of Zululand.

From *Black and White in Love*, pp. 1–2.

71   *To Paveba*

GABRIEL OKARA

When young fingers stir
the fire smouldering in my inside
the dead weight of dead years rolls
crashing to the ground
and the fire begins to flame anew,

The fire begins to flame anew
devouring the debris of years—
the dry harmattan-sucked trees,
the dry tearless faces
smiling weightless smiles like breath
that do not touch the ground.

The fire begins to flame anew
and I laugh and shout to the eye
of the sky on the back of a fish
and I stand on the wayside
smiling the smile of budding trees
at men and women whose insides
are filled with ashes, who
tell me, 'We once had our flaming fire'.

Then I remember my vow.
I remember my vow not to let
my fire flame any more. And the dead
years rise creaking from the ground
and file slowly into my inside
and shyly push aside the young fingers
and smother the devouring flame.

And as before the fire smoulders in water,
continually smouldering beneath
the ashes with things I dare not tell
erupting from the hackneyed lore
of the beginning. For they die in the telling.

So let them be. Let them smoulder.
Let them smoulder in the living fire beneath the ashes.

From *The Fisherman's Invocation*, pp. 33–4.

72 *Fado Singer*

WOLE SOYINKA

For Amalia Roderiguez.

My skin is pumiced to a fault.
I am down to hair-roots, down to fibre filters
Of the raw tobacco nerve

Your net is spun of sitar strings
To hold the griefs of gods: I wander long
In tear vaults of the sublime

Queen of night torments, you strain
Sutures of song to bear imposition of the rites
Of living and of death. You

Pluck strange dirges from the storm
Sift rare stones from ashes of the moon, and rise
Night errands to the throne of anguish

Oh there is too much crush of petals
For perfume, too heavy tread of air on mothwing
For a cup of rainbow dust

Too much pain, oh midwife at the cry
Of severance, fingers at the cosmic cord, too vast
The pains of easters for a hint of the eternal.

I would be free of your tyranny, free
From sudden plunges of the flesh in earthquake
Beyond all subsidence of sense

I would be free from headlong rides
In rock seams and volcanic veins, drawn by dark steeds
On grey melodic reins.

From *Poems of Black Africa*, p. 323.

73 *Christmas in Biafra (1969)*

CHINUA ACHEBE

This sunken-eyed moment wobbling
down the rocky steepness on broken
bones slowly fearfully to hideous
concourse of gathering sorrows in the valley
would yet become in another year a lost
Christmas irretrievable in the heights
its exploding inferno transmuted
by cosmic distances to the peacefulness
of a cool twinkling star.... To death-cells
of that moment came faraway sounds of other
men's carols floating on crackling waves
mocking us. With regret? Hope? Longing? None of
these, strangely, not even despair rather
distilling pure transcendental hate....

Beyond the hospital gate
the good nuns had set up a manger
of palms to house a fine plastercast
scene at Bethlehem. The Holy
Family was central, serene, the Child
Jesus plump wise-looking and rose-cheeked; one
of the magi in keeping with legend
a black Othello in sumptuous robes. Other
figures of men and angels stood
at well-appointed distances from
the heart of the divine miracle
and the usual cattle gazed on
in holy wonder....

Poorer than the poor worshippers
before her who had paid their homage
of pitiful offering with new aluminium
coins that few traders would take and
a frayed five-shilling note she only
crossed herself and prayed open-eyed. Her
infant son flat like a dead lizard
on her shoulder his arms and legs
cauterized by famine was a miracle
of its own kind. Large sunken eyes
stricken past boredom to a flat
unrecognized glueyiness moped faraway
motionless across her shoulder....

Now her adoration over
she turned him around and pointed
at those pretty figures of God
and angels and men and beasts—
a spectacle to stir the heart
of a child. But all he vouchsafed
was one slow deadpan look of total
unrecognition and he began again
to swivel his enormous head away
to mope as before at his empty distance.
She shrugged her shoulders, crossed
herself again and took him away.

From *Beware, Soul Brother*, pp. 13–14.

74   *By the Waters of Babylon*

DENNIS BRUTUS

By the waters of Babylon
    the brackish wastes of alienness
    lie like dust on heart and throat,
    contour and curve of hill and field
    unspeaking and meaningless
    as a barbarous foreign tongue

by the waters of Babylon
we sat down and wept
    the mind yearns over the low horizon
    to other familiar friendly haunts
    not unlike these gracious scenes

when we remembered thee
O Zion
    these trees; these hills; this sky, this sun
    evoke a dearness that lacerates;
    the heart heels from this wounding loveliness

how can we sing our songs
in a strange land?
    wordlessly
    one turns from such beauty and such pain:
    weeps.

In a strange land.
By the waters of Babylon
we sat down
and wept.

Bamako, Mali

From *Seven South African Poets*, p. 18.

Caribbean Poetry

75   *So that We Build*

MARTIN CARTER

In a great silence I hear approaching rain:
There is a sound of conflict in the sky.
The frightened lizard darts behind a stone.
First was the wind, now is the wild assault.

I wish this world would sink and drown again
So that we build another Noah's ark
And send another little dove to find
what we have lost in floods of misery.

From *Poems of Succession*, p. 65.

MARTIN CARTER   *Born in 1927 in Georgetown, Guyana (then British Guiana). A gifted, complicated politician and writer. A revolutionary who has also worked in the private sector, and a historian, he is one of the few West Indian poets to have been in prison for his political activities. He has represented his government at many international conferences. Appears to have become somewhat disillusioned over the lack of progress made since Independence.*

76   *A City's Death by Fire*

DEREK WALCOTT

After that hot gospeller had levelled all but the churched sky,
I wrote the tale by tallow of a city's death by fire;
Under a candle's eye, that smoked in tears, I
Wanted to tell, in more than wax, of faiths that were snapped like wire.
All day I walked abroad among the rubbled tales,
Shocked at each wall that stood on the street like a liar;
Loud was the bird-rocked sky, and all the clouds were bales
Torn open by looting, and white, in spite of the fire.
By the smoking sea, where Christ walked, I asked why
Should a man wax tears, when his wooden world fails?
In town, leaves were paper, but the hills were a flock of faiths;
To a boy who walked all day, each leaf was a green breath
Rebuilding a love I thought was dead as nails,
Blessing the death and the baptism by fire.

From *Caribbean Voices*, Vol. I (2nd ed.), p. 103.

DEREK WALCOTT   *Born in 1930 in St Lucia. By any standards a remarkable poet and playwright. Made his name very early, and was well known before he left the West Indies first to travel and to study, and then on a semi-permanent basis, teaching and producing in the USA. But he still maintains a home in the Caribbean. As he grew up in St Lucia he commands the French Creole of that interesting country, and has written in it. He commands many varieties of English and uses these to great artistic purpose and effect. In* The Schooner Flight *he has the narrator of the poem speak in a special form of Trinidadian English which enables a unique form of communication to take place (Reading 114, p. 280). In* The Saddhu of Couva *(Reading 104, p. 266) he explores an aspect of the Caribbean heritage which is often forgotten, that of the culture of the indentured labourers who were brought to the Caribbean after the abolition of slavery. Walcott's work, not least of all his autobiographical poem,* Another Life, *(London: Cape, 1973), evinces the rich possibilities of life in the Third World, even while it criticizes the philistine aspects.*

77   *For the Altar-Piece of the Roseau Valley Church, Saint Lucia*

DEREK WALCOTT

I

The chapel, as the pivot of this valley,
round which whatever is rooted loosely turns
men, women, ditches, the revolving fields
of bananas, the secondary roads,
draws all to it, to the altar
and the massive altar-piece;
like a dull mirror, life
repeated there,
the common life outside
and the other life it holds
a good man made it.

Two earth-brown labourers
dance the botay in it, the drum sounds under
the earth, the heavy foot.

                    This is a rich valley,
It is fat with things.
Its roads radiate like aisles from the altar towards
those acres of bananas, towards
leaf-crowded mountains
rain-bellied clouds
in haze, in iron heat;

This is a cursed valley,
ask the broken mules, the swollen children,
ask the dried women, their gap-toothed men,
ask the parish priest, who, in the altar-piece
carries a replica of the church,
ask the two who could be Eve and Adam dancing.

II

Five centuries ago
in the time of Giotto
this altar might have had
in one corner, when God was young
ST OMER ME FECIT AETAT whatever his own age now,
GLORIA DEI and to God's Mother also.

It is signed with music.
It turns the whole island.
You have to imagine it empty on a Sunday afternoon
between adorations

Nobody can see it and it is there,
nobody adores the two who could be Eve and Adam dancing.

A Sunday at three o'clock
when the real Adam and Eve have coupled
and lie in re-christening sweat

his sweat on her still breasts,
her sweat on his panelled torso
that hefts bananas
that has killed snakes
that has climbed out of rivers,

now, as on the furred tops of the hills
a breeze moving the hairs on his chest

on a Sunday at three o'clock
when the snake pours itself
into a chalice of leaves.

The sugar factory is empty.

Nobody picks bananas,
no trucks raising dust on their way to Vieuxfort,
no helicopter spraying

the mosquito's banjo, yes,
and the gnat's violin, okay,

okay, not absolute Adamic silence,
the valley of Roseau is not the Garden of Eden,
and those who inhabit it, are not in heaven,

so there are little wires of music
some marron up in the hills, by AuxLyons,
some christening.

A boy banging a tin by the river,
with the river trying to sleep.
But nothing can break that silence,

which comes from the depth of the world,
from whatever one man believes he knows of God
and the suffering of his kind,
it comes from the wall of the altar-piece
ST OMER AD GLORIAM DEI FECIT
in whatever year of his suffering.

III

After so many bottles of white rum in a pile,
after the flight of so many little fishes
from the brush that is the finger of St Francis,

after the deaths
of as many names as you want,
Iona, Julian, Ti-Nomme, Cacao,
like the death of the cane-crop in Roseau Valley, St Lucia.

After five thousand novenas
and the idea of the Virgin
coming and going like a little lamp

after all that,
your faith like a canoe at evening coming in,
like a relative who is tired of America,
like a woman coming back to your house

that sang in the ropes of your wrist
when you lifted this up;
so that, from time to time, on Sundays

between adorations, one might see,
if one were there, and not there,
looking in at the windows

the real faces of angels.

From *Sea Grapes*, pp. 52–5.

78 *History Makers*

GEORGE CAMPBELL

Women stone breakers
Hammers and rocks
Tired child makers
Haphazard frocks
Strong thigh
Rigid head
Bent nigh
Hard white piles
Of stone
Under hot sky
In the gully bed
No smiles
No sigh
No moan.

Women child bearers
Pregnant frocks
Wilful toil sharers
Destiny shapers
History makers
Hammers and rocks.

From *Caribbean Voices*, Vol. I (2nd ed.), p. 66.

GEORGE CAMPBELL   *Born in 1918 in Jamaica. Poet and playwright. Lived for many years in New York, but has returned to Jamaica.*

79   *Theophilus Jones Walks Naked Down King Street*

HEATHER ROYES

On Monday, October 18th,
Theophilus Jones took off
his asphalt-black, rag-tag pants
and walked naked down King Street.
It was a holiday—
and only a few people saw
his triumphant march,
his muscular, bearded-brown body,
his genitals flapping in front.
Theophilus Jones had wanted
to do this for a long time.

At Tower and King, three carwash boys
shouting 'Madman!', followed him to Harbour Street,
but seeing his indifference, turned
and dribbled back up the road.
Down on the Ferry Pier, a handful of people
waiting for the boat, stared out to sea
but did not see
Theophilus enter the water.
He walked out as far as possible,
then began to swim, strongly and calmly,
into the middle of the harbour.
Eventually, way out in the deep,
he stopped,
floated for a while, enjoying the sun,
watched a plane take off from the green-rimmed palisades,
and then, letting himself go,
allowed the water
to swallow him up.

Theophilus Jones went down
slowly,
slowly his bent legs, slowly
his arms above his head,
slowly his locksed hair,
slowly.
Until nothing could be seen of him.

Some orange peel, an old tin-can
and a sea-saturated cigarette box
floated over his demise,
while near by,
a kingfisher—scavenging for sprats
on a low current—veered down
and landed,
in a spray of sunlit water.

From *Jamaica Woman*, pp. 73–4.

HEATHER ROYES   *Born in Jamaica. First degree, UWI, Mona, Jamaica. Post-graduate work in communications abroad. Now working with Jamaican Government in communications. One of the new Jamaica women poets represented in the interesting collection,* Jamaica Woman.

80   *No Sufferer*

DENNIS SCOTT

No sufferer,

but in
the sweating gutter of my bone
Zion seems far
also. I have my version—
the blood's drum is
insistent, comforting.
Keeps me alive. Like you.
And there are kinds of poverty we share,
when the self eats up love
and the heart smokes
like the fires behind your fences, when my wit
ratchets, roaming the hungry streets
of this small flesh, my city

: in the dread time of my living
while whatever may be human chains me
away from the surfeit of light, Mabrak
and the safe land of my longing,
acknowledge I.

From *Uncle Time*, p. 53.

DENNIS SCOTT   *Born in 1939 in Jamaica. Playwright, poet, author and dancer, who did his first degree at UWI, Mona, Jamaica. Recently won the Commonwealth Poetry Prize.*

81 *Lala: The Dressmaker*

HONOR FORD-SMITH

Across from Chang's Green Emporium,
at Halfway Tree, near the fish fry sidewalk
where the men now sit to play at winning
crown and anchor—the dress shop circled her.
Inch measure of her life's scramble—
mountain range of chequered scraps
scent of fabric satin and taffeta—
on the wheels of the foot machines
tread-treading on the raw edges of
parties, teas and mothers' union's socials,
she was drawn into town, moving yard
by yard on the trains of bridal gowns,
fashioning a living from these things.
There was nothing else to do.

The rack of finished dresses, hanging, linings out,
concealed the beadwork her fingers were known for.
(A bald pink mannequin stood in the window—
Issa's had made them necessary.)
She, seated behind the children's magic mahogany
and glass case cargo of the trade's beads, buttons,
zippers, a bangle, pencil, candle—even fruit,
finished collars. The firm fat of her hands
dissolved by time into a skein of thin brown linen.
One son. No husband. In silence
she stitched the distant canefield's cotton trees,
her shame-me-lady face half hidden by the shoulder length
crisp straightened hair. Occasionally, laughter
like a sluice gate crinkled the black black eyes.

*   *   *

Once, before, in the town's taboo, Mohammed's
secret raft of tissue paper and bamboo stood among the
indentured ready to float back to him,
the Indian women chanting
'Allah man say husseh'
She earned her name Lala mingling with the chant
then
breaking, climbing, tearing at the women's work
to see the forbidden centre of the thing.

And afterwards, the dry red heat of malaria,
journeying, fighting, fighting through the hot cloth
covering a sea of seaweed, to the place where
years later, behind the hidden patterns in the stripped
backroom of the shop, between rough walls
across the naked cedar table, she gambled on futures,
staring into the muddled darjeeling leaves
calling the good fortunes of the women to life.

*   *   *

When Lala died
in the backroom of the shop
the girlchildren she had clothed,
whose futures she chose from those cupped in her hand
unpicked the beaded dresses to find what she hid
stitched in the lining.
They put the beads in the locks of their hair
their needles flashing (dangerous and quick)
collecting the light
opening
opening
their laughter strikes the centre of the clock
at Halfway Tree and the flames of the alleys
lick the rotten wooden walls.

HONOR FORD-SMITH   *One of the new Jamaican women poets who is also an actress
and producer.*

82   *Mother of Judas, Mother of God*

MERVYN MORRIS

For Sheila and the company

Curtain
Kettledrum.
Two women meet
in an empty place.

The traitor's mother, jittery,
darting behind her grief,
explores
the calm authority of love.

She understands, she knows,
an inner voice
advises, *Give.*
And gradually

vibrations, bond
of blood, the shawl
transfigured,
canopy.

The women grieve together
now, acknowledging
the sanguine promise
of the cross.

Crescendo.
Fade.
A rope hangs
from the tree.

From *Shadow Boxing: Poems*, p. 35.

MERVYN MORRIS   *Born in 1937 in Jamaica. Lecturer in the Department of English,
UWI. Highly sophisticated poet and critic. Did his degree at St Edmund Hall, Oxford.*

83   *Grampa*

DENNIS SCOTT

Look him. As quiet as a July river-
bed, asleep, an' trim' down like a tree.
Jesus! I never know the Lord could
squeeze so dry. When I was four
foot small I used to say
Grampa, how come you t'in so?
An' him tell me, is so I stay
me chile, is so I stay
laughing, an' fine
emptying on me—

laughing? It running from him
like a flood, that old molasses
man. Lord, how I never see?
I never know a man could sweet so, cool
as rain; same way him laugh,

I cry now. Wash him. Lay him out.

I know the earth going burn
all him limb dem
as smooth as bone,
clean as a tree under the river
skin, an' gather us
beside that distant Shore
bright as a river stone.

From *Uncle Time*, p. 37.

84 *Searching for Grandfather*

OLIVE SENIOR

I
In Colón I searched for my
grandfather without connection.
Not even the message of his
name in the phone book.

II
Along the Line I found my
grandfather disconnected
at Culebra.

Hacking at the Cut
he coughed his brains loose
and shook

(but it was only malaria).

You're lucky they said as they
shipped him home on the deck
of the steamer, his mind
fractured but his fortune intact:
Twenty-eight dollars and two
cents. Silver.

III
What he had learnt to do really
well in Colón was wash corpses.
At home the village was too poor
to patronize. He was the one
that died.

His sisters laid him out in a
freshly-made coffin and cried:
there was nothing left of the
Silver Roll to weigh down his
eyes

for although his life has been
lacking in baggage, they didn't
want him to see that on this
voyage out he still travelled
steerage.

From *Jamaica Woman*, pp. 75–6.

OLIVE SENIOR   *Jamaican journalist and critic. Held important post at the Institute of Social and Economic Research, UWI, Mona, Jamaica. Worked closely with Rex Nettleford's Jamaica Dance Company. She is currently Editor of* Jamaica Journal.

85 *Terminal*

MERVYN MORRIS

She's withering
before our eyes

and no one
noticeably

cries
We do

the hopeful
ritual

each day
we bring

fresh fruit
we prattle

and we pray
for hours

Her room
is heavy

with the scent
of flowers

From *Shadow Boxing*, p. 50.

86 *Spring Feast*

JOHN FIGUEROA

When the Roman soldier laughed
And showed his money
I was Magdalene.

When Judas counted coins
With double-entry envy,
Finding no means to appropriate,
I was he.

I was Peter
When he warmed himself
By the burning coals
And looked not at the accusing maid.

I was the darkened sun,
My heart the riven earth.
Now I am the Easter sun arisen.
The wing-tipped eagle
Scalloping across the sky.

Magdalene I was,
Judas, Peter;
Now I am the risen Lord.

From *Ignoring Hurts*, p. 97

87   *At Easter*

FRANK COLLYMORE

No winter in this equinoctial land, though the shrunken
Trees still share old rhythms;
Their emerald pales, through filigree of bated
Branches Orion marches westward,
And the grass is stubbly as an old toothbrush, thirsty
For rain. Then Easter comes and new
Life bursts from the dark tomb;
Gold is showered upon the blistered fence,
Gold gleams in the gutter; soon
Flamboyant's[1] arching flame will run
Along the backyard and the rusty lawn,
And the lilyblade be thrust from the grey mould.

Only a shower or two in the long interim
When day after day the windbare skies
Mock the tawny mantle of our land,
And foraging roots scrabble in dust.
Only a shower or two, and yet the miracle
Re-enacted; life unprisoned, beauty
Foiling dark bonds. The winds
Will soon despoil the gold, brief
Fruit for dreams; golden shower
And little crocuses all gone, gone
Back to oblivion. Always the cycle
Returning to rejoice parched hearts, each
Resurrection a remembrance, a valediction.

From *Caribbean Voices*, Vol. I (2nd ed.), p. 104.

---

[1] Flamboyant: This poem comes from Barbados; in some other parts of the
Caribbean the flamboyant plant is called the poincianna.

88 *Spring*

GLORIA ESCOFFERY

Do you know why the sun shines
And the breeze throws
Small seeds across the sky?

Do you know why the seas heave
And the young sing
Small songs without a sound?

The universe spins, the world reels, and I
See the street shining. Upside down
You are steady—or do you spin too?

From *Caribbean Voices*, Vol. I (2nd ed.), p. 27

GLORIA ESCOFFERY   *Born in 1923 in Jamaica. Better known as a painter, but has written poetry and criticism for many years. Has lived in Canada and Barbados, but Jamaica has always been her home.*

89 *To an Expatriate Friend*

MERVYN MORRIS

Colour meant nothing. Anyone
who wanted help, had humour or was kind
was brother to you; categories of skin
were foreign; you were colour-blind.

And then the revolution. Black
and loud the horns of anger blew
against the long oppression; sufferers
cast off the precious values of the few.

New powers re-enslaved us all:
each person manacled in skin, in race.
You could not wear your paid-up dues;
the keen discriminators typed your face.

The future darkening, you thought it time
to say good-bye. It may be you were right.
It hurt to see you go; but, more,
it hurt to see you slowly going white.

From *The Pond: A Book of Poems*, p. 14

90   *On Tour: Boston '74*

SALLY HENZELL

lured
out on to the black stage
by the animal cry
of a people
lusting to see their own soul's
mirror
the music maker
steps into the dazzle of his sound
spilling spells
flooding worlds
building highs
with the magic reflection of dreamers

From *Jamaica Woman*, p. 44.

SALLY HENZELL   *Member of a well-known Jamaican country family; married to the man behind the famous Jamaican film,* The Harder They Come.

91   *An Even Shape*

CHRISTINE CRAIG

Her garden looks in through my window
Criss-crossed by the white lattice.
Coolers they call them but they are also
Hiding places for small girls playing.

Her garden stands neatly round her house
Travels politely unto the verandah
To sit in pots or hang
Leafily down from large, earth-coloured urns.

She lives with Mama, shepherding with her full body
The hesitant ins and outs of Mama's half-blind days.
Feeding her frail consciousness with edited Gleaner news
And homemade chicken soup.

In her home, borrowed children touched her china birds with hands
Wiped clean from eating sticky cakes, each with a cherry on top
Or press moist, breathless kisses round
The corners of her smile.

Sometimes she fills the spaces out
With music. Spreading out nostalgia through
Strings and flutes, old fashioned love songs
Of blue moons and forever and until.

Shameful peeping Tom, I sit silent in
My lattice watching the even shape of her days
To catch, just once, a wider open door behind
Her steady eyes.

But in her green edged privacy, self-contained
She keeps the half-drawn shutters of her life
Open just so, and mocks my greed and restlessness
With a calm refusal to be other than she seems.

From *Jamaica Woman*, pp. 5–6.

CHRISTINE CRAIG   *Born in Jamaica. Lived and worked in England. Has written children's stories illustrated by Jerry Craig. Now lives and works in Jamaica.*

92 *All Men Come to the Hills*

ROGER MAIS

All men come to the hills
Finally....
Men from the deeps of the plains of the sea—
Where a wind-in-the-sail is hope,
That long desire, and long weariness fulfils—
Come again to the hills.

And men with dusty, broken feet;
Proud men, lone men like me,
Seeking again the soul's deeps—
Or a shallow grave
Far from the tumult of the wave—
Where a bird's note motions the silence in....
The white kiss of silence that the spirit stills
Still as a cloud of windless sail horizon-hung
    above the blue glass of the sea—
Come again to the hills....
Come ever, finally.

From *Caribbean Voices*, Vol. I (2nd ed.), p. 98.

ROGER MAIS *Born in 1905, died 1955. Best known as a novelist, Roger Mais was also an outstanding painter and poet. He was imprisoned for six months in 1944 for writing what was considered a 'treasonable article' called* Now We Know.

93 *At Home the Green Remains . . .*

JOHN FIGUEROA

In England now I hear the window shake
And see beyond its astigmatic pane
Against black limbs Autumn's yellow stain
Splashed about tree-tops and wet beneath the rake.

New England's hills are flattened as crimson-lake
And purple columns, all that now remain
Of trees, stand forward as hillocks do in rain,
And up the hillside ruined temples make.

At home the green remains: the palm throws back
Its head and breathes above the still blue sea,
The separate hills are lost in common blue
Only the splendid poinsettias, true
And crimson like the northern ivy, tack,
But late, the yearly notice to a tree.

From *Ignoring Hurts*, pp. 84–5.

94   *We Who Do Not Know the Snow*

DANIEL WILLIAMS

We who do not know the snow
And the white teeth of the cold,
Who are not friendly with the quick turn of the season,
And the chill inability of the summer plaid,
Still know the light bright cotton cushioning the breeze;
Not cold but warm in the drowsy pillow,
Lazy under the blanket, steeped in the drug of night;
Untrampled by passing foot blow. . . .

Now the clouds are a flock of sheep,
Grazing over the fertile vault, and the fishermen sweep
Over the high home of the fishes, down in the tall ditches
Of the sea chasing through mossy reef and coral the inhabitants
Of the salt kingdom, seeking flesh to silver dinner dishes.

The uncertain seine, a bundle of nerves, molests the sad sand,
Twitching with its wet colony as dawn catches the strands
Of morning in a ribbon of light and the glad embrace of her hand
Hugs archipelago of ships and the ripple-dimple with brine the planks.

From *Caribbean Voices*, Vol. I (2nd ed.), p. 29.

DANIEL WILLIAMS   *Born in 1927 in New York, of St Vincent, West Indies parentage. Died 1972. He was a barrister who was always generously involved in his community.*

95   *A Mountain Carved of Bronze*

H. D. CARBERRY

How curious is language and the web we weave in it
And the sense of colour in it—
What does colour mean to man?
It speaks to him in many languages
Emphasizing danger or seeking friendship. . . .

Red of fire that burns or fire that warms
Blue of sea that drowns or bears us on its breast
Black of the storm in a sky still brooding
Or black of the night that brings us sleep
White of dusty earth on a mountain road
Or white of the light that warms and sees.

Black for the colour of mourning
White for the colour of death
Yellow the colour of flowers in spring
Grey the colour of the burnt out hearth
Green the colour of leaves and grass
Symbol of softness and of fertile earth.
Red the colour of blood or passion
Red ambivalent speaks of love or hate
Gold the splendour beloved of fashion
Shadows economy of a nation's fate . . .

Oh the riot of colour in the world of earth
Blackman, redman, brownman, yellow man
Man of colour, man of white . . .
Parrot and peacock, bird and beast . . .
All speak to all in the language of colour
Colours of danger, colours of peace
Colours of friendship or hate or spite . . .

Colour of sun, colour of sea,
Colour of mountain, colour of stream,
Shivering green of humming bird
Thin black wing of hawk
Red of the flaming poincianna[1] tree
Dull mossy brown of alligator's back
Floating by in the silty river
River of fish with silver bellies
And thin black fin of white toothed shark
With pallid under-flesh the colour of lizards' legs . . .

World of colour, world of life . . .

And I saw once a mountain carved of bronze
Stand out against a sky of green, bright green . . .
Almost yellow
But shot with red
Like a Chinese silk . . .

And it came to me that that moment was electric
And never again would I see the hills that bronze
The sky that green and red
The sea that blue, and all . . . gleaming like a parrot's breast . . .

World of colour, world of life
World of movement, world of life . . .
Parrot and peacock, bird and beast
All speak to all in language of colour
Colours of danger, colours of peace
Colours of friendship, colours of strife . . .

From *Caribbean Voices*, Vol. I (2nd ed.), pp. 56–7.

H. D. CARBERRY   *Born in 1921 in Montreal of Jamaican parentage. He has made his home in Jamaica from an early age. Qualified as a barrister in England, where he was active in West Indian student affairs.*

[1] Poincianna: A flowering tree more commonly known in many parts of the Caribbean as the flamboyant, a word which well describes its striking colourfulness.
    'Poincianna' is said to derive from a French West Indian Governor M. Poinci. (The plant is of the family *leguminosi*, suborder *cesalpinaceae*.)

96   *Colonization in Reverse*[1]

LOUISE BENNETT

Wat a joyful news, Miss Mattie,
I feel like me heart gwine burs'
Jamaica people colonizin
Englan in reverse.

By de hundred, by de t'ousan
From country and from town,
By de ship-load, by de plane-load
Jamaica is Englan boun.

Dem a-pour out o' Jamaica,
Everybody future plan
Is fe get a big-time job
An settle in de mother lan.

What a islan! What a people!
Man an woman, old an young
Jusa pack dem bag an baggage
An tun history upside dung!

Some people don't like travel,
But fe show dem loyalty
Dem all a-open up cheap-fare-
To-Englan agency.

An week by week dem shippin off
Dem countryman like fire,
Fe immigrate an populate
De seat o' de Empire.

Oonoo see how life is funny,
Oonoo see de tunabout,
Jamaica live fe box bread
Outa English people mout'.

For wen dem catch a Englan,
An start play dem different role,
Some will settle down to work
An some will settle fe de dole.

Jane say de dole is not too bad
Because dey payin' she
Two pounds a week fe seek a job
Dat suit her dignity.

Me say Jane will never find work
At the rate how she dah-look,
For all day she stay pon Aunt Fan couch
An read love-story book.

Wat a devilment a Englan!
Dem face war an brave de worse,
But I'm wonderin' how dem gwine stan'
Colonizin' in reverse.

From *Jamaica Labrish*, pp. 179–80.

LOUISE BENNETT   *Born in 1919 in Jamaica. Outstanding actress and singer. Her poetry exploits many varieties of Jamaican English. Her humour is always humane, but often goes sharply to the point.*

[1] Jamaicans, who have been migrating since the late 19th century (to Panama, Central America or the USA), turned in the early 1950s to Britain, where some 200,000 first generation Jamaicans now reside. Truly a paradox of colonial history —this colonization in reverse to the mother country which once settled her colonies with Britons who came as planters, traders, administrators, technicians, etc....!!

97   *In the Middle of the Night this Howling*

JOHN ROBERT LEE

In the middle of the night this howling.
We will have to wait until the morning
papers come to understand that prowling

messenger's lament.
                    Without warning,
this solitary hound which moves about
our dangerous streets before the dawning

hours, has come to plead with loud devout
insistence right beneath our shutters.
We yearn to know of what he cries throughout

the dark.
            Dear Lord Jesus, what soul utters
with such keening sorrow, gnashing, gnashing
at the night, what soul is lost beneath my shutters?

My life cannot bear this gashing.
It crumbles from my face's edge, crashing

in the middle of the night.

Church of Christ, St Lucia

JOHN ROBERT LEE   *Born in 1948 in St Lucia. Poet and critic. Has been running a theatre workshop for some time in St Lucia. Recently did a special course at UWI, Mona, Jamaica. He also worked successfully as a writer in Barbados. Worked for two years in the Royal Bank in St Lucia where he met MacDonal Dixon, himself an outstanding young St Lucian poet who encouraged Lee to concentrate on poetry and the theatre. Has taught at St Mary's College which was Walcott's old school.*

98   *The Song of the Banana Man*

EVAN JONES

Touris', white man, wipin' his face,
Met me in Golden Grove market place.
He looked at m' ol' clothes brown wid stain,
An' soaked right through wid de Portlan' rain,
He cas' his eye, turn' up his nose,
He says, 'You're a beggar man, I suppose?'
He says, 'Boy, get some occupation,
Be of some value to your nation.'

I said, 'By God and dis big right han'
You mus' recognize a banana man.

'Up in de hills, where de streams are cool,
An' mullet an' janga¹ swim in de pool,
I have ten acres of mountain side,
An' a dainty-foot donkey dat I ride,
Four Gros Michel,² an' four Lacatan,²
Some coconut trees, and some hills of yam,
An' I pasture on dat very same lan'
Five she-goats an' a big black ram.

'Dat, by God an' dis big right han'
Is de property of a banana man.

'I leave m' yard early-mornin' time
An' set m' foot to de mountain climb,
I ben' m' back to de hot-sun toil,
An' m' cutlass rings on de stony soil,
Ploughin' an' weedin', diggin' an' plantin'
Till Massa Sun drop back o' John Crow mountain,
Den home again in cool evenin' time,
Perhaps whistling dis likkle rhyme,

(Sung) 'Praise God an' m' big right han'
I will live an' die a banana man.

'Banana day is my special day,
I cut my stems an' I'm on m' way,
Load up de donkey, leave de lan'
Head down de hill to banana stan',
When de truck comes roun' I take a ride
All de way down to de harbour side—
Dat is de night, when you, touris' man,
Would change your place wid a banana man.

'Yes, by God, an' m' big right han'
I will live an' die a banana man.

'De bay is calm, an' de moon is bright
De hills look black for de sky is light,
Down at de dock is an English ship,
Restin' after her ocean trip,
While on de pier is a monstrous hustle,
Tallymen, carriers, all in a bustle,
Wid stems on deir heads in a long black snake
Some singin' de songs dat banana men make,

'Like, *(Sung)* Praise God an' m' big right han'
I will live an' die a banana man.

'Den de payment comes, an' we have some fun,
Me, Zekiel, Breda and Duppy Son.
Down at de bar near United Wharf
We knock back a white rum, bus' a laugh,
Fill de empty bag for further toil
Wid saltfish, breadfruit, coconut oil.
Den head back home to m' yard to sleep,
A proper sleep dat is long an' deep.

'Yes, by God, an' m' big right han'
I will live an' die a banana man.

'So when you see dese ol' clothes brown wid stain,
An' soaked through wid de Portlan' rain,
Don't cas' your eye nor turn your nose,
Don't judge a man by his patchy clothes,
I'm a strong man, a proud man, an' I'm free,
Free as dese mountains, free as dis sea,
I know myself, an' I know my ways,
An' will sing wid pride to de end o' my days

(Sung) 'Praise God an' m' big right han'
I will live an' die a banana man.'

From *Caribbean Voices*, Vol. I (2nd ed.), pp. 4–6.

EVAN JONES   *Born in 1927 in Jamaica. Playwright and poet who has done a great deal of work in TV. Has lived in Europe for many years.*

¹janga: a crayfish, found in some of the rivers of Jamaica.
² 'Gros Michel' (pronounced 'grow mee-shell') and 'Lacatan' are two varieties of banana.

99   *The Flag of My Country*

ANDERSON PETER DÉSIR

The Flag of My Country . . .

. . . and my excursions into flights
    of geography
    of unvisited,
    Caribbean places,
    drive nails of patriotic fire
    through the armour
    of my originality.

I see visions of scientists,
and sharp,
        short,
        shock
        showers
of benediction
stretching in the dawn
of my mighty country,
although geometrically
small.

I shed my blood
for saint and sinner.

The sanctuary of Parliament,
I insist,
must be measured by the barometer
of changing times,
sufficiently,
dimensionally exemplary
to embrace
the thorough involvement
of my people,
in the reconstruction
of an eternal
Utopia.

And aim at pumping cylinders
of oxygen
into the mood
and mechanics
of our political system,
thus purifying the plasma
of our common understanding.

and to make bubbling babies
    and babbling brooks
appreciate our humble beginnings.
we must gladly observe
the birds and the bees,
as they oscillate between
their flowers of natural perfection,
So they root
into the volcanic dominion
of our turbulent civilization.

We are free—first: 'ceremonially';
and the echoing voice
of my renewed vision
represents the embryo,
the interaction between the alpha
                and omega
of Europe's long standing partition
in my house
of several
lingual audiences.

'We are free'—we boast,
partly because economic slavery
is being re-abolished.

Our hardy race,
the ambrosial fabric
of our cultural heritage,
is growing splendidly
under ripe bamboo skies
sustaining the bonfire
of animation!
and excitement!
and bonne fête!

Turn about the axis
of your own initiative,
and watch the lightning
flashes
of our staccatoed progress,
illuminating
the farthest point
on our intellectual
horizon.

Say nothing long
    and loud
    and new
    and now
about those precious
        parasites
of history,
who migrated to our shores
in order to create,
    to perpetrate,
I suppose to perpetuate
somewhere in the rendezvous
of forced labour,
a paradise
of suffering
for my brainwashed,
    THIRD WORLD
    ancestors.

c'est impossible!
but what?
Superlatively
we cannot afford
to formulate
prescription
for panacea
for the resuscitation
of our weeping
dead;

but,
paradoxically,
we can realize
the beauty
of justice,
by looking
carefully
through the mirrored
eye
of conscience,
in order to discover
the consequence
of our own injustice.

ANDERSON PETER DÉSIR   *Born in St Lucia. One of the most remarkable of new poets writing in the West Indies. Won the 1980 BBC Caribbean poetry prize. Schoolteacher in St Lucia; poet and essayist.*

100   *Like a Strong Tree*

CLAUDE McKAY

Like a strong tree that in the virgin earth
Sends far its roots through rock and loam and clay,
And proudly thrives in rain or time of dearth,
When dry waves scare the rain-come sprites away;
Like a strong tree that reaches down deep, deep,
For sunken water, fluid underground,
Where the great-ringed unsightly blind worms creep,
And queer things of the nether world abound:
So would I live in rich imperial growth,
Touching the surface and the depth of things,
Instinctively reponsive unto both,
Tasting the sweets of being, fearing no stings,
Sensing the subtle spell of changing forms,
Like a strong tree against a thousand storms.

From *Caribbean Voices*, Vol. I (2nd ed.), p. 88.

101   *Poor Gum!*

LOUISE BENNETT

An attendance at a Fabian Bureau weekend conference in England leaves the Jamaican conferee cold and crestfallen. A lot was apparently said but to the conferee the speakers merely 'murder up dem gum!' [. . .] Poor gum!

De sun was there, de day was fair,
De FB group an me
Jump offa train, strole eena Hall,
At Clacton-pon-de-sea.

Black an wite an some wee-droppers,
From near an far dem come,
Fe spen week-en', have conference,
An murder up dem gum!

Dem lick dem gum gains Politics,
Dem beat it up pon War,
Dem batter it wid Colour-Prejudice
An Colour-Bar.

Dem jam teet eena Exploitation,
Bite hypocrisy,
Dem gnaw pon Complete Freedom
An pon Race-Equality.

Dem chaw Colonial Policy,
Walla it eena gall,
Dem grine de way dem country people
Suffer one an all!

Me say no meself, 'though tings may
Be bad, me don't see how
Dem country can suffer more than
Dem gum dah-suffer now!'

Me listen to big-wud a-bus,
Me listen to de prattle,
Me hear po' gum dah-groan wid pain
An po' false-teet' a-rattle.

As me got noh fambily who use
Dentis' noh me chile,
Me never want fe go home back
Wid toot-ache an gum-boil!

An though me mighta got some grievance
Gains' society,
Me can't afford fe meck me poor
Gum pay de penalty.

For after all de gum-maltreatment
Conference discover
Dat all we-all need is, 'to understan
Each other better'.

Me coulda tell dem dat from me
Did lan eena de place,
An shake some people han an look
In a some people face!

So all me do was clap an smile,
An roam de road-side free,
An have a boonoonoonoos time,
At Clacton-pon-de-sea.

From *Jamaica Labrish*, pp. 182–3.

102 *Afro-Saxon*

MERVYN MORRIS

I

Another friend arraigns me:
too detached, he says,
absurdly free
of all the ways of feeling
true blacks, as a rule,
now share: Be funky, brother,
or be cool!

Okay. Though blackness isn't new
to me: ten, fifteen years ago
I didn't need
a uniform, my skin would do:
but I am learning, brother;
I'll succeed. . . .

II

He never made it. Thought-
inspectors, quivering at the sight
of an Afro-Saxon on the road
towards the border, caught
him sneaking in-
to Blackness, radioed:
Don't let that nigger fool you, he is WHITE!

From *Shadow Boxing: Poems*, p. 16.

103   *A Letter from Brooklyn*

DEREK WALCOTT

An old lady writes me in a spidery style,
Each character trembling, and I see a veined hand
Pellucid as paper, travelling on a skein
Of such frail thoughts its thread is often broken;
Or else the filament from which a phrase is hung
Dims to my sense, but caught, it shines like steel,
As touch a line, and the whole web will feel.
She describes my father, yet I forget her face
More easily than my father's yearly dying;
Of her I remember small, buttoned boots and the place
She kept in our wooden church on those Sundays
Whenever her strength allowed;
Grey haired, thin voiced, perpetually bowed.

'I am Mable Rawlins,' she writes, 'and know both your parents';
He is dead, Miss Rawlins, but God bless your tense:
'Your father was a dutiful, honest,
Faithful and useful person.'
For such plain praise what fame is recompense?
'A horn-painter, he painted delicately on horn,
He used to sit around the table and paint pictures.'
The peace of God needs nothing to adorn
It, nor glory nor ambition.
'He is twenty-eight years buried,' she writes, 'he was called home,
And is, I am sure, doing greater work.'

The strength of one frail hand in a dim room
Somewhere in Brooklyn, patient and assured,
Restores my sacred duty to the Word.
'Home, home,' she can write, with such short time to live,
Alone as she spins the blessings of her years;
Not withered of beauty if she can bring such tears,
Nor withdrawn from the world that breaks its lovers so;
Heaven is to her the place where painters go,
All who bring beauty on frail shell or horn,
There was all made, thence their lux-mundi drawn,
Drawn, drawn, till the thread is resilient steel,
Lost though it seems in darkening periods,
And there they return to do work that is God's.

So this old lady writes, and again I believe,
I believe it all, and for no man's death I grieve.

From *Caribbean Voices*, Vol. II, pp. 99–100.

104   *The Saddhu of Couva*

DEREK WALCOTT

For Kenneth Ramchand

When sunset, a brass gong,
vibrate through Couva,
is then I see my soul, swiftly unsheathed,
like a white cattle bird growing more small
over the ocean of the evening canes,
and I sit quiet, waiting for it to return
like a hog-cattle blistered with mud,
because, for my spirit, India is too far.
And to that gong
sometimes bald clouds in saffron robes assemble
sacred to the evening,
sacred even to Ramlochan,
singing Indian hits from his jute hammock
while evening strokes the flanks
and silver horns of his maroon taxi,
as the mosquitoes whine their evening mantras,
my friend Anopheles, on the sitar,
and the fireflies making every dusk Divali.

I knot my head with a cloud,
my white mustache bristle like horns,
my hands are brittle as the pages of Ramayana.
Once the sacred monkeys multiplied like branches
in the ancient temples; I did not miss them,
because these fields sang of Bengal,
behind Ramlochan Repairs there was Uttar Pradesh;
but time roars in my ears like a river,
old age is a conflagration
as fierce as the cane fires of crop time.
I will pass through these people like a cloud,
they will see a white bird beating the evening sea
of the canes behind Couva,
and who will point it as my soul unsheathed?
Neither the bridegroom in beads,
nor the bride in her veils,
their sacred language on the cinema hoardings.

I talked too damn much on the Couva Village Council.
I talked too softly, I was always drowned
by the loudspeakers in front of the stores
or the loudspeakers with the greatest pictures.
I am best suited to stalk like a white cattle bird
on legs like sticks, with sticking to the Path
between the canes on a district road at dusk.
Playing the Elder. There are no more elders.
Is only old people.

My friends spit on the government.
I do not think is just the government.
Suppose all the gods too old,
Suppose they dead and they burning·them,
supposing when some cane cutter
start chopping up snakes with a cutlass
he is severing the snake-armed god,
and suppose some hunter has caught
Hanuman in his mischief in a monkey cage.
Suppose all the gods were killed by electric light?

Sunset, a bonfire roars in my ears;
embers of blown swallows dart and cry,
like women distracted,
around its cremation.
I ascend to my bed of sweet sandalwood.

From *The Star-Apple Kingdom*, pp. 33–5.

105   *After One Year*

MARTIN CARTER

After today, how shall I speak with you?
Those miseries I know you cultivate
are mine as well as yours, or do you think
the impartial bullock cares whose land is ploughed?

I know this city much as well as you do,
the ways leading to brothels and those dooms
dwelling in them, as in our lives they dwell.
So jail me quickly, clang the illiterate door
if freedom writes no happier alphabet.

Old hanging ground is still green playing field.
Smooth cemetery proud garden of tall flowers.
But in your secret gables real bats fly
mocking great dreams that give the soul no peace,
and everywhere wrong deeds are being done.

Rude citizen! think you I do not know
that love is stammered, hate is shouted out
in every human city in this world?
Men murder men, as men must murder men,
to build their shining governments of the damned.

From *Poems of Succession*, p. 71.

106   *Conqueror*

EDWARD BRATHWAITE

1
From quiet shires of church bells, falling leaves,
to this salt turbulence
sand under my feet, pebbles, powdery hills

halting my innocence

from the wooden bridge, pub on the corner, its sign swinging,
willows in winter,
to this empty house, these windmills turning, turning

this midnight drummer

there was a king and his court, archbishops, churchmen,
I had nothing to do with them
I obeyed the laws, poured my soft head of ale in the evening, fished in all
    weathers

hauled my revenge of pale women

now I am king of the court, pay churchmen
to pull weeds from the pathway to heaven, send them
back home with the children as soon as the girls' pains grow red with the
    moon's change of weather.

before the boys breed loyalties out of these strange women

at home there is a wooden bridge, pub on the corner, its sign swinging
willows in winter;
here there is this empty house, these windmills turning turning

this midnight drummer

2
like a rat
like a rat
like a rat-a-tap tappin

like a rat
like a rat
like a rat-a-tap tappin

we eyes we teet we eatin

like a rat
like a rat
like a rat-a-tap tappin

like a rat
like a rat
like a rat-a-tap tappin

an we burnin babylone
              haile selassie hallelu/ja
              haile selassie hallelu/ja
              haile selassie hallelu/ja

              an we burnin babylone

3
it was a victory for the chapels
blowing their bibles
black preachers speaking with the voices of conches

as toussaint did in haiti
as christophe died in haiti

speaking from the tongues of whips
tonelles
speaking from the lips of limp-
ing angels: loa

as the gods do in haiti
in liberated haiti

it was a victory for prayers
starched linen halleluja
pressed pants
barefoot respectability

drought no law no land
the pastors almost doubted

you ask for bread and they fling you a stone
no loaf no love no miracle

you ask for a roof: ceremony of the mounted dead
and your spiked head rots by the roadside

and then those eyes

            that could speak so sweetly
            burn so softly

            farms by the sea-
            side: green growing on green
            green glowing against the blue

            for now I would obliterate you
            from the obscurity of yourselves'
            uncertain silver
            from the feint hearts of your mind-

            less architects
            from the starless dampness of your leaking corners

I would obliterate you
from your self-cement of fist of rise of rocket
from the hatred of your dolour
from the inhabited dungles of no hope

I would take you into the home of the brick
the flat foot of the mortar
the spinning industrial space of the spider
the hounforts of favella vision

I would ask you to walk the four corners of your understanding
rum cocksblood spirit liberation

humbly to step from slave to certain owner
humbly to acknowledge mother father brother sister
humbly to break forth song psalm handclap petal
from the dungeons of unrighteousness

into light into stone into pathway into leaf
of hope
and the rope: whip tomb boulder:
that had bound you

now talisman now twisted into prayer shredded into
timeless stars

like a rat
like a rat
like a rat-a-tap tappin

like a rat
like a rat
like a rat-a-tap tappin

and we burnin babylone. . . .

From *Other Exiles*, pp. 38–41.

EDWARD KAMAU BRATHWAITE   *Born in 1930 in Barbados. One of the best
known and most prolific of Caribbean poets. Also a historian who works in the history department of the University of the West Indies. Won the Barbados Scholarship in 1949; BA
Pembroke College, Cambridge, 1953. Worked in the teaching services in Ghana for some six
years then became Extra Mural Tutor, UWI. PhD, Sussex. Outstanding reader of his own
poetry, he can be heard regularly in England and the USA. Writes in a variety of English
'dielects'. Can be heard on Caedmon Record No. TC 1379, Poets of the West Indies.
Brathwaite has explored in his poetry, among other things, the African heritage in the West
Indies. Editor of the West Indian literacy journal* Savacou.

107   *New Year Letter*

EDWARD BRATHWAITE

For Mexican

The burnt out year
dies as the rocket
dies: cold sparks
to earth and ashes
to the earth, while
church bells mark
its passing

A brave new world
bursts as the rocket
bursts: hot sparks
to heaven and heaven
in the stars, while
church bells ring
the changes.
we too have known
this passing

We too have felt
the change. the cold
midnight unites and cleaves us.
hope dies, despair
like sparks is born,
bursts on our helpless
heaven in the brilliant air

And falls now
silently, dry
rain.
and falls now
soundlessly: the sky's
harsh waters will not flare
again

So softly now this moment fills
the darkness with its difference.
earth waits. trees touch
the dawn. despair, like sparks,
soon dies. so difference
dies. so darkness.
so let us face the new year
with clear eyes

From *Other Exiles*, pp. 51–2.

108   *Ragged Point*

EDWARD BRATHWAITE

New year's morning and we searched
in vain for the dawn: cloud-
carpet over the sea, light
seeping through like a slow stain

we watched what there was to watch
saw the cold rocks come clearer
sky rise. and we knew then

that this would be the year
of the great failure: what
we had always expected, feared,
never really wanted

next morning the weather was clear
we'd forgotten our notions: blue
sky and a beach black with bathers,
pleasure boats, horns hooting, steamed into the harbours

we travelled

far-off places seemed nearer: the telephone,
letter, personal messages, kept us content
like ships near a harbour. no danger
lurked in the postman's nook,

in the envelopes opened and read

and then one innocent weekday
just before lunch, mind only on lunch
not on fear or on failure
I switched on the news and heard

you were dead

banged head against the walls
of a bank, burst brains out
chained in the mad house
soft in a sad cell

shot in the neck as you turned
to smile and the heart's beat-
en drum, dumb in the sun-
light forever

and this failure returns me now

to that new year's morning: the dawn
coming up, the sun silent light
on the rocks, on the edge
of our island and the sea

saying silence unshattered
by wounds and by bullets
but the fear of it there in the cold
and the dark wind

From *Other Exiles*, pp. 1-2.

109   *Heretic*

EDWARD BRATHWAITE

The little speaker, with his red
spade beard, twinkled at us for an hour
or so on the various themes of the age
five feet tall, but jaunty and fat,
he was dwarfed by the tall dark tales that he said

he threw the silhouette of sigmund freud
across our apprehensiveness, made him
hunchbacked and sinister, unshaven,
with blue jowls; showed us his satchel
of smooth instruments: psychoanalysis and
sex: saw how he chopped his mother, murdered
the thick-lipped saints and turning with his humped
up, dromedary back, jumped from the shore in a cockle-shell boat,
hooting his horn on the long dark seas of subconscious self that he sailed.

we were relieved this dangerous quack was gone
shaken, we settled back
our lecturer assuaged our hopes and soothed
our fears, sipping cold water from his glass. . . .

the glass of water where it stood,
shining against the books and stones
was towering and cool
we longed to climb this tower
and escape this heretic and all the shams he showed
to feel the blue ice on our effort as we climbed
rung after rung of our exertions to achieve the top.
would breeze away and leave us strength for further rungs and heights
'til laddering up into the smooth and round running rim—
aquamarine and green like brightest alps—
we walked its purest apogee, surveyed
our scaled achievements, the tilted landscape way below and temperate. . . .

but suddenly the tower of our safety was the tower of a town
translucent tint of water turned to blood.
the table that it stood on heaved and cracked
the flat walls bulged and bent. the dust was deafening.
the classical renaissance ceiling of our lecture room,
before this, smooth and bland, was blotched like sour milk
before the roof ripped off and showed the sky
confused and coiled, a boiling bowels of entangled intestines and wires:
rockets and wreakage, meteors and panic-stricken planes,
sky larks of parachutes picked out by lights
and stiller than the stars, grey weather
from the spreading bombs, roses and wreaths,
clouds funerals and broken jarrs, and all hearts
howling from the mosque of death. . . .

he paused again to drink. and in the pause,
we picked our powers up; stacked stone on polder stone
back to the speckless sky; rolled
carpet-grass and lawns, orchards and walks;
cut stone again and carved
it, moon-marble hard and smooth to represent our memories and scars.
this time, it seemed, these things would hold. . . .

our speaker paused: the glass half drained, our fears half
dwindled, heights unclaimed, the vision still foundationless
and taking up his notes again, continued

From *Other Exiles*, pp. 23–4.

110   *Schooner*

EDWARD BRATHWAITE

A tossed night between us
high seas
and then in the morning
sails slack
rope flapping the rigging
your schooner came in

on the deck, buttressed
with mango boxes, chicken-
coops, rice: I saw you:
older than I would wish you
more tattered than my pride
could stand

you saw me
moving reluctant to the quay-
side, stiff as you knew me
too full of pride.
but you had travelled
braved the big wave
and the bilge-swishing stomach,
climbed the tall seas
to come to me

*ship was too early
or was I too late?*

walking still slowly
(too late or too early?)
saw you suddenly turn
ropes quickly cast off from the capstan
frilled sails were unfurled
water already between your hull and the harbour

*too late too late
or too early?*

running now
one last rope stretched
to the dockside
tripping over a chain—
chink in my armour—

but the white bows were turning
stern coming round squat in the water

and I
older now
more torn and tattered than my pride
could stand
stretch out my love to you across the water
but cannot reach your hand

From *Other Exiles*, pp. 33–4.

111   *Love Letta*

LOUISE BENNETT

Me darlin Love, me lickle Dove,
Me dumplin, me gizada,
Me Sweety Sue, I goes for you
Like how flies goes for sugar.

As ah puts me pen to paper
An me pen nib start to fly,
Me remembrance remember
De fus day you ketch me y'eye.

You did just come off o' tram-car,
A bus was to you right,
A car swips pass you lef-aise
An you stan up stiff wid fright!

You jaw drop, you mout open,
Jus like wen jackass start yawn,
Me heart go boogoo-boogoo
An ah know wha meck ah born!

Noh scorn me lickle letter Love,
Noh laugh after me yaw,
Me larnin not too good, but wat
Me kean spell, me wi draw!

De ting eena de corner wid
De freckles is me heart,
An de plate o' yam an salfish mean
Dat we can never part.

See how me draw de two face dem
Dah-look pon one anada
Well one is you an one is me,
Teck anyone you rada!

Is not a cockroach foot dis, is
A finger wid a ring,
An it mean ah want to married you
Dis line is piece o' string.

Teck it put roun de wedden-finger
A you wedden-han,
Careful fe get de right size, an
Den gi it to dis man.

De man is me. Now sweet-rice,
Keep swell til ah see you nex',
Accep me young heart wile ah close
Wid love an bans o' X.

From *Jamaica Labrish*, pp. 201–3.

112   On Seeing the Reflection of Notre Dame in the Seine

JOHN FIGUEROA

For Louis Arnaud Reid

A man builds better than he knows
The cathedral, stone before floodlight's invention,
Through floodlight's shimmering reflection
On matted water long after renews perfection
A man builds better than he knows.

What he seeks is not hereafter
But everlasting now well done
The answer in stone or images
Built for the now that is forever
With every invention finds further perfection.

He makes the poem, the cathedral
The image, the tune, the stone
So sweetly stretched the tension—
That is perfection—in stone
He cuts stone's dreams, and the world's and his

A man builds better than he knows.

A poet at the crossroads
In a strange land,
Caught by his long forgotten song
As it falls from a curtained window,
Suddenly hears it as I see
This night's reflection
Steady in the moving stream
Knowing that he builds well
Who builds better than he knows.

May 1960

From *Ignoring Hurts*, p. 5.

113   *Children Coming from School*

ROGER MAIS

I can hear the gospel
Of little feet
Go choiring
Down the dusty asphalt street.

Beneath the vast
Cathedral of sky
With the sun for steeple
Evangeling with laughter
Go the shining ones
The little people.

From *Caribbean Voices*, Vol. I (2nd ed.), p. 2.

114   *The Schooner* Flight

DEREK WALCOTT

1   *Adios, Carenage*

In idle August, while the sea soft,
and leaves of brown islands stick to the rim
of this Caribbean, I blow out the light
by the dreamless face of Maria Concepcion
to ship as a seaman on the schooner *Flight*.
Out in the yard turning gray in the dawn,
I stood like a stone and nothing else move
but the cold sea rippling like galvanize
and the nail-holes of stars in the sky roof,
till a wind start to interfere with the trees.
I pass me dry neighbor sweeping she yard
as I went downhill, and I nearly said:
'Sweep soft, you witch, 'cause she don't sleep hard,'
but the bitch look through me like I was dead.
A route taxi pull up, park-lights still on.
The driver size up my bags with a grin:
'This time, Shabine, like you really gone!'
I ain't answer the ass, I simply pile in
the back seat and watch the sky burn
above Laventille pink as the gown
in which the woman I left was sleeping,
and I look in the rearview and see a man
exactly like me, and the man was weeping
for the houses, the streets, that whole fucking island.

Christ have mercy on all sleeping things!
From that dog rotting down Wrightson Road
to when I was a dog on these streets;
if loving these islands must be my load
out of corruption my soul takes wings,
But they had started to poison my soul
with their big house, big car, big-time bohbohl,
coolie, nigger, Syrian, and French Creole,
so I leave it for them and their carnival—
I taking a sea bath, I gone down the road.
I know these islands from Monos to Nassau,
a rusty-head sailor with sea-green eyes
that they nickname Shabine, the patois for
any red nigger, and I, Shabine, saw
when these slums of empire was paradise.
I'm just a red nigger who love the sea,
I had a sound colonial education,
I have Dutch, nigger, and English in me,
and either I'm nobody, or I'm a nation,

But Maria Concepcion was all my thought
watching the sea heaving up and down
as the port side of dories, schooners, and yachts
was painted afresh by the strokes of the sun
signing her name with every reflection;
I knew when dark-haired evening put on
her bright silk at sunset and, folding the sea,
sidled under the sheet with her starry laugh,
that there'd be no rest, there'd be no forgetting.

Is like telling mourners round the graveside
about resurrection, they want the dead back,
so I smile to myself as the bow rope untied
and the *Flight* swing seaward: 'Is no use repeating
that the sea have more fish. I ain't want her
dressed in the sexless light of a seraph,
I want those round brown eyes like a marmoset, and
till the day when I can lean back and laugh,
those claws that tickled my back on sweating
Sunday afternoons, like a crab on wet sand.'
As I worked, watching the rotting waves come
past the bow that scissor the sea like silk,
I swear to you all, by my mother's milk,
by the stars that shall fly from tonight's furnace,
that I loved them, my children, my wife, my home;
I loved them as poets love the poetry
that kills them, as drowned sailors the sea.

You ever look up from some lonely beach
and see a far schooner? Well, when I write
this poem, each phrase go be soaked in salt;
I go draw and knot every line as tight
as ropes in this rigging; in simple speech
my common language go be the wind,
my pages the sails of the schooner *Flight*.
But let me tell you how this business begin.

2   *Raptures of the Deep*

Smuggled Scotch for O'Hara, big government man,
between Cedros and the Main, so the Coast Guard couldn't touch us,
and the Spanish pirogues always met us halfway,
but a voice kept saying: 'Shabine, see this business
of playing pirate?' Well, so said, so done!
That whole racket crash. And I for a woman,
for her laces and silks, Maria Concepcion.
Ay, ay! Next thing I hear, some Commission of Inquiry
was being organized to conduct a big quiz,
with himself as chairman investigating himself.

Well, I knew damn well who the suckers would be,
not that shark in shark skin, but his pilot fish,
khaki-pants red niggers like you and me.
What worse, I fighting with Maria Concepcion,
plates flying and thing, so I swear: 'Not again!'
It was mashing up my house and my family.
I was so broke all I needed was shades and a cup
or four shades and four cups in four-cup Port of Spain;
all the silver I had was the coins on the sea.

You saw them ministers in *The Express*,
guardians of the poor—one hand at their back,
and one set o' police only guarding their house,
and the Scotch pouring in through the back door.
As for that minister-monster who smuggled the booze,
that half-Syrian saurian, I got so vex to see
that face thick with powder, the warts, the stone lids
like a dinosaur caked with primordial ooze
by the lightning of flashbulbs sinking in wealth,
that I said: 'Shabine, this is shit, understand!'
But he get somebody to kick my crutch out his office
like I was some artist! That bitch was so grand,
couldn't get off his high horse and kick me himself.
I have seen things that would make a slave sick
in this Trinidad, the Limers' Republic.

I couldn't shake the sea noise out of my head,
the shell of my ears sang Maria Concepcion,
so I start salvage diving with a crazy Mick,
name O'Shaugnessy, and a limey named Head;
but this Caribbean so choke with the dead
that when I would melt in emerald water,
whose ceiling rippled like a silk tent,
I saw them corals: brain, fire, sea fans,
dead-men's-fingers, and then, the dead men.
I saw that the powdery sand was their bones
ground white from Senegal to San Salvador,
so, I panic third dive, and surface for a month
in the Seamen's Hostel. Fish broth and sermons.
When I thought of the woe I had brought my wife,
when I saw my worries with that other woman,
I wept under water, salt seeking salt,
for her beauty had fallen on me like a sword
cleaving me from my children, flesh of my flesh!

There was this barge from St Vincent, but she was too deep
to float her again. When we drank, the limey
got tired of my sobbing for Maria Concepcion.
He said he was getting the bends. Good for him!
The pain in my heart for Maria Concepcion,

the hurt I had done to my wife and children,
was worse than the bends. In the rapturous deep
there was no cleft rock where my soul could hide
like the boobies each sunset, no sandbar of light
where I could rest, like the pelicans know,
so I got raptures once, and I saw God
like a harpooned grouper bleeding, and a far
voice was rumbling, 'Shabine, if you leave her,
if you leave her, I shall give you the morning star.'
When I left the madhouse I tried other women
but, once they stripped naked, their spiky cunts
bristled like sea eggs and I couldn't dive.
The chaplain came round. I paid him no mind.
Where is my rest place, Jesus? Where is my harbour?
Where is the pillow I will not have to pay for,
and the window I can look from that frames my life?

3   Shabine Leaves the Republic

I had no nation now but the imagination.
After the white man, the niggers didn't want me
when the power swing to their side.
The first chain my hands and apologize, 'History';
the next said I wasn't black enough for their pride.
Tell me, what power, on these unknown rocks—
a spray-plane Air Force, the Fire Brigade,
the Red Cross, the Regiment, two, three police dogs
that pass before you finish bawling 'Parade!'?
I met History once, but he ain't recognize me,
a parchment Creole, with warts
like an old sea bottle, crawling like a crab
through the holes of shadow cast by the net
of a grille balcony; cream linen, cream hat.
I confront him and shout, 'Sir, is Shabine!
They say I'se your grandson. You remember Grandma,
your black cook, at all?' The bitch hawk and spat.
A spit like that worth any number of words.
But that's all them bastards have left us: words.

I no longer believed in the revolution.
I was losing faith in the love of my woman.
I had seen that moment Aleksandr Blok
crystallize in *The Twelve*. Was between
the Police Marine Branch and Hotel Venezuelana
one Sunday at noon. Young men without flags
using shirts, their chests waiting for holes.
They kept marching into the mountains, and
their noise ceased as foam sinks into sand.
They sank in the bright hills like rain, every one
with his own nimbus, leaving shirts in the street,
and the echo of power at the end of the street.

Propeller-blade fans turn over the Senate;
the judges, they say, still sweat in carmine,
on Frederick Street the idlers all marching
by standing still, the Budget turns a new leaf.
In the 12.30 movies the projectors best
not break down, or you go see revolution. Aleksandr Blok
enters and sits in the third row of pit eating choc-
olate cone, waiting for a spaghetti Western with Clint Eastwood and featuring Lee Van Cleef.

4   *The* Flight, *Passing Blanchisseuse*

Dusk. The *Flight* passing Blanchisseuse.
Gulls wheel like from a gun again,
and foam gone amber that was white,
lighthouse and star start making friends,
down every beach the long day ends,
and there, on that last stretch of sand,
on a beach bare of all but light,
dark hands start pulling in the seine
of the dark sea, deep, deep inland.

5   *Shabine Encounters the Middle Passage*

Man, I brisk in the galley first thing next dawn,
brewing li'l coffee; fog coil from the sea
like the kettle steaming when I put it down
slow, slow, 'cause I couldn't believe what I see:
where the horizon was one silver haze,
the fog swirl and swell into sails, so close
that I saw it was sails, my hair grip my skull,
it was horrors, but it was beautiful.
We float through a rustling forest of ships
with sails dry like paper, behind the glass
I saw men with rusty eyeholes like cannons,
and whenever their half-naked crews cross the sun,
right through their tissue, you traced their bones
like leaves against the sunlight; frigates, barentines,
the backward-moving current swept them on,
and high on their decks I saw great admirals,
Rodney, Nelson, de Grasse, I heard the hoarse orders
they gave those Shabines, and that forest
of masts sail right through the *Flight*,
and all you could hear was the ghostly sound
of waves rustling like grass in a low wind
and the hissing weeds they trailed from the stern;
slowly they heaved past from east to west
like this round world was some cranked water wheel,
every ship pouring like a wooden bucket
dredged from the deep; my memory revolve
on all sailors before me, then the sun
heat the horizon's ring and they was mist.

Next we pass slave ships. Flags of all nations,
our fathers below deck too deep, I suppose,
to hear us shouting. So we stop shouting. Who knows
who his grandfather is, much less his name?
Tomorrow our landfall will be the Barbados.

6   *The Sailor Sings Back to the Casuarinas*

You see them on the low hills of Barbados
bracing like windbreaks, needles for hurricanes,
trailing, like masts, the cirrus of torn sails;
when I was green like them, I used to think
those cypresses, leaning against the sea,
that take the sea noise up into their branches,
are not real cypresses but casuarinas.
Now captain just call them Canadian cedars.
But cedars, cypresses, or casuarinas,
whoever called them so had a good cause,
watching their bending bodies wail like women
after a storm, when some schooner came home
with news of one more sailor drowned again.
Once the sound 'cypress' used to make more sense
than the green 'casuarinas', though, to the wind
whatever grief bent them was all the same,
since they were trees with nothing else in mind
but heavenly leaping or to guard a grave;
but we live like our names and you would have
to be colonial to know the difference,
to know the pain of history words contain,
to love those trees with an inferior love,
and to believe: 'Those casuarinas bend
like cypresses, their hair hangs down in rain
like sailors' wives. They're classic trees, and we,
if we live like the names our masters please,
by careful mimicry might become men.'

7   *The* Flight *Anchors in Castries Harbour*

When the stars self were young over Castries,
I loved you alone and I loved the whole world.
What does it matter that our lives are different?
Burdened with the loves of our different children?
When I think of your young face washed by the wind
and your voice that chuckles in the slap of the sea.
The lights are out on La Toc promontory,
except for the hospital. Across at Vigie
the marina arcs keep vigil. I have kept my own
promise, to leave you the one thing I own,
you whom I loved first: my poetry.
We here for one night. Tomorrow, the *Flight* will be gone.

8   Fight with the Crew

It had one bitch on board, like he had me mark—
that was the cook, some Vincentian arse
with a skin like a gommier tree, red peeling bark,
and wash-out blue eyes; he wouldn't give me a ease,
like he feel he was white. Had an exercise book,
this same one here, that I was using to write
my poetry, so one day this man snatch it
from my hand, and start throwing it left and right
to the rest of the crew, bawling out, 'Catch it,'
and start mincing me like I was some hen
because of the poems. Some case is for fist,
some case is for tholing pin, some is for knife—
this one was for knife. Well, I beg him first,
but he keep reading, 'O my children, my wife,'
and playing he crying, to make the crew laugh;
it move like a flying fish, the silver knife
that catch him right in the plump of his calf,
and he faint so slowly, and he turn more white
than he thought he was. I suppose among men
you need that sort of thing. It ain't right
but that's how it is. There wasn't much pain,
just plenty blood, and Vincie and me best friend,
but none of them go fuck with my poetry again.

9   Maria Concepcion & the Book of Dreams

The jet that was screeching over the *Flight*
was opening a curtain into the past.
'Dominica ahead!'
                          'It still have Caribs there.'
'One day go be planes only, no more boat.'
'Vince, God ain't make nigger to fly through the air.'
'Progress, Shabine, that's what it's all about.
Progress leaving all we small islands behind.'
I was at the wheel, Vince sitting next to me
gaffing. Crisp, bracing day. A high-running sea.
'Progress is something to ask Caribs about.
They kill them by millions, some in war,
some by forced labour dying in the mines
looking for silver, after that niggers; more
progress. Until I see definite signs
that mankind change, Vince, I ain't want to hear.
Progress is history's dirty joke.
Ask that sad green island getting nearer.'
Green islands, like mangoes pickled in brine.
In such fierce salt let my wound be healed,
me, in my freshness as a seafarer.

That night, with the sky sparks frosty with fire,
I ran like a Carib through Dominica,
my nose holes choked with memory of smoke;
I heard the screams of my burning children,
I ate the brains of mushrooms, the fungi
of devil's parasols under white, leprous rocks;
my breakfast was leaf mold in leaking forests,
with leaves big as maps, and when I heard noise
of the soldiers' progress through the thick leaves,
though my heart was bursting, I get up and ran
through the blades of balisier sharper than spears;
with the blood of my race, I ran, boy, I ran
with moss-footed speed like a painted bird;
then I fall, but I fall by an icy stream under
cool fountains of fern, and a screaming parrot
catch the dry branches and I drowned at last
in big breakers of smoke; then when that ocean
of black smoke pass, and the sky turn white,
there was nothing but Progress, if Progress is
an iguana as still as a young leaf in sunlight.
I bawl for Maria, and her *Book of Dreams*.

It anchored her sleep, that insomniac's Bible,
a soiled orange booklet with a cyclop's eye
centre, from the Dominican Republic.
Its coarse pages were black with the usual
symbols of prophecy, in excited Spanish;
an open palm upright, sectioned and numbered
like a butcher chart, delivered the future.
One night, in a fever, radiantly ill,
she say, 'Bring me the book, the end has come.'
She said: 'I dreamt of whales and a storm,'
but for that dream, the book had no answer.
A next night I dreamed of three old women
featureless as silkworms, stitching my fate,
and I scream at them to come out my house,
and I try beating them away with a broom,
but as they go out, so they crawl back again,
until I start screaming and crying, my flesh
raining with sweat, and she ravage the book
for the dream meaning, and there was nothing;
my nerves melt like a jellyfish—that was when I broke—
they found me round the Savannah, screaming:

All you see me talking to the wind, so you think I mad.
Well, Shabine has bridled the horses of the sea;
you see me watching the sun till my eyeballs seared,
so all you mad people feel Shabine crazy,
but all you ain't know my strength, hear? The coconuts
standing by in their regiments in yellow khaki,

they waiting for Shabine to take over these islands,
and all you best dread the day I am healed
of being a human. All you fate in my hand,
ministers, businessmen, Shabine have you, friend,
I shall scatter your lives like a handful of sand,
I who have no weapon but poetry and
the lances of palms and the sea's shining shield!

10   Out of the Depths

Next day, dark sea. A arse-aching dawn.
'Damn wind shift sudden as a woman mind.'
The slow swell start cresting like some mountain range
with snow on the top.
                          'Ay, Skipper, sky dark!'
'This ain't right for August.'
                          'This light damn strange,
this season, sky should be clear as a field.'

A stingray steeplechase across the sea
tail whipping water, the high man-o-wars
start reeling inland, quick, quick an archery
of flying fish miss us! Vince say: 'You notice?'
and a black-mane squall pounce on the sail
like a dog on a pigeon, and it snap the neck
of the *Flight* and shake it from head to tail.
'Be Jesus, I never see sea get so rough
so fast! That wind come from God back pocket!'
'Where Cap'n headin? Like the man gone blind!'
'If we's to drong, we go drong, Vince, fock-it!'
'Shabine, say your prayers, if life leave you any!'

I have not loved those that I loved enough.
Worse than the mule kick of Kick-'Em-Jenny
Channel, rain start to pelt the *Flight* between
mountains of water. If I was frighten?
The tent poles of water spouts bracing the sky
start wobbling, clouds unstitch at the seams
and sky water drench us, and I hear myself cry,
'I'm the drowned sailor in her *Book of Dreams*.'
I remembered them ghost ships, I saw me corkscrewing
to the sea bed of sea worms, fathom pass fathom,
my jaw clench like a fist, and only one thing
hold me, trembling, how my family safe home.
Then a strength like it seize me and the strength said:
'I from backward people who still fear God.'
Let Him, in His might, heave Leviathan upward
by the winch of His will, the beast pouring lace
from his sea-bottom bed; and that was the faith

that had fade from a child in the Methodist chapel
in Chisel Street, Castries, when the whale-bell
sang service and, in hard pews ribbed like the whale,
proud with despair, we sang how our race
survive the sea's maw, our history, our peril,
and now I was ready for whatever death will.
But if that storm had strength, was in Cap'n face,
beard beading with spray, tears salting his eyes,
crucify to his post, that nigger hold fast
to that wheel, man, like the cross held Jesus,
and the wounds of his eyes like they crying for us,
and I feeding him white rum, while every crest
with Leviathan-lash make the *Flight* quail
like two criminal. Whole night, with no rest,
till red-eyed like dawn, we watch our travail
subsiding, subside, and there was no more storm.
And the noon sea get calm as Thy Kingdom come.

11 After the Storm

There's a fresh light that follows a storm
while the whole sea still havoc; in its bright wake
I saw the veiled face of Maria Concepcion
marrying the ocean, then drifting away
in the widening lace of her bridal train
with white gulls her bridesmaids, till she was gone.
I wanted nothing after that day.
Across my own face, like the face of the sun,
a light rain was falling, with the sea calm.

Fall gently, rain, on the sea's upturned face
like a girl showering; make these islands fresh
as Shabine once knew them! Let every trace,
every hot road, smell like clothes she just press
and sprinkle with drizzle. I finish dream;
whatever the rain wash and the sun iron:
the white clouds, the sea and sky with one seam,
is clothes enough for my nakedness.
Though my *Flight* never pass the incoming tide
of this inland sea beyond the loud reefs
of the final Bahamas, I am satisfied
if my hand gave voice to one people's grief.
Open the map. More islands there, man,
than peas on a tin plate, all different size,
one thousand in the Bahamas alone,
from mountains to low scrub with coral keys,
and from this bowsprit, I bless every town,
the blue smell of smoke in hills behind them,
and the one small road winding down them like twine
to the roofs below; I have only one theme:

The bowsprit, the arrow, the longing, the lunging heart—
the flight to a target whose aim we'll never know,
vain search for one island that heals with its harbour
and a guiltless horizon, where the almond's shadow
doesn't injure the sand. There are so many islands!
As many islands as the stars at night
on that branched tree from which meteors are shaken
like falling fruit around the schooner *Flight*.
But things must fall, and so it always was,
on one hand Venus, on the other Mars;
fall, and are one, just as this earth is one
island in archipelagoes of stars.
My first friend was the sea. Now, is my last.
I stop talking now. I work, then I read,
cotching under a lantern hooked to the mast.
I try to forget what happiness was,
and when that don't work, I study the stars.
Sometimes is just me, and the soft-scissored foam
as the deck turn white and the moon open
a cloud like a door, and the light over me
is a road in white moonlight taking me home.
Shabine sang to you from the depths of the sea.

From *The Star-Apple Kingdom*, pp. 3–20.

115   For the Last Time, Fire

DENNIS SCOTT

That August the birds kept away from the village, afraid:
          people were hungry.
The phoenix hid at the sun's centre and stared down
          at the Banker's house,
which was plump and factual, like zero.
Every good Banker knows
there's no such bird.

She came to the house like an old cat, wanting
a different kind of labour.
But the Banker was busy, feeding his dogs, who were nervous,
Perhaps she looked dangerous.
The child threshed in her belly
when she fell. The womb cracked, slack-lipped,
leaving a slight trace of blood on the lawn. Delicately,
the phoenix placed the last straw on its nest.

Mrs So-and-so the Banker's wife beat time
in her withdrawing room. Walked her moods
among the fluted teacups, toying with crusted foods.
The house hummed Bach, arithmetic at rest.
The phoenix sang along with the record,
and sat.
But the villagers counted heads, and got up.

So, logical as that spiral worming the disc to a hole in the centre
one night there were visitors, carrying fire. The dogs died first.
then they gutted everything.

Something shook itself out of the ash.
Wings. Perhaps.

From *Uncle Time*, p. 46.

116   *Love Overgrows a Rock*

E. M. ROACH

Only the foreground's green;
Waves break the middle distance,
And to horizon the Atlantic's spread
Bright, blue and empty as the sky;
My eyot jails the heart,
And every dream is drowned in the shore water.

Too narrow room pressed down
My years to stunted scrub,
Blunted my sister's beauty
And my friend's grave force,
Our tribe's renewing faith and pride:
Love overgrows a rock as blood outbreeds it.

We take banana boats
Tourist, stowaway,
Our luck in hand calypsoes in the heart:
We turn Columbus's blunder back
From sun to snow, to bitter cities;
We explore the hostile and exploding zones.

The drunken hawk's blood of
The poet streams through climates of the mind
Seeking a word's integrity
A human truth. So, from my private hillock
In Atlantic I join cry:
Come, seine the archipelago;
Disdain the sea; gather the islands' hills
Into the blue horizons of our love.

From *Caribbean Voices*, Vol. II, p. 216.

E. M. ROACH   *Born in 1915 in Tobago; died in 1974. One of the outstanding poets of the West Indies with a particularly fine lyric gift.*

Bibliography

African Prose Fiction

Achebe, Chinua, 'Civil Peace' and 'Girls at War', *Girls at War* (London: Heinemann Educational Books, African Writers Series No. 100, 1972) pp. 82–9 and 103–23.

Ekwensi, Cyprian, 'Rikku and the Cattle Thieves', *Burning Grass* (London: Heinemann Educational Books, African Writers Series No. 2, 1962) pp. 65–75.

Emecheta, Buchi, 'A Short Journey', *The Slave Girl* (London: Collins/Fontana Books, 1979) pp. 29–61.

Equiano, Olaudah, 'Equiano on His Way to Slavery', *Equiano's Travels*, ed. Paul Edwards (London: Heinemann Educational Books, African Writers Series No. 10, 1967) pp. 10–33.

Ngugi wa Thiong'o, 'Wedding at the Cross', *Secret Lives* (London: Heinemann Educational Books, African Writers Series No. 150, 1975) pp. 97–112.

Nicol, Abioseh, 'The Truly Married Woman', *Modern African Stories*, ed. Charles R. Larson (London: Collins/Fontana Books, 1978) pp. 28–39.

Nwankwo, Nkem, 'Rain', *Reflections*, ed. F. Ademole (Lagos: African Universities Press, 1962) pp. 18–24.

Okara, Gabriel, 'The Crooks', *More Voices of Africa*, ed. Barbara Nolen (Glasgow: Collins, 1975) pp. 66–70.

Opara, Ralph, 'Lagos Interlude', *Reflections,* ed. F. Ademole (Lagos: African Universities Press, 1962) pp. 100–5.

Radin, Paul (ed.), 'How Contradiction Came to the Ashanti', *African Folktales and Sculpture* (Bollinger Foundation, Patten Books, 1952) pp. 101–3.

Rive, Richard, 'Rain', *Quartet,* ed. Richard Rive (London: Heinemann Educational Books, African Writers Series No. 14, 1974) pp. 142–50.

Wannenburgh, Alf, 'Debut', *Quartet,* ed. Richard Rive (London: Heinemann Educational Books, African Writers Series No. 14, 1974) pp. 117–28.

Caribbean Prose Fiction

Collymore, Frank A., 'RSVP to Mrs Bush-Hall', *BIM,* Vol. 9, No. 35 (1962) pp. 199–217.

Courlander, Harold, 'Bouki and Ti Malice Go Fishing', *Treasury of Afro-American Folklore,* ed. Harold Courlander (New York: Crown Publishers, 1976) pp. 584–5.

Dawes, Neville, 'Scholarship Exam', *Interim* (Institute of Jamaica, 1978) pp. 44–9.

Figueroa, John J., 'The Red Square Just Before Spring', *BIM,* Vol. 9, No. 35 (1962) pp. 154–6.

Hearne, John, 'At the *Stelling*', *West Indian Stories,* ed. Andrew Salkey (London: Faber and Faber, 1960) pp. 51–68.

Lamming, George, 'Women at the Hairdresser', *The Emigrants* (USA, McGraw-Hill, 1955) pp. 148–55.

Lamming, George, 'A Wedding in Spring', *West Indian Stories,* ed. Andrew Salkey (London: Faber and Faber, 1960) pp. 28–41.

McKay, Claude, 'I Meet an English Gentleman', *My Green Hills of Jamaica* (Kingston, Heinemann Educational Books, 1979) pp. 65–72.

Mittelholzer, Edgar, 'A Morning at the Office', *A Morning at the Office* (London: Heinemann Educational Books, Caribbean Writers Series No. 11, 1974) pp. 51–67.

Naipaul, V. S., 'B. Wordsworth', *Miguel Street* (London: Heinemann Educational Books, Caribbean Writers Series No. 14, 1974) pp. 56–65.

Naipaul, V. S., 'The Baker's Story', *Caribbean Rhythms*, ed. James T. Livingstone (New York: Washington Square Press, 1974) pp. 116–28.

Wickham, John, 'The Old Man and the City', *BIM,* Vol. 16, No. 16 (June, 1977) pp. 18–33.

African Poetry

Achebe, Chinua, *Beware Soul Brother* (London: Heinemann Educational Books, African Writers Series No. 120, 1972). Poems 28, 55, 73.

Dipoko, Mbella Sonne, *Black and White in Love* (London: Heinemann Educational Books, African Writers Series No. 107, 1972). Poems 42, 67, 70.

De Graft, Joe, *Beneath the Jazz and Brass* (London: Heinemann Educational Books, African Writers Series No. 166, 1975). Poems 26, 44, 45, 65.

Feinberg, Barry (ed.), *Poets to the People* (London: Heinemann Educational Books, African Writers Series No. 230, 1980). Poems 29, 33, 46.

Mapanje, Jack, *Of Chameleons and Gods* (London: Heinemann Educational Books, African Writers Series No. 236, 1981). Poems 30, 35, 53, 68.

Okara, Gabriel, *The Fisherman's Invocation* (London: Heinemann Educational Books, African Writers Series No. 183, 1978). Poems 38, 60, 64, 66, 69, 71.

Okigbo, Christopher, *Labyrinths with Path of Thunder* (London: Heinemann Educational Books, African Writers Series No. 62, 1971). Poem 47.

Pieterse, Cosmo, *Seven South African Poets* (London: Heinemann Educational Books, African Writers Series No. 64, 1971). Poems 27, 36, 37, 39, 48, 49, 50, 51, 54, 74.

Soyinka, Wole, *Poems of Black Africa* (London: Heinemann Educational Books, African Writers Series No. 171, 1979). Poems 31, 32, 34, 40, 41, 43, 52, 56, 57, 58, 59, 61, 62, 63, 72.

Caribbean Poetry

Bennett, Louise, *Jamaica Labrish* (Kingston: Sangster, 1966). Poems 96, 101, 111.

Brathwaite, Edward Kamau, *Other Exiles* (Oxford: Oxford University Press, 1976). Poems 106, 107, 108, 109, 110.

Carter, Martin, *Poems of Succession* (London: New Beacon Books, 1977). Poems 75, 105.

Figueroa, John, *Caribbean Voices,* Vols. I and II (London: Evans, 1970). Vol. I, poems 76, 78, 87, 88, 92, 94, 95, 98, 100, 113: Vol. II, poems 103, 116.

Figueroa, John, *Ignoring Hurts* (Washington, DC: Three Continents Press, 1976). Poems 86, 93, 112.

Livingston, James T. (ed.), *Caribbean Rhythms* (Washington: Washington Square Press, 1974).

Mordecai, P. and Morris, M. (eds.), *Jamaica Woman* (London and Kingston: Heinemann Educational Books, Caribbean Writers Series No. 29, 1980). Poems 79, 84, 90, 91.

Morris, Mervyn, *The Pond: A Book of Poems* (London: New Beacon Books, 1974). Poem 89.

Morris, Mervyn, *Shadow Boxing: Poems* (London: New Beacon Books, 1979). Poems 82, 85, 102.

Scott, Dennis, *Uncle Time* (Pittsburgh: University of Pittsburgh Press, 1973). Poems 80, 83, 115.

Walcott, Derek, *The Star-Apple Kingdom* (New York: Farrar, Straus and Giroux, 1979). Poems 104, 114.

Walcott, Derek, *Sea Grapes* (London: Faber & Faber, 1976). Poem 77.

Other Sources of Information

The following authors who appear in this Anthology are also included in the *Caribbean Sampler* prepared by John J. Figueroa for the Open University Course *U204 'Third World Studies'*: Derek Walcott, Frank Collymore, George Campbell, Evan Jones, Louise Bennett, Martin Carter, Claude McKay, Edward Brathwaite, Eric Roach, and John Figueroa. There is cultural and background information in that Sampler which might be of interest to readers of this Anthology. They should also consult *Caribbean Writers* by D. Herdeck, J. J. Figueroa *et al.* (Washington DC: Three Continents Press, 1979).

Index